# REBEL AMERICA

# REBEL AMERICA

The Story of Social Revolt
in the United States

by
Lillian Symes
and
Travers Clement

Introduction by
Richard Drinnon

Beacon Press    Boston

Introduction copyright © 1972 by Richard Drinnon
Copyright 1934 by Lillian Symes and Travers Clement
Library of Congress catalog card number: 71–181068
International Standard Book Number: 0–8070–5433–X
First published by Beacon Press in 1972 by arrangement
  with Harper & Row, Publishers
*All rights reserved*
Beacon Press books are published under the auspices
  of the Unitarian Universalist Association
Published simultaneously in Canada by Saunders of Toronto, Ltd.
Printed in the United States of America

# Contents

# INTRODUCTION
## by Richard Drinnon

### I

WHEN this book was first published the old gods seemed dead or dying. In the early thirties the Boom Decade was already a bad memory—who could hum the popular tune of "Brother, Can You Spare a Dime?" and still believe the economy had reached "a permanently high plateau"? The celebration of "the American System" also seemed fulsome and hopelessly dated, for even professional patriots lost heart as they looked out upon smokeless factory chimneys and fallow fields. The System was crumbling before their eyes: about fifteen million persons were out of work; food was destroyed as hundreds of thousands went hungry; many families lived in shacks or makeshift shelters; others were shattered, with children placed in orphanages or with relatives, while the father sank out of sight in one or another of the skid rows or hobo jungles across the country. The Great Depression meant want and wretchedness, confusion, bewilderment, and dejection. But it also meant spurts of anger and an edge of bitterness, and therein lay opportunity for what we have since come to call the Old Left.

Lillian Symes, with the help of her husband, could thus bring this valuable study of American radicalism to a close on a note of hope: "the objective conditions favorable for the rapid growth of a revolutionary climate of opinion were at hand." It was indeed hard not to see the graphic lesson of breadlines and bursting granaries. Though the unemployed were demonstrating unbelievable patience and passivity, urban workers were stirring rebelliously and farmers angrily took to direct action against the forced sale of their property. As John A. Simpson, president of the Farmers Union, declared to a Senate Committee just before Roosevelt's inauguration in 1933, "the biggest and finest crop of little revolutions I ever saw is ripe all over the country right now." Even members of the owning class took the possibility seriously, as Lillian Symes points out, betraying their apprehensiveness by "stocking their country homes with canned goods in preparation for a possible state of siege." But talk of revolution was most common and intense within intellectual and professional circles. It was the day of the "turn to the left," a chance for radicals to keep their own rendezvous with destiny.

Of course we all know now that the opportunity was muffed and can admire Lillian Symes for being hopeful but not confident that the Left could take advantage of the favorable conditions. As she pointed out, the avowed forces of the Revolution, battered by a decade and more of sectarian infighting, had split into Socialist and Communist Party wings, each of which was further rent by left and right caucuses or oppositions. The Communist Party labored under the further burden of being directed from Moscow and of having to fit Russian directives to American circumstances. The Socialist Party, by contrast, drew upon social democratic European models and was tied to their failures. Mrs. Symes perceptively saw some hope in third-party farmer and labor movements and closed by emphasizing the need for revolutionary unity and an end to scholastic theoretical controversies.

Unity alone, alas, was not enough. As it happened, the Communist Party was on the eve of its own plunge into consensus via the Popular Front. At the Seventh World

Congress in the summer of 1935, the Comintern declared Fascism the main enemy. In the United States this meant that Communists should stop fighting capitalism and ally themselves with FDR's Democratic Party, which was held to be the liberal wing of the ruling class. Thereafter the Communist Party discouraged third-party proposals and eventually, as Staughton Lynd's recent research shows, even blocked the independent action of left-wing unions within the CIO. Had there been no betrayal of the Spanish Revolution, no Moscow trials, even no Nazi-Soviet pact, which temporarily interrupted the Popular-Front period, the Communist Party support of the New Deal bureaucracy was in itself sufficient to discredit it as an agency of fundamental change.

The Socialist Party pursued a different course to the same end. In the 1936 national convention the Party split three ways, with the followers of Norman Thomas vying with young Militants on the left and Old Guardists on the right. When Thomas sided with the former, the Old Guardists withdrew and wound up in the American Labor Party, which was dominated by Communists and which therefore committed these former Socialists to the New Deal. The Militants, curiously enough, came round to essentially the same position. Though they had furiously opposed the inactivity of the Old Guard and objected to the moderation of Thomas, their sympathies for the Popular-Front tactic led many of them to join the ranks of the New Deal where they quietly or openly supported Roosevelt. At the end of the decade, therefore, the Party had lost both wings. It had lacked legs throughout: the Socialist platform in 1932 and in the succeeding elections hardly went to the root of anything and was without the imagination and daring to pose a serious challenge to the System. FDR could easily rip off planks for his inconclusive steps toward welfare capitalism. New Dealers could say of the platform itself: "Roosevelt carried it out." "On a stretcher," Thomas always replied wryly, but the contention

[ ix ]

was uncomfortably close to the full truth. As World War II approached, interventionists who were still in the Party dropped out to support Roosevelt's foreign policy; after Pearl Harbor, Thomas himself gave it his "critical support."

The decade that began with self-scrutiny and criticism ended in what Alfred Kazin justly characterizes as a "thundering flood of national consciousness and self-celebration." The few remaining questioners of national greatness were isolated and held in high disesteem while erstwhile radicals mobilized in support of the common cause against Fascism.

The *de facto* Popular Front on which the Left fought Hitler finally smashed on the rocks of the Cold War. Those who had joined to support the two superpowers against a common enemy then faced a forced choice of either the US or the USSR. Most of the Old Leftists continued to give America their uncritical support, while the Communist Party continued its abject dependence on directives from Russia. The Heresy Hunt, which dated at least from Truman's loyalty directives in the late forties, was demoralizing primarily because of the earlier failure of a generation of radicals to establish their own independent base.

American radicalism had thus largely ceased to exist when Senator Joseph R. McCarthy began his swift rise to infamy— its absence gave his investigations their truly hallucinatory quality. Certainly it will not do to say, as does Michael Harrington, Thomas' heir to leadership of the social democrats, that there were "discontinuities created when McCarthyism all but wiped out the radical youth movement." What radical youth movement? What discontinuities? To blame McCarthy and his malevolent influence for the demoralization on the Left is to forget or sidestep the fact that it was all but wiped out not so much by overwhelming external forces as by its own internal weaknesses. It is to miss the historical truth that the frightened, silent fifties flowed uninterruptedly from debacles which had their roots in the Great Depression and

[x]

before. Not until the sixties did the Left surface again, and then it earned the right to be called New.

## II

Imagine, for a moment, that the "progressive" parties and groups of the thirties had somehow established a coalition which went on to win elections and effective political power. Would that have mattered very much? Perhaps there would have been more experiments like the Tennessee Valley Authority and the Resettlement Administration; more workers organized in industrial unions like the CIO; more extensive and adequate coverage of welfare measures such as Social Security. Maybe steel and some other basic industries, along with the railroads, would have been nationalized. No doubt there would have been some other changes of relatively comparable importance. But the end result would have been somewhere along a continuum stretching from the Russian model to the British experience from 1945 to 1950. By no stretch of the imagination could any of the possible changes and reforms, in any combination, have announced the beginning of the end for the American System.

The truth is that the revolutionary socialist tradition had run down by the time Lillian Symes turned to it with the qualified expectation that it spoke for the future. From our own vantage point we can see more easily that its outworn formulas were as lacking in promise for America as Marxism-Leninism proved to be for Soviet Russia and Fabian Socialism for postwar England.

Some of the weaknesses of the Old Left were outlined or suggested by the final chapters of *Rebel America*. Its members were, with exceptions like Norman Thomas and A. J. Muste, dogmatic, ill-tempered, puritanical, and humorless. Many shared an embarrassing conviction that all history had come to a culmination in their own scientific understanding of its motive powers. Their thinking was mechanistic, unimaginative, derivative. Apparently no one thought of undertaking anything comparable to George Lukács' *History and Class Consciousness* (1923), a creative restatement of Marxism which placed economics *within* a field of forces and conceived of man dialectically as both the subject and object of the social system. Lacking such suppleness of mind and riches of experience, American Marxists drew on the most reductive sections in the canon to strip man down to his economic functions and place in the class structure. In the name of objectivity they dismissed emotion from their thinking, only to have it return by the back door to pervade their polemics and vindictive personal attacks. For all their emphasis on objective consciousness, they lived in an abstract paper world. Political victories were verbal victories, awarded to those who advanced just the right or, better, the *correct* ideology in a manifesto, tract, or book. And their claims to egalitarianism were betrayed by their impoverished vocabulary: *"Under the dynamic leadership of disciplined cadres, the mass revolutionary party marched irresistibly forward to programmatic conquests . . ."* and so on to further proof that their view of the Revolution was from the top down.

I speak of this radical style without much admiration, obviously, but not as an outsider lacking in sympathy for those individuals who tried to do something about a collapsing system. After the Second World War I was myself a member of the Socialist Party and supported Norman Thomas in his last campaign and in the first presidential election in which I was old enough to vote. My own experience in the almost nonexistent Left of those years between the Old and the New makes me keenly aware that I have been describing general characteristics only; memories surface to remind me of good comrades who had quite different views and attitudes rooted in the more freewheeling Debsian past. Nevertheless, after all the necessary qualifications and exceptions, there was still a certain Old Left configuration. Its common aspects disenchanted radicals faster than conditions could create them. As Lillian Symes said of the Communist Party, so one could say in some measure of the other sects and groups: "thousands of convinced radicals and potential recruits sickened and turned away."

Thousands were sickened and turned away by a politics which did not speak to their deepest needs. The truth about the mainstream Old Left must be put bluntly: it was not radical at all. Instead of confronting a technological process which was destroying the last possibilities of individuality and community—not to speak of the destruction of the environment—it uncritically embraced industrialism in the name of Progress, Science, and Reason. It merely demanded that the managerial elites be staffed by Socialists or Communists, for they, so the argument went, would be more efficient, less corrupt, and less self-serving than their Capitalist counterparts. In an age when all the dominant political and economic forces were centripetal, the Old Left threw its weight in the same direction by demanding greater concentrations of authority. It glorified organizations at a time of overorganization and celebrated collectivities when individuals faced an ever more hopeless fight to keep from being swallowed by them. The mainstream Old Left promised no transcendence of the given reality, in short; and proof of this can readily be obtained by traveling from Capitalist to Communist Bloc countries, with a stopover in Scandinavia on the way. "Whatever the political regime and system, 95 percent of the nation's activities are quasi-identical from country to country. We are dominated by a mechanical system. It is the same from one end of the world to the other, at least in the countries at a similar level" —or so charged M. Edgar Pisani, a conservative assemblyman and former cabinet official, in explanation of his vote against the Pompidou Government in May 1968. His words on the Paris uprising might have come from a young student in the

Sorbonne, or in Tokyo, Prague, or Berkeley.

In the sixties, from whatever quarter and by whatever route, an increasing number of young people came to recognize—along with a few of their elders—that they were the victims of a worldwide dehumanized system of things. This was the underlying message, whatever its particular formulation, of the movement called the New Left. In France, for instance, Daniel Cohn-Bendit and his brother wrote a book with the suggestive title, *Obsolete Communism: The Left Wing Alternative* (1969), which dispenses with the need for "leaders," discusses the repressive nature of all hierarchies, attacks *la maladie sénile* of communism, and extols the kind of auto-organization which can arise from the insurrectionary ferment of a minority which pushes for action but does not seek to direct. Across the Channel Bernadette Devlin's *The Price of My Soul* (1969) expresses the same contempt for those to whom politics means debate and not action, the same concern for organizing a people's democracy on the local level, and, though written by a Socialist Member of Parliament from Northern Ireland, the same distrust of the State. "Basically I believe that the parliamentary system of democracy has broken down," writes Miss Devlin. "What we have now is a kind of *Animal Farm,* all-pigs-are-equal system, whereby the pigs with MP after their name are entitled to sit in the farmhouse, and the rest of us are just common four-footed animals." Across the Atlantic Abbie Hoffman's *Revolution for the Hell of It* (1969) enjoins readers never to forget "that ours is the battle against a machine not against people" and insists on the need to maintain a sense of humor. "People who take themselves too seriously are power-crazy," asserts Hoffman. "If they win it will be haircuts for all. BEWARE OF POWER FREAKS." For an epigraph Hoffman uses a graffito from the Paris May Days: "BE REALISTIC. DEMAND THE IMPOSSIBLE," which brings us back to where we started. The common attitude toward those in power, from one end of this circuit to the other, was deftly captured by a London *Daily Express* cartoon, which showed five aging heads of state before mirrors: Johnson, Wilson, De Gaulle, Franco, and Brezhnev each asks, "Mirror, mirror on the wall, who's the most hated of them all?"

In the United States the New Left came into being through student, civil rights, and anti-war groups such as the Berkeley Free Speech Movement (FSM) and the national Students for a Democratic Society (SDS), the Student Nonviolent Coordinating Committee (SNCC) and the Southern Students Organizing Committee, the Committee for Nonviolent Action and the New Mobilization Committee. Why these or like organizations were so notably absent in the fifties is perhaps an even better question than why they got underway during a decade of relative affluence and peace. A thorough inquiry and analysis, manifestly beyond the scope of this introduction, may well reveal that the sense of needs unmet, of dead ends, and nausea, had to continue to mount over the years before some individuals would move together to save their humanity. There were, of course, precursors. When Rosa Parks refused to move to the back of the bus and in so doing set off the 381-day Montgomery bus boycott in the mid-fifties, she acted in direct anticipation of the four black freshmen at North Carolina Agricultural and Technical College, who tired of walking the two miles into Greensboro without being able to get a bite to eat and a cup of coffee: their sit-in at the local F. W. Woolworth lunch counter on 1 February 1960 was the unofficial beginning of a decade of direct action against racism.

The origins of the movement were similar on the West Coast. As early as 1957 students at Berkeley had organized SLATE, an issues-oriented party, to oppose the usual "sandbox" politics of student government. In 1959 SLATE took up, along with such campus-based issues as compulsory ROTC, the case of Caryl Chessman, who had awaited execution for eleven years after being convicted of rape and kidnaping. As a participant in the unsuccessful campaign to save his life, I came to know growing numbers of students—and even some Beat-Bohemians from nearby North Beach—who saw in Chessman an existential hero, a man who had somehow matured as a writer of promise while living literally at the gates of death. Capital punishment seemed to them legitimate murder and an absurd contradiction of all the verbiage about "rehabilitation." When they learned that Chessman had killed no one and had been convicted under most dubious circumstances, they were appalled and, toward the end, infuriated. One student got at the tense and bitter mood in his report to the *Daily Californian:* As Chessman was readied for the gas chamber on 2 May 1960, a demonstrator outside San Quentin cried: "Violence? Who's violent?! . . . go on, kill Chessman, you bastards!" That they did and, eleven days later, police clubbed and washed down the stairs inside the San Francisco City Hall some of the same students who had gone on to protest hearings of the House Un-American Activities Committee. The widening circle of events had already proved powerfully educational for these young middle-class whites.

Every authentic rebellion is both pushed and pulled into existence. The push-part of this one is clear: Bob Moses made his legendary descent into Amite County, Mississippi; and other SNCC workers there and elsewhere braved beatings, shootings, gassings, and jailings for what seemed to them good reason—Moses likened racism to Camus' plague. Add to this atmosphere of racial bigotry that of the universalized hate expressed by the Cold War and you have what the students, black and white, found most intolerable. As David Horowitz, then a teaching assistant, wrote in *Student* (1962), "we have been made to live, as no other generation has, on the edge of the world's doom." The fine SDS Port Huron Statement of 1962 said the same thing: "Our work is guided by the sense that we may be the last generation in the experiment with

[ xvi ]

living." For them all the leading symbols of the age were the gas ovens and concentration camps and atomic bombs—Horowitz insisted it was no exaggeration to say "that we began our maturity with Hiroshima."

The cry that "we are children of the Bomb" is easily ridiculed but at the cost, invariably, of missing one of the key characteristics of the New Left. Almost as if they alone had been properly attentive to the lessons of the Bomb, young radicals lived on a time dimension which did not reach indefinitely into the future and which allowed for a flash ending tomorrow or the next day. It provided the context of urgency within which they fought racism and sought survival and the continued flow of generations. It fueled their impatience with institutionalized hypocrisy, with "Brotherhood Week," for instance, and the assorted crusades of "the Free World Family of Nations." It helped shape the tactics of their protests and demonstrations against economic manipulation and against those bureaucratic definitions of life which contribute, in the words of the Port Huron Statement, "to the sense of outer complexity and inner powerlessness." The sense of crisis unlimited has also led many of the young to burn themselves out quickly and others to the puerile habit of demanding instant solutions for deep-set ills. But who is to say that their eschatological sense of time is inappropriate in the Atomic Age?

The pull-part of their rebellion is more elusive. Originally black students in the South, for instance, merely demanded what white students in the North and West had already experienced as empty and degrading. Moreover, the "personalistic" manner, which Kenneth Keniston found common among the young, produced almost as many versions of the Good Society as there were persons in the movement. It may be, as Keniston implies, that the young were simply trying to make the American Dream come true in a time when it had been forsaken or betrayed by their elders. Certainly this was true for most of them at the beginning. But the focus became increasingly international or anti-national, a shift suggested by the title *The Making of an Un-American* (1970), Paul Cowan's book on his experiences in the civil rights struggle and the Peace Corps. The discovery of the Third World and a heightened awareness of the role therein of the American Empire led to formulations of ideals which went beyond nationalism to anticipate the cosmopolitanism of the French students of 1968: "We are all German Jews." The young radicals dared to speak of emotions more tender than those usually associated with nationalism: Carl Oglesby, onetime president of the SDS, says simply that he wants a society in which love is more possible. "We regard *men*," reads the Port Huron Statement, "as infinitely precious and possessed of unfulfilled capacities for reason, freedom, and love."

The forces generated by the negative and positive poles of this rebellion produced a novel style. Among its key words are love, gentleness (scarcely a traditional masculine virtue), freedom, imagination, directness, honesty, immediacy, experience (over theory), body (sensuousness), compassion, community, and—for the early SNCC and SDS—nonviolence. It reaches out to touch the outcasts of society and expresses a primary concern for loneliness, estrangement, isolation. It has a sense of humor and an attitude of political irreverence: The so-called Filthy Speech Movement in Berkeley, for instance, explained that one of its four-letter signs meant merely Freedom Under Clark Kerr. Or as the "Together" of the Jefferson Airplane confessed: "We are the forces of anarchy and chaos/ We are everything they say we are/And we are proud of ourselves." Finally, it squarely confronts the issue of power: "As a *social system*," reads the Port Huron Statement, "we seek the establishment of a democracy of individual participation, governed by two central aims: that the individual share in those social decisions determining the quality and direction of his life; that society be organized to encourage independ-

ence in men and provide the media for their common participation."

The New Left, in short, is almost everything the Old was
not. Consider this illustrative passage from an essay in *Root
and Branch* by Robert Scheer:

> To speak of society and to ignore the spirit is to forget the real
> root which is man. Life has been too long politicized by the Left,
> which has proposed the transformation of life as if it meant the
> simple change from one set of political terms to another; no, we
> are against this, against the politicization of man. Men's politics
> must be an extension of their beings, and not the other way
> around.

Here the thought cuts down through the conventional political categories to the person and his plight in a commercial,
racist, militaristic, bureaucratic society. Scheer and other
young radicals have had the intelligence and courage to see
that the way out, the great leap to the kingdom of freedom, is
fundamentally a spiritual journey.

### III

Now as *Rebel America* reappears the American System is in
deeper crisis. Inflation *and* unemployment make something
comparable to a depression real for vast numbers of people.
But this time the crisis goes beyond the economy to raise
doubts about the entire structure of power and privilege. In
the summer of 1971 one national survey by the Gallup organization shows that almost one of every two Americans believes
that current unrest "is likely to lead to a real breakdown in
this country" and another by the Roper organization reveals
that nearly two of every three Americans believe that their
country has lost its proper sense of direction.

The background of the crisis is well known. Cities are
bankrupt and crumbling. The Ecology Crusade inadvertently
reveals that the destruction of the environment proceeds

apace. The War on Poverty slips to disclose the extent of wretchedness in the world's richest republic. Benign Neglect of racial justice shows the depth of liberalism's failure to deal with the American Dilemma. The long War in South East Asia has slaughtered a million Indochinese and cost fifty thousand American lives. Other tens of thousands of young men have gone into exile to escape service in the dirty cause. Hundreds of others resist from their jail cells. The Pentagon Papers on the origins of the war disclose that Americans have been consistently deceived by their leaders and furnish substantial grounds for believing that their government has fallen into the hands of war criminals.

The New Left can take credit for exposing this state of the country. Its anti-poverty and anti-racism actions, waged in behalf of pretty much the same people, helped make poor blacks, browns, reds, and whites visible even in the suburbs. Women's Liberation has exposed the indefensible submission of woman to man, even within the movement, and has gone beyond to herald the breakup in the larger society of ancient patterns of male domination. The anti-war movement has done a great deal—though admittedly less than the Vietnamese collectively —to expose America's unbenign policies abroad. The exclusive Executive conduct of foreign relations, the anachronistic pieties of the Cold War, the wisdom of the nuclear buildup and US global messianism—all are being questioned and attacked as never before. Young radicals have even got their message through to the men of power in Washington: "A feeling is widely and strongly held that 'the Establishment' is out of its mind," John T. McNaughton, Assistant Secretary of Defense, reported to his chief Robert McNamara in May 1967. "The feeling is that we are trying to impose some U.S. image on distant peoples we cannot understand (any more than we can the younger generation at home), and that we are carrying the thing to absurd lengths."

These absurd lengths do present radicals with another moment of opportunity. Whether the New Left will prove any more capable of taking advantage of circumstances than was the Old, however, is questionable. So far the former has been able to shake up and occasionally alarm power-holders, but it has not been able to turn Washington round to stop the War and begin the work of recovery and renewal at home. It has not been able to build durable organizations or to maintain its earlier mood of expansive possibility—*the imagination takes command!* I know that it has received scores of premature obituary notices during the past few years and have no wish to join the ranks of gleeful undertakers. The latter laid away nonviolence and pronounced the day of mass demonstrations safely past, only to have the May Day Tribe and other New Left groups take to the streets of Washington, as recently as the spring of 1971, in the largest civil disobedience action in American history. The movement is obviously still ambulatory. Nevertheless, signs mount that its original energy has been pretty well played out. Many activists express a felt need for self-criticism, deeper analysis of options, a chance for effective redirection.

Those who share a sense of "a falling-apart present and a future full of fears," as one young radical recently put it, will find that the re-publication of this book comes at a good time. And there is irony in the fact that it is still so timely.

Lillian Symes and her husband quite clearly set out to write a study which would be immediately useful to their contemporaries. That they failed in large part was due to their virtues. Mrs. Symes, who had married Travers Clement in 1929, was a former journalist with a lively style and, as one reviewer noted, "a fine, strong, richly informed intellect." She also had an aversion to sectarian quarrels. As she noted in the Foreword, "though the writers have a point of view, and a definite one . . . they are members of none of the radical factions and under no obligation, emotional or otherwise, to make a case for any special group." But the price of this independence, given the internecine warfare among all the special groups, was that none had much use for what they wrote.

The other main reason their work suffered relative neglect is more complex. Writing when she did, Mrs. Symes naturally shared some of the Marxist presuppositions of the day. Insofar as she did, she had to see the thirties as the culmination of all the activity of the past and to see present radicals working, as she put it in the final chapter, "on the side of the angels. In the general direction toward which they are pointing may well lie the only alternative to social chaos." So said her mind but her heart was not in this general direction, with all its hair-splitting controversies, dissensions, and schisms. Her prose reveals that her real feelings were with the idealistic radicals of the preceding century. The pages on Robert Owen and Frances Wright, Margaret Fuller and George Ripley glow with sympathetic understanding. Those on William Z. Foster, Jay Lovestone, James Cannon, and Norman Thomas are dutiful. Moreover, Mrs. Symes recognized that "anarchism is undoubtedly the philosophy most native to the American temperament" and honestly refused to shape her evidence to fit the presumed needs of the machine age. As an unintended consequence of this recognition and these sympathies, I am suggesting, *Rebel America* spoke less to the Old Left than it speaks over the decades to the anarchist perspective at the core of the New.

And a final bit of irony lies in the fact that this perspective draws on a native past older than that of the Old Left. Marxism in the United States goes back only to the post-Appomattox decades, while the anarchist/libertarian–socialist tradition is rooted in the idealistic eighteen thirties and forties. Intellectuals and the generous young then made their first "turn to the left," after the Revolution, in sharp reaction against the materialistic values of an increasingly commercial civilization. The outburst of creative energies then produced the "American Renaissance" in literature and a whole series of individual and communitarian experiments in living. The dominance of the machine was challenged; root and branch questions were posed about state authority, the bases of individuality, the grounds of genuine community.

To be sure, Mrs. Symes does poke gentle fun at the utopians and their efforts "to usher in the millennium through establishing green plots of social righteousness in a world already badly smudged with factory smoke." Choking on the air we breathe, we have more difficulty in seeing them as very funny and may rather regard them as forerunners of recent and much more desperate experiments in survival. Fortunately Mrs. Symes does not lack a basic respect and liking for the men and women of the Romantic period, as I have noted, and thus offers us a valuable introduction to a tradition which has immediate relevance to our present. The little groups of artistic and social radicals who then had "their community flings" would have no trouble today finding their place in a commune in New Hampshire or Oregon. And, after all, what is the SDS motto of "One man, one soul" but a modern restatement of the great Emersonian theme of self reliance?*

Mrs. Symes also reminds us that the general American response to authentic individualism has remained relatively constant. From Tocqueville's time to ours, Americans have never found it easy to tolerate protest, dissent, even difference. In their harsh prescriptions for "yippies" the modern champions of law and order are no more generous or imaginative than were the editors quoted by Mrs. Symes, who proposed to give the "tramps" of the eighties "leaden" meals or offered as "the simplest plan . . . to put strychnine or arsenic in the meat and other supplies furnished." So it went, on down to the "passion of Sacco and Vanzetti," which Mrs. Symes quite properly gives considerable space, and beyond.

* Which is not to say that the present is the past or that the Woodstock Nation is Brook Farm writ new and large. Origins and similarities can only be traced sensitively by the wary reader who keeps differences in mind.

Histories of the victims of the American System have long been in short supply, as concern for those run over by what is called Progress has never been a national virtue. *Rebel America* comes close to being such a history. There are some very good sections on the response to the immigrants and on the early attempts to crush labor organization. But there are some surprising omissions as well: Blacks are rarely mentioned and seem to exist only as the objects of abolitionist and radical efforts. The Indians are truly invisible. Moreover, women, of whatever ethnic background, only rarely appear in the person of an exceptional Fanny Wright or Victoria Woodhull; feminist movements receive only a line or two. This relative neglect of the roles of race and sex in American history, however surprising in a writer of Mrs. Symes' breadth of sympathy, is readily traceable to the pervasive economism of the period in which she wrote. The Marxist focus on class determinants also leads her to overemphasize the importance of organized labor to radicalism and to underemphasize the importance of nationalism as an obstacle to its growth.

But these criticisms are more than counterbalanced by the strengths of *Rebel America*. It remains, in my judgment, the best single volume survey of American radicalism. Mrs. Symes knowledgeably introduces a long, honorable list of rebels, from John Humphrey Noyes to John Reed, from communitarians to the Wobblies, who were said to be "the greatest conglomeration of freaks that ever met in convention." All those who think of seizing control of their lives might well begin by striking up an acquaintance with such freaks: if we ever discover a usable past in this New World, many of them are likely to be in it.

*Bibliographical Note*

Lillian Symes and Travers Clement could carry their discriminating "Selected Bibliography" no farther than 1933. Readers

[ xxiv ]

who wish to pursue the story of social revolt in the United States on down to the present can turn to an already extensive body of work. Perhaps the most thoughtful of the general interpretations is Theodore Roszak's *The Making of a Counter Culture* (Anchor Books, 1969). Jack Newfield's *A Prophetic Minority* (Signet, 1966) has insight and verve and is nicely complemented by Paul Jacobs and Saul Landau, *The New Radicals* (Vintage Books, 1966). One of the most recent attempts to interpret the events of the sixties is Michael W. Miles, *The Radical Probe* (Atheneum, 1971). David Horowitz, *Student* (Ballantine, 1962), remains helpful. Alfred F. Young has edited a collection of essays which explore various facets of *Dissent* (Northern Illinois University Press, 1968). One essay which should not be overlooked is C. Wright Mills' "Letter to the New Left," *New Left Review*, no. 5 (September–October 1960), 18–23. For the hostile response of the Old Left, see Irving Howe's *The Radical Papers* (Doubleday, 1966) and *The Radical Imagination* (*Dissent*, 1967); see also Lewis Feuer, *Conflict of Generations* (Basic Books, 1969). There are good books on the problems of growing up in America, the best of which, to my mind, is Edgar Z. Friedenberg's *The Dignity of Youth and Other Atavisms* (Beacon, 1965); see also Kenneth Keniston's *Young Radicals* (Harcourt, Brace & World, 1968); and Paul Goodman's *Growing Up Absurd* (Random, 1960). On the black revolt, see above all *The Autobiography of Malcolm X* (Grove, 1966); Eldridge Cleaver's *Soul on Ice* (Dell, 1968) is important for understanding the Black Panthers and LeRoi Jones' *Home: Social Essays* (Morrow, 1966) for understanding the general perspective of black nationalism. For the background and origins of the black student movement, Howard Zinn's *SNCC: The New Abolitionists* (Beacon, 1964) is outstanding. On the new Indian resistance, see Vine Deloria Jr.'s *Custer Died for Your Sins* (Avon, 1969), William Meyer, *Native Americans* (International Publishers, 1971), and the issues of *Akwesasne Notes*, the Indian newspaper published at Rooseveltown, N.Y. On Women's Liberation, see Cellestine Ware, *Woman Power* (Tower, 1970); Caroline Bird, *Born Female* (David McKay, 1968); and Eva Figes, *Patriarchal Attitudes* (Faber, 1970). A good collection of readings is *Masculine/Feminine,* edited by Betty and Theodore Roszak (Harper Colophon Books, 1969). On specific student insurrections, see, in addition to Daniel Cohn-Bendit's work, the collection edited by Hervé Bourges, *The French Student Revolt* (Hill & Wang, 1968). On Berkeley, see Sheldon S. Wolin and John H. Schaar, *The Berkeley Rebellion and Beyond* (Vintage, 1970); on Columbia, see Jerry Avorn *et al.,* eds., *Up Against the Ivy Wall* (Atheneum, 1968). For immediate forerunners of the young radicals, see Thomas F. Parkinson, ed., *Case on the Beats* (Crowell, 1961); Allen Ginsberg, *Howl & Other Poems* (City Lights, 1956); Lawrence Ferlinghetti, *Coney Island of the Mind* (New Directions, 1958); Gary Snyder, *Earth House Hold* (New Directions, 1969). Important for any understanding of New Left thought are Herbert Marcuse's *Eros and Civilization* (Beacon, 1955) and *One-Dimensional Man* (Beacon, 1964) and Norman O. Brown's *Life Against Death* (Wesleyan University Press, 1959). For some of the radicals, outside the mainstream Old Left, who contributed directly or indirectly to the rise of the New, see the autobiographical writings of Edmund Wilson, A. J. Muste, Bertrand Russell, and Jean-Paul Sartre. Nat Hentoff's *Peace Agitator* (Macmillan, 1963) is a competent study of Muste, one of the over-thirty radicals the young could and did trust. So was Ammon Hennacy, whose *Autobiography of a Catholic Anarchist* (Catholic Worker Books, 1954) is well worth reading, and so would have been Emma Goldman had she lived, as I hope my biography *Rebel in Paradise* (Beacon, 1970) makes clear.

Weekapaug, Rhode Island
2 August 1971

# FOREWORD

TO WRITE an informal history of social revolt in America which is not at the same time a history of the American people, is to indulge necessarily in a somewhat arbitrary limitation of subject-matter. Using the term in its broadest sense, such a story might begin with the rebellions of Roger Williams and of Anne Hutchinson in the 1630s against the theocratic tyrannies of the Pilgrim Fathers, or in another and possibly more accurate sense with the uprisings of the Virginia frontiersmen in 1676. Besides these, its roster of heroes would include, certainly, the names of Patrick Henry and Thomas Paine, of Daniel Shays, Henry Thoreau, Elijah Lovejoy, and John Brown. There is no decade in American history since the founding of the first Colonies which has not had its gestures of protest and rebellion against some specific social injustice or outworn code—religious, political, economic, or cultural. For the purposes of this book, however, the term "social revolt" is used to describe primarily the activities of those groups which have aimed at the complete transformation—by whatever means—of the whole social order. *Rebel America* is the story of our social revolutionaries and of those allied movements of protests with which their activities have, at various times, overlapped.

In almost any other nation such a story would be practically synonymous with the history of its labor movement.

But certain anomalies, which in the past have distinguished the social scene in the United States from that of Europe, have helped to create a fatal division between the labor and radical movements which the latter, for all its persistent efforts, has never been able completely to overcome. The existence of vast tracts of Western land open for settlement, the creation of a large and aggressive class of small-owning farmers which was neither peasant nor proletarian in the European sense, mass immigration, the shifting and heterogeneous character of our industrial populations, the fluidity of our social strata and opportunities for individual advancement—often more apparent than real—all tended to defeat for many years the advance of those philosophies of social change which in Europe were finding validity in the experiences of the masses and which permeated their organizations. The American tradition of rebellion has found expression more frequently outside than inside the labor movement. Much of the history of radical activity in the United States has consisted of the struggles of contending groups of radical intellectuals for the soul of labor.

The comparative weakness of our movements of social rebellion and the apparent stability and vigor of the American social structure have made for a general indifference—rarely found in Europe—to the meaning, history, and purposes of radical movements. The events of the past four years, however, have indicated that the problem of social revolt is not an academic one, even in the United States. In a world that is obviously torn asunder by economic contradictions and beset everywhere by conflicting winds of doctrine, past and present efforts to revolutionize the social order, whether purely native or international in complexion, take on a new relevance. The present volume makes no pretense to being a general interpretation of social forces in American history. It is merely what the subtitle implies.

It would be impossible to discuss a subject more controversial, more befogged by factional prejudices, than the past twenty years of radical history. Each group has its own interpretation of events, its own rationalizations, its own passionate historians. It is obviously impossible for any contemporary to discuss so turbulent a scene with complete objectivity. But though the writers have a point of view, and a definite one, toward their subject, they are members of none of the radical factions and under no obligation, emotional or otherwise, to make a case for any special group.

# ACKNOWLEDGMENTS

THE authors are indebted to The Macmillan Company for permission to reprint the brief quotations contained in this book from *American Syndicalism: The I.W.W.*, by John Graham Brooks, *Social Forces in American History*, by A. M. Simons, *Brook Farm: Its Members, Scholars, and Visitors*, by Lindsay Swift, and *The Rise of American Civilization*, by Charles A. and Mary R. Beard; to Harcourt, Brace and Company, Inc., for the quotation from *Chicago, the History of its Reputation*, by Lloyd Lewis and Henry Justin Smith; to D. Appleton-Century Company, Inc., for the excerpt from *The Labor Movement in the United States: 1860-1895*, by Norman J. Ware; to International Publishers for the selection from *Bill Haywood's Book*; to Farrar and Rinehart for permission to use the paragraph from *Homecoming: An Autobiography*, by Floyd Dell; to the Columbia University Studies in History, Economics and Public Law, and to the respective authors for quotations from *The Decline of the I.W.W.*, by John S. Gambs, and *Frances Wright*, by William Randall Waterman. The writers are particularly indebted to the last-named study for material on the life of Frances Wright, to the *History of Labour in the United States*, by John R. Commons and Associates, for material on the early labor movement, and to an unpublished manuscript by Walter Wilson for certain facts concerning the Garland Fund.

PART ONE

*THE UTOPIANS*

# I

## REVOLUTION BY BENEVOLENCE

SINCE the beginning of history, thoughtful and sensitive men have looked at the scene about them and finding it wanting in justice, kindliness and sanity have proceeded to spin out of their sympathies and imaginations pictures of an ideal world. The societies they have envisaged have differed as widely as their times and temperaments—the Republic of Plato, the Utopia of Sir Thomas More bearing only the vaguest resemblance to the decorative Nowhere of William Morris, the disciplined World State of H. G. Wells. The kinship of the utopians through the ages has been primarily a moral and æsthetic one. The creation of social harmony out of social chaos has been the very essence of the bright utopian dream— a dream quite unrelated to historic processes, social evolution and economic reality in general.

Down to the beginning of the Industrial Revolution such concepts remained, for the most part, mere literary and philosophic exercises of the creative imagination. Men read of the Republic, of Christianopolis, the New Atlantis, the City of the Sun, as they read of Ulysses, Beowulf, Siegfried and King Arthur. It was not these literary inventions, but a tradition of primitive and medieval communism, which inspired such mass movements as the peasant revolts of the fourteenth century and much of the equalitarian social criticism of the eighteenth. Not until the machine had begun its conquest of

British industry and the hopes aroused by the French Revolution had failed—so far as the masses were concerned—to materialize, did the utopian dream assume the reality of a concrete social program in the minds of a few scattered social philosophers and altruistic laymen. It was then that the movement known as Utopian Socialism was born.

During the last decades of the eighteenth century, the factory system arose in England and was later to be extended to the Continent and across the sea to the New World. The day of domestic industry was passing. Manufacturing shifted from the cottages and small shops of rural villages to the towns and cities of the North, and the rural population, which since the closing of the commons had been partially or wholly dependent on this industry, shifted with it. Out of the ranks of agricultural workers, town laborers and their women and children, a new social class appeared—a class which a German-Jewish economist, who was to have much to say on this subject many years later, was to designate as "the industrial proletariat."

Poverty and degradation had existed among the masses through all time but hardly in that wholesale and obviously man-made form which they now assumed. Control over machine production, vested in men actuated solely by their predatory instincts in a society which had not yet developed the rudiments of a social conscience, introduced a new set of incongruities into human society—hunger and cold in the midst of plenty, superabundance and privation side by side. In the words of Mr. Lewis Mumford in *The Story of Utopias*: "Those machines whose output was so great that all men might be clothed; those new methods of agriculture and new agricultural implements which promised crops so big that all men might be fed—the very instruments that were to give the whole community the physical basis of a good life, turned out, for the vast majority of people who possessed

[ 4 ]

neither capital nor land, to be nothing short of instruments of torture."

The first chapters of modern industrial history constitute a story of incredible misery and inhumanity punctuated by flashes of blind and bitter revolt in which the workers smashed machinery, rioted for political representation, and to which the government responded with ever-increasing repression.

If the privileged classes, as a whole, remained quite indifferent to the social consequences of this new dispensation, individuals here and there, usually from the ranks of the well-fed liberal and intellectual groups, revolted against its brutality and its ugliness. Poets like Coleridge, Wordsworth, Southey and Shelley, already fired by the libertarian political philosophers of France, were outraged by the blackening of the English countryside, the dehumanization of the mill workers. Shelley wrote in poetic anticipation of the theory of surplus value:

> The seed ye sow, another reaps;
> The wealth ye find, another keeps;
> The robes ye weave, another wears;
> The arms ye forge, another bears.

Humanitarian and radical philosophers like Jeremy Bentham, Thomas Spence, Charles Hall and William Godwin inveighed in their separate fashions against the social and industrial injustices of the time. Even from members of the landed aristocracy came protests against the ruthlessness of the new industrial "vulgarians" pushing their way to power unhampered by traditions of *noblesse oblige*. And in the forefront of that brilliant array of reformers which arose in England in the wake of the factory system was a man who began to suspect—after twenty years of agitation for more civilized industrial practices—that reform was not enough. This was Robert Owen.

Of the other outstanding utopians both in England and

[ 5 ]

France who were contemporaries of Owen in that socialistic Age of Innocence of the early 1800s, only one, Charles Fourier, is destined to play an influential part in our story. Both Owen and Fourier believed that the new social order could be ushered in by the good-will of the rich and powerful rather than by the aggressions of the poor and oppressed. Both were also convinced that they could demonstrate the practicability of their utopian vision by the establishment of successful oases of coöperation in a desert of competition. It was inevitable that the American continent with its cheap land, its pioneering possibilities and still fluid social standards should suggest itself as the most appropriate setting for such schemes.

Though the community experiments of the 1820s marked the first conscious efforts in America to reconstruct society upon an entirely new model, they did not mark the beginning of either communism or class conflict in the New World. Not all the immigration from Europe to America during our Colonial period had consisted of religious dissenters fleeing ecclesiastical tyranny to a land in which they might worship God in their own fashion. Probably half our Colonial settlers landed as indentured servants and many thousands of these were unemployed and undernourished men and women who had sought to escape their misery at home by selling themselves for a period of years in exchange for their passage to America. Once their indenture was worked out, many settled along the adjacent frontier while others remained in the towns as artisans and laborers. From the beginning their interests, like those of the small shopkeeper, conflicted with the interests of the wealthy planters and merchants. As far back as 1676, Virginia, under Governor Berkeley, had had its Bacon's Rebellion in which the frontier farmers to the west had risen against their rich creditors of the coast and had burned Jamestown to the ground. In 1769 New York had seen

[ 6 ]

an armed rebellion under Jacob Leisler in behalf of the rights of the artisans and small shopkeepers. A little later, South Carolina, North Carolina, Pennsylvania, Maryland and Vermont had experienced agrarian revolts similar in spirit to Bacon's; and the armed frontiersmen, marching against Philadelphia, had frightened that city out of its wits. After the Revolution came the desperate uprising of the debt-laden farmers under Daniel Shays against the rich creditor class of Massachusetts—a rebellion in which the militia fired upon the rebels and set a precedent which was to be followed in similar disturbances for a hundred and forty years. These early Americans were decidedly not a docile lot. They were rugged individualists given to violent though sporadic outbursts against specific injustices. These outbursts had nothing to do, however, with the practice of communism in the same period.

Pre-Owenite American communism was almost exclusively the offspring of religious dissent. It was rooted in primitive Christianity and the ethics of the New Testament. It was concerned with individual salvation rather than with social revolt, but its success served as an inspiration and encouragement to the social radicals.

The first two experiments in religious communism were short-lived—the Labadist Community settled by a group of Protestant mystics in northern Maryland in 1680 and the Women in the Wilderness Community established shortly after. The earliest communist settlement about which much of anything is known remained in existence for one hundred and seventy-five years. This was Ephrata, settled in Lancaster County, Pennsylvania, in 1732 by a group of German Anabaptists under Conrad Beisel.

Nearly fifty years after the founding of Ephrata, the hysterical young Quakeress, Jemima Wilkinson, arose from a two-day coma to announce that she had been divinely inspired to lead a new sect into a new Jerusalem. The Jerusalem

[ 7 ]

Community in upper New York State was the result. Seven years later, the Shakers, after having been similarly inspired by a similar vision on the part of Ann Lee, completed their first permanent home at Mount Lebanon, New York. The Shakers were the most successful of all the Christian communists in America.

Of numerous communistic settlements founded by religious dissenters from Germany, the Harmony Community in Indiana, established by 600 Würtembergians under George Rapp in 1814, is the most significant, for Harmony was destined to become, under Owen, the first of the American utopias. After the coming of the Owenites, the Rappites moved on to Economy near Pittsburgh and prospered there all during the remainder of the century. Other communistic German dissenters settled and prospered at Zoar in Ohio, Amana in Iowa, Bethel in Missouri and Aurora in Oregon.

The most famous and certainly the most interesting American experiment in religious communism owed less to the New Testament than to the secular socialism of the '40s, and so will be discussed in relation to that movement. This was Oneida, one of the last episodes of the utopian period. Its founder, John Humphrey Noyes, was the first and the most astute historian of American communities and his *History of American Socialisms*, written in the late '60s, is an amazing and salutary document now out of print. In this autoptic study, founded partially on an unpublished manuscript left to him by a painstaking Scotch investigator named William MacDonald, Noyes chronicles the rise and fall of some thirty communistic communities, or "American Socialisms" as he calls them, in the United States; and most of these were secular. It was his opinion at this time that the experimental phase of American communism was now passed and that henceforth "communism or nothing" was likely to be the demand of the American people!

A glance at the American social scene between 1820 and

[ 8 ]

1860 could easily have led a more sophisticated observer than Noyes to the conclusion that there was something inherently utopian in the American temperament itself, an irrepressible impulse to individual and social salvation by "getting away from it all." The continent had been and was still being peopled not by groups and individuals inclined to stand and fight on the old ground but by those who sought escape to some freer and more wish-fulfilling environment. It is not surprising then that the various movements of still further escape—both religious and social—should find a ready response in the American breast of this unsettled time. Except in the period immediately following the European upheavals of 1848, it was more frequently the romantic than the revolutionary who turned a hopeful gaze westward as factory chimneys multiplied against the sky. The social unrest that smoldered in the Chartists' agitations and flamed in the rebellions of the '40s was translated into other terms in the New World with its far-flung frontier and varied environments. Having attracted the ambitious individualist, the restless dissenter, the social dreamer and experimentalist, the believer in the Kingdom of God on Earth, it provided him not only with physical space but with a setting in which social traditions had not yet crystallized. Anything was possible and salvationists were legion.

The wave of secular socialism which swept the country from the '20s through the '40s had its spiritual counterpart in a wave of hysterical revivalism—one of those prolonged debauches of emotional religious excitement to which undeveloped Anglo-Saxon communities, largely bereft of satisfactory cultural releases, seem particularly prone. Powerful throughout the '30s, it reached its final absurd culmination in the activities of the Millerites, the followers of one William Miller who, by some amazingly complicated calculations based on Biblical prophecy, proved to the satisfaction of thousands from Maine to New Orleans that the Second Coming

[ 9 ]

of Christ was at hand. So credulous were his converts and so convincing his data that the price of muslin—the approved material for ascension robes—soared heavenward, even though its wearers, trailing white clouds of glory through parks and country fields when the appointed day arrived, did not.

"There was a time between 1831 and 1834," writes Noyes, "when the American people came as near to a surrender of all to the Kingdom of God as they came in 1843 to a socialistic revolution." Realizing how far the rank and file of the American people actually were from a socialistic revolution in 1843, we may conclude that Noyes had, likewise, a somewhat exaggerated notion of the power of the national revival. Nevertheless, it is obvious, when we consider that Owen propagated his schemes to the applause of Congressmen and Senators and that Fourierism won the support of the country's foremost intellectuals, that the American people were extremely susceptible at this time to intimations of a new deal and that both Socialism and the Kingdom of God were seriously considered by large numbers of persons as possible ways out.

The pursuit of the ideal society on American soil as expressed in utopian experiments never constituted one coherent movement. It has never really ended. The utopian hope still springs eternal in many a dissenting breast, but as a dominant phase in revolutionary history it ran its episodic course in the first half of the nineteenth century. It is the story of little groups of idealists and serious-thinkers who sought by precept and moral suasion to turn the advancing tide of industrialism into channels prescribed by their eighteenth-century libertarian theories and their timeless dreams of social harmony. American utopianism was a compound of Owenite communism, Fourieristic socialism and rugged individualism of the Thomas Paine-Thomas Jefferson-Declaration of Independence brand. Even that French utopian anarchist, Pierre-Joseph Proudhon, exerted an indirect influence on its later phases. Its adherents reflected the philosophic confusions of their time. But in one rôle or another, some of the most brilliant names in American annals are listed in its cast.

The first attempt to demonstrate socialism on American soil was but an episode in a career that was, in itself, a prolonged utopian gesture. Robert Owen was one of those fairly numerous figures in the history of radical movements whose activities seem to violate every canon of their own class interests. A self-made man of humanitarian instincts, originality of thought and unbounded self-confidence, he came into power as an industrialist in an era of industrial barbarism. Early in his career he reached a conclusion which mid-century philosophers were still to popularize; namely, that man is the creature of his environment and that his character is made *for* him not *by* him. Owen, who was nothing if not vocal, held this theory in its most dogmatic and uncompromising form, much to the irritation of his friends, Harriet Martineau and Francis Place. "Man," he would declare, "becomes a wild, ferocious savage, a cannibal or a highly civilized and benevolent being according to the circumstances in which he may be placed from his birth." Once off on this track, nothing could stop him. It was a theme upon which he could —and did—expatiate for hours.

In 1800 he came into control of the New Lanark Mills in Scotland which had previously been the property of his father-in-law, David Dale, and Sir Richard Arkwright, the inventor, and on the basis of his faith began a thorough housecleaning immediately. From the standpoint of working conditions, the mills had been generally considered the best in Great Britain. To Owen, a hundred years ahead of his time in his conception of industrial relations, they were shocking. Of the 2,000 villagers, 500 were child laborers recruited at the ages of five to seven from the foundling asylums of Edinburgh, who worked from six in the morning until seven at night. The village was dirty, bedraggled, unsanitary; the villagers, according to Owen, "a collection of the most ignorant and destitute from all parts of Scotland, possessing the usual characteristics of poverty and ignorance."

Within a few years, New Lanark and its inhabitants were transformed. In place of the typical mill village of the period there appeared a model industrial community with schools, clean, comfortable cottages, and clubrooms. The wage and hour standards were unheard of at the time. By 1816 the experiment was world-famous and Owen had gained an international reputation as the man who had "made philanthropy pay." Liberals, reformers, statesmen, aristocrats and princes —even Nicholas of Russia—came to see the miracle. Owen was now deep in the struggle for general factory legislation. Reaction against the worst abuses of the system was coming to a head. Conditions disclosed by investigations of the Select Committee of 1816 were shocking even to the hardened sensibilities of that day—as, for example, the testimony that in the Backbarrow mills, five-year-old children worked the year around from five in the morning to seven at night with one hour out for meals and in addition were required by their pious employers to spend several hours on Sunday cleaning the machinery. The *Report of the Committee on the Education of the Lower Orders in the Metropolis* disclosed the widespread illiteracy of the London poor. The Upper Orders were impressed with the need for concessions. But Owen, radiating energy in the midst of all this, was evolving a new social philosophy.

Up to this point Owen had been an enlightened philanthropist, the foremost social and educational reformer of his day, an exponent of "the new capitalism" a hundred years ahead of his time. The revolution in the mental, moral and physical characteristics of the New Lanarkers under his dispensation had confirmed his convictions regarding the decisive nature of environmental factors. But now, looking at the world beyond New Lanark, he was rapidly coming to the conclusion that such isolated experiments in good-will by an occasionally enlightened employer were altogether inadequate. It was the pressure of industrial competition, he began to suspect, not the hard-heartedness of the individual industrialist, that was operating to produce the misery and degradation which accompanied the rise of the new industrial order. Competition must give way to coöperation, private to coöperative ownership, if the Machine was to be a Deliverer rather than a Juggernaut to the human race. In short, Owen passed from reformism to socialism.

As a utopian socialist, Owen imagined that the new coöperative system could be inaugurated by the establishment of small, self-sustaining coöperative units. As a utopian again, he believed that it could be superimposed upon the world by wealthy and altruistic individuals, and so proceeded at once to the business of converting the upper classes to his plan for the regeneration of society. He could scarcely have chosen a more inopportune time.

The collapse of industry at the close of the Napoleonic Wars had spread unemployment and misery in its wake, resulting in violent disturbances among the workers, urgent demands for reform among the radicals, the suppression of public meetings and the suspension of the Habeas Corpus Act by the authorities. It was anything but a propitious moment for the promulgation of socialistic doctrines among the socially elect when Owen fired his first gun in a report made for the Committee of the Association for the Relief of the Manufacturing and Labouring Poor under the presidency of the Duke of York and the chairmanship of the Archbishop of Canterbury in 1819. The report contained an outline for the social salvation of the unemployed by the establishment of coöperative communities and a prophecy that "when

[ 13 ]

Society shall discover its true interests," these communities would gradually supersede the existing social order.

Heretofore Owen had had the support and friendship of the aristocratic classes and of the press, but now his influential friends began to fall away and Fleet Street turned against him. He continued his efforts, even naïvely submitting his plan to Czar Alexander and the Congress of Sovereigns at Aachen. He soon discovered, however, that he was no longer Owen the Philanthropist, but Owen the Infidel, the Socialist, the "gentleman who makes much noise in the public prints" in the words of the rather feeble-witted Lord Lascelles. The Duke of Kent, Victoria's father, supported him long after lesser lights had ceased to regard him with approval. He finally became convinced that it would be necessary for him to demonstrate his theories on his own responsibility and began to watch for an opportunity to do so. It came when an agent of the Rappite Community in Indiana visited England in 1824 looking for a possible purchaser. Owen returned with him to America and some months later bought the village of Harmony with all its improvements, "infant industries," and 30,000 acres of land for $150,000.

The New Harmony Community, as the former Rappite settlement was now to be called, began its existence in a blaze of glory and nation-wide publicity. When Owen arrived in America in 1824, the community idea was already in the air. His fame and theories had preceded him and 1822 had witnessed the formation of a Society for Promoting Communities inspired principally by a collection of his essays entitled *A New View of Society*.

Already intoxicated with the idea of his new enterprise, the welcome Owen received intoxicated him still further, but it is difficult to understand how the man whose practicality and sound judgment had made a success of every business project he had undertaken could have been so blinded by evangelical zeal as not to have moved more cautiously in this preliminary experiment that was to serve as a model for the new society. All of the Christian communist colonizers before and after Owen showed better judgment in this respect than did the famous industrialist. But the latter's faith in human nature and its essential goodness—if given half a chance—was boundless. It never occurred to him that a vague desire for "social justice" does not necessarily prepare one for all the exigencies of pioneer communism even under such comparatively comfortable conditions as those which the Rappites had left behind them.

Immediately after the purchase of the community and even before the Rappites had completed their orderly withdrawal, Owen left his inexperienced 23-year-old son, William, in charge of this large and complicated enterprise and set out enthusiastically on a lecture tour to spread the glad tidings and gain recruits. Soon he was speaking in the House of Representatives before distinguished audiences that included not only Congressmen and Senators, but Supreme Court justices, Cabinet members, the Vice President and even the President himself. After explaining that New Harmony was but a preliminary project in a general scheme for the transformation of society, Owen announced "a new empire of peace and good-will to men" in the heart of the United States and proceeded to invite everyone in sympathy with its development to pack up and leave at once for the Promised Land. He repeated the invitation wherever he went.

The response overwhelmed the little community. Within a few weeks more than eight hundred assorted utopians—some with their household goods, some empty-handed, and almost all without any ready cash—arrived at New Harmony ready to take the initial plunge into the Brotherhood of Man. Some of them were sincere adherents of Owen's doctrines; others were merely restless and dissatisfied souls looking for some new adventure; a few were downright crooks. All were accepted without test of their qualifications or fitness to take part in the colony's industrial and agricultural program. Visitors, fed at Owen's expense, came and went continuously. The small community inn overflowed with "guests" and they invaded the community houses. William, struggling desperately under the burden of his responsibilities, wrote protesting letters to his itinerant father whose increasingly glowing word-pictures of "the good life," painted far behind the battle-lines, were threatening the very existence of the enterprise.

By October, when Owen, returning on a visit to England, had removed himself still further from the realities of New Harmony life, the resident membership had increased to nine hundred, and William wrote: "We have been much puzzled to know what to do with those who profess to do anything and everything; they are perfect drones and can never be satisfied here. We have got rid of a good many such although we still have a few left."

Owen's eldest son, Robert Dale, who came to New Harmony the following spring, described the colonists as "a heterogeneous collection of radicals, enthusiastic devotees to principle, honest latitudinarians and lazy theorists, with a sprinkling of unprincipled sharpers thrown in." Not all of the recruits, of course, belonged to these categories. Owen's glowing phrases and high idealism attracted to the enterprise several men whose names are significant in American scientific and educational history. The most prominent of these was William Maclure, the foremost geologist of his time, a founder of the Philadelphia Academy of Natural Sciences and a man of wealth, who invested considerable money in the venture. Maclure undertook the supervision of the New Harmony schools which were intended to demonstrate the most advanced principles of education and child-training of the period. Other notables were Thomas Say, famous zoölogist; Charles Alexander Lesueur, the French naturalist; Dr. Gerard

Troost, a distinguished Dutch chemist; and three former associates of Johann Pestalozzi, the Swiss educational reformer. Among the last was William Phiquepal d'Arusmont, who was later to find himself the inconspicuous husband of the brilliant Frances Wright. With such an array of talent at his elbow, it is no wonder that Owen's enthusiasm refused to be dashed by initial difficulties. When he returned from England in January, 1825, his confidence was so great that he reduced the preliminary period, during which the community was to have remained under his personal control, from three years to one and set out to institute full communal ownership immediately.

During the next year and a half New Harmony operated under seven successive constitutions and oscillated all the way from a temporary dictatorship by Owen (at the colonists' request) to a decentralized group of ten separate community units. The atmosphere crackled with conflicting theory. At each reorganization, each tussle of utopian egos, each small tempest over religion, education or bookkeeping, small groups withdrew to set up for themselves or return to the world outside.

Despite dissensions and upheavals, however, life in the community was not without its compensations—mainly social and intellectual. The *New Harmony Gazette*, ably edited by William Pelham, who had been a surgeon in the American Revolution, contained vigorous articles on current political, social and philosophical questions as well as poetry, essays and belated items of European news. No religious observances were provided for, but in conformity with the new freedom any outside preacher who wished to occupy the old Rappite pulpit on Sunday could do so—subject, however, to the condition that he permit questions at the end of the service. Few preachers, after once facing the barrage laid down for them by New Harmony's eager, inquiring minds, ever tempted fate in a like fashion again. There was an abundance of musical talent

[ 17 ]

and dancing was evidently a passion with the younger set. While the official program called for one dance a week in the old Rappite church, the Duke of Saxe-Weimar, who visited the community during his American tour in 1826, reported that he witnessed dancing every evening, *including Sundays* —a scandalous proceeding in the 1820s. Debates alternated with picnics, philosophic discussions with boating parties. Everybody, even the more "delicately reared" young ladies who grumbled on occasion at their chores, seemed, on the whole, to have an exceedingly good time.

New Harmony reached its high water mark in 1826. Its co-educational school was thriving with four hundred pupils from two-year-old kindergartners up. The curriculum was vocational as well as academic and the last word in progressive pedagogy. Maclure and his assistants had established an experimental farm with granaries, stables, workshops and lecture halls which was almost exclusively a children's community. The business and administrative sides of the venture, however, were growing increasingly difficult. The handling of accounts became particularly complex and it was here that one of the colonists, Josiah Warren, a musician and inventor, who, in his reaction from the coöperative life after the failure of New Harmony, was to become the founder of the American school of anarchism, conceived his pet Time Store scheme with which he experimented later in Cincinnati and in his own community, Modern Times, on Long Island.

By 1828 even the optimistic Owen had to admit that New Harmony was a failure. "I tried here," he declared in a farewell address to the members, "a new course for which I was induced to hope that fifty years of political liberty had prepared the American population—that is, to govern themselves advantageously. I supplied land, houses and the use of much capital. . . . But experience proved that the attempt was premature . . ."

When Owen left the community behind him and returned

to England that summer, he also left behind him some four-fifths of his entire fortune. The experiment gradually lapsed into individualism, though all during the nineteenth century the town of New Harmony bore the imprint of the Owen family and has even now, in its library, some of the fruits of Maclure's educational dream. Owen's four sons, William, Robert Dale, Richard and David, remained, each to become a distinguished citizen of his adopted land, but it was Robert Dale who was a true chip from the Owenite block, an inveterate radical, a constitutional dissenter. As associate and boon companion of Frances Wright, he was to plunge into free thought, journalism and the labor movement; and thereafter his name occurs in every movement of protest from birth control to Negro emancipation in the next thirty years. In 1841, his plain-spoken treatise on family limitation startled the country. As a member of the Indiana legislature and of Congress, he battled for social legislation that was considered radical at the time. He ended his career in the American diplomatic service, a convert, like his father, to spiritualism.

New Harmony was by no means the sole expression of Owenism in America, although it was the only American utopian experiment under the master's personal supervision. The '20s saw at least half a dozen other brief-lived communities on the New Harmony model. The most interesting of these was the Yellow Springs Community in Ohio on what is the present site of Antioch College. This settlement, inspired by Owen's visit to Cincinnati in 1824, was established by a group of Swedenborgians under the leadership of their minister, Dr. Daniel Roe. "This society," in the words of an anonymous member quoted by Noyes, "was composed of a very superior class of people" who were "fascinated by Owen and his communism." The community with its walks, rides, plays, "pleasing exercises," dancing and public lectures, its free opinion

[ 19 ]

on all subjects, its official indifference to religious matters (although "there was no free-lovism or other looseness of morals allowed") provided, at the outset, a delightful environment for the "intelligent, liberal, generous and cultivated men and women, many of them wealthy and highly educated" who played such brave rôles in this cultural aristocrat of Owenite utopias. Unfortunately, however, it seems to have had an insufficiency of mechanics, farmers and common laborers, and the experiment, which resembled in many ways the still unborn Brook Farm venture, lasted barely a year.

Another Owenite colony, the Franklin Community at Haverstraw, New York, founded by one of the New Harmony seceders, drew the following withering comment from an erstwhile member in a pamphlet published in New York in 1826:

The amusements mentioned in their [the Frankliners'] constitution as one of the privileges of members consist of piping, drumming, dancing and card-playing every evening. Rational amusements these and worthy of an immortal soul! Ye who love the music of the spirit-stirring fife, ye who love to trip the light, fantastic toe and gamble away the hours which might be devoted to reflection and religious meditation, go to the Franklin Community; there, undisturbed by thought or religious melancholy, you may pass your evenings in threading the giddy mazes of the ball and laugh at the stings of remorse and the upbraidings of a guilty conscience!

Incidentally, the above gives an excellent indication of the general temper and tone of the storm of criticism eventually stirred up by Owen in the United States. American opposition to his theories did not come primarily from the traditional antagonists of the radical—the intrenched, propertied classes. These saw little danger to their privileges in such bucolic and romantic experiments in the Brotherhood of Man. It arose instead among the religionists, who, though theoretically friendly to the coöperative ideal, were dead set

[ 20 ]

against anyone's having a good time. Unfortunately, from this point of view, the coöperative life tended to be a jolly one.

The failure of the Owenite experiments, both official and unofficial, did little to disillusion the redoubtable Owen himself. Again and again he returned to the New World on lecture tours to expound his socialistic doctrines and to attempt the establishment of coöperative communities, first in Texas and finally in Mexico. Almost until his death in 1858, he was continuously engaged in some effort to inaugurate communism by boring from within the prevailing system in England and America. But most of his later life, until he finally became a spiritualist shortly before his death, was devoted to improving the condition of the English working class, through his Equitable Banks of Labour Exchange, coöperative stores, factory legislation, trade unions, or his Association of All Classes and Nations, the first organization whose members were officially to call themselves Socialists. His self-confidence and enthusiasm never admitted defeat. He was probably one of the world's worst bores and poorest listeners, a visionary, and at times, no doubt, pretty much of a fool. But he was also one of the most disinterested, benevolent and farsighted men modern England has produced.

While the New Harmony experiment was running its course and the Owenite movement in general was still in full swing, the South furnished the setting for still another utopian project that was to serve the double purpose of demonstrating the coöperative ideal and of emancipating the southern Negro from chattel slavery. Nashoba in Tennessee, idealistically the most ambitious and actually the most futile communistic venture of the period, was the brain-child of one of the most brilliant women of the nineteenth century. Like so many radicals of her day, Frances Wright was a product of the upper middle class, the daughter of a wealthy Dundee merchant. In her early teens she was something of an intellectual *Wunderkind* and by her early twenties had won the attention and friendship of Jeremy Bentham, Benjamin Constant, and other philosophic radicals and libertarians including General Lafayette, whose confidante she became and whom she later assisted in connection with the conspiracies of the French Carbonari.

To the average idealistic radical of the early 1800s, our youthful Democracy was the very embodiment of political and social promise—just such a symbol of the social ideal made real as is Soviet Russia to the contemporary communist. To Frances Wright, in particular, it seemed a stage upon which the drama of human brotherhood and justice could unfold without political or ecclesiastical hindrance; and in 1818, with her sister Camilla, she paid her first visit to the New World. New York society received her with open arms. A poetic tragedy she had written based upon the struggle of the Swiss against Austrian tyranny was produced anonymously at the Park Theatre shortly after her arrival and drew a letter of praise from Thomas Jefferson. The sisters traveled about the northern and central states, but refused to visit the South because of its chattel slavery. Surveying the American scene through the rosy glasses of libertarian idealism, they were charmed with the country and the vigorous, independent spirit of its people.

The comparative peace of Frances Wright's first American visit was suddenly interrupted by stirring events back home. The industrial collapse following the Napoleonic Wars which did so much to render Owen *persona non grata* among British conservatives had occurred but recently and spontaneous riots were breaking out all over England. The "splendid patience" of the long-suffering poor, mercilessly ground down under incredible toil and hardships, seemed to be at an end. The workers, bitter and rebellious, were demonstrating a revolutionary mood. The radical intelligentsia was seething with excitement. *Der Tag,* or what contemporary radicals would call a "revolutionary situation," seemed at hand.

All of this Frances Wright gleaned from the letters of her friends across the Atlantic and to be more than three thousand miles from the scene of a revolution was more than she could bear. She hurried home in order to assist in and await its coming, but arrived just in time to see the spirit of revolt, already appreciably weakened by ruthlessly repressive measures, collapse completely with the first signs of recovery.

Much of her time during the next four years was spent in France at the home of Lafayette, working on the General's biography, assisting in his various conspiratorial efforts and becoming entangled in his family affairs. The modern psychoanalyst would probably have little hesitancy in diagnosing this young girl's devotion to the aging French patriot as a bad case of Œdipus complex. A contemporary describes her at this period as "a beautiful, slender girl," and her portraits prove that she was as attractive as she was brilliant. In the 1820s, this last quality might easily have proved fatal to romance, but to offset such a disadvantage was the fact that she was also wealthy. Yet she seemed obsessed at this time, to the practical exclusion of all other personal attachments, with the idea of becoming Lafayette's adopted daughter—an ambition to which his family of grown children strenuously objected.

When Frances returned to the United States, it was with Lafayette's party on the triumphal tour of 1824. During this year two things occurred which were to determine the course of her life for some years to come. She visited the Rappite community at Harmony and received her first introduction to a communistic colony in operation; and traveling with the Lafayette party in Virginia, she had her first contact with chattel slavery. Out of these two events Nashoba was born.

The Emancipation movement was still in its infancy when "Fanny" Wright—as she was now to be called by the plain-spoken American press and laity—conceived her plan for freeing the Negro. She had met and talked with Benjamin Lundy, famous editor of *The Genius of Universal Emancipation;* and at the home of President Madison, during Lafayette's visit, she had discussed the slavery question with visiting planters, many of whom deplored the institution but saw no practical solution for it—meaning, of course, no solution that would not incur serious financial loss to themselves. But The Plan was Fanny's own—a combination of communist idealism and emancipationism that was to provide a painless cure for a national cancer. In true utopian fashion, it was to proceed from the top down by a gradual process of ethical persuasion, precept and education. It is not surprising, therefore, that The Plan was greeted with promises of coöperation from a few of the more liberal slave-holders. It aroused the enthusiasm of Lafayette, of such hard-headed American political leaders as Madison, Jefferson and Monroe, and even, it was claimed, of Chief Justice Marshall. Fanny tried to secure Jefferson's participation in the actual experiment itself, but while assuring her of his hearty moral support, he declined on the ground of his advanced years. The shrewd old Democrat probably realized the chimerical nature of the undertaking while applauding its ethical intent.

The Wright Plan for the Gradual Abolition of Slavery in the United States Without Danger of Loss to the Citizens of the South was outlined in a pamphlet published in Baltimore in 1825. It called for a trial project in the form of a community controlled by a small group of sympathetic whites and operated somewhat along the lines then being laid down by Owen at New Harmony. From fifty to a hundred slaves, purchased outright or contributed by interested planters, were to perform the work of the plantation on a coöperative basis. One half of their labor was to be allocated for the purpose of working out their purchase price, the other half to their maintenance. It was calculated that in this way the slaves could attain their freedom in five years. Meanwhile they would be prepared for equality, self-support and self-reliance through their training in the community schools which were to be attended by both blacks and whites. The initial cost of the venture was estimated at $41,000 and it was expected to show a profit of $10,000 a year!

The sagacious Noyes describes the arrangement as a "Brook Farm plus a negro basis" and quotes Hawthorne to the effect that the amateurs who took part in that "pic-nic" (the Brook Farm experiment) did not like to serve as "chambermaids to the cows." "This difficulty," Noyes points out, "was provided against at Nashoba."

The actual experiment, as was invariably the case in utopian enterprises, was on a much less ambitious scale than the one outlined in its prospectus. It took place on 2,000 acres of poor land about thirteen miles from Memphis. Only five slaves were purchased outright at the start, but a South Carolina planter contributed a family of several more. By the end of the experiment the number had increased to thirty.

All went well for a time, though the white members, consisting of Fanny, her sister Camilla, an experienced Illinois colonizer, George Flower, and his family, a Scotchman named James Richardson, and one Richeson Whitby, a former member of a Shaker community, had to work from dawn to dusk clearing ground, building fences and planting patches of corn. Fanny herself worked as hard as any female slave and as she was totally unaccustomed to any physical labor, to say nothing of the intense heat and malarial atmosphere of the section, she became dangerously ill in the summer of 1827 and was ordered to take a complete rest in a cooler climate.

It was the little community's first blow and the colonists watched her depart for England with misgivings. Before she left, she deeded the entire enterprise, the slaves, the plantation and all her personal property thereon, to a committee of trustees consisting of Lafayette, Robert Owen and his son, Robert Dale, William Maclure, Cadwallader Colden, Robert Jennings and the then resident members of Nashoba to "hold in perpetual trust for the benefit of the negro race."

She was accompanied to England by young Robert Dale Owen who had come to Nashoba in the spring, expecting to find it an Eden of kindred spirits but who discovered instead "land, all second rate only and scarcely a hundred acres of it cleared; three or four squared log houses and a few cabins for the slaves the only buildings; slaves, released from the fear of the lash, working indolently under the management of Whitby whose education in an easy-going Shaker village had not at all fitted him for the post of plantation overseer."

Fanny's departure at this critical time, followed by the withdrawal soon after of the practical Flower, and the rapid ascendancy to power of the erratic James Richardson hastened the debacle at Nashoba. Richardson's communism and emancipationism were complicated by a violent anti-clericalism and by frequent attacks of that acute verbal exhibitionism to which so many social rebels have been subject. Camilla and the gentle Whitby were completely under his sway, and as he had charge of the community's "public relations," he was soon sending out compromising excerpts from Nashoba's daily records to Lundy's sympathetic emancipationist journal. Some of these selections, quoted by William Randall Waterman in his excellent biography of Frances Wright, are as eloquent of the utopian emancipators' general social naïveté as of Richardson's atrocious judgment.

Friday, June 1, 1827.
Met the slaves after dinner time—Isabel had laid a complaint against Redrick for coming during the night of Wednesday to

[ 26 ]

her bedroom uninvited and endeavoring without her consent to take liberties with her person. Our views of the sexual relation had been repeatedly given to the slaves; Camilla Wright again stated it and informed the slaves that as the conduct of Redrick, which he did not deny, was a gross infringement of that view, a repetition of such conduct by him or by any other of the men ought in her opinion to be punished by flogging. She repeated that we consider the proper basis of sexual intercourse to be the unconstrained and unrestrained choice of *both* parties. Nelly had requested a lock for the door of the room in which she and Isabel sleep . . . the lock was refused as being in its proposed use, inconsistent with the doctrine just explained; a doctrine . . . which will give every woman a much greater security than any lock can possibly do.

Wednesday, June 13, 1827.

Willis having reported to us that Henry declined coultering today on the plea of a pain in his knee joint to which he is subject —we met the slaves at breakfast time and told them that though we do not doubt that Henry's knee gave him more or less pain, we had not sufficient confidence in his veracity to trust to his statement regarding the degree of the ailment, that we would therefore take their vote respecting the capacity of Henry to follow the oxen today. From this vote we stated that we would exclude . . . Maria because she now cohabits with Henry. As there were ten votes, five each way, we gave our opinion as the casting vote in support of Henry's capacity to coulter.

Sunday evening, June 17, 1827.

Met the slaves—James Richardson informed them that last night, Mamselle Josephine [a quadroon] and he began to live together; and he took this occasion of repeating to them our views on color and on the sexual relation.

The reverberations caused by the publication of these and similar extracts rocked the liberal and emancipationist world of the '20s and eventually reached the ears of Fanny herself, recuperating at the Lafayette home in France. While her views on "the sexual relation" were undoubtedly as liberal as those of Richardson, she would never have prejudiced the cause of Nashoba by a totally unnecessary and irrelevant public statement of them. The little southern colony suddenly became notorious. One emancipationist referred to it

[ 27 ]

as "a great brothel." Lafayette, Lundy and other influential friends of the cause protested. Nashoba was unalterably damned so far as the public was concerned. In a long letter to Richardson, Fanny wrote most reasonably:

Were our own happiness the sole object, it might be indifferent in what manner we addressed ourselves to the world we had left —though in that case I should say it were wiser not to address it at all. . . . But surely, Richardson, that is not our only object, at least not mine. I am far from the conceit that it lies with us to convert the world. But I do believe that it is in our power to influence it. . . . To shrink from criticism would mark us indeed unfit for the work we have undertaken. But to provoke abuse would mark us for equally unfit. If we have in view the conversion of men or if we have simply in view our own happiness and dignity, the manner of all our communications is of equal import with the matter. Let us not throw stones at the world we have left.

When Fanny returned to hard-pressed Nashoba later in the year, she brought back with her that finicky and caustic Englishwoman whose *Domestic Manners of the Americans* was to arouse so much resentment in the patriotic American breast a few years later—Mrs. Frances Milton Trollope, mother of the novelist, Anthony. The lady had evidently failed to visualize in advance the primitive nature of her friend's American enterprise, and upon her arrival was profoundly shocked "at the savage aspect of the scene." She fled almost immediately to Cincinnati where she spent the next two years.

Discouraged at the state of affairs upon her return, Fanny decided to abandon the coöperative and emancipationist basis of the enterprise. She realized at last that she and her friends were unfitted for the hard pioneering work they had undertaken. (By this time Whitby had collapsed from overwork and had gone off with Camilla.) Moreover, she was losing faith in such isolated attempts at emancipation and was coming to the conclusion—no doubt in part at least a rationalization of her failure—that slavery was already on the wane due to economic developments in the South and that Negro labor would soon be displaced by an influx of white labor from the North. She pinned her hopes for a solution of the Negro problem, therefore, on the gradual education of Negro children and on subsequent racial amalgamation. Racial amalgamation was as explosive a subject then as now and the name of Fanny Wright became anathema to Southerners as well as to most of the northern whites who, though they might be eager to free the slaves, were in no manner prepared to meet them as members of the family. Hopelessly ostracized so far as the South was concerned, a little awed no doubt by the violence of the storm she had aroused, and none too well, this "slender girl"—she still seemed that despite her thirty-two years and her intellectual maturity—at last turned her back on the wilderness and accepted Robert Dale Owen's invitation to come to New Harmony and help him edit the *Gazette*.

Though she left the colony in the hands of a caretaker, this was virtually the end of Nashoba. Eighteen months later, the plantation having gone from bad to worse, she decided to abandon it altogether, to emancipate the slaves and to colonize them, at considerable expense to herself, in Haiti, where they would be free to work out their own destinies. She took time off from her editorial duties to accompany the expedition to the West Indies and there, in January, 1830, she settled the thirty Negroes on land provided for the purpose, together with equipment and some preliminary provisions, by the Haitian government. Thus ended the first American attempt at the self-emancipation of the Negro.

The Nashoba experiment in itself might have proved somewhat more successful in the hands of a more practical, experienced and single-minded director. But there were too many facets to Fanny Wright's revolutionary and humanitarian program for her to concentrate her energies exclusively on Negro emancipation. And it was the fate of the little plantation colony, as it has been of every other secular

[ 29 ]

coöperative enterprise, to attract to itself too many well-meaning but ineffectual individuals imbued with too many assorted and extraneous notions.

The end of Nashoba was by no means the end of Fanny Wright as the foremost woman radical of her time. Freed from its demands upon her, she was able to give herself to the revolution on all fronts. Free thought, educational reform, and especially women's rights—from the vote to family limitation—were her chief concerns. While acting as editor of the *Gazette,* she discovered in herself the possibilities of a first-class public speaker, and a brilliant and highly successful lecture tour took her from New England to New Orleans.

The country at this time was going through the worst throes of that hysterical national revival described by Noyes; and the Protestant clergy, projecting an interdenominational organization, the Christian Party in Politics, was attempting something of that same invasion of political life as was to be accomplished by our Methodist Board of Temperance, Prohibition, and Public Morals in the second decade of the twentieth century. The American Tract Society, the American Society for Educating Pious Youth for the Clergy, the Sunday School Union, the American Bible Society, the General Union for Promoting the Observation of the Christian Sabbath united to sanctify the nation for Christian orthodoxy. Unitarians and Free Thinkers, scenting the danger of a new tyranny, were up in arms. The free-thought reaction, particularly, assumed the nature of a countercrusade and journals of protest against the new Calvinism sprang into existence all over the country. The principal free-thought organ appeared in New York under the editorship of George Houston, a disciple of Thomas Paine, who had once been imprisoned for blasphemy in England. He was assisted by Robert Jennings, formerly of New Harmony. All the free-thought journals were widely read and the meetings and debates of the Free

Press Association, the Society of Free Enquirers and similar agnostic groups in the principal cities from Boston to Cincinnati drew large and enthusiastic audiences.

The popular growth of anti-orthodoxy and agnosticism as expressed in the free-thought movement was more than a mere reaction against the aggressions of organized evangelism. It was an intellectual reflection of the industrial changes that had been taking place since the War of 1812. The self-contained handicraft era with its settled institutions and settled religious concepts was passing. The machine basis of the new order called for a spiritual rationalization based on "reason," "progress," "enlightenment" and "science." Until religion adjusted itself in some fashion to these new demands, "infidelity" ran riot.

Fanny Wright sailed into this infidel crusade with all the energy at her command and soon became its best-known spokesman. Cincinnati was at the moment the center of revivalism and here Fanny made her first valiant stand. Her friend, the sharp-tongued Mrs. Trollope, was still living there and has left us a vivid description of the unprecedented event in her famous book:

That a lady of fortune, family and education whose youth had been passed in the most refined circles of private life should present herself to the people as a public lecturer would naturally excite surprise anywhere and the *nil admirari* of the old world itself would hardly be sustained before such a spectacle; but in America where women are guarded by a seven-fold shield of habitual insignificance it caused an effect which can hardly be described.

After recording the hesitations of herself and friends as to the wisdom of attending the lecture, she rushes on enthusiastically:

We congratulated ourselves that we had had the courage to be among the number [of those present], for all my expectations fell far short of the splendor, the brilliance, the overwhelming eloquence of this extraordinary orator. . . . Her tall, majestic figure, the deep, almost solemn expression of her eyes, the simple

[ 31 ]

contour of her finely formed head, unadorned except by its own natural ringlets, her garment of plain white muslin which hung about her in folds that recalled the drapery of a Grecian statue, all contributed to produce an effect unlike anything I had ever seen before or ever expect to see again.

It was not until Fanny reached New York in January, 1829, after her reputation as a "free lover," a "bold blasphemer" and a shameless woman generally had had time to precede her, that she received the full blast of disapproval from the conservative press. But the attacks aroused more curiosity than indignation on the part of the public. Her course of lectures at the Park Theatre, the scene of her theatrical triumph of eleven years before, was highly successful in spite of the efforts of the *Commercial Advertizer*, the *Evening Post* (under editorship of William Cullen Bryant) and the New York *American* to incite the populace against her. "Is there no danger," asks the *Post* rhetorically, and no doubt hopefully, "of collecting an unruly mob which nothing can restrain short of public force and bloodshed itself?" But in spite of one near-riot, precipitated by hoodlums, the speeches continued to attract overflow audiences and had to be repeated in nearby towns.

The whole nature of the New York response to her message convinced Fanny and Robert Jennings that here was the proper home of the radical renaissance and the *Free Enquirer* was transferred from New Harmony to carry on the fight, not only against clericalism, but also against capital punishment, and imprisonment for debt, for political and social equality of all classes and both sexes, free and non-sectarian education, and free support of school children by the State. Robert Dale Owen followed soon after. The little group of free-thought and radical evangelists bought the old Ebenezer Church on Broome Street and turned it into a Hall of Science to house lectures, a progressive school, and the *Free Enquirer* and to be a general center of radical propaganda. Fanny rented a rambling old house and ten acres of ground in what

[ 32 ]

is now the Yorkville section on the East River and here the Free Enquirers, Fanny, Robert Dale Owen, Camilla and her baby, together with William Phiquepal d'Arusmont, who had also come on from New Harmony with three of his pupils to print the paper, lived a simple and frugal life.

Her lecture tours took Fanny to New England where she was bitterly assailed by the Rev. Lyman Beecher; but in Auburn, New York, she won the enthusiastic support of that strange, childlike creature, Orestes Augustus Brownson of whom we shall hear more later. Her discussions of such "indecencies" as birth control and marital reform probably shocked her middle-class listeners more than did her infidelism. It was her advocacy of these sensational causes which was to prove so embarrassing to that industrially rebellious but socially conservative labor movement into which she and Robert Dale Owen were soon to pour their intellectual fire— a phase of her career which belongs to the next chapter.

It was after this labor interlude and several years abroad that Fanny returned to the lecture platform as Mme. d'Arusmont. She was soon estranged from her husband, however, and a few years after the birth of her daughter (who was to become the mother of that stormy petrel of New York theological circles, the Rev. William Norman Guthrie) she divorced him.

Fanny died, after a long illness, in 1852 at Cincinnati, the scene of her first platform triumph. Only seventeen years after her death, Noyes wrote of her in his *History of American Socialisms*:

This woman, little known to the present generation, was the spiritual help-mate and better half of the Owens in the socialistic revival of 1826. Our impression is not only that she was the leading woman in the communistic movement of that period but that she had an important agency in starting two other movements that had far greater success and are at this moment strong in public favor; viz, Anti-Slavery and Woman's Rights. . . . She was indeed, the pioneer of the "strong-minded women."

# II

## WORKING-CLASS INTERLUDE

WHILE the Owenite phase of utopianism, as exemplified in New Harmony, Yellow Springs and Nashoba, was drawing to a close, the first organized labor movement in America was getting itself born of a carpenters' strike in Philadelphia for the ten-hour day. Though comparatively untouched by utopian collectivism, it was almost as naïve socially as those native radicals and British intellectuals who espoused its cause and kindly offered to lead it the way it should go. Like these intellectuals, it thought in terms of those elastic eighteenth century generalities so eloquently stated in the Declaration of Independence; but while its sublime faith in such panaceas as free public education—a cause for which it pioneered and which it helped to win for the American people—must seem a little pathetic to us now, the actual conditions of its daily struggle tended to make it the most realistic of all the social movements of its time. In its brief history we have the rise of trade and industrial unionism, a labor party and a labor press.

Labor unions of a sort—loose associations of skilled artisans gathered together for mutual benefits and indulging in small sporadic strikes—dated from the banding together of Philadelphia printers in 1786 and their strike (the first authentic one on record in the United States) for a minimum wage of $6 a week. But this vague and early groping of skilled craftsmen in no sense constituted a "movement." The early American workingman, not yet divorced from the handicraft stage of production, often found himself an employer one week, an employee the next. Many of the early so-called strikes were not strikes of wage-earners against employers, but strikes against conditions imposed by the terms of some unfair contract in which the immediate employer and employees stood shoulder to shoulder.

The factory system did not become fastened upon the United States until after the War of 1812. When it came, it repeated most of the abuses of its English prototype. Women and children formed the bulk of the workers, having followed industry out of the home into the factory. They worked at starvation wages for as long hours as their employers—many of them hard-bitten New England Puritans to whom Industry was the mother of all virtues—chose to exact. As late as 1835, women and children, the latter between the ages of seven and sixteen, in a Paterson, New Jersey, mill were required to work from four-thirty in the morning until dark. "Is it to be wondered at," asks a statement issued by a strikers' committee and published in the *Radical Reformer and Working Man's Advocate* for September 19 of that year, "that our country has become a great theatre of mobs, yea, we may say, of murderers too, when we remember that the poor and their children in manufacturing towns and districts are kept in ignorance and regarded as but little superior to the beasts that perish?" It seems to have been the fact that the long factory hours precluded any opportunity for educating these working children—rather than the physical dangers and moral injustices involved—that most impressed the awakening working-class consciousness of the skilled artisans in the '20s and '30s.

The factory workers, who—after all—were a very small proportion of the American working class of this period, were not the only group to suffer from the industrial confusions of the new order. Americans had seen hard times before, notably in 1802 and 1808; but in 1819 the country had passed through its initial "panic," first of those periodical depressions which were to be repeated in one form or another at almost regular intervals during the subsequent history of the nation. The collapse had followed a period of feverish speculation in western land, overcapitalization of the new joint-stock companies, chaotic banking conditions and the prostration of European markets following the Napoleonic Wars. Thomas H. Benton in *Thirty Years' View* has left us a graphic account of that early breakdown which could as easily have been written of '73, '93 or 1933:

The years 1819 and 1820 were a period of gloom and agony. . . . No price for property or produce. No sales but those of the sheriff and marshal. No purchasers at the execution sales but the creditor or some hoarder of money. No employment for industry —no demand for labor—no sale for the produce of the farm—no sound of the hammer but that of the auctioneer knocking down property. . . . *Distress*, the universal cry of the people: *Relief*, the universal demand thundered at the doors of all legislatures, State and Federal.

It was during this panic that soup kitchens made their initial appearance in our principal cities, the first official survey of unemployment and public charities was launched in Philadelphia and mass misery became too obvious to be ignored by the daily press.

In the slow return to normality which followed, the new manufacturing class and its creditors were determined to keep production costs at their lowest ebb, even by the introduction of convict labor if necessary. The new industrial order which was exploiting the factory workers so ruthlessly was also engaged in an intense competitive struggle for expanding markets. This avid competition among employers, who depended largely upon credit for their growing operations, exercised a constant downward pressure upon the living standards and bargaining power of the formerly independent mechanic and artisan. And it was among these skilled workers who could recall happier days, not among the oppressed and enfeebled factory hands, that the first signs of revolt appeared.

The six hundred journeymen carpenters of Philadelphia who threw down their tools during the sumer of 1827, thereby firing the first gun for labor in an epic battle that was to echo down the ages, had—we may be sure—little understanding of the real significance of their act. The immediate impetus behind the strike was a simple one. The men were fed up with working from sunrise to sunset; they wanted a little leisure, they wanted—to be exact—a ten-hour day. But behind all this were vague yearnings, as in the case of the utopian radicals, for a better world. The essential difference between the two forces was that the utopians began with the dream and tried to work back toward reality, while labor, at constant grips with the latter, naturally tended to reverse the process.

Despite the forebodings that contemplation of the downtrodden factory workers may have aroused in the breasts of the relatively free and independent mechanics, it was less a consciousness of *class* than of *citizenship* which inspired this first labor movement. These early aristocrats of labor objected particularly to the long regulation working-day because it precluded their participation in public and political affairs and left these in the hands of the idle and wealthy who manipulated government to their own advantage. The lack of free public education, they believed, kept the worker in a state of helpless ignorance in which he could easily be exploited by the better educated and more ruthless members of society. In short, they were convinced that it was leisure and education which gave the rich their advantage over the poor, and that an educated working class with sufficient leisure in which to participate in public affairs could easily rectify all its other abuses, such as imprisonment for debt, the lack of a lien upon its own wages, the obnoxious militia requirements of the day, etc.

The Philadelphia carpenters' strike failed, but it aroused the sympathy and increased the restlessness of a great many other Philadelphia artisans. A ten-hour agitation was whipped up and the various labor forces involved came together in the Mechanics' Union of Trade Associations, a union of unions and the first central labor body in the world. This historic organization soon found a voice in the *Mechanics Free Press* and out of the movement, which spread rapidly to other cities, the world's first labor party, the Working Men's Party, was born.

The franchise had come early and easily to the American workers, and, plunging into politics at a time when they had little understanding of their interests as a class, they were to be misled again and again by professional politicians. High hopes would give way to black despair; until, as one bitter disillusionment followed another, they tended to develop a distrust for "labor politics" that was never to be completely eradicated. In Europe, on the other hand, the fierce struggle for the ballot was itself to be a stimulant to working-class solidarity and by the time labor had won the vote, it had become sufficiently conscious of its own interests to use it more or less as a class weapon.

With the formation of the Working Men's Party, the scene shifts to New York, for it was the New York section which almost immediately became the battle-ground of the radical theorists. The Pennsylvania workers remained more conservative in every way than their New York comrades, although a statement issued by their Political Association of Penn Township when Karl Marx was but a boy in knee trousers throws an interesting light on the early stirrings of American "class consciousness." It reads in part:

There appear to exist two distinct classes, the rich and the poor; the oppressor and the oppressed; . . . the one apparently desirous and determined to keep the people in ignorance of their rights and privileges, that they may live in ease and opulence at the expense of the labor and industry of others; and the other showing that they are acquainted with the nature of their rights and are determined to maintain and possess them.

The Working Men's Party in New York came into existence in the bitter spring of 1829, the second year of the then current depression. The New York workers were in a desperate mood after a winter of serious unemployment. "It is almost impossible to imagine and consequently beyond the reach of our pen to describe the suffering under which the poor of our city are at this time laboring by reason of Cold and Hunger," remarked the *Morning Courier* of February 26, 1829.

Two important radical factions came to grips in the new party almost immediately. These were the Free Enquirers under the joint leadership of Frances Wright and Robert Dale Owen and the so-called Agrarians under the wing of Thomas Skidmore, then engaged in writing *The Rights of Man to Property! Being a Proposition to make it Equal among the Adults of the Present Generation: and to Provide for its Equal Transmission to Every Individual of Each Succeeding Generation, on Arriving at the Age of Maturity.* (Titles meant something in those days!)

Skidmore was called an agrarian because his theories seemed, at first glance, to derive from Thomas Paine's *Agrarian Justice.* In reality, however, he had little more in common with Paine and with the land reformers who followed him than has a modern Communist with a Single Taxer. His program struck not only at land tenure but at the whole system of private ownership. He was frankly for "dividing up," for taking away from the rich and giving to the poor, for liquidating all debts; in short, for starting all over again with a clean slate under an arrangement by which extremes of wealth and poverty would be eliminated forever. To this end, he declared himself in no uncertain terms:

Inasmuch as great wealth is an instrument which is uniformly used to extort from others their property, it ought to be taken away from its possessors on the same principle that a sword or pistol may be wrested from a robber, who shall undertake to accomplish the same effect in a different manner. . . .

Such unequivocal words were not calculated to endear him to the propertied classes. Imprecations arose on every hand. Even the word "Agrarianism" was enough to make the merchant-capitalist of the period see red.

Skidmore, when judged in relation to his time, was undoubtedly a fanatic, but one who saw more clearly the nature of the new industrialism than did most of the early nineteenth-century agitators.

The steam engine [he declared] is not injurious to the poor, when they can have the benefit of it, and this, on supposition, being always the case, instead of being looked upon as a curse would be hailed as a blessing. If, then, it is seen that the steam-engine [as private property] for example is likely greatly to impoverish or destroy the poor, what have they to do, but to lay hold of it and make it their own? Let them appropriate also, in the same way, the cotton factories, the iron foundries, the rolling mills, houses . . . ships, goods, steam-boats, fields of agriculture, etc., etc., etc. . . . as is their right.

Skidmore had the undeniable advantage, so far as his activities in the Working Men's Party were concerned, of having been himself a mechanic and at the outset he impressed upon the comparatively inarticulate, confused and much more conservative rank and file a program which they would undoubtedly have repudiated had they understood its implications. But he was not to have things all his own way for long. The equally articulate Free Enquirers entered the fray, marshaled by Fanny Wright, Robert Dale Owen and George Henry Evans, one of Fanny's many devoted admirers.

The Wright-Owen group early gained an advantage that more than offset Skidmore's proletarian origin. Evans started and assumed editorship of the New York *Working Man's Advocate*, America's second labor paper; and with the *Free Enquirer*, their personal free-thought organ espousing the cause, the Owenites had a virtual monopoly of the party press. Later another labor paper, the *Daily Sentinel*, edited by several enthusiastic young converts to the cause from the staff of the Tammany-controlled *Courier and Enquirer*, came into the field; but this too, being financed in part by a loan from Fanny Wright, leaned toward the Owenite faction.

Along with a general reform program, the Owenites directed their agitation toward what was called "State Guardianship Education," a proposal to have the State afford free support as well as free education to all children from the age of two. This was to be accomplished by the establishment of great boarding schools, owned and controlled by the State—a scheme that was immediately discerned as one of those well-known plots to break up the American family. Needless to say, the Owen group and the Skidmore faction each heartily detested the other's formula and a battle royal was on.

Externally, however, the new party managed to present a more or less united front during the brief election campaign into which it immediately plunged. The "capitalist press" of the period made no discrimination between the party's official program and the private views of its supporters. Vilification, ridicule and misrepresentation were the opposition's chief weapons. Skidmore's agrarian "dividing up" views were lumped together with the Wright-Owen atheistic doctrines and State-guardianship plans and passed out as the program of the mechanics' movement. Their organization was called indiscriminately "The Fanny Wright Party," "The Agrarian Party," "The Infidel Party." At the close of the first day of the three-day election, the *Courier and Enquirer* and *Evening Post* grew fairly hysterical. Cried the former:

We understand with astonishment and alarm that the Infidel Ticket, miscalled the Working Men's Ticket, is far ahead of every other assembly ticket. What a state of things we have reached! A ticket got up openly and avowedly in opposition to all banks—in opposition to social order—in opposition to the rights of property—running ahead of every other!

The vote of the limited electorate was split five ways, but with the closing of the polls the Working Men's ticket was found to have received 6,000 out of 20,000 votes and to have elected one of its candidates, a carpenter, to the state legislature.

This unexpected showing in no way silenced the ranting of the conservative press—quite the contrary. The respectable *Commercial Advertizer* referred to the workers as "poor and deluded followers of a crazy atheistical woman," and proceeded to denounce their leadership in the best rhetoric of the day:

Lost to society, to earth and to heaven, godless and hopeless, clothed and fed by stealing and blasphemy . . . such are the apostles who are trying to induce a number of able bodied men in this city to follow in their own course . . . to disturb the peace of the community . . . betake themselves to incest, robbery, and murder; die like ravenous wild beasts, hunted down without pity; and go to render their account before God, whose existence they believed in their miserable hearts, even while they were blaspheming him in their ignorant, snivelling, and puerile speculations.

Such names as "The Infidel Party" were now too mild and gave way to "The Dirty Shirt Party," the "ring-streaked and speckled rabble." The opposition elsewhere took its cue from New York and the relatively conservative Philadelphia workers soon discovered to their amazement that they were "aiming at an agrarian law for equal distribution of property" and were "in league with foreigners to overthrow religion, and the existing system of government."

Both in Pennsylvania and in New York the vast majority of the workers who made up the rank and file of the movement were in no sense radical. They were concerned primarily with the correction of certain specific political and social abuses, not with altering the structure of a society of the nature of which they had little understanding. They were, in short, reformistic, not revolutionary, in spirit. They might follow complacently those extremely articulate revolutionary theorists in their midst while all was going smoothly, but they were by no means eager to go through fire for beliefs they did not understand or share. They were startled by the charges of infamy flung at their head in the daily press and particularly shocked and angered to find themselves branded as atheists and moral degenerates. Was it possible that they were harboring serpents in their midst? Some of the more unguarded rhetorical flourishes of Fanny Wright, Owen and Skidmore echoed in their ears and they grew uneasy in conscience. The New York Typographical Union adopted resolutions denouncing the Owenites, stating that they hoped "to be always found labouring in better company than with those who would destroy the dearest of social ties, and the hope of the great reward of the 'good and faithful servant.' "

Other factors besides the growing distrust on the part of the rank and file for the intellectuals were operating at this time to cause dissension in our first labor party. The strength shown in the New York and Philadelphia elections—the Philadelphia party gained and held the balance of power in both city and county for a short time—attracted the attention of numerous hack politicians. With the invasion of the movement by these professionals both the Owenite and so-called Agrarian leaders found themselves at an immediate disadvantage. The new element was not only articulate, but it talked the language of the rank and file and, unhampered by any particular principles, resorted from the outset to all the tricks of the trade, cajolery, flattery and misrepresentation. If the Owen and Skidmore factions had been able to forget their differences for awhile, they might have been able to hold the line, but their quarrel had become too bitter for that. In New York, where the real battle was waged, the Skidmore faction was the first to go down to defeat. Skidmore and a few of his loyal disciples immediately founded the Poor Man's Party, but remained a small isolated group without influence. This left the field to the new "Politicals" and the Free Enquirers. The newly converted *Evening Journal* espoused the cause of the former and, in the bitter factional fight which followed, the conservative press of the city, particularly the Tammany contingent, directed most of its shafts at Fanny Wright. These ranged from slander to facetious satire.

> There is a scandalous report about town [remarked the *Courier and Enquirer* on May 8, 1830] that Miss Epicene Wright has abstracted, or rather Agrarianized, a pair of Mr. Jennings' inexpressibles and means to appear in them at her next lecture, which reports say, is to be delivered at the sign of "All Things in Common," Five Points.

So determined and bitter did the attack upon her become that Fanny decided that her presence was injuring the legitimate cause of the workers and left for Europe, leaving Owen, Jennings and Evans to carry on. They soon split away and in the following elections the Skidmore group polled a mere handful of votes, the Owen group, under the name of Liberal Workingmen's Party, polled a little under two thousand, and the Politicals—as the Owenites had predicted—fused with the Adams-Clay Party. This was practically the end of the movement in New York, although a semblance of an organization was maintained, together with the *Working Man's Advocate*, until it was swallowed up by Tammany in 1834. The Working Men's Party in Philadelphia had come to an end in the presidential election in 1832.

While the Working Men's Party was disintegrating there was coming to life in New England, where the labor party idea had also penetrated, an independent but closely related organization known as the New England Association of Farmers, Mechanics and Other Workingmen, the first American industrial union and the precursor of that behemoth of unions destined to startle the country in the '80s, the Noble and Holy Order of the Knights of Labor.

The New England Association, which also grew out of the ten-hour agitation, was composed in the main of skilled craftsmen, but it made a much more concerted effort to broaden the field of its operations than did the Working Men's Party. The latter was primarily a city movement, even though it showed signs at one time of becoming national in scope. The Association made an eloquent bid for the support of the farmers on the ground that "there is an indissoluble connection between the interests of the cultivators of the soil and the mechanics and every class of laborers." It also tried, with little success, to sink its roots into the seemingly fertile recesses of the factory system. (One of the Association's moving spirits was Seth Luther, America's pioneer in the crusade against child labor.) The New Englanders soon discovered that they could expect little response from the downtrodden mill hands. "The absence of delegates from the mill villages," declared a speaker at the 1833 convention, "gives reason to fear that the operatives in the factories are already subdued to the bidding of the employers." The delegates then proceeded to draw conclusions that will have a familar and prophetic ring to the radical ear. "The Farmers and Mechanics, then, are the last hope of the American people. If they falter from ignorance or from fear, if they are diverted from their object by deception or by reproaches, the next generation will find its 'workingmen' pusillanimous subjects of an aristocratic government, naked, famished and in hovels, spinning that others may be clothed, sowing that others may reap, and building palaces for others to inhabit."

In 1834 the New England Association made a brief and unsuccessful excursion into state politics; and in the following year it became immersed in the Loco Foco Party, the anti-monopolist wing of the Jacksonian Democrats. That was the end of it, but in its brief span of life it had given an effec-

[ 45 ]

tive impetus to factory legislation, the shorter workday and the public school system.

With the return of comparative prosperity and the disintegration of the various politically-minded labor groups in the early '30s, the workers were apparently right back where they had started. The conservative press, however, which jumped only too eagerly to this conclusion and rejoiced at considerable editorial length at the end of what it termed "workeyism," soon had reason to doubt the logic of its optimism. It had overlooked one extremely vital factor. The workers, their political offensive crushed, might fall back to their old lines, but they were no longer, psychologically at least, the same workers. Their venture into politics, bitterly disillusioning though it had turned out to be, undoubtedly had done much to increase their self-confidence. They might be defeated again and again in their daily struggle for higher wages, better conditions and shorter hours, but never again would they look upon themselves as humble servants. Politicians had flattered them and that flattery, while it had no doubt gone to their heads and had been instrumental in wrecking their movement, nevertheless had given them— both as individuals and as a class—a sense of power. Consequently, when industry began to hum again, as it did in the middle '30s, they wanted a larger share of the profits and were determined to get it.

In spite of the rapid expansion of industry during this period and the comparative plenitude of work, the skilled mechanic was facing serious dangers. The new industrial development with its rapid introduction of machine invention was already beginning that division of labor which was destined to become an outstanding feature of large-scale production. Boys and women were flooding the trades, and the apprentice system, which was the foundation of the journeyman's status, was breaking down. The grim specter of technological unemployment was already haunting the dreams of the more thoughtful toiler. In a quaint little volume published in 1834 entitled *The Radical* appeared an exhortation that might have been set down yesterday by a rhetorical disciple of Mr. Howard Scott:

In the name of Nature! can no way be found out to make machinery beneficial to the whole mass of the poor and common people who stand in need of facilities to produce or procure the necessaries of life? Is it not in the power of a republic—a nation of people that claims the dignity of representative government, that boasts of independence and a knowledge of liberty and equal rights, to convert the products of genius to the use of all or make them available to promote equally the welfare of everyone that stands in need of their service? Is it impossible that social men shall ever become so humanized and enlightened as to make a common cause of their greatest refinements, that the poor may be equally interested with all others, in every facility of subsistence?

The pressure of these adverse factors and the soaring prices which accompanied a new era of speculation forced the unionists into closer affiliation and a National Trades Union was formed. It survived but three years and was never more than an agitational and advisory body, but it helped to stimulate the phenomenal growth of unionism during this period. In 1836, it was estimated that more than 300,000 workers were affiliated with it.

Capitalism, as well as labor unionism, was having its innings in this brief period before the deluge. An employers' association had preceded the National Trades Union. It found an ally in the courts and "anti-conspiracy" cases against the unions became the order of the day. Labor held indignant mass meetings and burned judges in effigy. "If an American judge," declared a New York labor journal, "will tell an American jury that these barriers which the poor have thrown up to protect themselves from the gnawing avarice of the rich are unlawful, then are the mechanics justified the same

[ 47 ]

as our Fathers were justified in the days of the Revolution in 'Arming for Self-Defense.' "

The prosperity of the period, while it affected materially the skilled city workers and more efficient farmers, scarcely reached down to the unskilled masses, recruited largely from the Irish immigrants now beginning to pour into the country. The cities grew with their numbers and the slums, rivaling those of Great Britain, grew with them. Stevedores, riggers and particularly canal builders were grossly underpaid for incredibly long hours and dangerous work. Their desperation expressed itself in unorganized strikes and riots crushed with vigor and cruelty by police and militia. To the New York *Journal of Commerce* these strikes were "exotic phenomena," the immigrants themselves "the dregs and scum of the Old World."

All during these boom years, the subject of labor politics was taboo. Sure of its economic might, labor wanted nothing of those radicals, agrarian or socialistic, who had seemed to bring so much confusion and odium to their movement in its early phases. Politically, the workers functioned mainly through the Democratic Party, although one year in New York, in a moment of disillusionment with Tammany, they bolted, united with the Loco Focos in an Equal Rights Party, and administered a defeat to the Tiger. Two years later, however, believing that they had again converted Tammany to righteousness, they drifted back into the Democratic fold.

By this time the debacle was upon them and in the fourteen years of almost continuous hard times which followed, the young American labor movement was practically wiped out. It had accomplished much, not only for its own constituents, but for the American people. It had initiated and fought for reforms which to the propertied classes of that day were utterly subversive and revolutionary but which the successors of those selfsame classes now consider "intrinsically American." "Measured by the success in the attainment of its objects," writes A. M. Simons in *Social Forces in American History*, "this first American labor movement has but few equals in the history of the world. A study of the list of things for which it worked is a study of the establishment of what is best in present society."

Though 1837 marked the beginning of the end for the first labor movement, a few words must be added on the long depression itself. It had its beginnings in the winter of 1836, though the general collapse did not come until the following year. In February, 1837, unemployment and suffering were already intense and a "bread, meat, rent and fuel" meeting called by the Equal Rights Party in Chatham Square, New York City, culminated in the Flour Riot in which a part of the vast audience stormed and ransacked a flour warehouse after driving the police and mayor from the scene.

Conditions did not reach their lowest ebb until 1841, but the winter of 1838-39 saw indescribable suffering among the poor. There was no pretense that "no one need starve." Many did starve and many others froze to death. Working among the unemployed of New York City during that dreadful winter, Horace Greeley probably received his first impulse toward radicalism. After describing in his autobiography the wretched conditions of the families he found burrowing in the city's cellars, he adds: "But the worst to bear of all was the pitiful plea of stout, resolute single young men and young women: 'We do not want alms; we are not beggars . . . help us to work—we want no other help; why is it we can have nothing to do?'"

The depression was world-wide, but coming on top of the frenzied land speculation that had accompanied the settlement of the West, the wildcat banking practices, and—for the day—the tremendous industrial expansion of Jackson's second administration, it seemed to hit with particular severity in the United States. By 1841 the nation was prostrate, the workers helpless. New York, Philadelphia and Boston were like dead cities. Practically all shipping, building and manufacturing were suspended. Nine-tenths of the New England factories were shut down. Over six hundred banks had closed their doors in 1837 alone and now others were closing daily. Scrip made its appearance and the people in the rural districts resorted to barter.

Although there was a slight "lift" in 1842-43, complete recovery did not come until nearly 1852, after the discovery of gold in California had not only increased the gold supply but had drawn many workers westward. In Europe, the long depression with its intense suffering resulted in that serious industrial and social unrest that furnished the impetus for the revolutions of 1848. But in the United States, the workers seemed, for the most part, too crushed for aggressive action. Social protest during the late '30s and the '40s was left again to the utopians and humanitarians. The radicals now take the center of that stage so recently held by the trade unionists. Faced with a world they could neither accept nor conquer, people again began to cast a hopeful eye in the direction of Utopia.

# III

## THE INTELLECTUALS TURN LEFT—
## INFINITUDE TO FOURIER

A MERICA had provided the stage and the supernumer-
aries in the cast; but, as we have seen, it was Great
Britain with its Owens and its Wrights that had supplied the
script and filled the stellar rôles in the first act of the serio-
comic drama of Utopian Socialism. Where, meanwhile, were
the American intellectuals? While Owen was dickering for
New Harmony and Nashoba was yet unborn, their energies
were engaged in laying the ghost of grim Calvinism in New
England; and in the '30s, while the young labor movement
was struggling for a foothold, they were erecting on a ledge
of Unitarian dissent an ivory tower of transcendental speculation.

But the camp of the Revolution—particularly of Utopian
Revolution—may be reached by numerous winding bypaths,
and of all the various approaches the one used by those who
travel the way of religious dissent is not the least worn. Many
a pure young man fresh from the theological seminary has set
out to question only some detail of the Nicene Creed and has
found himself in the end challenging the whole social order.
From religious unrest through philosophic heterodoxy to the
dream of a new society ran the path which led to the full-
blown utopianism of the '40s.

As late as 1840, that lofty organ of the Transcendentalists, the *Dial*, was launched with the following typical statement of individualist liberalism:

A perfectly free organ to be offered for the expression of individual thought and character. There are no party measures to be carried, no particular standard to be set up. A fair, calm tone, a recognition of universal principles. . . .

But a few years later, when the *Dial* had been succeeded by the *Harbinger*, published at Brook Farm by George Ripley and the brilliant Charles Dana, the transition had taken place; the ivory tower stood deserted. The new announcement read:

We shall suffer no attachment to literature, no love of purely intellectual theories to seduce us from our devotion to the cause of the oppressed, the down-trodden, the insulted masses of our fellow-men. Every pulsation of our being vibrates in sympathy with the wrongs of the toiling millions; and every wise effort for their speedy enfranchisement will find in us resolute and indomitable advocates. If any imagine from the literary tone of the preceding remarks that we are indifferent to the radical movement for the benefit of the masses which is the crowning glory of the nineteenth century, they will soon discover their egregrious mistake. . . . We look for an audience among the refined and educated circles . . . but we shall also be read by the swart and sweaty artisan; the laborer will find in us another champion; and many hearts struggling with the secret hope, which no weight of care and toil can entirely suppress, will pour on us their benediction as we labor for the equal rights of all.

The intellectuals of the 1840s had—in the phrase of the 1930s—turned to the left. Such transcendental Edens as Brook Farm had become phalanxes of the New Order.

The two forces—authoritarian religion and the rising tide of industrialism—which had threatened the idealist's conception of the "free man" in the '20s and '30s had both centered in New England. The first was old and clearly defined; the second, new and but vaguely comprehended. The shock troops of the revolt against Calvinism had been recruited largely from among the Harvard intellectuals, rallying under the banner of Unitarianism. But by the time the smoke of battle had cleared away and the liberal forces were revealed as more or less in possession of the field, Unitarianism itself had become what seemed to many of the more ardent spirits a new and confining orthodoxy. The answer was Transcendentalism.

New England Transcendentalism, though it had its roots in German philosophy, in the speculations of Fichte, Schelling, Hegel and Kant, was primarily a New World product reflecting all the quirks of that Yankee temperament which has played such a prominent rôle in reform and radical movements in the United States. It brought to the realm of social uplift the same drive and emotional intensity, coupled with a certain poetic mysticism, which the Puritan puts into his religion. Aimed at deifying Man, the Individual, it sought to release him from the authoritarian strait-jacket of Calvinist doctrine, from all that cramped the free play of his innate religious impulses, and to put him in direct contact with the Infinite. It was a tendency destined, obviously, to react just as vigorously against the soul-destroying routine of the new factory system as against the shackles of dogma. For of what benefit to free mankind from religious dogmas only to render him up to "the exploitations of trade and commerce . . . the vicious round of unpaid labor, vice and brutality"?

The Transcendentalists (the term was originally one of derision applied to them by contemporary skeptics, one of whom declared that they "dove into the infinite, soared into the illimitable and never paid cash") were never a formally organized body. They were at the outset merely a group of congenial, intellectually restless and somewhat lonely New England souls who met at Dr. Peabody's convenient bookshop or at one another's houses to discuss "openly and candidly" such dangerous topics as Revelation, Inspiration, Providence and Divine Law; or to listen—no light duty—to Bronson Alcott read Plato, to attune their minds "to the Immensities and Eternities" and to decide whether "omnipotence abnegated attribute." Ralph Waldo Emerson, whose star was destined to outblaze those of all the others, was usually there. So were the Rev. George Ripley, who was to abandon his pulpit and found Brook Farm; William Ellery Channing, whose great blasts against Calvinism had made him the outstanding rebel of his day; his nephew, William Henry Channing, suffering from his "disease of disproportionate speculation"; and Frederick Henry Hedge, the New England scholar. Bronson Alcott, father of Louisa May, whose Fruitlands was to be quite the maddest and—for those not engaged in it—probably the most hilarious adventure in utopia the world has ever known, often lent his benign and incoherent presence. Young Nathaniel Hawthorne came later. Margaret Fuller, whose brilliance never ceased to irritate her masculine contemporaries; Elizabeth Peabody (Henry James' "Miss Birdeye"); her sister Sophia, who was to become Mrs. Hawthorne, and several other transcendental vestals attended regularly.

The disputatious Orestes Augustus Brownson was not invited after the first few sessions; but though his associates dismissed him abruptly, the social historian cannot. He stands as a symbol—tending toward caricature, to be sure—of all the unquenchable unrest, the earnest soul-seeking, the mystical radicalism of the period. Reared in the strictest Puritanism, he passed rapidly through Presbyterianism, Congregationalism, Universalism to skepticism, complete atheism and—under the Owenite influence—to radical social reformism: then, swinging back, through Unitarianism, Transcendentalism, Saint-Simon utopianism, and, after a brief flirtation with the Democratic Party, straight—in one last giddy swoop—into the arms of the Holy Roman Catholic Church!

By 1840 the little band felt the need of a literary organ and the *Dial,* a quarterly, was launched under the editorship of

Margaret Fuller with Emerson and Ripley as her associates. Later, when the magazine failed to achieve financial success—it probably never attained a circulation of two thousand—it was handed over to Emerson and Thoreau; but even their genius, its undoubted literary merit and its many famous contributors failed to attract the necessary support. Carlyle wrote, on receiving copies: "Too aeriform, aurora-borealis-like. I can do nothing with vapours but wish them condensed." For some of the group at least, those "vapours" were about to be condensed in the Brook Farm experiment.

Of all the attempts to usher in the millennium through establishing green plots of social righteousness in a world already badly smudged with factory smoke, none has won as secure a place in social history as this little colony founded some nine miles from Boston in 1841. The importance which this experiment of a small band of romantics assumes in the annals of utopian communities or the prestige it gained in its day can scarcely be attributed to its contribution to social philosophy, its size, span of life or measure of success. It had, in the beginning, little but vague idealism behind it; it survived but a bare six years and ended in dismal failure. Nevertheless, it stirred the imaginations of vast numbers of Americans as has no other community enterprise. But what is more important, it marked the first actual participation, on any scale worth mentioning, of the American intellectual in a movement which, while its well-bred converts would have shuddered at anything approaching violence, came to have definite, even though utopian, revolutionary implications.

Its renown was due chiefly, of course, to the intellectual caliber of its sponsors. Born of Transcendentalism, it basked in the light of reflected glory—a light that shed brilliance over all New England in the '30s and '40s. To be sure, few of the exalted philosophers, humanitarians and literary lions of that movement ever, as John Thomas Codman puts it, "soiled their ink-stained fingers with the grass-green sod of Brook Farm." Hawthorne did, going there directly from his desk in the Boston Custom House. After various bucolic adventures, which included difficulties with the famous recalcitrant and anti-social transcendental heifer, his "remarkable energy," we are told, "employed itself on a heap of manure." Though the impetuosity of youth carried him in where transcendental angels feared to tread, he discovered in himself, after his first burst of enthusiasm, what his publisher called "a physical affinity with solitude." In spite of the idyllic memories of this experience which color the pages of *The Blithedale Romance*, he was probably as much at home at Brook Farm as Marcel Proust would have been in Soviet Russia.

Among the twenty or more individuals who first came to the farm in the spring of 1841, the restless, energetic Ripley was the moving spirit. Emerson, after temporizing, clung to his peaceful Concord. Like others, he was content to pay occasional lordly visits to the Farm and was not above having his joke now and then at the expense of this embarrassing brainchild. It was Emerson who referred to the experiment as "an Age of Reason in a patty-pan," and who, according to Lindsay Swift, "never refers to Brook Farm without conveying to the finest sense the assurance that some one is laughing behind the shrubbery." Alcott, who could talk himself into physical exhaustion, wrote in his diary of "our community," bombarded Ripley with encouraging advice and inspiring platitudes, but never came to the point.

There were two distinct periods of the experiment: the first, or pioneer stage, in which the transcendental influence was dominant and academic life was varied by farm and household labor; and the second, or Fourieristic phase, in which the former idols were repudiated as "extinct volcanoes of Transcendental nonsense and humbuggery," and mechanical industries were introduced.

The community site, for which Ripley himself first assumed financial responsibility, was a dairy farm near the village of West Roxbury. It covered 160 acres of beautiful rolling hills, with a brook, pine woods, broad meadows, and with the Charles River within easy walking distance. It was in this idyllic setting that the Brook Farm Institute forAgriculture and Education, incorporated as a joint-stock company, was "to promote the great purposes of human culture; to establish the external relations of life on a basis of wisdom and purity; to apply the principles of justice and love to our social organization in accordance with the laws of Divine Providence; to substitute a system of brotherly coöperation for one of selfish competition," and finally "to guarantee to each other the means of physical support and of spiritual progress and thus to impart a greater freedom, simplicity, truthfulness, refinement and moral dignity to our mode of life." Administration was vested in four committees. A uniform wage-scale and maximum working-day of ten hours were adopted. Provision was made for free support of children under ten and adults over seventy, for free education and medical service.

In spite of the emphasis on brotherly coöperation, the Brook Farmers never approached real communism. Ripley could write of "securing to them [his agrarian intellectuals] the fruits of their industry," but he did not mean what the Marxist does when he speaks of "securing for labor the full product of its toil." The Brook Farmers were firm believers in the right of individuals to accrue capital.

As was fitting with its cultural heritage, the Brook Farm school was the community's pride and glory and its methods anticipated those of progressive schools of today. There was a minimum of discipline and regularity. Efforts were directed rather toward arousing in the pupil a "passion" for both intellectual and manual labor. The results are open to varying interpretations. The school had an unusual quota of distinguished names. The two Curtis brothers, George and James Burrill, studied there. (George later became editor of *Harper's Weekly* and contributed some fifteen hundred essays to the new *Monthly;* James ended his career as a curate at Cambridge.) Both were "young Greek gods" in the eyes of the susceptible Brook Farm maidens, one of whom wrote to a Boston friend as follows: "Burrill is a perfect beauty, entirely unconscious and then (as Sarah says) so human! George has a rich voice and they sing duets together. . . . Is it not grand to see them come out so independently and work away at the peas! ! !" Orestes Brownson and George Bancroft, the historian, each sent two sons to the school. James Lloyd Fuller, young brother of Margaret, enlivened the scene through the habit of writing in his diary exactly what he thought of everybody and then leaving the pages strewn about for his victims to read.

Visitors came to the Farm by the thousands. Among the more intimate friends who sometimes stayed for several days were Margaret Fuller, of whom all the Brook Farm women stood in awe; Emerson, smiling benignly at the "unsullied youth" of the school; Henry James and Elizabeth Peabody; the Channings, and Alcott, accompanied occasionally by Charles Lane, his eccentric English co-partner in the Fruitlands venture who, refusing to wear cotton because it was the product of slave labor and wool because the shearing of it "robbed sheep of their natural defenses" found it difficult to put in an appearance at all. After the conversion to Fourierism, Albert Brisbane, Horace Greeley and Parke Godwin came up often from New York. The more casual visitors were of every class and description—poverty-stricken workers, wealthy curiosity-seekers, Abolitionists, wild-eyed inventors, health faddists, and religious cranks of every sort.

Life at the Farm was strenuous and varied to say the least. One of the students has left us a brief account of his program:

I rise in the morning at six to half-past; breakfast at seven, chat with the people; get to my studies at eight; work an hour in the garden; recite, dine at noon; take an hour in the afternoon on the farm; drive team; cut hay in the barn; study or recite; walk; dress up for tea at six. In long days the sunset and twilights are delightful and pass pleasantly with a set of us who chum together. I am so near Boston that I go to concerts and lectures with others, or to the theatres or to the conventions, the anti-slavery ones being the most exciting. In summer, I join the hay-makers. In winter, we coast, boys and girls, down the steep though not high hills, in the afternoon or by moonlight or by the light of the clear sky and bright stars, or we drive one of the horses for a ride, or we skate on the frozen meadow or brook to the Charles River where its broad surface gives plenty of room.

Impromptu tableaux, charades and dancing seem to have been the chief evening diversions; but, all in all, a high cultural tone was rigidly—and very consciously—maintained. "Nothing," writes Swift, "better evinces the fine zeal of these Brook Farmers—some of them simple folk enough—than their journeying to Boston to hear good music and then walking back a good nine miles under the stars in the middle of the night with an early morning's work before them."

This early Golden Age of Brook Farm was filled with gayety, all-conquering enthusiasm and a tremendous amount of hard, grinding toil by people whose hands were easily blistered. But by 1843 a new movement was sweeping the liberal and radical intellectual circles of the country. Beginning in New York, it almost immediately caught the attention of the New England advance guard and Brook Farm faced a crisis. While youth at Brook Farm "danced or played," writes Codman, "acted in charades or masquerades, wove garlands of green around their straw hats or amused themselves by wearing long tresses and tunics," the patriarchs pondered. Would they take among them "men and women endowed only with practical every-day talents . . . but who had never read Goethe or Schiller or possibly even Shakespeare, Scott or Robert Burns and might not care to read or study Latin, French, German or Philosophy?"

[ 59 ]

The decision came hard but the Brook Farm elders, prodded by Ripley, were equal to it. The classics went up on the shelf. The "swart and sweaty artisan" was to have his place in the utopian sun. The Transcendental dream survived in its most rarefied form, as we shall see, at Alcott's Fruitlands, but Brook Farm opened its arms to the social gospel according to François-Charles-Marie Fourier.

Even in a decade which has witnessed the sudden sweep and recession of the technocratic formula, it may seem strange that the fantastic notion of an eccentric little Frenchman should, several years after his death, leap some three thousand miles of ocean and take the intellectually and socially restless elements of a whole nation by storm; but in the turbulent and visionary '40s it was the most natural thing in the world. The depression which followed the panic of 1837 dragged out its weary length, its misery and despair, all through the following decade and engendered in many thousands of persons a disposition to try anything. The religious colonists, the Owenites and other utopians had already directed considerable attention to coöperative community life as a way out. The early disciples of Fourier in America were not called upon, therefore, to start from scratch and to nurse the new doctrine along while it sank its roots into a fertile soil. They could graft their system onto a movement which already—if we date from the founding of Ephrata—had been in existence for over a hundred years. Moreover, intellectual America was still turning unanimously to the Old World for philosophic guidance, and the mildly religious and nonreligious reformers, such as the Brook Farmers, who were a little weary of wrestling with the mystifying vapors of ethical speculation, could turn with relief to a system, equipped with a ready-made, psuedo-scientific jargon, that was as complete and definite as Fourier's. Granting the existence of vast numbers of liberal-minded men and women, most of them reacting from a rigid religious code, lost in a fog of vague good-will, and yearning to establish the Kingdom of Heaven on Earth, Fourier's blueprint of the New Order—every bit as detailed as the Calvinists' blueprint of Heaven—was bound, if it reached them at all, to come with the force of a revelation.

To understand something of this dominant utopian theme of the '40s, it is necessary to consider for a moment the career of this dry little French traveling-salesman, or "shop-sergeant" as he called himself, who had died in comparative obscurity in Paris a few years before and whose tombstone bore the curious legend: "Here lie the remains of Charles Fourier. The Series distribute the harmonies. The Attractions stand in relation to the destinies."

Fourier, born at Besançon, France, in 1772, was the son of a French linen draper. Upon the early death of his father, he inherited a small fortune which was wiped out during the course of the French Revolution. As a result, he lived in mortal terror of popular uprisings ever after, and his entire complicated and elaborately detailed system for the regeneration of society sprang—in the main—from this obsession, from his desire to circumvent what he believed to be the inevitable consequences of *laissez faire*, the recurrence at intervals of violent and bloody revolution.

Like Owen and so many other utopians, Fourier believed in beginning at the top and set his net to catch some prince, banker or philanthropic millionaire. Unlike the others, however, he based his system upon observation—no matter how inaccurate—of human beings in their relation to their environment rather than upon dreams of the Ideal State and an *a priori* faith in the Perfectability of Man. In a sense, therefore, he was not a utopian at all, but a forerunner of our whole modern school of social planners. The fact that his so-called "science" was pre-scientific, bearing about the same relation to modern sociology as does astrology to modern astronomical research, and led him to conclusions which, in the light of modern knowledge, seem fully as wild as those of the maddest of utopians, has little to do with the soundness of his method.

Fourier's theories as they gradually take form in his various works—he was a prolific writer, producing rambling, disordered tomes without tables of contents or consecutive paging—are too complicated to be set forth in detail here; but, in the light of the enormous vogue certain of them were to have in America, some outline of his system is necessary.

Termed the first of the "efficiency socialists," Fourier was not concerned primarily with the condition of the poor, but with the anarchy and wastefulness of modern industry and with the fact that labor, which he believed should be a pleasure, had become repellent to man. From his analysis of human nature, he reached the conclusion that Mankind was motivated by some twelve instincts or passions, all of them legitimate and useful in a properly organized society. Only through the "associative" communal life, in which all men could be free to be all things, he argued, could the individual find an outlet for these various instincts of his many-sided nature and realize his ultimate destiny. The social unit in this "associative" life, as planned by Fourier, was to be the Phalanx. The Phalanx was to occupy an area approximately three miles square, the center of which was to be the site of an enormous building, the Palace or Phalanstery.

Fourier was a confirmed bachelor, which no doubt does much to account not only for his love of cats, hatred of children and abhorrence of a society in which the family was the social unit, but also for the fact that life in his Phalanstery—with its palatial as well as modest suites and its table-d'hôte meals—was to be very much like life in a first-class European hotel. The members of the Phalanx were to divide themselves into Groups and Series—Fourier had a numerologist's preoccupation with numbers—for the performance of useful tasks. This division was to be carried out in accordance with individual abilities and the "passional attraction" one showed for various types of work.

Some notion of how far Fourier carried his idea of "passional attraction" for work may be gained from his conception of the Little Hordes. In his observations, he had noted that children have a marked passion for dirt. To harness this energy which he saw going into the making of mud pies and being expended in other forms which were not only non-social but often unmentionable, he conceived the brilliant plan of organizing all the children of his Phalanx into small bands which would take upon themselves such work as blacking boots, cleaning streets and sewers and spreading manure. In compensation, the Little Hordes would not only find their peculiar passion gratified, but they were to be honored with the title "Militia of God," given first place in all parades, and receive the salute of supremacy as leaders in the service of Industrial Unity!

Fourier, like the Brook Farmers who were to become enamored of his theories, was no communist. He stated emphatically that "no community of property can exist in the Phalanx," and his scheme was one of universal harmony which was to include Capital, Labor, and—for that matter—everything else under the sun as well as beyond it. For the brain which conceived the Little Hordes was not content to confine its imaginings to this earth, but must project them into interstellar space. The polar regions were to be warmed by a new aurora borealis, our planet was to gain four new satellites, the ocean was to give up its salt and take on a most agreeable acid taste, and lions, sharks and all other disagreeable creatures were to make way for "anti-lions," "anti-sharks," etc., which would become peaceful domestic animals and a great boon to Man!

It is easy to conclude from all this that the little Frenchman

[ 63 ]

was stark mad, but many of his previsions were amazingly accurate. "When we read his pages upon the adulteration of merchandise, upon speculation and monopolies, the new industrial feudalism . . . the approaching piercing of the Isthmus of Suez and the Isthmus of Panama 'by canals through which the largest vessels will be able to pass' . . ." remarks Charles Gide, a modern French scholar, "we cannot conceive that these pages were written as much as three-quarters of a century ago."

Fourier, however, considered all the details of his system from his Groups and Series to his "anti-sharks" as equally infallible. The establishment of one Phalanx in strict accordance with his specifications, he imagined, would prove all this. Then Phalanx after Phalanx would spring into existence until they covered the whole globe. This world would hold, he figured out in his usual plodding and meticulous fashion, exactly two million Phalanxes.

America in the '40s, as we have seen, was fertile soil for the utopians. All that was necessary for a Fourieristic vogue was some one to transport the seed from France. This man of destiny appeared at the psychological moment in the person of the cultured Albert Brisbane, father of Mr. Hearst's Arthur Brisbane and son of a well-to-do landowner of Batavia, New York.

Young Brisbane, in the late '20s, chose to round out his education by travel and study abroad. In Europe he came into contact with many of the outstanding intellectuals and humanitarians of the day, became converted to the socialism of Saint-Simon, and later to Fourierism. Returning to the States in 1834, he at once set about spreading the light and recasting the Fourieristic formulæ into terms more intelligible to Americans. His first work—he was, like his son, a most able popularizer—published in 1840 and entitled *Social Des-*

*tiny of Man*, swept the country. Half of the book consists of direct quotations from the saner portions of Fourier's work; the other half is Fourierism *à la Brisbane*.

The spread of Fourierism in America, however, was not destined to depend upon one man, able advocate though he was. At the suggestion of a friend, Brisbane submitted advance proofs of his book to Horace Greeley, then the young editor of the *New Yorker*, who was immediately fired with enthusiasm for Fourier and all his works. Two years later, Greeley, now a national figure in the realm of journalism with his *Tribune* exceeding the unheard-of daily circulation of 20,000, opened his columns to Brisbane for the good of the cause. Moreover, Greeley himself grasped every opportunity to speak and write on the subject which had so quickly won his heart. The two eloquent propagandists were soon joined by an able third, Parke Godwin, associate editor of the New York *Evening Post* and son-in-law of its editor, William Cullen Bryant. Journalistic circles and lecture halls resounded with the name of the eccentric Fourier. Pamphlets and books on his system poured from the presses, classes and clubs were organized, debates were held. In October, 1843, Brisbane established the *Phalanx*, a monthly magazine devoted to the cause, and kept it alive until 1845 when its place was taken by the *Harbinger*, published at Brook Farm.

The Brook Farmers turned to Fourierism in 1844, when enthusiasm for the new movement was at its height. A young member, Marianne Dwight, bears witness to the ardor with which the little New England group embraced the new doctrines. In informing a friend of three new babies born at the Farm—potential recruits, no doubt, for the Little Hordes —she writes: "They are all *fine* babies—*beautiful* babies, etc., etc.,—so smart that they go a-visiting, and will no doubt soon be able to utter their first words,—which of course we expect will be 'groups and series' and 'associations.'"

Emerson and others of the transcendental galaxy looked

[ 65 ]

with disfavor upon this turn of affairs and came less often to the Farm, but the espousal of the new cause won the colonists many new friends. Brisbane was now a frequent visitor, holding forth of evenings to a wide-eyed audience. Marianne Dwight records one of these occasions in one of her gossipy letters: "We had a great lecture from Mr. B. on the origin of evil. He traces it to three causes: matter, transition, and individuality; and gave the only satisfactory explanation I have ever heard."

Brook Farm, of course, had neither the funds nor the membership necessary for even the semblance of a Phalanx as conceived by Fourier. Nevertheless, the colonists did the best they could to allocate themselves to "groups and series" and carry on varied activities which would have taxed the strength and diversity of twenty times their numbers. A large part of their funds, which no doubt should have gone toward enriching their land or developing their school, were poured into a barnlike structure that was to be the Phalanstery. Early in 1846 the building, then nearing completion, was destroyed by fire. This disaster, though many of the colonists lingered on for awhile, marked the virtual end of Brook Farm.

So far as Fourierism was concerned, the Farm was much more important as a propaganda center than as a testing laboratory. As part of the program of industrialization, the Brook Farmers installed a print shop and the *Harbinger*, the principal organ of Fourierism, was launched under Brisbane's benevolent eye. Ripley and Dana edited it and they, as well as several other Brook Farmers, contributed generously to its columns; but the *Harbinger* was never in any sense a Brook Farm organ. It reflected the life of the whole association movement and was seized upon from the beginning by the liberal-minded intellectuals as their mouthpiece. Henry James, John Greenleaf Whittier, James Russell Lowell, as well as the full galaxy of Fourieristic leaders, contributed to its pages. It survived four years, finally being moved to New York, and there, after a brief struggle, it quietly expired.

In a few years beginning with 1842 some twenty-nine associations, or phalanxes, were established in the eastern and middle western states more or less in accordance with Fourier's system, and every one failed. Brisbane had drastically modified Fourier's original and practically impossible conditions by drawing up specifications for a model community based on a membership of 400 persons and a capital of $400,-000; but filled with naïve enthusiasm, small groups here, there and everywhere, with little or no capital, rushed forward to greet the dawn of the new day. Some bare plot of heavily mortgaged land in the wilderness would take the place of that Garden of Eden envisaged by Fourier; a few squalid log huts would occupy the site of his gorgeous but mythical Phalanstery.

Of all the Fourieristic experiments in America, the North American Phalanx was the most carefully and scientifically planned and came nearest to fulfilling Brisbane's conditions. All the brilliant exponents of Fourierism—Brisbane, Greeley, Godwin, William H. Channing and Ripley—officiated at its birth. The site chosen was a good-sized tract of fertile land near Red Bank, New Jersey. A three-story Phalanstery and grist mill were erected, an immense orchard planted, and the members organized by "groups and series." Full trust was never placed in Fourier's theory of "passional attraction" for work, however, and various wage-scales were set, the maximum being ten cents an hour with bonuses for special skill. While their earnings were never munificent, the colonists received the benefit of extremely low living costs.

The North American Phalanx survived for twelve years, but in 1854, after the $12,000 mill was destroyed by fire, it was dissolved. This marked the end of Fourierism in America.

Only one other Phalanx is important enough to be considered here, the Wisconsin Phalanx in Fond du Lac county of that state. This colony, founded in 1844, is significant primarily because it was the only experiment of its type that resulted not in financial loss but in a small profit to its founders and stockholders. The factors which contributed to this unusual achievement were good management, a rise in land values, and the fact that the majority of the colonists—whatever their cultural shortcomings—were experienced dirt farmers. The formal dissolution of the enterprise, for no apparent reason other than the general irritability of its members, occurred in 1850.

Though Fourierism was the dominant note in the radicalism of the '40s, other schools of utopianism—some of them purely native—existed side by side with it. Despite the desertion of the Brook Farmers in the face of the new revelation, the coöperative school of Transcendentalism was continued for a time under the leadership of Alcott and Lane at Fruitlands. The Brook Farm experiment had never been sufficiently exalted in its aim to satisfy the Fruitlanders. They looked upon themselves as one large (they termed it "consociate") family, disclaimed all rights to private property, refused to deal in money or to use any animal substance either internally or externally. They would not even employ manure to enrich their land, holding that this was an unjustifiable means of forcing nature. In this, and many other curious respects, they rivaled in eccentricity a certain Brook Farmer who refused to drink milk because he held that "his relation to the cow did not justify him in drawing upon her reserves." A sharp distinction was drawn between foodstuffs such as wheat, corn and fruit, which grew into the air, or "aspired," and those products such as beets, turnips and carrots which grew downward into the soil. These latter, Alcott, at least, would not touch. Life at Fruitlands was so hedged in by "Shalt Nots" that it is difficult to see how its members could have kept body and soul together had the community been located in a tropical paradise instead of on an impoverished New England farm.

Fruitlands has been described as "a place where Mr. Alcott looked benign and talked philosophy, while Mrs. Alcott and the children did the work"; and the most famous of these children, Louisa May, in her sketch *Transcendental Wild Oats* does much to give credence to this estimate. "About the time the grain was ready to house," she writes, "some call of the Oversoul wafted all the men away." It was not long before discord racked the consociate family and the gentle Alcott lay down upon his couch and turned his face to the wall. It took the combined efforts of Mrs. Alcott and all the little Alcotts to get that usually beaming countenance turned back toward the world again; and, though they succeeded, the incident marked the end of Fruitlands as well as the end of Transcendentalism on any but the purely ethereal plane.

Two other strictly Yankee attempts to regenerate society deserve mention. The religious unrest, early in the century, had split the Congregational Church, and the seceders had divided roughly into two camps, the Unitarians and the Universalists. A small group of Unitarians, as we have seen, came by way of Transcendentalism to Brook Farm. In a somewhat similar manner, a small group of Universalist coöperators expressed themselves through the Hopedale experiment. This colony, founded at Milford, Massachusetts, by the energetic Rev. Adin Ballou in 1841, managed to prolong its existence well into the '50s, outlasting all the portentous experiments of the Fourier epoch. The Hopedale philosophy, if one could call it that, was a vague Christian Socialism; its members, for the most part, were strong Abolitionists, non-resistants and firm believers in women's rights. The community succumbed at last to a combination of internal dissension and financial difficulties.

The remaining venture, the Skaneateles Community,

started in 1843 when Fourierism was sweeping the country, but it did not spring from that movement. Its founder, J. A. Collins, was a rabid Abolitionist and iconoclast, many of whose doctrines had much in common with the later Proudhonist anarchists. He repudiated all creeds, held that governments were but "organized bands of banditti," refused to vote, pay taxes, serve on a jury or appeal to the law for redress. He took an uncompromising stand against private property, favored vegetarianism and orthodox marriage, though in reference to the latter a visitor to the community speaks of some "affinity" affairs among its members and the storm of gossip these had aroused. As might be expected, Collins' extremely radical views, which he flaunted in his paper, the *Communitist*, brought down upon his head the anathemas of the orthodox, and the whole coöperative cause fell into such disgrace in central New York State, where the colony was located, that two eminently respectable Brook Farm lecturers, who passed through this territory later in behalf of Fourierism, bewailed their cold reception and wrote home disgustedly of Collins' "No-God, No-Government, No-Marriage, No-Money, No-Meat, No-Salt, No-Pepper system." Outside pressure and a little practical experience soon caused Collins greatly to modify his views; but the peace of the colony was shattered almost from the beginning by bitter quarrels and after a few years, convinced his attempt was premature, Collins turned the deed of the property over to his followers and withdrew, as a radical paper of the day sarcastically expressed it, "to the decencies and respectabilities of orthodox Whiggery."

The end of the '40s marked the end of the utopian impetus to social revolution. It did not, to be sure, mark the end of utopianism. That was to survive in one form or another down to the outbreak of the World War. But if the utopian dream persisted in the minds of scattered, and occasionally scatterbrained, individual radicals, it no longer occupied the center of the revolutionary stage. It was a mere intermittent side-show.

The utopian period did not close, however, before it had, at its very end, given birth to two more important experiments in small-scale communism which were to live far down into the more "scientific" decades. One of these was the quite successful Christian-Utopian communism of the Oneida Perfectionists inspired in part by the theories of Fourier. The other was that ill-starred but gallant attempt at emancipation, the French Icarian community of Etienne Cabet.

Oneida, except for the fact that it had its philosophic roots in Fourierism, was a one-hundred-per-cent American product and a thoroughly Christian one at that, but no other venture of its kind, not even Nashoba, has ever so scandalized the American public. The "free love" onus has been fastened upon almost every effort at social emancipation from that of the earliest utopians down to that of the contemporary communists; but Oneida was not only charged with "free love," it actually espoused the doctrine (though scarcely in that libidinous form conjured up by the imaginations of its critics) and vigorously imposed it as a duty upon its membership. There was much more than "free love" to the Oneida experiment, however, even though that aspect of its life, and the storm of controversy it aroused, have tended to blot out all other consideration of it from the public mind.

The Oneida Perfectionists bridged the gap between the pure Christian communism of the Shakers, Rappites and other religious sects and the secular utopianism of the Fourierists. John Humphrey Noyes, their leader, was a cultured Vermonter, a graduate of Dartmouth who later studied law and theology at Andover and Yale.

The Perfectionists were a purely religious group of more than average intelligence. Originally, they had no interest in, or sympathy with, communistic theories. But in the middle

[ 71 ]

'40s, Noyes and some of his friends began reading the *Harbinger* and the *Phalanx* regularly, and became convinced that communism was the best—as well as the most Christian—basis for the practice of Perfectionism. Thereafter, communism became an integral part of their religious system and they carried its implications far beyond anything dreamed of by the secular radicals of the period.

The Oneida Community in New York State was not established until 1848 when Fourierism was already on the wane. Socially the most eccentric of all the communities, it was financially the most successful. By 1874 its members owned over 300 acres of rich land and were doing a thriving business in manufacturing a number of commodities from silk to silverware. While most of its members were now skilled mechanics and farmers, their general cultural standards were far above those of the average American of the day. In many of its features their educational technique antedated Dr. John B. Watson and his school by half a century.

The main tenet of the Perfectionists was "the immediate and total cessation of sin." But the sex relation, when practiced by the pure of heart and bereft of selfish, monogamistic exclusiveness, was not included in this category. Their Compound Marriage System decreed that, within the limits of mutual consent, every man in the community was the husband of every woman. This polygamous-polyandrous arrangement was, however, in no sense a concession to licentiousness. It was merely an extension of the Perfectionist's rejection of private property in things to a rejection of private property in persons. Only those who, in the opinion of the community, had achieved "holiness of heart" were fitted for "liberty in love." Moreover, the right to cohabit freely with any man or any woman in the community was not looked upon as an indulgence, but as a duty—sometimes a painful one. The annals of Oneida bear witness to the fact that man is not invariably a promiscuous animal and that sinful temptations to monogamy—"that exclusive and idolatrous attachment of two persons for each other"—had to be constantly and rigorously combated.

The Oneidans, in short, were attempting to reshape the entire pattern of emotional response. In this field of sex relations, which the average economic radical leaves strictly alone, they were attempting to initiate that emotional revolution which modern Russia—without any interference with the normal mating instincts—is seeking in its cultural life, the substitution of the communal stimulus for the individual one, the replacement of the individual hero or heroine by the heroic mass, the transference of loyalties from persons to principles.

But in the realm of sex, the Oneidan found the individualist impulse a persistent one. Writing soon after his visit to the colony in 1874, Charles Nordhoff, the historian of religious communities, records:

Finally, they [the Oneidans] find in practice a strong tendency to what they call "selfish love," that is to say, the attachment of two persons for each other and their desire to be true to each other; and here and there in their publications are signs that there has been suffering among their young people on this account. They rebuke this propensity, however, as selfish and sinful, and break it down rigorously.

A feature of the Oneidan discipline was the periodical subjection of each member to a "criticism cure" by his fellow members. On one of these occasions, when the victim was a young man named Charles, Father Noyes offered, as an extenuating circumstance in the young man's behalf, his recent victory over serious temptation.

In the course of what we call stirpiculture, Charles is in the situation of one who is by and by to become a father. Under these circumstances he has fallen under the too common temptation of selfish love, and a desire to wait upon and cultivate an exclusive intimacy with the woman who is to bear a child through him. This is a very insidious temptation, very apt to attack

[ 73 ]

people under such circumstances; but it must nevertheless be struggled against."

In a "praiseworthy" spirit, Charles agreed to leave his wife and allow another comrade to take his place.

The "stirpiculture," or eugenics, of the Oneidans was not rigidly enforced and no undue pressure was brought to bear to influence individual choice. For breeding purposes, however, an attempt was made to pair the young of one sex with the older members of the other and to confine breeding to the most physically fit. The contraceptive methods of the Perfectionists grew out of their therapeutic-mystical attitude toward the sex relation and were only incidentally contraceptive. Their doctrine of "Male Continence," minutely described in their privately printed religious documents, has been advocated by various later "sexologists" under the name of Karezza.

It was in their attitude toward children and child-care that the Oneidans so closely paralleled our contemporary behaviorists. The Oneidan children were left with their mothers until they were weaned and then were placed in a general nursery under trained caretakers, both men and women. Here, their reflexes were carefully conditioned to community life and Oneidan mores. In view of the importance ascribed to the child's need for personal love and care by so many present-day psychiatrists and educators, the following comment by the sympathetic and far from sophisticated Nordhoff, written early in the '70s, is interesting:

The children I saw were plump and sound; but they seemed to me a little subdued and desolate, as though they missed the exclusive love and care of a mother and father. This, however, may have been only fancy; though I should grieve to see in the eyes of my own little ones an expression which I thought I saw in the Oneida children—difficult to describe—perhaps I might say a lack of buoyancy, or confidence or gladness. A man or woman may not find it disagreeable to be part of a great machine, but I suspect it is harder for a little child.

Whatever may have been the private frustrations of its individual members, young and old, Oneida prospered steadily; its social life was outwardly calm, healthful and happy. All of this might have continued indefinitely perhaps but for outside interference. It was probably too much to be expected of the United States in this period—or any other, perhaps—that it should leave such a self-contained group of high-minded, though naïve, idealists to reap the fruits of their own experiments. The Compound Marriage System was too much for the clergy and religious laity of up-state New York in the '70s and '80s. Imprecations rose to heaven from a hundred pulpits.

Much of the campaign against the Oneidans was founded, of course, on rumor and consisted of sheer vilification. The colonists stood up courageously under the bludgeoning, but by 1879 it became obvious that the very existence of the community was threatened by the tempest, and, because of this fact, they abandoned Compound Marriage.

For some reason, economic communism did not long survive the abolition of marital communism. Dissolution of communal ownership followed within a year and the scholarly Noyes and a few of the faithful moved to Canada. Oneida was reorganized as a joint-stock company under the name "Oneida Community, Limited."

Privation, hardship and downright misery have dogged the footsteps of so many would-be travelers to Utopia that studies in utopian adventure often become studies in sheer courage and the establishment of communistic communities not so much a test of theory as of human endurance. Though the Icarian experiment was an exclusively French venture and had little or no influence on American utopian socialism, it deserves brief mention because of the unparalleled heroism and persistence of its members. Etienne Cabet, its leader, had come under the influence of Robert Owen while in exile

[ 75 ]

in England in the '40s. Evolving his own communistic theories, he gave them to the world in a utopian novel, *Voyage en Icarie*. The book was a sensation and became a best-seller among French workers. Cabet's call for volunteers for a projected colony in the New World received such wholesale response that he expected to start the enterprise with a million members. After negotiating for a million acres of land in Texas, an advance guard of sixty-nine members set forth from France to New Orleans to take possession in 1848. The story of how they had been swindled by the American land company, their terrible trek inland through swamp and forest, their futile attempt to meet the impossible legal requirements for holding at least a part of the land, the illness, starvation and insanity which pursued their efforts, and their final abandonment of Texas for a new site in Illinois, is a story which must be told in all its nightmarish detail to be fully appreciated. Even after their final settlement at a former Mormon community in Illinois and the arrival of more recruits, misfortune continued to dog them. Internal dissension, coming on the heels of comparative security, split their ranks again and again. Seceding factions settled all the way from St. Louis to California. And yet, each faction attained comparative prosperity in the end. The last of the Icarian communities did not disappear until 1895.

The community phase of revolt had dissipated itself long before this last utopian child of the '40s collapsed in the '90s. The main stream of social revolution had found another channel and the main army of the Revolution was inclined to frown upon such futile gestures of escape. But even in this main army, there were occasional individuals and groups, who, while recognizing all the implications of "the class struggle," could not resist the utopian temptation. Down to our own time little groups of social and artistic radicals have had their community flings, ranging from the "Polish Brook

Farm" established by Mme. Modjeska and her friends in Southern California during Grant's administration to the anarchistic Home Colony and Upton Sinclair's little Helicon Hall in the new century.

But meanwhile those "masses," in whose behalf utopias are usually conceived, were looking elsewhere for salvation.

# IV

## TRANSITION AND WAR

THOUGH "coöperation" and "association" were the chief
watchwords of the early nineteenth-century utopians, they
were by no means the only concepts which stirred the social
thinkers of their day. With the twilight of Utopian Socialism,
came an effulgence of Utopian Anarchism, an expression of
that intellectual individualism which was to furnish a political philosophy for American middle-class protest down to the
present day. It expressed itself principally in the activities of
two groups, the exchange reformers and the land reformers.
To the proponents of these movements in the '40s and '50s,
they had, of course, a far-reaching and revolutionary significance.

The bank of exchange or currency reform theories were
promulgated by men whom we now recognize as the pioneers
of American philosophic anarchism. The spiritual descendants of Thomas Paine and Thomas Jefferson, the intellectual
brethren of Herbert Spencer, and the philosophic first cousins
of the French economist, Pierre-Joseph Proudhon, they were
actually much closer to the native American tradition than
were the socialist coöperators. They did not constitute at
this time one definite and clear-cut school, but while their
schemes differed somewhat in detail, their dominating purpose—the elimination of the financier and middleman by
the exchange of commodities on the basis of labor costs, this

exchange to be handled by some sort of "mutual banks" or "banks of exchange"—makes it possible to group them together.

Josiah Warren, philosopher, musician and inventor, who has been called "the father of American anarchism," was the group's foremost apostle. Warren, it will be remembered, was that member of Owen's New Harmony community who had reacted so violently from its paternal communism that he had evolved an extreme individualistic philosophy of his own. This system, in which coöperation and authority were whittled down to that irreducible minimum necessary for the maintenance of commercial relations, he called Individual Sovereignty.

As early as 1827 Warren had proposed that labor be paid in kind and reproduced a sample of what he declared money should be. This specimen labor note bore the inscription, "Due to bearer, Eight Hours Labor in Shoe-Making, or One Hundred Pounds of Corn." Money, he argued, should be issued by those who perform some useful service, but by no one else.

Warren attempted to put his theories into practice first at his Cincinnati Time Store and later at an anarchistic colony, Modern Times, which he established on Long Island, but without success. Like most anarchist theories, his were conceived in relation to a much more simple and primitive economy than actually existed even at this period.

In common with other individualist radicals of his time— men like Edward Kellogg, John Campbell and William Beck —Warren looked upon the *capitalist* and *banker* as the villains of the social drama and pinned his hopes for a more equitable distribution of wealth and a general solution of the labor problem, not upon a revolution in the ownership and control of industry, but upon a revolution in the system of banking and exchange. The shafts of these pioneer monetary reformers were directed, therefore, at the monopoly of the media

[ 79 ]

of exchange and at the money changers who exercised it, just as the resentment of their spiritual descendants was to be directed at the "Wolves of Wall Street" in the '70s, '80s and '90s, and at the "International Bankers" in the 1930s. Like the Fourierists and "profit-sharers," they carried their message direct to labor, but their early converts, as might be expected, were largely from among the ranks of the intellectuals and middle classes. Some twenty years later, however, Edward Kellogg's *Labour and Other Capital* became the bible of the theoreticians of the infant Greenback movement, and thus the ideas of the group, and—in a sense—of Proudhonist anarchism, reached the great American masses, though in drastically modified form.

While the monetary reformers originally made little impression upon native American labor, they discovered a strange ally in the German immigrant workers who poured into this country during the '40s, especially after the European disturbances of 1848, many of whom had come into contact with Proudhon's teachings abroad. Wilhelm Weitling, one of their leaders, evolved a bank of exchange theory of his own which was closely allied to the ideas developed by Robert Owen in connection with his Equitable Labour Exchange Bank in England.

Prior to 1847, Weitling had been a leading spirit in Brussels of that secret Society of the Just (later the Communist League) to which two other young German exiles, Karl Marx and Friedrich Engels, also belonged. After coming to America, however, the vague Utopian Communism of this man who saw in Marx "nothing else than a good encyclopaedia" became diluted more and more by that Proudhonist anarchism which was the especial *bête noir* of his former German comrades. While this served to alienate him from his more hard-headed European contemporaries, it undoubtedly brought him into closer touch with the native American radicalism of his day. A large body of Negroes assembled at a mass meeting in New

York in 1850 went on record in favor of his labor exchange bank scheme; similar action was taken at a general working-man's convention at Philadelphia in the same year, and even a group of American farmers organized an association for the purpose of experimenting with his theories. Weitling became so encouraged that he himself called a workers' convention, which, though little resulted from it, is particularly significant in that it marked the first national gathering, as a class, of German workers on American soil and the first move toward national organization of that element which was to play the dominant rôle in introducing Marxian socialism to the New World.

When his exchange banks failed to materialize, Weitling became discouraged, put behind him all radical and reform notions, accepted a job with the Bureau of Immigration, and finally became obsessed with the notion that he was a great inventor and that other men were amassing fortunes by stealing his ideas.

The much more important and far-reaching land reform movement of the '50s and '60s, or "the new agrarianism," was sponsored by that same George Henry Evans who had helped to defeat the older agrarianism of Skidmore in the first labor party. When Evans began the publication of a new *Working Man's Advocate* in New York in 1844, the "right to labor" of his earlier, more socialistic days gave way to the "natural right to the soil." While the new agrarians did not dispute the necessity for organized labor action, they saw in the vast land resources of the West the American worker's most effective avenue of escape from the rigors of the fast-spreading factory system, from the competition of cheap immigrant labor and from the low living standards of the slums. At the time, this vast domain, with the exception of that goodly portion of it which was already in the hands of speculators, was being held for sale by the government at prices prohibitive to the average wage-earner. The new agrarians demanded that it be given free to actual settlers in parcels of one hundred and sixty acres each. Under the slogan, "Vote yourself a farm," they also urged the inalienability of homesteads, a general bankruptcy law and abolition of monopoly, of the existing laws for the collection of debt, and of the United States Bank. It is also interesting to note in this later phase of agrarianism, the recurrence at the bottom of the list of two demands from Evans' early labor days: "Equal rights for women and men in all respects" and "the abolition of chattel slavery and of wages slavery."

This program found considerable support among the eastern trade unionists, and prominent union officials sat on agrarian committees.

Energies which in the normal course of affairs would have been devoted to building trade unions and framing schemes of social revolution [write the Beards in *The Rise of American Civilization*] were diverted to agitation in favor of a free farm for every workingman whether he wanted it or not. A Homestead Act, ran the argument, would emancipate him from the iron law of misery; it would enable him either to go West and take up an estate, or, as the price of staying home, to demand higher wages from his industrial employer. Thus in the literature of the great social debate, land reform assumed a radical color.

The movement won over many of the German communists under the leadership of Herman Kriege, some of whom, no doubt, hoped to direct it into more revolutionary channels.

The subsequent history of the free land struggle which culminated in the Homestead Act of 1862 need detain us but briefly here. While in the beginning, in spirit at least, the movement had been a revolutionary one, it fell increasingly under the sway of the Westerners who looked upon it not as a means of relieving the hard-pressed city worker but as a means of opening up the West for further development and of bringing about a boom in land values. These Westerners, in true boosting spirit, even favored huge grants to the railroads, a fact that must have set many of the more class-conscious comrades of the East to communing with their souls. Nevertheless, Homesteadism, as the agrarian movement shorn of its industrial demands now came to be called, advanced by leaps and bounds both in the West and in the East, where an older and more staid Horace Greeley and other liberals threw their energies into the cause. By the late '50s it had assumed the proportions of a great national issue and the party politicians began to sit up and take notice. In the field of national politics other liberalizing forces were at work, but when the Republican Party, in which they found expression, finally emerged, it was more the party of Homesteadism than of Anti-Slavery. But it was also the party of the northern manufacturers and in exchange for their Homestead Act the Westerners were forced to accept the principle of the high protective tariff. The final triumph of Homesteadism was a more than questionable victory—even from the Westerners' point of view, as they were to discover in the '70s. George Henry Evans, speaking for the eastern agrarians, hailed it with enthusiasm as a practical realization of his doctrine of natural rights; but from the viewpoint of a later generation of labor radicals, it was less beneficent. The frontier that it opened tended to deplete the labor movement of its most aggressive elements and to create a new army of small independent landowners. It helped to postpone labor's coming to grips with American industrialism until that industrialism had so consolidated its position as to be almost impregnable.

The practical paralysis of the trade union offensive by the early '40s had, as we have seen, been reflected in the ascendancy of socialism, agrarianism and individualist anarchism. The terrible years from 1847 to 1849, in particular, marked a high point of radical idealism. It was during these two years of despair that the hopes and aspirations of the American radicals were most stirred by events abroad. Both in and out of

[ 83 ]

the labor movement there was an abundance of sympathy in all of the big cities with the revolutionary forces involved in the European uprisings of 1848. In Boston, where the Abolitionist and labor movements were both strong, mass meetings were called to felicitate the Parisians on the February insurrection, to encourage and congratulate the English Chartists and to express sympathy with the Irish Repealers. These meetings, as might be expected in view of conditions then prevailing at home, were not entirely hands-across-the-sea affairs. One of the resolutions passed by the Boston workers at a mass meeting in Faneuil Hall closed as follows:

> While we rejoice in the organization of free institutions in the Old World, we are not indifferent to their support at home, and we regret the despotic attitude of the slave power in the South, and the domineering ascendancy of the monied oligarchy in the North as equally hostile to the interests of labor, and incompatible with the preservation of popular rights.

These years marked vigorous efforts on the part of the radicals to consolidate and direct the forces of labor. The National Reform Association, dominated by the Evans agrarians, attempted to amalgamate the reform and labor movements by the organization of "industrial congresses," but these attracted more reformers than laborites. In New York, where Tammany made its usual bid for radical support, the New York Industrial Congress slipped down its maw with scarcely a struggle.

With the early '50s prosperity returned, and radicalism and humanitarianism again went into the discard. The unions revived and in this brief period of good times before the succeeding panic of 1857 we see the beginnings of that "pure and simple" trade unionism, that concern of exclusive crafts with their own immediate ends and that indifference to the plight of the unskilled and immigrant worker, which was to be the hallmark of our modern American labor movement. Politics, whether regulation or revolutionary, was taboo. The trade and even the shop strike became the weapon of the hour.

It is no wonder that humanitarians like Horace Greeley and radical agitators like Wilhelm Weitling looked with the utmost disapproval upon this "narrow and selfish" policy on the part of the skilled craftsmen who, to them, should have been in the very vanguard of the struggle for freedom. But if, from the viewpoint of the reformer and the radical, American labor was hopelessly opportunistic, the fires of idealism were being kept alight, feebly to be sure, in another quarter. This was in the trade and social organizations of the German workers, who, driven by both poverty and political persecution, arrived in the United States at the rate of 90,000 a year during the decade following the failure of the 1848 revolution.

Not all of these German immigrants were " 'forty-eighters" in the sense of having actively participated in the revolution. But their leaders and outstanding spokesmen were, and a large proportion of them had been involved, at least in sympathy, with the labor and republican struggles at home. Unlike the Irish immigrants, many of them were skilled workers with the German's ingrained tendency toward organization. Some of the more skilled trades were soon entirely in their hands. Politically, their sentiments ranged from a mild republicanism to a conscious philosophy of social revolution. Among those who possessed the latter in an unusually clear-cut fashion for this period was a German intellectual and 'forty-eighter named Joseph Weydemeyer. Weydemeyer, like Weitling, had known the two *émigrés*, Marx and Engels, in Brussels; but, unlike Weitling, he remained under their influence and kept up a constant correspondence with Marx. On his arrival in the United States, he sought to implant the germs of "scientific socialism" among the German unionists and also, in conformity with Marxian theory, to establish a national union of all wage-earners, irrespective of nationality, with a platform of both trade and legislative demands. But American

[ 85 ]

labor, with the hum of prosperity in its ears, was in no mood to listen, and he made little headway. He had better luck among his fellow Germans and remained an influential figure in their midst until the Civil War.

When the next depression, which was to culminate in the tail-spin of 1857, set in about the middle of the '50s, the radical philosophies then attracting so much attention in Europe would undoubtedly have gained a foothold in the United States had it not been for the increasing tension over slavery. For even as early as 1855, the trade unions had shown themselves helpless in the face of a new breakdown and among the rank and file were evidences of a revolutionary mood. In New York and Philadelphia in 1857, mobs roamed the streets shouting, "Bread or Death!" and in the former the Subtreasury Building was threatened with attack. The labor movement was infiltrated with a large body of foreign radicals and a new type of militant native labor leader, personified in W. H. Sylvis of the Molders' Union, was rising to power. But by this time the slavery issue was overshadowing every other. Harper's Ferry and the hanging of John Brown were focusing all liberal and radical attention upon this one immediate conflict. And within the radical and labor ranks it provided a bone of contention.

Organized propaganda against chattel slavery had begun when Lundy started his *Genius of Universal Emancipation* in 1812. The journal lived for twenty-four years; but it was too conservative for William Lloyd Garrison and, to express his more aggressive attitude, he founded the *Liberator* in 1831. The following year, together with several other Abolitionists, he established the New England Anti-Slavery Society.

The early labor movement of the '20s and '30s had opposed Negro slavery as a matter of course. But that demand

[ 86 ]

for "the abolition of chattel slavery and of wages slavery," which occurs in the labor press of both the '30s and '40s, indicates that they considered the plight of the white worker of equal seriousness with that of the black. This was an attitude which the early Abolitionists, most of them earnest, middle-class humanitarians motivated by a strong ethical indignation against Negro slavery, were totally unable to understand. So single-minded were they in their belief that Negro slavery was the one burning issue that many of them, including even the more radical Wendell Phillips, went so far at one time as to advocate secession of the anti-slavery states from the Union as a protest, a course which could only have fastened Negro slavery upon the South for many more years to come. More than this, Garrison and other Abolitionists of the '30s had opposed the New England Association of Farmers, Mechanics and Other Workingmen and its efforts in behalf of the white factory workers. The first issue of the *Liberator* contained a lengthy attack upon the Association's attempt "to inflame the minds of our working classes against the more opulent and to persuade them that they are contemned and oppressed by a wealthy aristocracy."

These attacks aroused spirited rejoinders from the Boston workingmen and particularly from their spokesman, William West. The growing consciousness of their own wrongs, which the Abolitionists tended to minimize or ignore, and the general attitude of the *Liberator* toward the unions increased the antagonism between labor and the Abolitionists all through the '30s.

In the '40s, the Fourierists—Greeley, Brisbane and the Brook Farmers, who were as interested in "wages slavery" as in chattel slavery—tended to bridge the chasm between the two groups. Brisbane wrote in the *Liberator* in 1845: "It would be a noble step, it strikes me, if the advance guard of the Abolitionists would include in their movement a reform of the present wretched organization of labor, called the wage system. It would add to their power by interesting the producing classes in the great industrial reform including chattel slavery and would prepare a better state for the slaves when emancipated, than that of servitude to capital, to which they now seem to be destined."

Needless to say, most of the Abolitionists failed to heed him, though the attacks upon organized labor gradually ceased. A few years later, Wendell Phillips, profiting by Brisbane's advice, adopted a conciliatory tone toward the labor movement and later still became one of its chief advocates. The New England workers continued to condemn slavery but also to emphasize the seriousness of their own plight. It was not, as William West expressed it, that "they hate chattel slavery less but they hate wage slavery more."

One labor spokesman remained outspokenly bitter toward the Abolitionists all through the '40s and '50s. This was George Henry Evans who never tired of taunting the followers of Garrison with their apparent indifference to the frightful conditions among the New England factory workers. Evans was convinced that the northern wage-earner was incomparably worse off than the southern slave, whose master was under the compulsion to care for him in good times or bad. In the *Advocate* of July, 1844, he declared that "to give the landless black the privilege of changing masters now possessed by the landless whites would hardly be a benefit to him in exchange for his surety of support in sickness and old age. . . ."

If the wage-earners of the North resisted the attempts of the Abolitionists to make chattel slavery the paramount issue of the day, the latter found strong allies among the English unionists. Even in the '30s, the Chartists had passed strong and indignant resolutions against the institution. When Garrison and Frederick Douglass, the Negro reformer, visited England in the '40s and founded an Anti-

Slavery League there, they discovered their most active supporters among the English unionists. So strong was this anti-slavery sentiment among the English workers that during the war, when upper-class and official England was on the verge of intervening in behalf of the South to lift the cotton embargo, the unionists and cotton mill workers, still imbued with the spirit of Chartism, resisted so violently as to defeat the movement, although its defeat meant hunger to many of the Lancashire cotton hands. In a letter to the workingmen of Manchester, written in January, 1863, Lincoln referred to their action as "an instance of sublime Christian heroism which has not been surpassed in any age or in any country."

The English unionists, as well as the revolutionary exiles gathered in London from all over the Continent in the '50s and '60s, undoubtedly had, like most European libertarians, a highly idealized concept of the American republic and of the aims of the North, particularly as embodied in the Republican Party. The radicals among them certainly recognized the economic as well as ethical factors involved in the struggle for control of the national government. But it is obvious from their resolutions that they invested first the Abolitionists, then the Republican Party, and finally the "Radical" Republicans with more *consciously* revolutionary motivations than they actually possessed. A letter of congratulation to Lincoln on the occasion of his second election, sent by the International Workingmen's Association in London and written by its secretary for Germany, Karl Marx, closed with the following paragraph:

The workingmen of Europe felt sure that, as the American War of Independence initiated a new era of ascendancy for the middle class, so the American Anti-slavery War will do for the working classes. They consider it an earnest sign of the epoch to come that it fell to the lot of Abraham Lincoln, the single-minded son of the working-class, to lead his country through the matchless

[ 89 ]

struggle for the rescue of the enchained race and the reconstruction of a social world.

This statment drew a letter of protest from the Communist Club of New York which was not so certain of "the reconstruction of a social world." But when the war ended, an equally exalted letter of congratulation was to be addressed to the American people from the same International:

Above all [it read in part], we congratulate you upon the termination of the war and the preservation of the Union. The Stars and Stripes which your own sons had brutally trampled in the dust, once more flutters in the breeze from the Atlantic to the Pacific Ocean, never again, we trust, to be insulted by your own children and never again to wave over bloody battlefields whether those of domestic insurrection or those of foreign war.

While the letter closed with an adjuration to the American people to grant full rights of citizenship to their newly emancipated brethren lest a new struggle should drench the land in blood, it is evident that the writers entertained a very sanguine picture of the effect of Union victory on the lives of American wage-earners. Twelve years later, the Stars and Stripes were to wave over federal troops as they shot down American workers in the "domestic insurrection" of 1877.

The enthusiasm of the European workers for the northern cause was not shared by all the German radicals in America prior to the war. Weitling remained indifferent to the slavery issue and had little use for the Abolitionists. Another German labor leader referred to them as "sentimental philistines" and "liberty intoxicated ladies." But the more definitely socialistic Weydemeyer and his companions in the *Arbeiterbund* lined up behind the anti-slavery forces in the Republican Party. Though they had as few illusions as the native unionists on the subject of "wages slavery," they saw that the new party was, as A. M. Simons has put it, "essentially revolutionary in many of its purposes. It was demanding that the control of the government be transferred to a new social class and that is the essence of revolution." Slavery was to them not only a shameful injustice but also an atavistic social institution which must be eliminated before capitalism itself, progressing toward its own fruition and inevitable doom, could prepare the way for a still newer order. It is not surprising, therefore, that they followed their liberal compatriots into the Union Army.

It was the more radical of the native unionists, those most influenced by revolutionary developments abroad, who, under the leadership of the incorruptible W. H. Sylvis and his Committee of Thirty-four, opposed the resort to arms even after the South had seceded. They continued to look upon the impending conflict as a quarrel between two sets of masters with which the workers had nothing to do. They adopted toward it, in short, the classic social revolutionary attitude toward all "capitalistic wars." Calling upon the workers of both North and South to prevent the war by every means in their power, they invoked huge mass meetings of protest from Boston to Louisville, Kentucky. When their efforts failed and war enthusiasm mounted, they too joined the colors. The labor offensive stood adjourned for the duration of the war.

The war was not to progress without violent opposition in other quarters and its quota of conscientious objectors. The violence occurred largely among the unorganized foreign workers of New York enrolled in the Democratic Party.

During the '30s and '40s, and especially after the Potato Famine of 1848, the Irish dominated those great floods of emigration that flowed westward toward our shores. While the Germans scattered throughout the country, most of the Irish settled in great solid blocks in the rapidly growing cities of the East, particularly in New York. Being poor and illiterate as well as unskilled, they were considered a potential menace to the standards of the native wage-earners. Being also Catholic, they inherited the full blast of the anti-Catholic sentiment that had marked the native labor movement since its early preoccupation with a free public school system. In the '30s and '40s they had been subjected to sporadic anti-Catholic and anti-Irish persecutions which did nothing to increase their American loyalty. It was to the gradual naturalization (frequently irregular) of these Irish workers that the northern section of the Democratic Party owed much of its strength.

"Copperhead" sentiment was not, of course, confined exclusively to the Irish. New York employers had, on numerous occasions, used Negro strike breakers in their struggle against white labor, and this fact, coupled with the idea that the Negro question had caused the war, accounted for the intense anti-Negro sentiment displayed by the Draft Rioters. In addition to all this, there was the class character of the Conscription Act which permitted the well-to-do classes, already profiting financially from the war, to slough off on the workers the entire burden of the fighting. Anyone able to do so could buy exemption from military duty by paying $300 for a substitute—a sum which few workers ever dreamed of possessing.

Though the Draft Riots have been pictured repeatedly as anti-Negro demonstrations on the part of the criminal and pauper elements of the New York slums, they had their origin in the legitimate grievances of the New York workers—"copperhead" in sentiment, to be sure—against the enforcement of what they believed to be a piece of class legislation.

When the federal provosts attempted to apply the Conscription Act in New York on July 13, 1863, the trouble began. The riots lasted from Monday to Friday, gathering momentum each day, and also gathering, unfortunately but inevitably, into the ranks of the rioters those brutalized groups bent merely on plunder and revenge which Marx has characterized as the most dangerous element in any revolutionary disturbance. At first only property was destroyed and telegraph wires cut. Then the rage of the mob turned against the Negroes and these were driven out of their homes, beaten, and a number of them killed. An attempt was also made to sack the offices of Horace Greeley's paper, the *Tribune*.

The later fury shown by the rioters was an answer undoubtedly to the relentless brutality of the police and of the soldiers called in from West Point and other garrisons. The mob was unarmed, for the most part, except for paving stones and clubs; and while only three policemen were killed during the entire five days, the number of persons shot by the police and military was estimated at nearly a thousand. Soldiers fired indiscriminately into the crowds. Slaughter, not arrest, was the order of the day.

The crowd made its most determined stand at barricades erected at the intersections of Eighth Avenue between Thirty-seventh and Forty-third streets. It was demonstrated then that, however effective barricades might be on the narrow, twisting streets of European cities, they were of little use on straight, wide American thoroughfares. The barricades of the Draft Rioters were carried by a small detachment of infantry and mounted police and a few days later 10,000 troops occupied the city. Nineteen persons were finally sentenced to prison in connection with the affair. The organized native workers and the Germans, definitely aligned by this time on the side of the North, had kept aloof from the struggle.

The Conscription Act was never enforced with anything like the severity of the Selective Service Act in 1917, but the Civil War had its conscientious objectors. They were mostly Quakers, Mennonites, Dunkards and other religious pacifists. While some of the District Boards in the North found a way to leave the Quakers unmolested, a number of Quaker objectors, including the well-known Cyrus Pringle, author of *The Record of a Quaker Conscience*, and Henry Swift, suffered severe persecution. Lincoln, however, was definitely sympathetic to the religious objectors and extended indefinite parole to many of them.

In the South, while exemption had been granted to the religious pacifists upon payment of $500, their position was much more difficult. The situation was complicated by the fact that they were also vigorous opponents of slavery and therefore, in southern eyes, northern sympathizers. Many of the young pacifists of the South were obliged to take to "bushwhacking"—hiding in the woods and mountains where they were surreptitiously cared for by relatives and friends. Some were imprisoned at Libby along with northern captives. In both North and South death sentences were passed against objectors—or resistors, as they were called—but there is no record of such sentences being executed.

While the war dragged on, industry hummed, prices rose and unemployment disappeared. The factory system expanded under the pressure of war-time demands, and the orgy of plunder, which marked the decade of reconstruction, had its beginnings while the hostilities were still on. Slavery was being abolished, to be sure, a clean gain for civilization, but in the process the worst fears of Sylvis and his group were being realized. While both farmers and industrialists were enjoying unprecedented prosperity, while tariffs rose higher and higher, while the cost of living jumped 78 per cent and wages only 55 per cent, a new financial and industrial oligarchy, with headquarters in New York, was arising out of the manipulations of war contracts, internal revenue taxes, gambling in gold, contraband trade in cotton, and out of plain, ordinary theft. J. P. Morgan was setting an example by selling condemned carbines to the Government. Robert Dale Owen, as head of an investigating committee, uncovered one minor steal of $17,000,000 in a $50,000,000 contract. The founders of our American dynasties had their feet in the trough.

And while in St. Louis, Missouri, at Louisville, Kentucky,

and at Cold Springs, New York, martial law was declared to suppress strikes and strike leaders were thrown into jail as "traitors," on the fields of Gettysburg and Appomattox, the Grand Army of the Republic was winning the Second American Revolution—a revolution of northern industry and western agriculture against the outmoded planter-aristocracy of the South.

PART TWO

*ENTER KARL MARX*

# V

## REVOLUTION AS A SCIENCE— THE FIRST INTERNATIONAL

THE Civil War placed a period at the end of the utopian rebellion in America. Attempts to change the basis of the social order by appeals to justice, reason, humanity, philanthropy, by experiments destined to show that the Good Life must necessarily be the coöperative life, by efforts to impose a ready-made millennium upon those who suffered most from a chaotic and ruthless industrialism in the first stages of its boisterous development, had, as we have seen, spent themselves by the '50s. A little tired and disillusioned, many of the utopians had then turned to more immediate and realizable social reforms.

As they did so, however, a new philosophy of revolution was being born in Europe—a philosophy which, according to its own implications, could have appeared at no previous epoch. It was not timeless, like the utopian dream. It was the child of its century, almost of its quarter-century, since it sprang out of the contemplation of the industrial process when it was achieving its most characteristic forms. While it contemplated a new wish-fulfillment, by the prophesied victory of a subordinate class, almost automatically attained, it sought to take the subject of social revolution out of the realm of speculative ethics and to put it into the realm of social science. It claimed that the current system of production and exchange was doomed, not because it was unjust or ugly, but because—like the systems which had preceded it—it rested upon certain inherent historical and economic contradictions; that this system—Capitalism—would be succeeded by a classless, socialist society because such a society would be the only one consistent with the development of modern modes of production; that the instrument of change from one society to the other would be that rising class which has everything to gain and nothing to lose by its introduction—the wage-earners. The man who formulated these new theories of revolution was Karl Marx, probably the most influential of modern social thinkers and the man whose philosophy was to become the faith of millions throughout the world during the next seventy-five years.

The first intimations of the new "scientific socialism" had, as we have seen, reached America in the early '50s when Joseph Weydemeyer had sought to proselyte the new faith among his fellow exiles. But the homestead and then the slavery issue were blotting out all others at this time and Weydemeyer made little impression. With the '60s came the war and revolution, whether utopian or scientific, was relegated to the background. As the war was drawing to a close, however, a far-reaching event took place in London. The International Workingmen's Association—the First International —had its first meeting, and a little later its communications, addressed to Lincoln, to Sylvis and the native unionists, and to the various German societies were read in America. A few years later, little groups, composed mostly of German immigrants, appeared in New York, Chicago and San Francisco and announced their affiliation with this body; and in 1869, the National Labor Union sent a fraternal delegate to the International's fourth congress at Basle. Thus Marxian socialism makes its first appearance on American soil. But before we enter this phase of our story it is necessary to go behind it, both to the International itself, with its conflicts of titanic egos, its stormy sessions in which republicanism, socialism, anarchism, syndicalism come into focus, and behind these, very briefly, to the career and theories of Marx himself.

The man who is so frequently credited with being the Darwin of social science was born at Treves, Germany, in 1818, into a German-Jewish family which later embraced Christianity. While an undergraduate at the University of Berlin—one of those intensely cerebral young Jews who, in the words of Marx's father, "undermine their health in order to snatch at the ghost of erudition"—he came under an influence that was to color most of his speculations thereafter: that of the philosopher Hegel. Marx was an unorthodox Hegelian, to be sure. Hegel's own system had led the master into a rationalization of the Prussian State; it led the disciple straight into the arms of socialism.

In attempting to explain the phenomenon of change and flux in a universe so long considered static, Hegel had formulated a system of logic the essence of which was "the dialectic method." The essence of the dialectic lay in the concept that all change is the result of a struggle between contradictory elements, a thesis or positive and an antithesis or negative and their resolution into another and new element; "only insofar as it contains a contradiction can anything have movement, power and effect." With this key to the process of change—and its corollary that every organism and institution carries within itself the germ of its own destruction—Marx formulated his philosophic system, the foundations of which were the materialist conception of history and the theory of class struggles. The first of these was, briefly, the doctrine that the *fundamental* factor in the development of any society is the economic factor, that "the mode of production in material life determines the general character of the social, political and spiritual processes of life"; the second, that the history of civilized society is a history of class struggles—based on contradictions of interests—and that these struggles are the force behind all social change. In the field of economics, Marx was to find his "antithesis" in the inevitable creation of masses of unconsumed goods—a situation inherent in a profit system and which was destined eventually to kill that system.

The essence of the Marxian philosophy was contained in a simple program and statement of principles which he and his lifelong friend and patron, Friedrich Engels, wrote for the second conference of the Communist League in 1847, while the two young men were revolutionary exiles in Brussels. (It was this League, formerly the Society of the Just, to which Weitling and Weydemeyer had belonged before their emigration to America.) This was the famous *Communist Manifesto* which has since sold by the million copies throughout the world.

Harold J. Laski has written of the Manifesto that it

gave direction and a philosophy to what had been before little more than an inchoate protest against injustice. . . . It freed socialism from its earlier situation of a doctrine cherished by conspirators in defiance of government and gave to it at once a purpose and an historic background. It almost created a proletarian consciousness by giving, and for the first time, to the workers, at once a high sense of their historic mission and a realization of the dignity implicit in their task. . . . It is a book of men who have viewed the whole process of history from an eminence and discovered therein an inescapable lesson. . . .

"It was at one and the same time," declares Otto Rühle, in his biography of Marx, "a historical demonstration, a critical analysis, a program and a prophecy. It was a masterpiece."

Into the confused revolutionary scene of the '40s and '50s —occupied by libertarians, republicans, utopians—socialistic and anarchistic—radical conspirators of every shade, the Manifesto penetrated like a beam of clear light. The various schools of radical thought had not yet emerged in their essential differences. The words "socialism," "anarchism," "communism" were used to cover a multitude of conflicting and overlapping theories. The word "socialism" had come to be associated with the utopianism of Fourier, Owen and Saint-Simon and was even used at times to describe the theories of the anarchistic Proudhon. To dissociate themselves and their activities from these elements, the group about Marx and Engels called themselves Communists; just as later, in order to dissociate themselves from the communist-anarchism of Bakunin, they were to revert to the term "socialism." That part of the Manifesto which deals with immediate political and social conditions and with a criticism of the then existing radical schools is of historical value only since both the special conditions and the groups involved have long since disappeared. But the essence of modern socialism or communism is all there in brief. An amazing job of condensation, the short document—beginning with the sentence, "A spectre is haunting Europe, the spectre of Communism"—presents Marx's historical analysis of past and present systems and his theory of the function of class struggles in social change. Its fundamental proposition, as later stated by Engels, was:

. . . that in every historical epoch, the prevailing mode of economic production and exchange and the social organization necessarily following from it, form the basis upon which is built up, and from which alone can be explained, the political and intellectual history of that epoch; that consequently the whole history of mankind (since the dissolution of primitive tribal society, holding land in common ownership) has been a history of class struggles, contests between exploiting and exploited, ruling and oppressed classes; that the history of these class struggles forms a series of evolution in which now-a-days, a stage has been reached where the exploited and oppressed class, the proletariat, cannot attain its emancipation from the sway of the exploiting and ruling class, the bourgeoisie, without at the same time and once for all emancipating society at large from all exploitation, oppression, class distinctions and class struggles.

In their preface to the edition of 1872, the authors of the Manifesto readily admit that already "this program has in some details become antiquated" and that "the practical application of the principles will depend as the Manifesto itself states, everywhere and at all times, on the historical conditions for the time being existing"; but they also insisted that "the general principles laid down in this Manifesto are on the whole, as correct today as ever."

The third and fourth corner-stones of the Marxian theoretical system were the labor theory of value and the theory of surplus value—the latter having borne the brunt of attack from conservative economists in the past sixty years. They were developed in Marx's critical examination of capitalistic economy, *Capital*. Neither the labor-value nor the surplus-value theory was wholly original with Marx. Both had been used by early English economists, but it is their use as class expressions of economic processes that is distinctly Marxian.

In Marxian terms, the value of a commodity is determined by the amount of *socially necessary* labor required for its production in a given state of society at a given time. Having already committed himself to the theory that the capitalist system of production was doomed to destruction by its own inherent contradictions, Marx looked for and found the *economic* contradiction in capitalistic economy in what he called surplus value. Labor power, according to Marx, is a commodity. The value of labor power, he declared, is determined by the value of the necessaries needed to maintain and perpetuate it. The employer buys this labor power, which is all the laborer has to sell, and applies it to the instruments of production, which by themselves can produce nothing. The laborer (meaning, of course, the laboring class) produces enough values in the first few hours of the day to pay his own wages, wear and tear on the machinery and proportion on raw material cost. The value of what he produces, but does not receive, in the remainder of the day belongs to his employer. This is surplus value. Labor is employed, in other words, not to make goods, but to make profits for the employer. All of this surplus value is not clear profit, naturally, for the immediate employer. Out of it the latter usually pays rent and interest. This merely means that the worker's surplus value is divided between two or three groups of capitalists. What his immediate employer receives is *industrial profit*. The whole situation is made possible because the employer owns the machinery of production which the worker must use in order to live. Out of this private ownership, with its inevitable creation of surplus value, a contradiction of interests arises—that fatal contradiction inherent in the nature of capitalism itself and which is certain to destroy it.

It is impossible here to go into all those developments through which Marx traces the course of capitalistic society —the concentration of production, the gradual disappearance of the middle classes, the increasing misery of the workers, the deepening and increasing frequency of economic crises, etc., to the point where it becomes a "fetter on production" and "the integument is burst asunder, the knell of capitalist private property sounds, the expropriators are expropriated" by a militant and united working class. Even among the Marxian radicals themselves there are certain differences of opinion regarding the details of some of these prognostications. But in the words of Scott Nearing, "the Marxian analysis of the probable line of capitalist development has proved to be more nearly correct than the analysis of any other 19th century economist."

Unlike the utopians, with their detailed schemes of the millennial society, Marx made no attempt anywhere in his work to draft a blueprint of the new order. What has been far more productive of dissension among his followers was his failure to chart the course of the social revolution itself except in the most general terms. Both Marx and Engels at first expected that revolution to result from the general European disturbances of 1848. Engels later expected an upheaval in Germany in the '80s. In the *Communist Manifesto* written in 1847, the inevitable conflict of proletariat and bourgeoisie

[ 105 ]

ends in the forcible overthrow of the latter by the former, though there is no specific prophecy of just how this is to be achieved. Writing after the counter-revolution which followed, Marx pointed out the ineffectiveness of the revolutionary *coup d'état* in countries where control was not centralized in one or two important centers— ". . . when, above all, there is no great center in the country, no London, no Paris, the decisions of which, by their weight, may supersede the necessity of fighting out the same quarrel over and over again in any single locality. . . ." Much later, in 1895, Engels, declaring that the days of street fighting and barricades were over, owing to the superior organization and armaments of the military forces, continued: "The time is past for revolutions carried through by small minorities at the head of unconscious masses. . . ."

This last is exactly what took place in Russia in 1917; but Russia, in spite of its huge area, also fulfilled that requirement which Marx gave for the *coup d'état*—the concentration of control in one or two large centers.

In his criticism of the Gotha Program, written in 1875, Marx makes his most specific reference to the "dictatorship of the proletariat" which has become the particular cornerstone of the contemporary Communist program: "Between the capitalist and the communist systems of society lies the period of the revolutionary transformation of the one into the other. This corresponds to a political transition period whose state can be nothing else but the revolutionary dictatorship of the proletariat."

In that long quarrel which has existed among Marxian disciples over the *inevitability* of a *catastrophic* revolution, both sides have been able to draw comfort and support from the words of the master. The Manifesto, as well as Marx's general analysis of capitalistic development, supports the theory of inevitable and general revolutionary cataclysm. On the other hand, in a speech made at the Hague congress of the First International in 1872, Marx declared:

> The worker must one day capture political power in order to found the new organization of labor. . . . But we do not assert that the way to reach this goal is the same everywhere. We know that the institutions, the manners, the customs of the various countries must be considered, and we do not deny that there are countries like England and America, and if I understood your arrangements better, I might even add Holland, where the worker may attain his object by peaceful means. But not in all countries is this the case.

Marx himself was not one of that proletariat whose "historic function" it is to conduct "the final conflict," and so rid the world of all class conflicts thereafter. He was the son of an intellectual middle-class family. He married Jenny Von Westphalen, the charming and intelligent daughter of Baron Von Westphalen, a Privy Councilor and an old friend of the Marxes. After a brilliant university career, Marx had looked forward to an academic appointment, but his radical sentiments made this impossible. As an exile in Paris in 1844, he met Friedrich Engels, the son of a German merchant who had made a fortune in the cotton business in Manchester, England. Their relationship is one of the classic friendships of history, in spite of the fact that Marx's irritability made him a difficult man with whom to maintain a friendship.

After the failure of the Continental revolutions Marx had been banished from Paris in 1849. He went with his family to London and lived there for practically the remainder of his life. Those first fifteen years in London were years of hardship, illness, worry and desperation. Engels, working in his father's office in Manchester, was as yet unable to send more than small and irregular contributions. (Later, after his father's death, he settled an annuity of 350 pounds on the Marxes.) The family's only regular source of income was the pound apiece which Marx received for his brilliant columns on European affairs in the New York *Tribune* when Dana saw fit to use them. Marx spent most of his time in the British Museum, working on the material for his study of capitalistic economy, but he found time, during the '50s, to engage in the numerous controversies which racked the revolutionary exiles of this period, to write polemics in defense of his theories, attacks upon those of his rivals. The family lived in two rooms in Soho and were frequently hungry. They were harassed by creditors, their furniture, even their clothing, was lost at times to the pawnbrokers. A more experienced housewife could undoubtedly have managed better than did the unpractical Jenny Marx on what income they received, but the entire Marx family was totally devoid of practicality. When the third of their six children died, probably as a result of the privations of their existence, a collection had to be taken among their friends for his burial. Marx was prostrated with grief and overwhelmed by his ever-recurring sense of inadequacy—a sense which undoubtedly contributed to his truculence outside the family circle. He was a devoted and loving father and husband, who adored children in general and was adored by them; but his intellectual and his public life were marked by an inordinate quarrelsomeness that was due probably to continuous poor health, to a consciousness of his own unquestioned intellectual superiority over the men about him, and possibly to what one of his biographers, Rühle, considers a deep-rooted sense of racial inferiority frequently encountered in Jewish families which have embraced the alien gods. (Though a thoroughgoing materialist, Marx had been raised in such a family.) He had, like another titan of his period, Carlyle, the dyspeptic's temper and disposition, and in his own revolutionary circle, he was, like Jehovah, a jealous god.

Living in a place and at a period—London in the '50s, '60s and '70s—rife with the differences and jealousies of exiled leaders, revolutionary careerists, thwarted messiahs and international political prima donnas in general, too much of

his valuable energy was wasted in fruitless personal controversies with real and imagined rivals. But in the scope and
clarity of his vision, his encyclopedic historical knowledge and
his economic realism, he towered above all the personally
more attractive revolutionary leaders and thinkers of his time.
For these reasons, his rapid ascent to leadership in the First
International is not surprising.

The International was not conceived, in the beginning, as
a revolutionary organization. In 1863, the English trade
unionists, together with delegates from the French unions,
held a great demonstration in London in sympathy with the
Polish revolutionaries then resisting the attacks of Russia.
Out of this demonstration came the suggestion for a permanent international body among the trade unions and the various revolutionary societies, mainly for the purpose of
preventing the laboring men of one country from "under-
cutting" the wage-rate of another country and of exercising
some influence over working-class immigration. "Whenever,"
ran a statement of the French delegates, "the workingmen of
one country are sufficiently well organized to demand higher
wages or shorter hours, they are met by the threat of the employer to hire cheaper foreign labor and this evil can only be
removed by the international organization of the working
class."

For the purpose of forming such an organization, a meeting was called at St. Martin's Hall in London on September
25, 1864. The gathering was made up of the most diverse
assortment of political, industrial and intellectual radicals
that has ever gathered under one roof. While the majority of
the delegates were trade unionists, the intellectuals dominated
by virtue of their greater articulateness. The meeting was
presided over by Professor Edward S. Beesley. Marx was present as a representative of the German workingmen. The
strongest element, numerically, consisted of the British labor

men, who, while thoroughly "class conscious" in the sense of being devoted to British working-class interests, were by no means revolutionists. Veterans of the '48 revolutions were there and to many of them—like the idealistic Mazzini, also an exile in London—the movement was essentially democratic, political and conspiratory. From France and Belgium came the followers of Proudhon and of Blanqui—individualist anarchists, or *"mutuellistes"* as they called themselves, and revolutionary conspirators expecting to capture France by a sudden *coup d'état*. (The communist-anarchists were yet to appear from Russia.) From Poland and Italy came revolutionary patriots on the order of Mazzini. Socialists, communists, collectivists of every type were drawn in.

Marx and Mazzini, elected on a subcommittee to draw up a declaration of principles, presented two quite different statements. That of Marx carried, almost unanimously. Except for the opening sentence which declared that the "emancipation of the working class must be accomplished by the workers themselves," the declaration was only a mildly radical statement that could not have offended the most conservative unionist present, but its acceptance gave Marx a leverage of power which he was now to use in his struggle with the rival factionalists.

In spite of its working-class character, the International was run by its intellectuals and it now became their battle-ground. Mazzini and the republicans soon withdrew, the Blanquists were expelled, but the Proudhonists held the balance of power and resisted the onslaught of the Marxians—backed up by the German and the British delegates—for nearly two years. By 1867 Marx was in the saddle, and the remaining sects within the ranks continued to battle or to adjust themselves to the course taken. That course was not an aggressive one. The solid British unionists, many of them former Chartists, steadied the keel of the new craft and held it down to specific realities. There was little or nothing that could be done at this time in the way of social revolution. The delegates turned their attention to the discussion of strikes, co-operative industry, hours of labor, woman and child labor, war, the effect of technological development, political action and—as we have seen—the sending of encouraging resolutions to groups engaged in various struggles abroad.

Actually the International was peacefully developing a philosophy and strategy of labor and socialism. But to the press of the period it was a dangerous conspiratorial body aiming at universal upheaval. Its influence was unquestionable. It had helped, for example, to line up the whole body of intelligent European working-class opinion on the side of the Union during the closing years of the Civil War. It represented the awakened, intelligent and purposeful section of the international working class, and though its constituent elements were not submitted to any centralized control, it managed to give them a definitely socialistic direction.

But the International no sooner reached its zenith, with Marx at the helm and the ghost of Proudhonism safely interred, than a new challenge appeared in the person of the brilliant and picturesque Russian anarchist, Michael Bakunin, and the real battle of the revolutionary titans for control of the International began. It was a battle that was to wreck the organization itself and have a far-reaching effect upon the revolutionary movement throughout the world.

Bakunin, known as the "father of terrorism," was the black sheep of an aristocratic Russian family and had been one of the most interesting and erratic figures in the revolutionary circles of Europe since the early '40s. Wherever he went he attracted the interest and admiration of literary, artistic and radical notables. As a result, he has been the hero of, or an active figure in, numerous novels. Marx had met him in Paris in the early '40s and had disliked him instinctively. He undoubtedly sensed in this equally arrogant, but more vigorous and romantic, figure a formidable rival. Soon after this first meeting, Bakunin had been banished to Siberia, but managed to escape. Thereafter he appeared in every revolutionary and terrorist event that startled the Continent during his lifetime. Frequently arrested and several times condemned to death, he managed always to escape or obtain commutation of sentence—a circumstance which raised the cry of *agent provocateur* among his rivals, a charge which Marx did not hesitate to use against him. In spite of these suspicions, Bakunin attracted to himself a large and devoted following, especially among the Russians and Latins. Possessed of tremendous energy and eloquence (the latter a quality for which Marx, a halting public speaker, must have detested him), he was infinitely less stable temperamentally and intellectually than his German opponent. But he was, on the other hand, much more likable as a human being. In the midst of his bitterest battles with the socialist leader, Bakunin was able to pay tribute to his rival's intellectual integrity and ability.

I have known Marx for a long time [he wrote once when Marx was under a fierce fire of criticism from his assorted enemies] and although I deplore certain defects truly detestable in his character, such as a tempestuous and jealous personality, susceptible and too much given to admiration of himself, an implacable hatred which manifests itself in the most odious calumny and a ferocious persecution against all those who, while sharing the same tendencies as his, have the misfortune not to be able to accept his particular system or his supreme and personal direction; . . . nevertheless I have always highly appreciated and rendered complete justice to the truly superior science and intelligence of Marx, and to his unalterable, enterprising and energetic devotion to the cause of the emancipation of the proletariat. I recognize the immense services he has rendered the International, of which he has been one of the principal founders and which constitutes to my eyes his greatest title to glory.

Bakunin was a born romantic, a congenital conspirator. Intrigue, secrecy, underground activity, police persecution were the breath of life to him. Turning his attention to the new International, he conceived of that organization as a vast, conspiratorial secret society for the forcible overthrow of all existing authority and the inauguration of the communist-anarchist régime—that is, of a loose federation of autonomous communes acting in voluntary association. Unlike the Proudhonists, Bakunin was a communistic rather than an individualistic anarchist, and he recognized the necessity of mass organization for the accomplishment of his revolution. Individual terrorism was but one plank in his program of action. Not education and peaceful penetration, as with the individualists, but revolutionary upheaval and violent seizure were the essence of the Bakuninist propaganda. (All the anarchist schools were equally opposed to the use of political action as urged by the Marxians.) Henceforth, the predominant anarchism of both Europe and America was to be communist-anarchism.

In 1867 Bakunin founded a semi-secret organization called the *Alliance Internationale de la Démocratie Socialiste* (a title which indicates that party labels had as little to do with social philosophies at that time as they have in contemporary European politics). The Alliance applied for admission to the International. The confusion of what modern communists would call "ideologies" was not sufficient even then to permit the admission of the Alliance to the fold. Its "propaganda of the deed" included political assassinations and other forms of sporadic violence, abhorrent both to Marx and to the German and English trade unionists. Marx contended that the Bakuninist tactics could lead only to brutal and crushing retaliations on the part of those in power, retaliations which the inadequately organized workers would be powerless to resist. He declared that revolutionary action must wait upon a more conscious, organized and disciplined working class. To his orderly and logical mind, Bakunin's underground conspiracies were a childish but dangerous indulgence in *opéra bouffe*; such radicals as the Russian anarchists, either sentimental imbeciles or paid *agents provocateurs*. The application of the Alliance was rejected but its members were not excluded as individuals. It was as individuals, therefore, that Bakunin and many of his followers, especially among the Belgian and Spanish radicals, joined. Within a year, they gained control.

Marx underestimated the influence of Bakunin, his persuasive eloquence, his genius as a conspirator. The former's strength lay in his appeal to the German and British workers. Bakunin won the Latins, the Russians, the Belgians. At the Basle Congress in 1869 he emerged victorious on every important issue. In the following year Marx rallied his forces and the battle continued. The International itself was the battle-field. Little bands of revolutionaries in every nation of Europe lined up behind the two polemical giants. It was not until after the failure of the Paris Commune, inspired for the most part by the Blanquists, whose revived influence in the International threatened at the moment to make the fight a three-cornered one, that Marx made his final desperate effort to extirpate Bakuninism altogether. At the Hague congress in 1872, the International was already showing signs of decline due both to changing political conditions in the world at large and to its own internal schisms. Only 67 delegates were present and the Bakuninists were caught napping. By methods that were not strictly ethical, but of a type which have marked practically all factional revolutionary struggles before and since, Bakunin was expelled. The Spanish, Belgian and Jurassian Federations, which looked upon him as their leader, went with him.

It was, in a sense, a Pyrrhic victory for the great socialist, though he must have realized by this time that the International had served its purpose and was doomed to extinction anyway. Rather than have its remains fall into the hands of the Blanquists or some other faction, the Marxians voted to move its general headquarters to New York. This was equivalent to signing its death warrant. In New York it lingered on, largely as a paper organization, for four years more, expiring in 1876.

The last fifteen years of Marx's life were his happiest and most comfortable, in spite of continued poor health. He was no longer financially harassed, and—though he quarreled as usual with most of his friends and disciples, with Ferdinand Lassalle, the brilliant but histrionic leader of the German socialists, even with his two devoted sons-in-law, Charles Longuet and Paul LaFargue, active among the French radicals—the more genial and human elements in his character had an opportunity to unfold. He died in March, 1883, and was buried at Highgate Cemetery. Engels and Wilhelm Liebknecht conducted the simple funeral services. Both men had loved Marx dearly and both had seen a side of his character usually hidden from the world and particularly from his revolutionary associates. Liebknecht later wrote a touching and beautiful memoir of his friend and teacher. "Mankind is less by a head," wrote Engels to his American friend, Friedrich Sorge, "and indeed by the most important head it had today."

The International did not die, as we have seen, until it had borne fruit on American soil.

Those trade unions which had survived the depression of 1857 were even further demoralized during the first two years of the war. But by 1863, with the unemployed absorbed into the army and industry humming with war orders, the unions revived. A labor press, labor libraries, even legislative lobbies developed. There was no central body, however, to weld them together. But in 1864, thanks largely to the efforts of a militant leader of the iron molders, William H. Sylvis, the National Labor Union was formed in Baltimore. Its existence was to be almost contemporaneous with that of the First International.

[ 115 ]

Sylvis might be called America's first real labor leader. In certain respects, he bore a strong resemblance to the man who was to become the foremost figure in early twentieth-century socialism—Eugene V. Debs. He was neither an intellectual, drawn into the labor movement through humanitarian motives, nor a hard-headed, practical trade unionist of the Gompers-Green type. He knew little of the various radical philosophies then agitating the labor world of Europe; and yet, by himself, he arrived at definitely radical conclusions on the position and function of labor. With practically no formal education, a wage-earner from the age of eleven, his many speeches and letters, later collected and published by his brother, indicate wide reading, a remarkable understanding—for his time—of economic issues, and a gift of expression much like that of Debs. As president of the Iron Molders' National Union, his activities represent a striking contrast to those of many contemporary labor executives. All his days and nights were given to the actual job of organizing. He lived like an ascetic, giving every ounce of his energy to the cause, and died at the height of his career in extreme poverty.

Under the influence of Sylvis, the National Labor Union established cordial relations with the First International and at its second convention passed a resolution pledging its support to "the organized workers of Europe in their struggles against political and social injustice." In a letter addressed to the general council of the International, Sylvis declared:

We have a common cause. It is a war of poverty against wealth. In all parts of the world, labor occupies the same lowly position, capital is everywhere the same tyrant. In the name of the workingmen of the United States I extend to you and through you to all of those whom you represent and to all the downtrodden and oppressed sons and daughters of labor in Europe, the right hand of fellowship. Continue in the good work you have undertaken until a glorious success shall crown your efforts! Such is our resolve. Our recent war has led to the foundation of the most infamous money aristocracy of the earth. The money power saps the very life of the people. We have declared war against it and

[ 116 ]

we are determined to conquer—by means of the ballot, if possible —if not, we shall resort to more serious means. A little blood-letting is necessary in desperate cases.

Thus was the threat of revolution (if only rhetorical) flung in the teeth of the new American oligarchy at the close of the Civil War.

Although the National Labor Union did not send a delegate to one of its conventions until 1869, the International, heartened by this demonstration of solidarity, kept a watchful and encouraging eye upon this American development. Had it not been for the untimely death of Sylvis, the alliance between the two groups would undoubtedly have become closer.

Meanwhile, however, the International, so far as the United States was concerned, had other irons in the fire—irons that even back in the '60s were beginning to give off a bright red glow. Scattered throughout the country were those thousands of German immigrants of whom we have spoken, many of them already deeply imbued with the principles of Marx or Lassalle and organized either in trade unions or social and gymnastic clubs. In 1867 a few such groups in and near New York coalesced to form the Social Party of New York and Vicinity, adopted a platform which drew heavily from both the International and the National Labor Union, and, after a brief and disastrous sally into local politics, gave way to the General German Workingmen's Association, the first strictly Marxian organization on American soil. The Association soon gravitated into the First International, becoming known thereafter as "Section 1 of New York." The era of modern socialism in the United States had definitely begun.

Unlike the vaguely socialistic National Labor Union, "Section 1" was purely an exotic growth. Its members were German workingmen, most of whom had learned their trade unionism as well as their socialism in Europe. Their meetings were conducted in the language of the Fatherland. Sorge, one of the most active and articulate of the socialist leaders of the period, wrote of them:

> The members, almost exclusively plain wage-workers of every possible trade, vied with each other in the study of the most difficult economic and political problems. Among the hundreds of members who belonged to the society from 1869 to 1874, there was hardly one who had not read his Marx, and more than a dozen of them had mastered the most involved passages and definitions, and were armed against any attacks of the capitalist, middle-class, radical, or reform schools.

It would probably be impossible to find such studiousness and devotion to doctrine among any group of native American workers at any time in our history. These Germans rightly regarded themselves as the keepers of the revolutionary covenant, as a little band of apostles dedicated to the mission of permeating the amorphous American "proletariat" with a vision of freedom based on something more tangible than a few phrases from the Declaration of Independence or the Bill of Rights. But their very intellectual integrity served to separate them from that very confused, essentially individualistic, and economically naïve mass which constituted at this time, and still constitutes in fact, the bulk of "the American proletariat." They were active in the German trade unions and even in some of the English-speaking unions and proselyted vigorously. In May, 1871, they addressed a circular to the trade unions of New York ending with that famous rallying cry of the *Communist Manifesto*: "Workingmen of all countries, unite!" But the response came mostly from the foreign-born. A French section was organized and its ranks augmented after the failure of the Paris Commune had driven many proscribed Communards to our shores. German branches sprang up in Chicago and even as far west as San Francisco and as far south as New Orleans. The active support which these Internationalists gave to a number of strikes won them a certain degree of friendship among the organized American workers, but comparatively few of these were drawn into the International itself. But this did not prevent the movement from receiving a rather remarkable degree of attention in the press. Its very exoticism, its definitely outspoken revolutionary position at a time when any actual possibility of revolution seemed so remote as to make discussion of it an agreeable academic exercise, tended to make it something to talk about. Then, too, its immediate program of working-class reforms was in line with a vaguely awakening social consciousness. The movement became widely discussed; its meetings and resolutions duly chronicled. It even won the attention of Congress when, during a discussion on the floor of the House of Representatives regarding the appointment of a commission to investigate labor conditions, a member quoted with approval a set of resolutions on this subject adopted by the General Council of the International in London. As a result of all this, the International became something of a local fad and was taken up, not by the American "proletariat," but by the American "intellectuals." The various sections became invaded by the strangest imaginable assortment of reformers and their lunatic hangers-on.

The American intellectuals had had a stormy time of it since the end of the simple, idyllic Brook Farm days, the decline of Fourierism and the rise of philosophic anarchism. Blown every which-way by the winds of conflicting doctrines, some embraced spiritualism, some Swedenborgianism, some turned to "free love" and others to Rome. Still others devoted themselves to women's rights or labor reform agitation. Many went in for almost all of these by turn and a few restless, advanced souls flirted with practically all of them at once. Free love and spiritualism, particularly, flourished in the '60s and '70s. Commenting on these movements as they existed in those days, Emanie Sachs writes in *The Terrible Siren*:

It [free love] had its own preachers, its poets and its colonies. It published newspapers and organized excursions and picnics. All the papers were full of it.

According to a loose estimate, there were four million Spiritualists in America then. Spiritualism was the first step from orthodoxy, and many Spiritualists regarded marriage as a doctrine of affinity to be made or unmade at will. Some believed that Heaven could be entered only with one's natural mate. Others, not all of whom were Spiritualists, simply held that the state had no jurisdiction over the affectional relations of the individual. Such was the creed of Stephen Pearl Andrews and the group of radical intellectuals who were his followers.

It was this Stephen Pearl Andrews and his little coterie who now came flocking into the International—much to the consternation of the solid German rank and file most of whom, no doubt, went from their solemn meetings in the rear room of some comrade's beer saloon to homes presided over by placid German *Hausfrauen* and who could see no more connection between the doctrine of free love and the emancipation of the working class than between table tappings and the theory of surplus value.

Andrews, as a disciple of Josiah Warren, had been one of the pioneer American exponents of philosophic anarchism, a religious dissenter, an abolitionist, a Fourierist of a sort, and later a Swedenborgian. In 1870 he was an ardent believer in women's rights and the doctrine of free love, and the leader of a little group of disciples made up largely of admiring women which styled itself the "Pantarchy." The principal business of the organization seems to have been that of freeing Andrews from all mundane pursuits, such as earning a living, so that he might turn his attention to the higher things of life. Just previous to becoming the center of such a charming circle, Andrews had been one of the moving spirits in a more clear-headed and purposeful group of advanced thinkers who advocated a sort of state socialism and called themselves the "New Democracy." In this capacity he had made overtures as early as 1869 to the General Council of the International in London seeking affiliation. Now that the International was beginning to attract attention locally, he renewed his efforts and succeeded in shepherding his Pantarchy flock, together with many former members of the New Democracy, into the International fold. The ranks of Pantarchy had been swollen recently by two prize recruits, probably the most seductive pair of reformers this country has ever known, the sisters Victoria Woodhull and Tennessee Claflin. They, along with the other Pantarchs, were swept into the International.

Born in a little Ohio town and into a family which, had it been located a little farther south, would certainly have been classed as "poor white," the Claflin sisters, after a checkered career in the Middle West during which they had set themselves up as magnetic healers, fortune-tellers, spiritualists, and no doubt at times as members of an even older profession, burst into sudden fame in New York City in the early '70s as "the lady brokers." Tennessee, the more hoydenish and less scrupulous of the pair, had obtained, soon after coming to New York, an audience with the ailing Commodore Vanderbilt, had subjected him to one of her famous "treatments," and had promptly become his mistress. Such a connection with the realm of high finance could not afford to be neglected, and a certain Colonel Blood, Victoria's lover, concocted the "lady broker" scheme and Vanderbilt was wheedled into backing it. Brokerage offices were opened under the firm name of Woodhull, Claflin & Company and the two charmers invaded Wall Street. The "female brokers" were a sensation; in fact they almost created a riot. They had to mount a sign on the wall: "All gentlemen will state their business and then retire at once."

Woodhull, Claflin & Company made a fortune out of the elder Vanderbilt's tips, but more important to the radical movement was the fact that Victoria, at the height of her fame as a financier, met Andrews. This gentle, polite scholar, then almost sixty years of age, and ever on the alert to advance his radical views, saw in her a charming and incidentally an eloquent mouthpiece. Colonel Blood was also something of a radical for the time, holding many of the beliefs of Andrews, though he was more of a soldier of fortune and less of a scholar than the older man. The two men became fast friends and Andrews easily won over the Colonel, as well as Victoria, to his sensational scheme. A paper was started entitled *Woodhull & Claflin's Weekly*, ostensibly edited by Victoria and Tennessee but in reality written almost entirely by Andrews and the Colonel. Underneath its title, the *Weekly* bore the legend: "Progress! Free Thought! Untrammeled Lives!"

For the first few months the new journal was a reasonably staid and ladylike affair, engaging in mild agitation on "the woman question," supporting Victoria, who, as a master-stroke of publicity, had announced herself a candidate for the office of President of the United States, and turning now and again to a gentle bit of muckraking. Then suddenly it launched into a series of articles on free love, abortion and prostitution and in 1872 gained a record circulation when it exposed the Beecher-Tilton affair.

Victoria later admitted, according to Benjamin Tucker, the American anarchist, who as a young man had been seduced by her, to having love affairs with both Henry Ward Beecher and his boyish friend and disciple, Theodore Tilton. The affair she chose to expose in the *Weekly*, however, was one between the great Brooklyn preacher and Theodore's attractive young wife, who was a Sunday-school teacher in Beecher's church.

The Beecher-Tilton exposé was the great scandal of the decade and men fought on the streets for the number of *Woodhull & Claflin's Weekly* containing the sensational story. Single copies sold as high as $40. But this startling issue was not that journal's only bid for fame. At the height of Victoria's and Andrews' interest in the International, there appeared in its lively columns—of all places—the first complete version in English of the *Communist Manifesto*!

While the free-love cause was undoubtedly the one closest to her heart, Victoria was a glorious rebel in whatever lists she chose to enter and she chose to enter more or less all of them. She nearly ran away with the early suffragist movement on several historic occasions; she brought great audiences howling to their feet with ringing phrases concerning "the principles of social freedom" and "the impending revolution." Her personality dominated Section 12 of the International, one of two native American sections which had resulted from the sudden descent of the Andrews-Pantarchy-New Democracy intellectuals upon that little band of amazed German workingmen who were hard put to it to find any explanation of these fantastic comrades even in the all-embracing theories of their beloved Marx. Tennessee, though but a tail to Victoria's kite, did her bit for the revolution too. A short time before Nast in *Harper's Weekly* portrayed Victoria as Mrs. Satan with horns and cloven hoofs tempting the poor with Free Love, *Frank Leslie's* published a sketch of a parade commemorating the Paris Commune with Tennessee at its head bearing proudly the banner of Section 12 with the legend: "Complete Political and Social Equality for Both Sexes."

The activities of what Horace Greeley was fond of referring to as "the Woodhull Brigade of Advanced Cohorts" soon caused a split between the native and foreign-born elements in the American branches of the International, but not before the organization on this side of the Atlantic had become practically synonymous in the public mind with the anathematized doctrine of free love. In the heated controversy that developed, both sides appealed to the General Council of the International in London, but it was a foregone conclusion that that group of serious thinkers and laborites would not rally to the defense of votes for women, sexual freedom and a universal language. The "intellectuals" were eventually expelled. The last act of the Woodhull contingent was the convocation of a convention of all "male and female beings of America" which took the name of "Equal Rights Party" and nominated Victoria as candidate for the presidency of the United States with Frederick Douglass, the Negro reformer, as her running mate.

As to the later activities of the Claflin sisters, they diverged farther and farther from the labor movement and, for that matter, from radicalism of any kind. They finally renounced "social freedom" in all its forms, and both married into wealthy and aristocratic English families, Victoria ending her days as the mistress of an ancient English estate, and Tennessee hers as the titled Lady Cook!

The remaining American branches of the First International held their first national convention soon after the expulsion of the Andrews-Woodhull brigade and assumed the official name of North American Federation of the International Workingmen's Association. New impetus was given the American movement at this time through the transference of the seat of the General Council from London to New York, but despite the heroic efforts of its new American general secretary, Friedrich Sorge, the International was doomed and expired in 1876. Meanwhile, it had a brief hour upon the stage during the panic of 1873.

# VI

---

## RED MENACE IN THE '70S

---

IN THE fifteen years following the Civil War, the Social Revolution flourished mainly in the immigrant quarters of our larger cities, among revolutionary exiles drawn from the more turbulent nations of the world. "Through the records of the American labor movement in the seventies," write the Beards, "stalk German refugees, English chartists, Italians of Garibaldi's red-shirt army, Irish Fenians, French communards, Russian nihilists, Bismarck's exiles and Marxian socialists bent on nothing less than a world revolution, philosophers of every school mingling with those hard-headed craftsmen who were indifferent to utopias and principally concerned with matters of fact—shorter hours and better wages."

Among these foreign radicals, the German socialists predominated. Guttural rumblings emanated late at night from the back rooms of humble *Ratskeller* where these solemn revolutionists, many of them veterans of the 1848 upheavals, sat muttering ponderous phrases over their lager, and dimly lit *Turnvereine* halls from New York to San Francisco echoed with debate over fine points in the Marxian dialectic.

The agitation of each little group of foreign radicals was conceived primarily in relation to the situations which they had left behind them in Europe. Their generalities were universally applicable, perhaps, but they were clothed in terms that had little meaning to the American masses. Even in the late '80s and early '90s, when the pattern of the American labor movement was becoming set, the Revolution was still primarily the concern of groups cut off by both language and social habits from the American rank and file. Emma Goldman's autobiography, expecially in its earlier chapters in which she recalls her first anarchistic activities in New York, indicates how essentially foreign the radical scene was to remain for many years. By the time she entered it, intense young Russian Jews, framing their manifestoes in lower East Side basements, vied with the less intense but no less determined Germans for the honor of emancipating those American masses whose language they could scarcely speak, but though this served to leaven somewhat the Revolution's heavy Germanic character, it can scarcely be said to have enhanced its prestige among American "proletarians."

From the very beginning, however, the immigrant radicals had their isolated English-speaking friends and champions—sympathizers like John Swinton of the New York *Sun* who in the '80s was to establish *John Swinton's Paper*, the best edited and most reliable of America's early labor journals; William West, whom we have already met as spokesman of the Boston workingmen in the Abolitionist controversy; Stephen Pearl Andrews and his Woodhull-Claflin contingent; Albert R. Parsons, who was to be a Haymarket victim, and others. Though some of these, it is true, did little more than to introduce extraneous issues which brought ridicule upon the movement, and though they were too few in number and too scattered to exert much influence toward its naturalization, they did serve to some extent as a connecting link between foreign and native radicalism. Moreover, certain of the more farseeing and adaptable immigrant leaders soon began to penetrate the ranks of American labor, and though this often resulted in their putting their radical theories behind them and becoming "renegades" in the eyes of their former comrades, such was not invariably the case. Yet even as late as 1885 we find the national secretary of the Socialist Labor Party, referring to that organization which was then carrying on almost single-handed the propaganda for Marxism on American soil, as "only a German colony, an adjunct of the German-speaking Social Democracy."

Through their English-speaking allies, their press, their manifestoes, their unions, the foreign radicals struggled manfully during all these years, in the face of misrepresentation, vituperation and ridicule, to carry the light to their native brethren. When strikes occurred in any section of the country, they gave the strikers their moral and often their financial support. In times of prosperity and trade union growth, they attempted, often with dire results, to infuse the American unions with an idealistic revolutionary fervor. In times of depression and widespread despair, they sponsored protest meetings, organized and led mass demonstrations which turned the spotlight of publicity upon the desperate condition of the unemployed, frightened city fathers out of their wits, and inspired relief measures which, though crude and inadequate, represented an enormous advance for the workers, both materially and in self-respect, over those days when their sole reliance had been upon so-called "benevolence." When, because of general hopelessness or some specific injustice, riots flared up among the workers, they tried, usually with little success, to direct the forces temporarily unleashed into channels which would bring some permanent gain to the working class. But to bring any sort of order out of American working-class chaos was an uphill job. For the most part, the native workers continued to fluctuate characteristically between violent spontaneous outbursts and a patriotic and respectable opportunism tinged with Greenbackism, agrarianism and temperance reform.

The isolation of the social revolutionaries from the main

[ 127 ]

currents of native unrest during one of the most turbulent periods in our history was not, of course, entirely due to the exoticism of their movement. The philosophy of the Marxists was a philosophy for wage-earners who knew that they were destined to remain wage-earners. Its raw material was an "industrial proletariat." But though the Civil War had sounded the political death knell of the southern planter-aristocracy and the northern industrialists were now firmly in the saddle, the United States was still predominantly agricultural—a nation of small farmers. Except during the violent and spontaneous labor outbursts in 1877, it was these farmers—not the industrial workers—who set the tune of revolt in the '70s and '80s. Labor, for the most part, merely joined in the chorus, associating itself with the rebellious agrarians as common members of a vague "producing class." It was not until the late '80s, when the frontier was rapidly disappearing, the eastern wage-earner was no longer a potential western farmer, and the grip of large-scale industry was firmly fastened upon the country, that labor began to sing its own tune and disentangle its demands from the aspirations of the debtor-agrarians.

The political revolts of the '70s, expressing themselves in farmer and labor Greenbackism, were but another expression of the individualist radicalism of the '40s and '50s—the free-landism of George Henry Evans, the Homesteadism of Horace Greeley, the currency reform theories of Edward Kellogg and the early Warrenite philosophic anarchists. The new movement, like the old, was directed against the middle-man and the financier—in this case specifically against the banker and the railroader—and not against the system of private ownership and control. In fact, it was a movement *for* private ownership and control on a small individualistic, rather than a monopolistic, scale. It followed the main tradition of American individualism tempered with labor reformism, the later manifestations of which were to range all the way from the single-tax doctrine of Henry George to the legal-tender theory of Jacob Coxey, from the sixteen-to-one *ignis fatuus* of William Jennings Bryan to the "little land and a living" propaganda of Bolton Hall in the early 1900s. Philosophically, it was as eloquently expressed by Paine, Jefferson and Thoreau as by the more sophisticated Albert Jay Nock in the brilliant pages of the *Freeman* in the 1920s.

The Homestead Act had ended the first phase of this struggle. Land could now be had for the asking. But after the Civil War the railroads took the place of the early land companies as holders of vast western grants; and, as intermediaries between the farmer and his expanding market, they held the former at the mercy of their exorbitant and preferential freight rates. The millions of acres distributed after the war were settled primarily by men without capital—many of them ex-soldiers driven west by the post-war deflation of 1866-67. They were necessarily borrowers. Even the older settlers nearer the eastern markets were forced to invest heavily in the new farm machinery which already was beginning to revolutionize agriculture. But the western farmer in particular was a farmer in debt to the eastern bankers and at the mercy of the railroad magnates, whose special privileges he had helped to win in the '50s. It was his grievances which were to set the keynote of political protest for a quarter of a century, a protest that expressed itself in Greenbackism, Grangerism, Populism, and Anti-Monopolism in general. With him enrolled the small business man, unable to compete with the new aggregations of wealth and industry in the interest of which both state and federal government was being quite shamelessly manipulated.

The Greenback movement of the '70s and '80s, as we have intimated, was primarily an agrarian-middle-class movement, an attempt, in the words of Selig Perlman, "to give the man without capital an equal opportunity in business with his rich competitor." It was a movement in which the more radi-

[ 129 ]

cal native labor elements were to lose themselves again and again. In a historical sense, it was essentially reactionary, an attempt to turn back the tide of economic evolution and revert to a simpler, more primitive economy; and, as such, it was doomed to failure.

With its attack upon the financier and the railroader—the latter was one of the greatest employers of labor in the decade—the Greenback movement struck a responsive chord in the breasts of the more advanced laborites. The humanitarian reformers of the period, men like Wendell Phillips, Peter Cooper, Benjamin Butler and John Swinton, were naturally drawn to all movements of dissent. As friends of labor, as well as of insurgency in general, they helped to cement together the two main trends of protest. Their type of radicalism, a combination of utopian socialism, American philosophic anarchism and labor reformism, dominated the intellectual insurgency of the decade. While the Marxians talked, mostly to themselves, of "the class struggle," the native radicals were drawn into a struggle for cheap money and against monopoly.

The native reform and labor scene seethed with ferment in the closing years of the '60s. The slaves had been freed from their planter-masters, but there were whole worlds of iniquity and injustice yet unconquered. There were the Negro's political rights to be enforced upon a reluctant South, there were women's rights, there were labor reforms—particularly the eight-hour day—and, most urgent of all in many minds, there was the currency question. The contraction of greenback currency, issued so freely during the Civil War, was now helping, so they believed, to intensify unemployment after a war-time period of scarcity, and the farmers, who had likewise prospered during the war, were at the same time bearing the brunt of falling prices. Monetary reform took on the status of a major issue not only with the humanitarians and reformers, but even in the mind of so clear-thinking a laborite as William Sylvis. Edward Kellogg's monetary theories were refurbished and introduced as the philosophic basis of a new labor Greenbackism and the program of the new National Labor Union—as of the short-lived political party to which it later gave birth—finally became one of Greenbackism plus labor reform.

Up in Massachusetts, which John Humphrey Noyes had called "the Great Mother of Notions," eight-hour leagues under the leadership of Ira Steward and his disciple, George E. McNeill, in close touch with the strong trade unions, were agitating for a universal eight-hour day. Here, too, enrolled in the New England Labor Reform League, were those irrepressible New England humanitarians who made every cause their own. Their energies released from the antislavery movement, they were now engaged in agitations on all fronts and the League became a haven for all the restless intellectuals of New England, many of whom were graduates of Brook Farm, Fourierism and Proudhonism. Wendell Phillips, whose enthusiasms now embraced the eight-hour movement, the new Negro movement, women's rights, temperance, Greenbackism, and laborism in general was the group's most eloquent advocate. The former Brook Farmers, Dr. Channing and John Orvis (the latter was to turn up again twenty years later as a worker for Bellamy Nationalism) were active, as were also Albert Brisbane and Jennie Collins, a wealthy young Boston woman who was devoting her life to the organization of women factory workers. As might be expected, in view of the Warrenite influence, the currency issue led all the rest in the League's program.

Wendell Phillips is probably the most striking personification of the pure New England brand of incurable intellectual insurgency which played so important a rôle in nineteenth-century American social protest. Down to the Civil War his enormous energies, like Garrison's, were given to Abolitionism. But after the war they spread in every direction. He helped Steward with the latter's eight-hour leagues, he fought for the establishment of the Massachusetts Bureau of Labor Statistics, he was active in the Labor Reform Party and later in the Greenback Party. Inclined at first to believe that the solution of "the labor problem" must wait upon the political enfranchisement of the Negro and of women, he could later be heard on the lyceum platform "dividing an evening's lecture between temperance, women's rights and labor reform." "Socialism had risen high enough at that time," wrote John Orvis many years later, "to float even Wendell Phillips. He came to see in these fragmentary reforms and the agitation which tossed them like rudderless ships on tempestuous seas, the background of action which was to culminate in the Co-operative Commonwealth." But the socialism of Phillips, as of Orvis himself, was distinctly a New England product, a brand which Marx would never have recognized as his legitimate offspring.

Meanwhile, labor unionism was achieving a national status. The National Labor Union reached its apogee in 1868, claiming 640,000 members. To its national congresses were coming delegates from two new elements in the labor movement: the women's unions, organized and led in the main by intellectual, leisure-class women like Elizabeth Cady Stanton, who were also the leaders of the suffrage cause, and the new Negro unions. The immediate political interests of white and black unionists were widely divergent. The National Labor Union was definitely committed to both Greenbackism and the eight-hour agitation; the Negroes were primarily interested in a Negro Homestead Act. The Union was pledged to independent politics; the Negroes were fanatically loyal to the Republican Party. Consequently they withdrew when the Union entered politics in 1870.

An independent labor party had always been an essential item in Sylvis' dream of a free American working class. "We have been the tools of professional politicians long enough," he proclaimed. "We must now cut loose from all party ties and form a workingman's party." He did not live, however, to see that party launched. In 1869 labor and reform tried its political wings in Massachusetts with considerable success, but when the popular Wendell Phillips ran for governor on both the prohibition and labor tickets the following year, he polled only a small vote and hope waned. The brief period of deflation which had furnished the impetus for this sally into politics also rendered abortive the National Labor Union's attempt to launch that national labor party of which Sylvis had dreamed. Moreover, by the time the presidential election year rolled around the Union itself was dying. Unsuccessful strikes and coöperative ventures had weakened its prestige. It had no outstanding leader of Sylvis' stature who was capable of inspiring the confidence of both the more hard-headed craftsmen and the reform elements. In spite of Sylvis' seduction by Greenbackism, he was a practical, stubborn fighter and a thoroughgoing radical so far as labor's interests were concerned.

As a political movement, the National Labor Union became infiltrated with all the unattached reformers and dissenting politicians of the period and the strongest labor bodies, centering their attention more and more on immediate demands, withdrew. Wendell Phillips, and Benjamin Butler, a Democrat, were the leaders of the National Labor Party in 1872 and they made strong bids for the support of the farmers, but the presidential candidate chosen by the new party "walked out on it" and joined Greeley's Liberal Republicans. This was the end of the first national labor party.

When the currency issue was revived as the basis for a new Greenback Party in 1874, it was the western farmers and not the eastern workers and reformers who dominated it. Labor and the Greenbackers, grangers and anti-monopolists were to form another transitory union later in the decade, but the Greenbackism of the late '70s and early '80s was more definitely a middle-class movement.

Except for the brief period of deflation in 1866-67, the industrialists and speculators had been riding high since the Civil War. It had been a period of unprecedented expansion, of rapid development in the West, of railroad projects requiring (for the time) tremendous outlays of capital. Each year the pace grew faster; the dreams of the Empire Builders dizzier; the American investing public more credulous and gullible. Then, with a suddenness which to the contemporary mind will recall October 1929, came the crash, heralded by the collapse of the Northern Pacific and the failure of the deeply involved Jay Cooke and Company on September 17, 1873. What has been termed the "mad gallop" of war and post-war capitalism came to an abrupt and disastrous end. The country was plunged headlong into the most severe panic it had ever known. Stocks dropped thirty and forty points a day. The exchanges closed. Bank runs, business failures— 20,000 of them in the next three years—and suicides were the order of the day.

The six years following were the most tragic the American worker had ever faced. Concentration in the industrial centers had gone on apace during the war and the boom period following it. Hundreds of thousands of workers with no recourse to the soil were thrown out of work. Those who succeeded in clinging to jobs were subjected to one wage cut after another until finally in sheer desperation many of them struck, though they knew that just outside the mill gates were a hundred half-starved applicants for every vacancy. Wages in the textile districts, hovering around the subsistence level even in good times, were cut almost in half. The flourishing trade union movement withered away. The unemployment figure, though unreliable, was set at three millions—this in a country of forty million inhabitants. In New York State alone approximately 182,000 skilled union workers were idle; trade union membership in New York City dropped from 44,000 to 5,000. Ten thousand homeless men and women wandered the streets, seeking shelter in doorways, sleeping on park benches, and lining up daily before the free soup kitchens which had been established in the working-class districts.

Demands for relief came from the unions and the humanitarians on every hand, but reached their highest pitch among the German socialists, particularly of New York and Chicago. In the latter city, sections of the International, acting jointly with other labor organizations, arranged a mass meeting in which some 5,000 persons took part. Speeches were delivered in five languages and a committee formed to submit relief demands to the City Council. To make the appeal more dramatic, it was decided to give the delegation a mass escort of unemployed workers. On a freezing winter day over 20,000 responded to the call, and marched in perfect order through the streets. (And in the little Indiana town of Terre Haute a lank, wiry youngster named Eugene Victor Debs, dollar-a-night fireman of a switch engine, read of their pathetic appeal and felt a surge of indignation and sympathy well up in his warm heart.) The pulses of the city officials who faced the delegation beat more quickly also, but for a different reason. Hastily they promised everything and anything. The demonstrators trudged away exulting in their "victory." Not a single promise was ever kept.

Similar mass meetings and demonstrations were held in various other cities, but it was in New York that the situation grew most tense. The agitation there culminated in a great open-air mass meeting at Tompkins Square on January 13, 1874, three weeks after the Chicago affair. As this demonstration was so typical of so many similar protests thereafter, it deserves special consideration. Substitute "Union Square" for "Tompkins Square" and it might have occurred yesterday.

Plans for the demonstration were announced at a mass meeting and a committee appointed to arrange for speakers and secure a permit from the city authorities. The permit was granted, but as the day for the demonstration approached, the authorities took fright from the hysterical tenor of the conservative press and at the last minute revoked it. It was too late for the leaders to inform their scattered cohorts even if they had desired to do so, and when the appointed hour arrived a great crowd of men, women and children poured into the square. The meeting started tamely enough. Tom-ri-John, eccentric editor of a little East Side radical journal, the *Volcano*, and father of three bounding daughters, Eruptor, Vesuvia and Emancipator, passed among the crowd and with the aid of his even more eccentric wife, who always wore masculine garb, sold his papers. The speakers harangued the multitude in the usual soap-box manner. (John Swinton, then on the ultra-respectable New York *Sun*, was one of these and the events of that day were to have much to do with transforming him from a vague humanitarian liberal to a militant radical.) Suddenly the whole atmosphere of the scene changed. A large body of police, mounted and afoot, trooped into the square. The crowd faced them, awed, silent. The Police Commissioner, who had come from the City Hall to take personal charge, promptly proceeded to lose his head. He shouted an order for the crowd to disperse and then, not waiting to see whether or not the command would be obeyed, sent his men into action. Police clubs rose and fell. Women and children ran screaming in all directions. Many of them were trampled underfoot in the mad stampede for the gates. In the street, bystanders were ridden down and mercilessly clubbed by mounted officers. A stocky and cautious little cigar-maker named Samuel Gompers barely saved his head from being split open by jumping down a cellarway. The incident instilled in him a respect for police clubs from which he was never to recover. "I saw," he wrote in recalling the experience many years later, "how professions of radicalism and sensationalism concentrated all the forces of organized society against a labor movement and nullified in advance normal, necessary activity. . . . I saw the danger of entangling alliances with intellectuals who did not understand that to experiment with the labor movement was to experiment with human life."

Meanwhile, within the square itself, all was tumult and wild confusion, a scene that even the graphic reporter for the New York *World,* whose adjectives rarely failed him, confessed was "indescribable." One little detachment of "New York's finest" miraculously kept their heads and in their quarter there was little violence, but their fellows elsewhere went berserk.

The day was not to be given up entirely, however, to the slaughter of the innocent. The committee, which had spent much official time and energy in preparing for a well-ordered, peaceful demonstration, evidently had harbored some flaming spirits who had considered it expedient to come prepared for emergencies. One man, referred to in the *World* the next morning as "a gray-headed communist named Hoefficher," wielded a heavy cane to distinct advantage. But the real villain or hero, depending upon one's point of view, was a stalwart little German with a claw hammer.

He had been ordered to fight or starve [runs the *World's* account] and, as he said afterwards, did the best he could being not of large intellect but quite zealous. . . . Sergeant Berghold sprang forward . . . and the hungry and zealous little German came to the front with his claw hammer. He was small, and had to strike at a disadvantage, but he struck with all his might and laid open the Sergeant's head, bringing him to the ground. Two officers seized the madman, but he partially freed himself, and struck the prostrate Sergeant a second blow on the head. Then he was clubbed and disarmed and stood panting looking in a scared way at the bleeding officer, either a very proficient dissembler or a very bewildered man. His more intellectual comrades ran away . . . and the police were masters of Tompkins Square.

One other, not mentioned in the above report, also stood his ground. This was a German refugee named Justus Schwab, whose saloon at 51 First Street, already known to the press as the "headquarters of the international infamies," was to remain a picturesque hang-out for radicals and bohemians for the next three decades. Schwab waved aloft a big red flag throughout the entire proceedings and was finally carted off to jail shouting the "Marseillaise" at the top of his voice. This was probably the first public appearance in America of that red symbol of the Revolution.

While the New York *World* tended to treat the whole matter in a humorous vein, it bitterly denounced, under the headline, "Communists At Every Post But Their Own," the leading agitators, who, having departed for the City Hall with a petition before the trouble began, escaped unscathed. Exactly one week later, however, it began publication of a series of feature articles in which it was shown that thousands in the city "lived on from 70 cents to $14 a week." The climax of the series was reached with the following description of conditions among certain families of the 70-cents-per-week class living in a tenement "just a block from Broadway."

No. 47 Crosby street is nearly given up to such families. The house contains twenty-four rooms, each on an average occupied by five persons at least. The staircases of this house, which has the population of an ordinary hamlet, are three feet broad, and at midday the sunlight never reaches them. The rooms themselves have never been opened [to the outside air], and the little colony sleeps composedly on a floor that has gathered grime and dirt since it was laid. The coal is picked up out of ash-barrels, the meat and vegetables come from the gutter. In days of exceptional prosperity the bread is bought. Many of the rooms have neither beds nor chairs, and in all of them the closet is used as a bedroom by those who are crowded out of the larger room. . . . In one of the rooms of the building an old Italian hag keeps a miniature provision store, which she stocks with the result of her quest for garbage. Cabbage heads that have seen better days, potatoes with rotten holes and spots, turnips half gone in decay, fruit thrown away from the stands, are picked up by her with discriminating care, washed, peeled, and sold to those around her. She not only lives on garbage but makes money out of it. Her balance at the savings bank makes her the aristocratic capitalist of 47 Crosby street. She has solved the problem of existence; she is living on nothing a year.

Few, if any, New Yorkers of that day probably saw any particular connection between this investigation and the events at Tompkins Square or realized just how it had happened that the attention of so many of their fellow townsmen, who had never before given the matter a thought, had suddenly become focused on "the social problem." Discussion in the city mounted until even the New York *Times* felt called upon to reassure its readers and to affirm its faith in some strenuously juggled unemployment figures:

> . . . a statement we published on Dec. 15, carefully compiled from trustworthy sources, showed that there were then only 4,050 more men out of employment in this city than there were at the same time last year. This fact proves that there is no such universal distress as the labor agitators and shallow politicians assert. There is no necessity for any resort to extraordinary measures. . . .

The New York conservative who unfolded his newspaper at breakfast on the morning after the Tompkins Square demonstration must—at first glance—have gained an impression that the world was going to the dogs. Aside from the colorful reports of that "rabble of blackguards, mostly foreigners" who had risen right under his very nose "to brandish red rags in public squares," there were dispatches from New Orleans telling of uprisings and "riotous demonstrations" among Negro plantation-workers, an account of a strike of engineers on the New Jersey Southern Railway in which tracks had been torn up, a report that the Delaware road was discharging men and that the latter were in an ugly mood, rumors of a great strike brewing in the coal fields. The Negro affair was so serious, it seemed, that the Governor of Louisiana had been asked to order out the militia. The financial columns, as usual, were unmitigated gloom. The only ray of hope appeared in the person of the Mayor of Boston. Approached by some busybodies who called themselves "reformers," (reformers, indeed, they were probably communists!) he had been asked to start a public building program to put men to work. Fundamentally unsound—he had called the proposal, adding that it would result in the creation of a large class who would lean upon the Government for support instead of depending upon their own energies. (There was a man with a head on his shoulders!) "The outlook," he had concluded as he ushered the delegation out of his office, "does not appear to me at all gloomy. The effects of the late financial disturbance are already passing away. Our manufactories will soon resume their wonted activity, and I have no doubt there will soon be plenty of work for all who desire it." We shall leave our conservative friend smiling happily over his second cup of coffee on this now fair morning in the fourth month of a depression which was to last six years!

The rumor of impending trouble in the coal fields, at least, was no idle gossip. Conditions in the coal regions, deplorable even in boom times, went from bad to worse in the early months of the depression. Finally, in December, 1874, a bitter strike broke out in the anthracite district of Pennsylvania. Lasting seven months and known as "the long strike," it resulted in the almost total destruction of the miners' unions, a reign of terror on the part of the operators, and widespread violence on the part of the desperate strikers which brought into national prominence the famous Molly Maguires, the first labor organization in America to resort frankly to terrorist tactics.

[ 140 ]

The Mollies, Irish-Catholics, workers, and a secret inner ring of the Ancient Order of Hibernians, traced their origin to the Irish Free Soil Party and their name to a picturesque figure in the Ireland of the 1840s, the widow Molly Maguire, who seems to have devoted her life to the systematic assassination of tyrannical landlords. Many of the Irish who had come to America had drifted to the Pennsylvania coal fields which, throughout the '60s, were drawing heavily upon the ranks of unskilled immigrant labor. Here they encountered conditions more brutalizing, perhaps, than feudalistic Ireland had ever known. Their answer was the Molly Maguires, an organization which promptly resorted to the tactics of its namesake except that now it was usually the corpse of a mine superintendent or boss that was being dragged from a ditch. Not all of these assassinations partook of a "class" character, to be sure. The Mollies were not philosophic radicals, motivated by a social vision. They were instinctive rebels, ignorant and often brutalized by the conditions of their life and labor, striking out blindly in their struggle for self-preservation. Their personal grievances and private quarrels were frequently settled in the same fashion as their class wrongs. On the whole, however, their "terrorism" was directed against the representatives of the "bosses."

During the strike of 1874, called and led by the Mollies, open warfare flared up between the operators and the miners. "An eye for an eye" was the policy of both sides. Killing succeeded killing, but finally the strike was broken. The aroused employers then promptly set out to get the Mollies. A Pinkerton detective, one James McParland, himself an Irishman and a Catholic, was sent into the mining regions. He hung about the saloons, drank with "the boys," plunged into the thick of every brawl, and soon won a reputation for toughness which out-Mollied the Mollies. As a result, he was invited to "join up," which he did. By the fall of 1875 he had gathered a mass of evidence, twenty-four ringleaders of the organization were arrested, tried and convicted. Ten were promptly hanged; the remaining fourteen sent to prison for terms ranging from two to seven years each. That marked the end of the Mollies. The Ancient Order of Hibernians, however, managed to escape responsibility for the escapades of its more adventurous sons and remains an influential organization among the Irish to this day.

The exposure of the Molly Maguires, a national sensation, coming upon the heels of the Chicago and Tompkins Square demonstrations, aroused dire misgivings in many conservative breasts. After all, men of property asked themselves, if simple workingmen in one section of the country could rise up and take the law into their own hands, why not elsewhere? Why not—perish the thought—everywhere at once? With such happenings and the Paris Commune fresh in their minds, every strike and riot took on the aspect of a "rabble" uprising. The gentlemen of the press had cried, "Wolf! Wolf" before, notably when the Owens, Wrights and Brisbanes had been airing their utopian views. Yet even the rock-ribbed conservatives, viewing these well-mannered, well-dressed and well-educated "fanatics" on the lyceum platform, must have found it difficult to believe in their hearts that they contemplated anything so "vulgar" as expropriation and bloodshed. Mobs and murder were another matter —a physical challenge to their well-ordered world. They were left, however, with two consoling thoughts. In the first place, the forces of law and order had been vindicated; secondly, the disturbances could undoubtedly be laid at the door of "those damn foreigners." The American worker, they assured themselves, was fundamentally sound. Their peace of mind, restored by such cogitations, was destined to be short-lived. The bodies of the ten unfortunate Mollies had scarcely been lowered into their graves when the "Great Riots" burst upon a startled land.

Contrary to the popular notion that violence in the American labor movement stems from European anarchism, it was this spontaneous uprising on the part of native American workers in the sultry dog days of July, 1877, that first directed the attention of European revolutionary anarchists—men like Michael Bakunin and Johann Most—to our revolutionary possibilities. The events that make 1877 the bloodiest year in the history of the American labor movement occurred without benefit of alien theories. There were, to be sure, many immigrants and foreigners involved in the 1877 upheaval. Most of these played no distinctive rôle and therefore may be dismissed at once. They were merely swept along with the tide. Like the native workers, by whom they were outnumbered a thousand to one, they were motivated not by social revolutionary theory but by hunger and privation. But what of the foreign revolutionaries, mostly German socialists? They had been trying, almost frantically, to stir the workers to organized protest ever since the beginning of the depression. Working through sections of the International and their radical unions, they had been the real motivating force behind the Tompkins Square affair, they had instigated and led the Chicago hunger march, they had even sought to extend their influence into the coal fields during the "long strike" of 1874. With all their agitation, however, they had made almost no headway in reaching the American masses. The fact was that figuratively—and usually literally—they did not speak the American worker's language. Exactly a year before the outbreak of the "Great Riots," the International was officially pronounced dead at a convention in Philadelphia. It had suffered the fate, in the words of Selig Perlman, "of every revolutionary organization of immigrants who, feeling unable to bring any power to bear upon the government and the ruling classes, eventually turn against each other."

Throughout the early and middle '70s, despite the crying need—from their point of view—for united action, the various foreign groups of socialists in America had been continually at each others' throats. Roughly, they were split into two main camps: one composed of uncompromising Marxians to whom the Communist Manifesto was sacrosanct and who were determined at all costs to keep their faith pure and undefiled; the other made up of more flexible elements who were ready to turn their back on the International and cast their lot with the more radically inclined native workers even at the expense of tossing overboard much of their revolutionary theory. The strict Marxians placed great emphasis on building up trade unions; the Opposition, taking its inspiration less from Marx than from Lassalle, was more open to the blandishments of politics. The times at first favored the latter.

With the coming of the depression and the shattering of the trade unions, the workers turned to politics for relief. In Chicago, as an aftermath of their march on the City Hall, the Labor Party of Illinois, dominated by the Lassallean socialists, sprang into existence. In New York a similar organization, the Social Democratic Workingmen's Party, took root shortly after the Tompkins Square incident. Finally, in the summer of 1876, delegates from these two organizations, together with delegates from the scattered American remnants of the International, convened in Philadelphia, put aside their personal and theoretical differences and launched a new united socialist party, the Workingmen's Party of the United States. For purposes of capitalizing on the rapidly spreading discontent among American workers, however, socialist unity had come too late. The new party had no time to consolidate its forces before the storm, threatening for so long, broke with all its fury. While its members tried here and there to ride the hurricane and met with partial success

[ 144 ]

in centers where they were strongest, the sweep of its force proved too powerful for them. Thousands of unskilled workers who knew little and cared less about organization were involved, as were also thousands of skilled native mechanics and even some American farmers totally untouched by radical theory. The scattered bands of Marxians and Lassalleans, though fighting shoulder to shoulder, were unable to exert any real influence over the widespread holocaust.

As wildcat railroading had been one of the factors in precipitating the financial collapse of 1873, it was inevitable that the railroad companies should be among the first to attempt drastic retrenchments. As the depression deepened, notices of wage-cuts appeared with increasing frequency on the bulletin boards of railway shops and yards. With each additional cut, an engineer or fireman here and there along the various lines would climb down from the cab of his locomotive, say in a few choice words what he thought of the company and stalk off toward home, a new recruit for the vast and scattered army of "the unemployed." Occasionally his words would inspire a few fellow trainmen to join him and some rails would be torn up or a locomotive disabled before the little group disbanded, but there was little concerted action. As things went from bad to worse, the grumbling of the railroad men took on a more threatening tone, but trains still continued to arrive on time and neither the railway magnates nor the general public saw any cause for alarm.

Thus matters stood in the early summer of 1877 when three major lines, the Pennsylvania, the Baltimore and Ohio and the New York Central, announced further reductions in trainmen's wages. On the day the reduction took effect on the Baltimore and Ohio lines, a gang of firemen and brakemen quit at a junction three miles out of Baltimore and began stopping freight trains. Police soon appeared and the

[ 145 ]

trains were once more set in motion. The trouble was viewed as a purely local disturbance of little importance.

News of the action of this one train crew, however, spread like wildfire and by midnight the most alarming reports began to trickle into B. & O. headquarters from Martinsburg, West Virginia. Strikers were stopping all trains. The company immediately appealed to Governor Matthews of West Virginia for troops, two volunteer companies marched on the strikers, shots were exchanged, and a locomotive fireman was wounded. Resentment immediately rose to fever pitch. Townsmen, unemployed workers generally, farmers from the surrounding countryside, and finally even the militiamen themselves joined the strikers. Meanwhile the trouble had spread to Wheeling, the state capital, and the Governor wired President Hayes for federal aid.

The entire Baltimore and Ohio system was now paralyzed and the trouble had spread to other lines. Edward Winslow Martin, a writer of the period, declares that "the entire country was startled by the simultaneous seizure by lawless men of the four great trunk lines between the Atlantic Seaboard and the Western States."

In a single day [he continues] the whole internal trade of the Union was suspended. Millions of dollars of capital were paralyzed, thousands of enterprises were confronted with ruin, and the whole of this great country was threatened with a crisis such as it had never experienced before. Instantly the whole military power of the general government and the great states involved in the trouble was called upon to give protection to the endangered commerce of the land. Our peaceful country resounded with the tramp of armed men hastening to assert the majesty of the law on one side; and with the rush of infuriated mobs on the other side, gathering to resist the execution of the statutes of the land and to overturn the very foundations of society.

Four hundred marines marched through the streets of Washington on the night of July 18 to entrain for Martinsburg. All along their route to the station they were hissed and jeered by an aroused populace. The following morning, to the accompaniment of more hisses, they took possession of the yards at Martinsburg and then pushed on as far as Cumberland, Maryland, where they fired on the strikers, killing ten and wounding many more. At Baltimore, where the ranks of the striking trainmen had been reinforced by thousands of sympathetic unemployed workers, the warfare raged for three days with frequent bloodly clashes between strikers and the militia. The former at one time gained practically complete possession of the city.

Nor were things any quieter along the route of the Pennsylvania. Thomas A. Scott, president of the Pennsylvania Central, was calling for the militia to give the strikers "a rifle diet for a few days and see how they like that kind of bread." At Reading thirteen strikers were killed and twenty wounded in a single day's fighting. On the night of Sunday, July 21, the skies above Pittsburgh glowed a sullen red from a fire raging through the Pennsylvania yards. Here, too, the locally recruited militia joined the strikers and reserves rushed from Philadelphia only served to incite the "rioters" to greater violence. They fell upon the Philadelphians in fury and, though it cost them twenty-six lives, bottled up the militiamen in a roundhouse. From here, after a night of terror—the mob raided ammunition stores and rained everything from stones to cannonballs onto the roundhouse from all sides— the harassed troops fled, leaving the city in the hands of the populace, who, before the excitement died down, brought the estimated damage to railroad property up to a total of $5,000,000.

Meanwhile, the storm was moving rapidly westward. In Chicago its approach was viewed with the most intense alarm not only because of the city's importance as a railroad center, but also because of the desperate hordes of unemployed who were beginning to give ear to the radical orators. The most able of these was a young man, a native of Alabama, who had come to Chicago a short time before and joined the Workingmen's Party, Albert R. Parsons.

On July 23 what Chicago had been awaiting in dread terror happened. The Michigan Central switchmen struck and by the following morning all roads leading from the city were tied up. The police moved swiftly. Parsons and his aide, Philip Van Patten, were arrested in a raid on socialist headquarters—a futile gesture, for the situation, so far as the socialists were concerned, was already out of hand. The real clash came when the police attempted to break up a general open-air mass meeting. A terrific battle followed in which nineteen persons were killed and many times that number wounded.

Twenty thousand men, police and citizens were under arms [write Lloyd Lewis and Henry Justin Smith in *Chicago: A History of its Reputation*]. Squads of householders shouldered rifles and patrolled the residence districts, fifty different mobs were chasing militiamen and volunteer "specials." Saloons were closed. . . . Terror had the business men by the throat, and at a meeting in the famous Moody and Sankey Tabernacle on Monroe between Franklin and Market, they demanded 5,000 additional militiamen to put down "the ragged commune wretches."

Two companies of United States regulars subsequently arrived under command of Lieutenant-Colonel Frederick Dent Grant, son of Ulysses, and put an end to both the strike and the rioting. The federal government, now fully aroused, was rushing troops to the various centers of disturbance from every point except from the capital itself. Official Washington was taking no chances. The Cabinet hastily convened and decided "that no further depletion of the military and naval forces at the capital ought to be made," warships were directed to bring additional troops from Norfolk and two ironclads were ordered to stand by for active service. Elaborate plans were laid for the defense of the Treasury.

But the storm had moved westward. In St. Louis the socialists were having their brief innings. Here the popular upheaval resulted in the disruption of all lines of communication, the factories closed, the strikers emerged in full possession of the city. The St. Louis socialists called a great mass meeting, elected a socialistic executive committee, restored order, organized a provisional municipal government and held sway for an entire week. At the end of that time, however, business leaders sponsored a counter-revolution. A citizens' vigilance committee, aided by the entire police force as well as several companies of militia, surrounded the socialists' headquarters and seventy-five persons, most of whom turned out to be mere loungers, were arrested.

The forces of "law and order" had their hands full even in far-away San Francisco. Labor on the Pacific Coast blamed its troubles primarily upon imported Chinese coolie labor and therefore the flare-up in San Francisco came to assume the aspects of a race riot. Here, too, the socialists had a finger in the pie at the very beginning, but were swept aside even more abruptly than in Chicago.

The San Francisco section of the Workingmen's Party, stimulated by events in the East, issued a call for a mass meeting to be held on the sand-lots before the new City Hall on the evening of July 23. Some 8,000 persons responded and all was proceeding peaceably when another group of workers, led by anti-Chinese agitators, descended upon the meeting. They demanded the socialists turn the meeting into an anti-Chinese demonstration, the latter indignantly refused, and at this tense moment a solitary Chinaman chanced to wander by. The mob was immediately off in hot pursuit and before it came under control of the combined forces of the police, state militia and specially organized vigilantes known as "the pick handle brigade," $100,000 worth of Chinatown property had been destroyed and four men killed. Dennis Kearney, an Irish drayman, who soon after was to become the fiery leader of the anti-Chinese agitation which culminated in the Exclusion Law of 1882, served at this time in "the pick handle brigade" and helped to quell the rioters.

The Great Upheaval came to an end almost as suddenly as it had begun. A spontaneous and undirected gesture, for the most part, it served as a temporary emotional release for the workers and threw the fear of God into the hearts of the employers. While it succeeded momentarily in solidifying the ranks of the former, it had a much more permanent effect upon the latter. The employers, their confidence in the docility of the American workers badly shattered, at once set about the business, not of removing the basic causes of unrest but of strengthening their defenses. New armories sprang up all over the land. State militias were reorganized with an eye to excluding those elements which in times of industrial war might find their sympathies enlisted on the side of the workers. Special manuals on riot duty became prescribed reading for state and federal forces.

But though in the main the events of that mad July thus played into the hands of the conservatives, they were not to be entirely without a salutary effect upon the radicals. In the first place, it was inspiring for the latter to learn that there were limits to the American worker's patience; secondly, the radicals' own ineffectiveness in the face of what had seemed a glorious opportunity gave them food for thought and brought fresh impetus to the struggle for socialist unity. At the second convention of the Workingmen's Party, held a few months later, the socialists succeeded in further consolidating their forces, a clearer and more vigorous program was adopted, and the name of the party changed to "Socialist Labor Party." The latter was destined to hold a remarkable domination over the socialist movement in this country for a period of more than twenty years and to make a heroic, even if futile, attempt to bring about its Americanization.

# VII

## PROPAGANDA OF THE DEED

THE lean and hungry '70s, a period of *Sturm und Drang* for both Capital and Labor, wrought such changes in the basic structure of our economic life that, with the '80s, a new economic pattern may be said to have emerged. It was a pattern no longer set by the pioneer, the independent farmer, the merchant-trader who swapped stories across the counter with his customers, the small producer who took a personal pride in the quality of his product. "Pioneering," in the words of R. L. Duffus, "had changed its emphasis from the settlement and cultivation of land to the exploitation of natural resources." And with this shift a whole new financial hierarchy was to arise, a hierarchy which was to perpetuate itself in the realms of coal, lumber, oil and steel.

In the world of labor, too, a new pattern was crystallizing at this time—one that was not to be seriously disarranged until the coming of communism following the Russian Revolution of November, 1917. For though modern American socialism stems from the '70s with the founding of the Socialist Labor Party, it was in the '80s that socialism, anarchism, an incipient syndicalism, and—to depart for a moment from the revolutionary field—"pure and simple" trade unionism all emerged as separate and distinct tendencies. The most dramatic features of the period, however, were the arrival in

[ 151 ]

America of Johann Most, the rise of communist-anarchism, and the Chicago Haymarket affair.

The Great Riots of 1877, as stated in the preceding chapter, first drew the attention of the European communist-anarchists, or Bakuninists, to America and convinced them that here was a new and fertile field for their propaganda. Bakunin himself, reading of the Tompkins Square fracas and the Chicago hunger march, contemplated coming to America as early as 1874, but became too ill to make the trip. By 1877 Bakunin was dead, but his disciples, avidly following the accounts in the European press of battles raging in the streets of American cities, were filled, in the words of James Guillaume, one of their number, "with a lively emotion." Prince Peter Kropotkin wrote in the *Bulletin* of the Jura Anarchist Federation of the "revolutionary qualities" of the American workers. "Its spontaneity," he declared in reviewing the upheaval, "its simultaneousness at so many distant points, the aid given by the workers of different trades, the resolute character of the uprising from the beginning, call forth our sympathies, excite our admiration, and awaken our hopes."

While the "riots" ended almost as abruptly as they had begun and comparative peace again reigned in the land, these "hopes" proved not entirely premature. The perfunctory and high-handed manner in which federal troops and state militias had been called out at the behest of the railroad officials, the brutality with which the police and soldiery had suppressed the aroused workers, the vitriolic tenor of the press in denouncing all strikers indiscriminately as communists and criminals, had served to shatter some of the illusions of even the so-called "honest" workingmen who had stayed with their jobs and had played no part in the disturbances. Those who had actually fought for what they considered their rights were filled, of course, with bitter resentment. There was peace,

but it was a sullen peace—a propitious moment for the introduction of more violent doctrines of revolt.

The European followers of Bakunin were not alone in
sensing this. Certain hot-heads of the Socialist Labor Party,
some of whom no doubt had been clubbed and shot at during
the 1877 uprising, began to adopt a much more strident tone.
Socialists in Chicago and Cincinnati organized rifle clubs
(*Lehr und Wehr Vereine*) and began holding secret drill
practice under the red flag. This development came to the
attention of the party's executive committee at its 1879 convention and, under leadership of the stricter Marxians, was
promptly repudiated. During the following year, however,
dissension broke out over this and other matters and the
party faced the first of many splits.

While its more impatient elements were trying to drag the
Socialist Labor Party leftward, it was being subjected to an
even stronger pull in the opposite direction by its more native
reformistic members. So long as the Greenbackers had limited
their agitation to currency reform, the socialists in America
would have nothing to do with them. But the Great Strikes
of 1877 had focused the attention of the reformer, as well as
that of the radical, on labor conditions. The Greenback Party
at its 1878 convention changed its name to Greenback Labor
Party and set its nets to capture the labor vote. In the following election, various sections of the Socialist Labor Party supported its ticket. Then in 1880 the party as an organization,
much to the disgust of the old-line Marxians and the new
hot-headed element alike, became entangled with the Greenbackers and gave their presidential candidate its half-hearted
support. Though the alliance was severed directly after the
campaign, it left a bad taste in the mouths of many socialists,
turned them against politics, increased internal tension and
played into the hands of the party's left-wing critics generally.

Matters finally came to a head when the more impatient
elements of the New York section split away from the party

to form what they called a "Revolutionary Club." Similar splits followed in Boston, Philadelphia, Milwaukee and Chicago. Two leaders of the new faction in the last-named city were Albert Parsons and August Spies, both of whom were to end their careers upon the gallows as a result of the Haymarket bomb. These various "clubs" soon came together to form the Revolutionary Socialist Labor Party which wavered between a fiery brand of socialism and out and out anarchism until the arrival in America of Johann Most in 1882. This violent and persuasive agitator soon won them completely to the Bakuninist cause.

Using the term in its broadest sense, America had a tradition of anarchism extending back more than sixty years when Most arrived on the scene. Those American individualists of the '20s, '30s and '40s who, frightened by the rising tide of industrialism, had developed a nostalgia for the good old decentralized days of small independent industry, the later advocates of free banking, free trade, and free land, were working strictly within the anarchistic tradition. The Jeffersonian Democrat with his doctrine of states' rights and his conviction that the best government is that which governs least was, from the anarchist's point of view, on the proper road. The avowed anarchist merely carries this philosophic individualism to its ultimate conclusion. It is, of course, a concept which envisages a utopia of utopias in which competition, individual greed, coercion, war, poverty and crime have disappeared and men live the good life together in peace and harmony, coöperating voluntarily where coöperation is necessary for social welfare. Such a goal is the ultimate objective of all social radicals. The anarchists are convinced that it is the next step.

More specifically, American anarchism, as a philosophy rather than a movement, was personified in its purest intellectual form by Henry D. Thoreau and in its more practical social applications by Josiah Warren and his disciples,

[ 154 ]

Stephen Pearl Andrews and Benjamin R. Tucker, whose theories were akin to those of Proudhon. When Most arrived to preach his "propaganda of the deed" in the early '80s, Tucker, no longer the unsophisticated youngster whom the seductive Victoria Woodhull had introduced to the facts of life, was propounding his theories of "Individual Anarchism" in Boston in a polite review entitled *Liberty*. (Proudhonism had received its first systematic presentation in America in a French journal, *La Libertaire,* published in New York by a French immigrant, one Joseph Dejacque, on the eve of the Civil War.) Tucker defined anarchism as "the doctrine that all the affairs of men should be managed by individuals or voluntary associations, and that the State should be abolished." Anarchists were "simply unterrified Jeffersonian Democrats." Unlike the communist-anarchists, he was not opposed to private property, and he believed that the Revolution was to be brought about by a civil disobedience campaign on the part of an increasing number of enlightened passive resisters rather than by force. Terrorism, he argued, might become necessary as a last resort, but if red revolution was the only way out, then it was to be relegated to some far distant future when the masses had been educated up to the responsibilities of their revolutionary rôle. Thus in the '90s, when Alexander Berkman made his attempt upon the life of Henry Clay Frick, we find Tucker expressing himself as follows: "The hope of humanity lies in the avoidance of that revolution by force which the Berkmans are trying to precipitate. No pity for Frick, no praise for Berkman—such is the attitude of *Liberty* in the present crisis."

The two principal schools of anarchism were epitomized in the characters of their two respective leaders in the America of the '80s. No greater contrast in temperament and background could be imagined than between those of the idealistic and scholarly Tucker and the fiery, impatient Most. The career of the former so typifies the development of the nineteenth-century American intellectual radical that an outline of it, set down by Tucker himself for Emanie Sachs' *The Terrible Siren*, deserves space here.

Born in 1854, in the town of Dartmouth, Massachusetts, adjoining the city of New Bedford, of Quaker and old Colonial stock; bred in New Bedford from the age of seven; sitting steadily under the very radical preaching of Rev. William J. Potter, at the Unitarian Church in that city; clever at school, but less interested in my studies than in my outside reading; a daily devourer of the *New York Tribune* from the age of twelve until Horace Greeley's death; a student of Darwin, Spencer, Buckle, Mill, Huxley and Tyndall from the age of fourteen; an absorbed listener every winter to lectures delivered before the New Bedford Lyceum by Wendell Phillips, William Lloyd Garrison, George William Curtis, Anna Dickinson, Ralph Waldo Emerson and many others; living in a community noted for the important part that it played in the long struggle for the abolition of slavery; and gifted with a thoughtful mind and a voracious appetite for the intellectual nourishment thus abundantly afforded,—I naturally took a decided stand on all religious, scientific, political and social questions, and cherished a choice collection of chaotic and contradictory convictions, which did not begin to clear until I reached the age of eighteen, when a lucky combination of influences transformed me into the consistent anarchist that I have remained until this day. In the meantime I had been an atheist, a materialist, an evolutionist, a prohibitionist, a free trader, a champion of the legal eight-hour day, a woman suffragist, an enemy of marriage, and a believer in sexual freedom.

While Tucker, inspired by brotherly love in peaceful New England, was advancing by easy stages from Unitarianism to philosophic anarchism, Most, the illegitimate and sickly offspring of a clandestine affair between a German army subaltern and a governess, was fighting a grim battle against poverty in Europe. Illness, a cruel stepmother and a vicious employer had made his boyhood years a horrible nightmare. As if this were not a cross heavy enough for one sensitive youth to bear, he was cursed with a hideous facial scar, the result of an operation. In later life, he managed to conceal his disfigurement to some extent behind an immense bushy beard, a feature of his appearance which undoubtedly had much to do with shaping that popular American conception of the anarchist that still finds its reflection in the work of our cartoonists. In Most's eyes, the severest punishment, the greatest indignity, he ever suffered at the hands of the American authorities was not the fact that they committed him to prison but the fact that upon beginning his term, he was forced to sacrifice his beard. In her autobiography, Emma Goldman, who was still his admirer at this time, relates how, after the prison barber had completed his destructive work, Most smuggled a piece of mirror into his cell and sat contemplating that "hideous image," the sight of which proved "more terrifying than the prison."

His illegitimate birth, his puniness as a youth, the scar which had made people shrink from him, the chastisements he had received, his lack of formal education and his poverty had combined to make Most an incurable neurotic. His hatred of society bordered upon the psychopathic, exceeding the normal bounds even for an extreme left-wing radical. In the '70s, Most had joined the radical Marxian wing of the German Social Democracy. After several prison terms—one in connection with the attempt on the life of William I—he settled in London and launched a weekly review, *Freiheit*. Soon thereafter he became a violent advocate of Bakuninism and was expelled from the German Social Democratic Party. When Czar Alexander II of Russia was assassinated, he wrote such a flaming editorial in praise of the deed that he was arrested by the London police and sentenced to sixteen months' imprisonment. Freed in October, 1882, he took a ship for New York.

It is doubtful if Most could have arrived in the United States at a more opportune time. The Revolutionary Socialist Labor Party—not to be confused, of course, with the Socialist Labor Party, which, taking its cue from the German Social Democracy, repudiated Most—received him with open arms.

A great mass meeting was arranged for his reception at Cooper Union Institute. Directly afterwards he toured the country and there sprang up in his wake a whole series of small anarchist "groups" and "clubs." The trip took on the aspects of a triumphal tour. Most was a brilliant platform orator, an artist in the use of invective. Once his tongue was unleashed he immediately seemed to transcend his physical imperfections. He became the very symbol of the suffering masses.

The full measure of Most's success, however, cannot be accounted for merely in terms of his personality. As stated previously, the time was ripe for his coming.

It had become evident by 1883 [writes Norman J. Ware in *The Labor Movement in the United States*] that political action in America on the part of the "proletariat" was a dismal failure. The campaigns of the seventies were flashes in the pan. When the farmers were miserable they would rush into politics, and when the workers were depressed they, or their leaders, would do the same. But their miseries seldom synchronized, were in fact of such a nature that synchronization was almost impossible. The wage-earners were hurt and the farmers benefited by high prices, while high wages put the shoe on the other foot. Only in long periods of depression was their misery common, as in the seventies, and then they seldom wanted the same thing. But America was predominantly agricultural and a pure and simple labor party had no chance at all. Politics then was a washout, and disappointment with politics turned the American wage-earner and his foreign adviser in other directions. . . . From impotent politics to arid trade unionism the foreign intellectuals were driven, until in desperation they listened to the voice of anarchy out of the oppressed past, and America was suddenly confronted with the black flag of assassination and terror.

In New York, after his lecture tour, Most resumed publication of the *Freiheit* which he had been forced to discontinue in London. He also published a pamphlet. Its title, *Science of Revolutionary Warfare: A Manual of Instructions in the Use and Preparation of Nitroglycerine, Dynamite, Gun-Cotton, Fulminating Mercury, Bombs, Fuses, Poisons, Etc., Etc.,* speaks for itself so vigorously that comment would be in the nature of anticlimax. It is interesting to note in passing, however, that among the various "instructions" is detailed information of just where and how to plant bombs in churches, palaces, ballrooms and at festive gatherings generally in order to obtain the happiest results. Also a complete dictionary of poisons is included for use against capitalists, politicians, spies and "other traitors." In the light of Most's favorite rallying cry—"Extirpate the miserable brood! Extirpate the wretches!" —it was, all in all, a thoroughly satisfactory performance.

The result of all Most's activity was that in October, 1883, when the Revolutionary Socialist Labor Party met in convention at Pittsburgh, with Most, Parsons and Spies prominent among the delegates, the radical socialist and anarchist "groups" joined forces to launch the International Working People's Association, more popularly known as the Black International, with a manifesto dedicating the organization to the "destruction of the existing class rule by all means, i.e., by energetic, relentless, revolutionary, and international action."

We could show by scores of illustrations [the manifesto continued in part] that all attempts in the past to reform this monstrous system by peaceable means, such as the ballot, have been futile, and all such efforts in the future must necessarily be so. . . . Since we must then rely upon the kindness of our masters for whatever redress we have, and knowing that from them no good may be expected, there remains but one recourse—FORCE!

Thus the so-called "black flag of assassination and terror" —though it was to require the flash of the Haymarket bomb almost two years later to bring it to the attention of the country at large—was unfurled to the American breeze.

The International Working People's Association was, in accordance with anarchist theory, an extremely loose organization, a series of small autonomous groups that supposedly kept in touch with each other through an "Information Bureau" in Chicago. But the fact that it was to give a very real impetus to the spread of Bakuninism in the United States and give the Marxians of the Socialist Labor Party a run for their money became apparent almost immediately. The circulation of *Freiheit* soared. So, too, did that of the Chicago *Arbeiter-Zeitung* and *Vorbote*, formerly socialist papers which had now been made safe for anarchism. On the eve of the Socialist Labor Party's 1883 convention some of its most prominent members made overtures to the Chicago anarchists for unity, but were rebuffed by Spies. When the convention met, only sixteen delegates were in attendance, but this little group, despite the terrific inroads the anarchists were making on their rank and file, stood manfully by their guns. "We do not share the folly of the men who consider dynamite bombs as the best means of agitation," they declared; "we know full well that a revolution must take place in the heads and in the industrial life of men before the working class can achieve lasting success." It was a declaration of war within the radical camp. From then on the lines between socialism and anarchism in the United States were to be tightly drawn.

Meanwhile the anarchists were holding the center of the revolutionary stage and making the most of it by the dramatic aspects of their propaganda. As early as 1881, the *Vorbote* set itself the task of laying down the conditions under which the assassination of a Gould or a Vanderbilt would be justifiable. "Whether one uses dynamite, a revolver, or a rope," it declared, "is a matter of indifference." A little later it was publishing poems with lines expressing such sentiments as follows: "Hurrah for science! Hurrah for dynamite, the power which in our hands shall make an end of tyranny."

When the depression of 1884 set in and the country was overrun with tramps—all homeless, unemployed workers were "tramps" in those days—and the New York *Herald* declared editorially that "the best meal that can be given to a regular tramp is a leaden one" and the Chicago *Tribune* echoed that "the simplest plan . . . is to put strychnine or arsenic in the meat and other supplies furnished" as "this produces death in a short time and a warning to other tramps to keep out of the neighborhood," the anarchists' counter-advice to the tramps themselves was, "Learn the use of explosives!"

This new agitational note reverberated throughout left-wing circles in the East but perhaps its most startling echo came from beyond the Rockies. In San Francisco, a group composed almost entirely of native Americans and under leadership of an eccentric lawyer named Burnette G. Haskell, met with elaborate and totally unnecessary precautions of secrecy, declared its allegiance to anarchism, and established a weekly entitled *Truth*. This lively little journal carried at its masthead the line: "*Truth* is five cents a copy and dynamite forty cents a pound," and underneath this the motto, "War to the palace, peace to the cottage, death to luxurious idleness!" "Every trade-union and assembly," it declared editorially, "ought to pick its best men and form them into classes for the study of chemistry." Finally, on November 17, 1883, Haskell could contain himself no longer. "We have no moment to waste," he wrote. "Arm! I say, to the teeth! for the Revolution is upon you!"

The influence of Haskell and his little group spread up and down the Coast and across the Great Divide. In Denver, Joseph R. Buchanan, author of *The Story of a Labor Agitator* and known as the "Riproarer of the Rockies," took up the cause and launched the *Labor Enquirer*. In place of the silver bullion quotation carried in a front page box by the other Denver papers, Buchanan substituted such lines as, "Dynamite is strong today at 47c." Haskell was so impressed by his disciple's zeal that he made him official organizer for "Colorado, Utah, Dakota, Montana, Idaho and the State of Chihuahua in the Republic of Mexico."

The depression which began in 1884 and lasted until 1886

added fresh fuel to the fires of discontent. As in 1877, throngs of idle, hungry workers roamed the streets. The anarchists, sensing their opportunity, increased the fervor of their agitation. In Chicago, looked upon as the headquarters of the movement, they were most active. In the first year of the depression Parsons launched the *Alarm* which immediately became the leading English organ of the anarchists. He was soon printing such sentiments as follows:

*Dynamite!* Of all good stuff, that is the stuff! Stuff several pounds of this sublime stuff into an inch pipe (gas or water), plug up both ends, insert a cap with a fuse attached, place this in the immediate vicinity of a lot of rich loafers who live by the sweat of other people's brows, and light the fuse. A most cheerful and gratifying result will follow. In giving dynamite to the downtrodden millions of the globe science has done its best work. The dear stuff can be carried in the pocket without danger, while it is a formidable weapon against any force of militia, police, or detectives that may want to stifle the cry for justice that goes forth from the plundered slaves. . . . A pound of this good stuff beats a bushel of ballots all hollow—and don't you forget it!

If the anarchists had remained merely a small sect crying alone in the wilderness, it is doubtful if such talk—much as it might have shocked those against whom it was directed had it come to their attention—would have aroused any widespread fear. After all, it was—during the early '80s at least—simply talk. It was no overt act on the part of the anarchists that shattered the relative calm which had descended upon the industrial world after the storms of the '70s. Yet by 1885 that calm was definitely shattered, there was a growing tension in the air and storm signals, in the form of repeated strikes, boycotts and blacklisting of workers, heralded the approach of what some acute observers believed might be a hurricane of terrific proportions. The first gusts came from quite another quarter than that occupied by the anarchists; namely, from the direction of the comparatively conservative unionists. It was only after the anarchists began to take advantage of the unrest of organized labor and direct it into revolutionary channels that their agitation gained a sinister significance in the eyes of the propertied classes and anarchism began to be referred to with increasing frequency in the conservative press of the day as "the menace." To understand this situation, which at its height was to give rise to a wave of hysteria almost as great as that which had swept across the land at the time of the Great Riots, it is necessary once again to leave the radicals for a moment and make an excursion into the realm of organized labor.

The unions had been dealt what was almost their death blow by the long depression of the '70s, but when the revival in trade finally set in, the workers, faced with the usual post-depression lag of wages behind soaring prices, flocked by the thousands back into their unions which were promising higher wages and shorter hours. The condition favorable to the rise of anarchism—i.e., disillusionment on the part of the underdog as to the effectiveness of political action—was also favorable to the spread of unionism. New unions sprang up on every hand; old ones revived and strengthened their position through amalgamation. But the most significant developments in the field of organized labor during this period were the tremendous spurt of the Knights of Labor and the founding in 1881 of the Federation of Organized Trades and Labor Unions, from the ashes of which five years later was to arise the powerful American Federation of Labor.

A few years after the close of the Civil War, nine obscure garment cutters had met in a small hall in Philadelphia and out of that meeting the Noble and Holy Order of the Knights of Labor had been born. The Order was undoubtedly the most representative American labor organization this country has ever known. Many radicals are inclined to reserve this particular place of honor for the Industrial Workers of the World, of which the Knights were a forerunner; but the I. W. W., despite its activity among eastern textile workers,

[ 163 ]

came primarily to be dominated by the spirit of the West and to represent workers of a particular type and section rather than that great amorphous mass which for convenience we label the "American working class." In fact, probably the principal factor in rendering the Knights so peculiarly representative of the American masses was its own amorphous and confused character. The organization, as Norman J. Ware has pointed out, "cannot be fitted into any conceivable classification of form, function, or theory. There was no form of organization they did not possess at one time or another, no function they did not perform or attempt, and almost no theory they did not hold either officially or unofficially."

If, from the outset, the Order was characteristically American in the very vagueness of its form and theory, it was to become equally so in terms of its subsequent history. The humble origin, the high ambition and noble aims, the steady plodding growth, the sudden dizzy ascent to fame at last—all the components of the American success story were there. Expressed, too, in most graphic form in this organization of humble, idealistic wage-earners was that peculiarly American sense of inferiority which seeks compensation in high-sounding ritual and grandiose titles. The Order was a secret, fraternal type of organization all during its formative years. The most downtrodden and harassed pants cutter, upon joining it, immediately found himself dubbed "Knight," possessed of secret grips and high-signs which set him apart from his non-union fellows. If he rose in the organization, the most elaborate titles were at his disposal.

Uriah S. Stephens, a bookish man who had originally been educated for the Baptist ministry but who had been forced to take to tailoring for a living, was the organization's first Grand Master Workman. Stephens was no radical—far from it. "We mean no conflict with legitimate enterprise," he declared, "no antagonism to necessary capital. . . . We mean to uphold the dignity of labor, to affirm the nobility of all who earn their bread by the sweat of their brows." Still he had visions of some far distant future in which the wage system would be abolished.

Stephens' successor in office was Terence V. Powderly, an American-born Irish Catholic and a machinist by trade, who led the organization all during its most active years. Powderly was a delicate, sensitive man with the vanity of a prima donna —about the last person in the world one would expect to become a labor leader. John Swinton, describing him when the Knights were at the height of their power, wrote: "English novelists take men of Powderly's look for their poets, gondola scullers, philosophers and heroes crossed in love but no one ever drew such a looking man as the leader of a million of the horny-fisted sons of toil." Overcautious, in fact downright timid, Powderly opposed strikes which he looked upon as "harassing details" serving to divert attention from his pet hobbies: land reform and prohibition. Always in favor of arbitration in industrial disputes, he was singularly inept as an arbitrator. Yet with all his timidity, conservatism and fear of public opinion, he never—like the hard-boiled leaders of the American Federation of Labor—committed either himself or his organization to the premise upon which the wage system is based. He was a great believer in the effectiveness of educational propaganda. When, in the '80s, other labor organizations and thousands of his own followers were ready for a general strike for the eight-hour day, he urged instead that members "write short essays on the eight-hour question." When unemployment was rife, Powderly issued instructions —incidentally one of the first instances of open advocacy of sabotage by an American labor leader—for all true Knights to smash their beer bottles after draining them, thereby doing their bit to end the depression by providing employment in the glass industry. Few labor leaders ever reached greater heights of absurdity than did Powderly at times. Perhaps his greatest asset was that he was an effective platform orator, a spellbinder, a tremendous windbag, and the masses adored him. "When I speak on the labor question," he once said, "I want the individual attention of my hearers and I want that attention for at least two hours and in that two hours I can only epitomize." The '80s were years of frills and furbelows in everything from oratory to dress and architecture. Powderly's grandiloquent rhetorical flourishes and amazing flights of fancy left the "horny-fisted sons of toil" positively ecstatic.

The Knights of Labor, as has been said, was originally a secret organization. For years its name was never referred to openly and was represented in all official documents and in the press by five asterisks (* * * * *). From its modest beginnings as a little local of Philadelphia garment cutters in 1869, it spread along the Atlantic seaboard, pushed westward into the coal and iron regions. Under pressure, principally exerted by the Catholic Church which was still shuddering over the fact that some of its sons had been at the bottom of the Molly Maguire affair, secrecy was abandoned. In 1878, the year after the Great Upheaval, the Knights held their General Assembly and permanent organization was established on a national scale.

Here was something decidedly new in the American labor world. While imposing arrays of labor leaders, assorted radicals and reformers had for years been coming together in conventions and industrial congresses and attempting to create a national organization by beginning at the top and working downward, this small band of rank-and-file laborites had gone quietly, even secretly, about the business of organizing from the very bottom, welding their local organizations into district assemblies, and had succeeded, where all the brilliant limelighters of labor and radicalism had failed, in launching the first great national labor organization in the United States.

The fundamental aim of the Order was to bring all workers, regardless of sex, creed, trade or color, together in one big union, "to teach," in the words of Norman Ware, "the American wage-earner that he was a wage-earner first and a bricklayer, carpenter, miner, shoemaker, after; that he was a wage-earner first and a Catholic, Protestant, Jew, white, black, Democrat, Republican, after." It was an ambitious aim—too ambitious and idealistic for the America of the '70s and '80s, and, for that matter, probably much too utopian for America today. It was difficult then, as it is now, for the highly skilled craft unionist to see that he had anything in common with the Negro hod-carrier, for the engineer at the throttle of the crack express to feel any great bond of brotherhood between himself and the pick-and-shovel workers along the right of way. Nevertheless the Knights made surprising headway in this respect. At its height, the Order had some 60,000 Negro members. The more tangible aspects of the Knights' program included the referendum, prohibition of child labor, graduated income and inheritance taxes, government ownership of telegraph and railroads, and the eight-hour day.

The Federation of Organized Trades and Labor Unions of the United States and Canada, precursor of the American Federation of Labor, which was organized in Pittsburgh in 1881 just as the Knights were getting nicely under way, was quite a different affair. Among the moving spirits of the Federation were Samuel Gompers, Adolph Strasser, and P. J. McGuire. Both Strasser and McGuire had played prominent rôles in the old Social Democratic Workingmen's Party and Gompers himself had toyed with the idea of becoming a socialist, but of recent years these men had been drawn deeper and deeper into the struggle of their unions for day-by-day concessions. Whatever radical idealism they may once have possessed, they were now hard-headed, practical men with but little interest in ultimate ends or high-sounding theories. They wanted something specific—mainly higher wages and shorter hours—for men of their own stamp, the highly skilled craft unionists, and they wanted it here and now. Like the leaders of the Knights, they sensed the need of a national or-ganization, but they had no intention of slowing up their own immediate progress by pulling the unskilled and unorganized workers up to their level. In effect, the Federation represented a revolt of the aristocrats of labor against the Knights whose organization was too broad for them, a "strategic retreat" of the craft unionist who sensed the fact that his superior skill gave him a distinct advantage over the common run of labor in bargaining with the employer.

The Federation failed to prosper, however, and is impor-tant today only because it served as a base for that impressive edifice, the American Federation of Labor. Perhaps its most significant act was one of its last, the passing of a resolution declaring that "eight hours shall constitute a legal day's work from and after May 1, 1886." This was by no means the first resolution of its kind, nor was the eight-hour outlook particu-larly hopeful at this time. But subsequent events were to rescue the resolution from oblivion in a startling fashion.

The chief argument advanced by proponents of the eight-hour day in the '80s was, as in the beginning of that move-ment, the simple one of the worker's need of leisure for self-improvement. But already the more thoughtful agitators were utilizing a more modern and scientific approach to this ques-tion. Even as early as 1879 we find one of these employing the technocratic argument in a letter to a Congressional com-mittee urging the shortening of the hours of labor. "In the manufacture of cotton fabrics," he pointed out, "one girl today can do what two generations ago would have required the united labor of 100 women, and in woolens the use of machinery has laid aside 70 per cent of the laborers."

Fresh views on time-worn questions, new ideas, new eco-nomic doctrines were gaining a popular hearing at this time. Labor was growing more militant. Radical and liberal ideas were spreading, even to the extent of penetrating such high citadels of respectability as the *Atlantic Monthly* which, in 1881, gave space to a scathing attack upon Standard Oil by Henry Demarest Lloyd, whose later book, *Wealth Against Commonwealth,* was to blaze the trail for the muckrakers of the Ida Tarbell-Lincoln Steffens school. Henry George's *Progress and Poverty*, published by Appleton & Company in 1879, was pouring from the presses in edition after edition. "Tens of thousands of laborers," wrote Professor Richard T. Ely in 1885, "have read *Progress and Poverty* who never before looked between the two covers of an economic book, and its conclusions are widely accepted articles in the working-man's creed."

The clearest indications of the mounting wave of discontent were to be found, however, in the deep rumblings from below in the form of strikes, boycotts and demonstrations in connection with the eight-hour agitation. The first great strike led by the Knights of Labor occurred in 1883 when the telegraphers walked out, demanding shorter hours and higher wages. Jay Gould, whose Western Union employed some 4,000 operators, succeeded in breaking it, but by the following year the depression had set in, general wage-cutting had begun, and fresh strikes were breaking out on every hand. In 1885 the Knights again clashed with Gould when he attempted to cut wages and enforce an anti-union policy over his railroad lines, known as the Southwest System. In the Great Southwest Strike, the Knights resorted to direct action and sabotage of a most violent sort, disabling locomotives, tearing up rails and halting trains. They won the strike, but trouble soon broke out again. Threatening to disorganize some 20,000 miles of road by refusing to handle Wabash rolling stock, the organized trainmen frightened Gould, whose proudest boast was that he could "hire one half of the working class to kill the other half," into conferring with their leaders, which virtually meant recognition of their union and wrung from him several concessions. The effect of this victory was electric.

Thousands of unorganized workers clamored to be taken under the protective wing of this organization powerful enough to bring such a financial titan to his knees. New locals sprang up so fast that finally the officials, fearing the organization would get entirely out of hand, refused to grant additional charters. To the newspapers, the victory over Gould was a subject for banner headlines. They now followed the story up with sensational reports in which the strength of the Knights was so grossly exaggerated that Powderly felt called upon to deny them.

No wonder that the employers—quite apart from any effect upon them of the anarchist agitation—were growing apprehensive. Along with strikes, boycotts—the boycott had become a favorite weapon of the Knights and almost two hundred of them were declared in 1885 alone—and the growing militancy of labor generally, they were faced with the eight-hour agitation which was now assuming alarming proportions. The unrest mounted steadily until we find General Phil Sheridan conferring with the Secretary of War on the danger of "entire cities being destroyed by the infuriated populace," and General Sherman, Chief of Staff, declaring: "There will soon come an armed contest between Capital and Labor. They will oppose each other not with words and arguments and ballots, but with shot and shell, gunpowder and cannon. The better classes are tired of the insane howlings of the lower strata, and they mean to stop them." It began to look—to the propertied classes at least—as if May 1, 1886, which had been set so innocently by the expiring Federation of Organized Trades and Labor Unions for the inauguration of the eight-hour day, might well be *Der Tag* the revolutionists had long been talking about.

Nowhere else in the country was the growing tension as apparent as it was in the great, sprawling city of Chicago. The New York *World* might once have editorialized as follows:

The American laborer must make up his mind, henceforth, not to be so much better off than the European laborer. Men must be content to work for low wages. In this way the workingman will be nearer to that station in life to which it has pleased God to call him.

But the Chicago *Times* now argued seriously that "hand grenades should be thrown among those who are striving to obtain higher wages."

The eight-hour movement was formally launched in Chicago by George A. Schilling, a socialist. At the outset the anarchists not only remained aloof, but opposed it, declaring that the eight-hour day, if attained, would amount to nothing but an ineffective compromise and that the only remedy for the ills of the workers was the abolition of the wage system. The movement immediately won the support of all the principal labor bodies in the city, however, including the local assemblies of the Knights; and the anarchists, afraid of becoming cut off from the unions in which they had already become influential, swung into line. Once they had done so, they agitated with such unrestrained enthusiasm that they soon assumed leadership of the local eight-hour struggle. In league with the socialists, with whom they now stood united so far as the hours question was concerned, they arranged a great mass demonstration for Christmas Day, 1885, the climax of which was a parade of ragged, half-starved men and women along the fashionable Prairie Avenue. The marchers waved black and red flags and stopped to hoot and jeer before the more ostentatious mansions.

The winter was an extremely severe one. Thousands wandered the streets out of work and gathered along the lake front to listen to socialist and anarchist speakers. In February a bitter strike broke out at the works of the McCormick Harvester Company; angry pickets clashed with strike breakers on the famous Black Road; police and privately employed Pinkerton men broke up the picket lines and clubbed the

[ 171 ]

strikers. The strike dragged on, the eight-hour agitation mounted in fervor, and as May Day approached the public in general and the propertied classes in particular became increasingly alarmed. It began to look as if anything might happen. But May Day came and passed and though there were 80,000 estimated strikers in Chicago and some 190,000 in the country as a whole, there was no revolution, no signs of any widespread violence. The most signal victory was that of the Chicago packing-house employees, 35,000 of whom gained, only temporarily to be sure, the eight-hour day merely by threatening a walkout. All in all, the employers who had been expecting the worst had much reason for rejoicing.

Two days later, however, Spies was addressing a group of McCormick strikers near the plant. As he concluded, a group of strike breakers came streaming past on their way from work. The provocation was too great for his aroused audience; stones began to fly, and a violent clash seemed inevitable when the police descended, opened fire and killed six strikers, wounding many others. Spies, witness of the slaughter, rushed to the office of the *Alarm* and in white heat wrote his famous Revenge Circular:

### REVENGE!
#### Workingmen, to Arms!!!

Your masters sent out their bloodhounds—the police—; they killed six of your brothers at McCormick's this afternoon. They killed the poor wretches, because they, like you, had the courage to disobey the supreme will of your bosses. They killed them, because they dared ask for the shortening of the hours of toil. They killed them to show you *"Free American Citizens"* that you *must* be satisfied and contented with whatever your bosses condescend to allow you, or you will get killed! . . .

If you are men, if you are the sons of your grandsires, who have shed their blood to free you, then you will rise in your might, Hercules, and destroy the hideous monster that seeks to destroy you. To arms we call you, to arms!

Five thousand of these were printed in English and German and distributed on the streets.

[ 172 ]

A protest meeting was announced for the following evening to be held in Haymarket Square to "denounce the latest atrocious act of the police." A crowd of perhaps three thousand men, women and children gathered at the appointed hour to listen to Parsons, Spies and Samuel Fielden. To those who had read the Revenge Circular and the editorials in *Vorbote, Alarm* and *Arbeiter Zeitung*, the meeting, until the arrival of the police, must have seemed a tame affair. The speeches were remarkably restrained, a fact testified to later by Mayor Carter Harrison who attended and who on his way home stopped at the Desplaines Street police station to report that nothing was likely to occur. Soon after the mayor's departure, rain set in and the meeting began to break up. At this moment, however, a large body of reserve police arrived on the scene under the leadership of Captain Bondfield of the Desplaines station. Fielden, who was just concluding his remarks, looked up with surprise. At a shouted order "to immediately and peaceably disperse," he replied, "Why, captain, we *are* peaceable." (In police testimony later this was rendered as, "Here are the bloodhounds! Men, do your duty and I'll do mine!") The words were scarcely out of his mouth when there was a blinding flash, a terrific explosion. A bomb, hurled from the general direction of a nearby alley, had fallen between the first and second companies of police, killing one officer instantly and wounding many more. The police, panic-stricken and blinded by smoke, fired into the crowd and even at one another. Some of the men in the crowd, who had doubtless taken Spies' advice to arm, fired back. The police reformed their lines and charged. It was all over in a few minutes, but at the end of that interval seven policemen lay dead and some sixty wounded. The casualties on the side of the workers were probably much greater but were never accurately determined.

The tension in Chicago—which can be fully comprehended perhaps only by one who has been in a southern town at the time of a lynching, in San Francisco during the early days of the Mooney case or in Boston on the eve of the execution of Sacco and Vanzetti—was now released in a wave of hysteria and mob spirit. Popular indignation throughout the country flared out not only against the anarchists but with almost equal intensity against the whole labor and radical movement and against anyone who had ever expressed the faintest sympathy with it. The hostility against even the conservative Knights, whose only connection with the Chicago affair was the part they had played in the eight-hour agitation and the fact that Parsons happened to be a member, can be judged by the extremes to which they went to offset it. No more hysterical outbursts could be found in all the rantings of the ultra-conservative press than the following quoted from the Chicago organ of the Knights of Labor:

> Let it be understood by all the world that the Knights of Labor have no affiliation, association, sympathy or respect for the band of cowardly murderers, cutthroats and robbers, known as anarchists, who sneak through the country like midnight assassins, stirring up the passions of ignorant foreigners, unfurling the red flag of anarchy and causing riot and bloodshed. Parsons, Spies, Fielden, Most and all their followers, sympathizers, aiders and abettors, should be summarily dealt with. They are entitled to no more consideration than wild beasts. . . .

A reign of terror was inaugurated in Chicago against labor and radicals of all degree. Meetings were raided indiscriminately; the *Arbeiter-Zeitung* was placed under police censorship; its entire staff, together with the Haymarket speakers, arrested. The Grand Jury convened and found an indictment against Spies, Parsons, Fielden, Michael Schwab, Adolph Fischer, George Engel, Louis Lingg, Oscar W. Neebe, and Rudolph Schnaubelt, charging them with murder. Two of these men were merely mild socialists and trade unionists. Even among those who had written and talked much about dynamite, it was little more than a mystical revolutionary symbol. Lingg was probably the only one of the lot who was temperamentally fitted actually to handle the "real stuff," and it was later established, practically beyond the shadow of a doubt, that Lingg, like several other of the defendants, was not at the Haymarket meeting at all. Schnaubelt, a labor organizer, at whom much suspicion was directed because he fled the country and also because of Frank Harris' highly inaccurate and fictional treatment of the case in his novel, *The Bomb*, denied repeatedly through the anarchist press that he had had any connection with the affair and no evidence ever came to light to cast the slightest doubt on the truth of his assertion. (He was never apprehended, by the way, and, making his way to South America under an assumed name, he settled there, and became a coffee planter of considerable means.)

The remaining eight defendants came to trial on June 21, 1886, before Judge Joseph E. Gary (not to be confused with Judge Elbert H. Gary of United States Steel fame) in an atmosphere of almost hysterical prejudice. The prosecution, in the words of Judge Gary, did not go "on the ground that they [the defendants] did actually have any personal participation in the particular act," but proceeded "upon the ground that they had generally by speech and print advised large classes to commit murder and had left the commission, the time, place, and when to the individual will, whim, or caprice or whatever it may be of each individual man who listened to their advice." All eight were declared guilty. Seven received the death sentence; Neebe was given fifteen years in the penitentiary. Upon appeal to the higher courts, the judgment was affirmed. As the date of execution drew near, a most frantic attempt was made to induce Governor Oglesby of Illinois to commute the sentences of the doomed men. George Bernard Shaw, William Morris and Frank Harris circulated petitions for reprieve in England. Oscar Wilde was one of the few who responded to their appeal. William Dean Howells, at the risk of complete social ostracism, spoke courageously in the anarchists' behalf. Robert Ingersoll and Henry George refused

[ 175 ]

to aid the cause, the former on the ground that Governor Oglesby had saved his life in the Civil War and he did not want to embarrass him. For organized labor, Gompers stepped forward with an eloquent plea. Powderly, though personally sympathetic at the end, was overcome by his timidity and blocked a resolution for clemency on the part of the Knights. Individual assemblies of the Order, however, even the one in Chicago which had so violently denounced the anarchists at first, defiantly urged commutation.

Schwab and Fielden were at last induced to put in a plea in their own behalf and at the last moment Governor Oglesby commuted their sentences to life imprisonment. Lingg committed suicide in his cell by exploding between his teeth a dynamite cartridge—believed to have been smuggled in to him by his sweetheart. Spies, Parsons, Fischer and Engel went to the gallows on November 11, 1887, a day that has ever since been known in radical circles as Black Friday. The last words of Spies, spoken through his black hood the moment before the trap was sprung, were: "There will be a time when our silence will be more powerful than the voices you strangle today."

Six years later, John P. Altgeld, liberal governor of Illinois, after a most painstaking investigation, granted a full pardon to Fielden, Neebe and Schwab, accompanying his decree with a scathing denunciation of Judge Gary's conduct during the trial. This act of mercy, one of the most courageous ever performed by any man in American public life, sealed Altgeld's political fate and undoubtedly had much to do with bringing about his financial ruin. The intense feeling had not even yet died down. Altgeld was branded as an enemy of society and portrayed by cartoonists as an anarchist himself with a bomb sputtering in each hand. Dr. Lyman Abbott denounced him from the pulpit as "the crowned hero and worshiped deity of the Anarchists of the Northwest," and Theodore Roosevelt characterized him as a man who "condones and encourages the most infamous of murders." When Altgeld died in 1902, two supposedly liberal clergymen found reasons not to officiate at his funeral, but it was not unfitting, perhaps, that the last rites should be performed by two of his friends, Jane Addams and Clarence Darrow.

# VIII

## DOCTRINE VERSUS REALITY

THE unknown hand, which on the rainy night of May 4, 1886, tossed a bomb into the ranks of the Chicago police, struck the radical movement in the United States a serious blow. It was not the immediate and inevitable reprisals that mattered so much. In fact, the hysterical tone of the prosecution and the conservative press, the high-handed manner of the court, the police repression and the vindictiveness of the employers raised the status of the Haymarket victims to that of martyrs and brought thousands of men and women who abhorred the anarchists' propaganda rallying to their defense. Between fifteen and twenty thousand people, singing the "Marseillaise," followed the bodies of the executed men to Waldheim Cemetery and 250,000 spectators lined the route.

Nevertheless, the ultimate effect of the disaster, as was to be the case many years later after the McNamara affair, was to drive American labor definitely to the right and to strengthen the influence of its more conservative leaders. However innocent they were of any actual connection with the Haymarket bomb, the anarchists had undoubtedly misjudged the temper of the American workers and had overshot the mark with their propaganda. The average wage-earner, even the average radical wage-earner, was by no means prepared for the advent of dynamite in "the class struggle" and, recalling the anarchists' phrases in the light of what had happened, he was profoundly shocked. To his customary distrust of politics was now added a deep distrust of radical leadership which played directly into the hands of practical men of the type of Samuel Gompers, who between the trial and execution of the Haymarket victims had been successful in raising, upon the foundations of the old Federation of Organized Trades and Labor Unions, the superstructure of the American Federation of Labor.

Antagonism between the radicals and the more conservative labor elements had had its genesis long before the Haymarket affair. As early as 1879, Uriah S. Stephens, first Grand Master of the Knights of Labor, had advised a fellow Knight: "You must not allow the socialists to get control of your assembly. They are simply disturbers and only gain entrance to labor societies that they may be in better position to break them up." As a result of the Haymarket debacle the arguments of the "pure and simple" unionists against radicalism gained a new authority. While the radical ranks were thinned out by the desertion of those who sought to escape the onus of "dynamiter," the stampede toward conservative unionism gained momentum. The revolutionaries were left high and dry. In the early '90s, particularly with the depression of '93, the radicals within the union ranks made threatening inroads on the power of Gompers and his friends. But on the whole the great battles of this period—Homestead, Coeur d'Alene, even the Debs Rebellion—were not their battles, hard as they struggled to make them so. Out of these grim hand-to-hand conflicts of capital and labor, militant labor leaders like Eugene V. Debs and "Big Bill" Haywood emerged, but they were not to assume their frankly revolutionary rôles until after the turn of the century. The great struggles of the '90s were fought, in the main, without benefit of theory for immediate, realistic ends which differed in few respects from

[ 179 ]

those being sought in less spectacular fashion by the plodding Gompers and his cohorts.

The widespread reaction against anarchism after the Haymarket affair left the Socialist Labor Party members more or less in possession of the revolutionary field. They had had an uphill battle since the organization of their party in 1877. Suffering from the inroads of the anarchists, they were barely able to maintain a skeleton of organization in the early '80s. In 1883, with the party at its lowest ebb, its national secretary, Philip Van Patten, gave up the struggle and mysteriously disappeared. A letter left behind him indicated suicide but he turned up later, as a federal employee. His successor, with more candor than is usually found among party executives, declared: "Let us not conceal the truth: the Socialist Labor Party is only a German colony, an adjunct of the German-speaking Social Democracy."

Fresh life was instilled into American socialism in the fall of 1886 by the visit of Wilhelm Liebknecht, eloquent leader of the German Social Democracy, together with Dr. Edward Aveling and his wife Eleanor, brilliant daughter of Karl Marx. (Aveling served as a model for Shaw's philandering artist, Louis Dubedat, in *The Doctor's Dilemma*.) Like Most, who had toured the country several years before in the interests of anarchism, these European advocates now invaded the hinterlands to spread the gospel of socialism. Together, they held some fifty meetings and penetrated as far west as Kansas City. Liebknecht spoke in German, the Avelings in English. Huge crowds flocked to their meetings. "The American people," wrote the Avelings in *The Working Class Movement in America*, "were waiting to hear in their own language what socialism was."

They were amazed at the prevalence of what they termed "unconscious socialism" and compiled a list—an incomplete one—of ninety-seven American labor papers which, while not altogether socialistic, were inclined in that direction. Extremes of wealth and poverty seemed to them more marked in the New World than in the Old and they prophesied that "the next years of the 19th century will be taken up chiefly by an internecine struggle that will end, as the capitalists hope, in the subjugation of the working class; as the working class knows, in the abolition of all classes." Their keenest observations, however, had to do with the state of American literature and might have been written by one of our contemporary proletarian critics.

Where [they inquire] are the American writers of fiction? With a subject and such a subject lying ready to their hands, clamoring at their very doors, not one of them touches it. Even in England where we have no novelist belonging to the schools of Henry James or W. D. Howells, some sort of attempt at dealing with the relative position of the rich and poor and even with their relative antagonism has here and there been made. . . . But of the American novelists, not one of repute has pictured the New York or Boston proletariat. . . . We have portraits of "ladies," of Daisy Millers, etc. But there are no studies of factory hands and of dwellers in tenement houses, no pictures of those sunk in the innermost depths of the Inferno. Yet these types must be dealt with and one of these days the Uncle Tom's Cabin of Capitalism will be written.

Though they spoke courageously for a new trial for the Chicago anarchists, the Avelings were bitterly assailed by some of the remaining adherents of that movement and they paid their respects to them as follows: "Where the working class has come to years of discretion and where, from a vague feeling of misery and unrest, it has grown to understand its true position, has awakened to class consciousness—Anarchism dies out."

What served more than anything else, perhaps, to lift the Socialist Labor Party from the obscurity into which it had fallen during the early '80s was the Henry George campaign in New York. The immediate impetus for "the United Front of 1886," as it came to be called, arose from the conviction of five New York unionists on the charge of conspiracy in boycotting a beer garden. Once again, as in the eight-hour fight in Chicago, unionists, radicals, liberals and reformers of all shades came together in a common cause. In seeking a champion to carry their banner into the fray they hit upon a man whose name was rapidly becoming a household word. This man was Henry George.

Probably no more incongruous figure ever appeared among the eastern industrial workers than this western land reformer. Though often referred to as the spiritual heir of George Henry Evans, Henry George had no such appreciation of the problems of the urban worker as had his predecessor, who, no matter how romantic his yearnings for the agrarian life, remained primarily a city man absorbed in industrial issues. George had gone to California in the late '50s and during the next two decades there—as prospector, printer, editor and inspector of gas meters—he had ample opportunity to observe the passing of the best of the free and easy frontier. Mining and agriculture, depending directly on a bountiful nature—and how bountiful nature could be in California!—were the main pursuits. Wages were high and land plentiful. But with the completion of the first transcontinental railroad in 1869, population soared, wages dropped and the desirable free land was gobbled up for speculative purposes. George, extremely naïve economically at this time, jumped to the conclusion that wages were falling solely because of land monopoly and exorbitant rental charges.

The early agrarians of the vote-yourself-a-farm school had been concerned primarily with opening up the frontier for harassed city dwellers. By the late '70s immense tracts of it had been seized by the railroads and the large speculators. The Northern Pacific alone had acquired a grant of 47,000,-000 acres. George undertook to fight the land battle all over again but discovered a more formidable foe in the persons of railroad kings and financiers than had his predecessors in politicians more or less subject to public pressure.

George's theory, popularly known as the Single Tax, was a scheme to open once more the door of opportunity to the city worker, the farm laborer and particularly the great American middle class already beginning to feel the increasing pressure of the monopolists and the Money Power. He proposed that the entire revenue for carrying on the government should be raised by a tax on land values alone (hence the term "single tax"). Such a tax, he argued, would make the holding of land for purely speculative purposes unprofitable and would strike at the root of all evil—land monopoly. Incidentally, of course, in common with all other social prophets, he held that his doctrine offered a panacea for all the ills from which society was suffering—a naïve assumption in the face of our modern industrial set-up.

Though repeatedly hailed as one by capitalist and reformer alike, George was no revolutionist. He had neither the temperament nor the background for one. He was eager to resolve the conflict between capital and labor; and, as John Chamberlain has pointed out in *Farewell to Reform*, "the problem of controls eluded him." He created no machinery and rallied no political or industrial army capable of enforcing the operations of his doctrine.

*Progress and Poverty* contained little that was new. George had been anticipated in all the essentials of his philosophy by Thomas Spence, Thomas Paine, Patrick Edward Dove (a Scotchman writing in the '50s) and Edwin Burgess, a Wisconsin tailor. Yet there is no doubt that he reached most of his conclusions independently and that his predecessors, while saying much the same thing, said it much less graphically. George's book was an eloquent portrait and indictment of a social order based on grotesque inequalities and injustices that were easily recognized and immediately conceded. Because of its oversimplified reasonableness it struck a respon-

[ 183 ]

sive chord in a public which still thought in social terms strongly colored by eighteenth-century physiocratic doctrines.

In a few years *Progress and Poverty* went through over a hundred editions and the New York *Independent* was declaring that George's books "are sold and read in America as no other books are sold and read: the sales are numbered by the hundred thousand, the readers by the million." It was this man of the hour whom the New York laborites—backed up by the socialists—prevailed upon to accept their nomination for mayor in the fall of 1886, just a few weeks after the conviction of the Chicago anarchists.

The New York socialists, while prepared to support George, were far from enthusiastic about him at the start, but as the short, spectacular campaign gathered momentum, their enthusiasm mounted. "A born American, Henry George, takes up our standard," declared *Der Sozialist* triumphantly. "We are living through a period of revolution in New York City."

In October, George's United Labor Party launched a daily, the *Leader*, under the editorship of Louis F. Post, later Assistant Secretary of Labor under Woodrow Wilson. The paper sold for a cent and gained a circulation of 100,000 before election. The Democrats put forward Abram S. Hewitt, philanthropic son-in-law of Peter Cooper who had established the Cooper Union Institute. The Republicans nominated a young man who had put his foot on the first rung of the political ladder by getting elected to the New York Assembly several years before—Theodore Roosevelt.

George's most able lieutenant was Father McGlynn, a fiery, plain-spoken Catholic priest who had espoused the single-tax cause. Deeply alarmed at his influence among the Irish Catholics, Tammany appealed to the Church for aid. The Vicar-General responded with a vigorous denunciation of George and all his works. The Archbishop declared that private property (which George was in no sense assaulting) was in accordance with God's law, that Christ had blessed the poor and that they should center their hopes on Heaven. McGlynn went on addressing overflow meetings until the Pope himself took a hand and summoned his wayward son to Rome on pain of excommunication. McGlynn refused to go and the order was executed. This action of the Holy See cost George the support of the *Irish World* and probably the election. McGlynn, shorn of his influence, remained faithful to the bitter end.

As election day approached the campaign grew turbulent. To the timorous conservatives, as well as to the more enthusiastic radicals, Revolution loomed over the Hudson. But when the votes were counted, the Tammany Tiger sat back on its haunches and licked its chops. Hewitt was first with 90,000 votes; George second with 68,000; Roosevelt, probably knifed in the back by his own party in an effort to save the city from George, came in third with 60,000. George's supporters always contended that he had been "counted out," a not unlikely assumption.

Under pressure of the campaign, the various elements which went to make up the United Labor Party had relegated their differences to the background; but as soon as outside pressure was removed, dissension rent the air. In the cold gray light of the morning after, it was again brought home to the socialists that George and his menagerie of assorted reformers made strange bedfellows for "scientific Marxian socialists." George himself turned on the radicals anything but a friendly eye. A battle ensued. The socialists were ousted.

They were never quite the same, however, after this experience with the United Front of 1886. Though their movement was still predominantly German, many of its more active spirits were no longer content that it should remain so. Rubbing shoulders with the native Americans in the United Labor Party, these militants had lost some of their alien ways and had gained some insight—however slight—into American

[ 185 ]

working-class and middle-class psychology. At the same time they had sown the seed of socialism within the United Labor camp and now, though they had brought about their own expulsion, all was not lost. They took some of the natives back with them into the socialist fold. Thus encouraged they redoubled their efforts to naturalize the Marxian philosophy. But suddenly—quite independently of their efforts—there appeared a new native movement that was eventually, and indirectly, to speed this process. It arose with the publication of Edward Bellamy's *Looking Backward* in 1888.

Bellamy was the cultured and unassuming son of a Massachusetts minister, a legitimate heir of the New England utopians. After a brief and unsatisfactory career as a journalist, he sought escape in the traditional fashion by writing a novel. It was a romance of the days of Shays' Rebellion and, published as a newspaper serial, it attracted little notice. But his second attempt, *Looking Backward*, created a new utopian era in America and sold over a million copies in ten years.

The hero of Bellamy's fantasy, a Bostonian named West, falls asleep under the influence of a mesmerist in 1887 and wakes up in the year 2000. In place of the squalid, slum-ridden Boston with which he is familiar, he is confronted with a shining new city *sans* politicians, graft, corruption and extremes of poverty and wealth—in short, by the Coöperative Commonwealth.

The response to the book, comparable to that which had greeted Etienne Cabet's *Voyage en Icarie* in France forty years before, overwhelmed the shy author. He suddenly found himself not only world-famous, but the idol of thousands of disciples who looked upon him as a revolutionary leader arisen at last to escort them out of the industrial wilderness. Under the influence of the book, Nationalist Clubs, as they were called, sprang up all over the country. At the height of the craze, according to a list published in the *Nationalist*, the monthly organ of the movement, there were some hundred and sixty of these in the country as a whole, of which over sixty were in California alone.

The Nationalists were far from ready to take up the class struggle according to Karl Marx.

We advocate no sudden or ill-considered change [they declared]; we make no war upon individuals; we do not censure those who have accumulated immense fortunes simply by carrying to a logical end the false principles on which business is now based. The combinations, trusts and syndicates, of which the people complain, demonstrate the practicability of our basic principle of association. We merely seek to push this principle a little further and have all industries operated in the interest of all by the nation. . . .

Nevertheless, with all the mildness of its wording, the above was the closest to the Marxian position that an appreciable number of native Americans had ever come. It is significant that the Nationalists, unlike the utopians who had preceded them, did not attempt to sidestep the implications of modern industrial concentration; but, like the Marxian socialists, met them head-on and showed how they could be turned to account in building the new order. What they envisaged, however, was a sort of state socialism and in their methods they followed the Owen and Brook Farm tradition. Their watchwords were "education," "enlightenment," "gradual change." But at least they stated the problem—the same problem that confronted the Marxists—and stated it in terms that Americans could understand. Though they were swallowed up for the most part in that great wave of reform known as Populism which swept the country in the early '90s, some of them, drifting to the left, had emerged as full-fledged socialists even before the Kansas farmers, on the advice of Mary Ellen Lease, "stopped raising corn and began raising hell." The most important of these new converts, so far as American socialism is concerned, was an ex-Columbia law student and lecturer named Daniel De Leon.

De Leon was probably the keenest theoretician the American radical movement has produced and the man to whom Lenin referred, shortly after the Russian Revolution, as "the only one who has added anything to socialist thought since Marx." He was born on the island of Curaçao in 1852. His father, a doctor, claimed to be a collateral descendant of Ponce de Leon, the Spanish explorer. Young Daniel was sent abroad to be educated. He studied at a *Gymnasium* in Hildesheim, Germany, and at the University of Leyden, showing remarkable talent as a linguist. Later, coming to New York, he entered Columbia Law School, graduated with honors—in the class which contained Samuel Untermeyer and several other later-celebrated New Yorkers. He was granted a prize lectureship in Latin-American diplomacy.

As we have pointed out, two will-o'-the-wisp pursuits brought a few choice and eager spirits within hailing distance of the Revolution in the late '80s and '90s. De Leon engaged in both. His first radical enthusiasms were aroused by George in the campaign of '86. He campaigned so vigorously for the Single Taxer that his academic standing was imperiled. After the collapse of that movement and the publication of *Looking Backward*, he joined the Nationalists. Meanwhile, however, probably at the suggestion of some German socialist with whom he came in contact during the George campaign, he began a concentrated exploration into the realm of Marxian economics. To an incisive, robust mind, stimulated by bouts with the Marxian formulæ, Bellamy nationalism could offer but little nourishment. In 1889, De Leon turned his back on utopianism, reformism and Columbia University alike and emerged as a full-fledged member of the Socialist Labor Party.

With his professorial dignity and Germanic thoroughness —the latter doubtless the product of those formative days at Hildesheim—De Leon was the answer to the Marxian comrades' prayers. Though not native-born, he had little of the foreigner about him. He was not "American" in the sense of Lincoln, Bryan or his later rival Debs; but, with his perfect

English and splendid platform presence, he was a man whom the radically inclined workers could "look up to" and with a little effort come to understand. Here, at last, was the man who could carry the revolutionary message to the natives with some chance of success. The Socialist Laborites welcomed him with open arms.

Almost from the time he joined the Socialist Labor Party in 1889, the history of De Leon becomes, in all essentials, the history of the Socialist Labor Party, the history of the party, that of De Leon. Perhaps no other man in the American labor and radical movements, not even the redoubtable Gompers, ever fastened so implacably upon an organization and shaped it so in accord with his own inflexible will. Certainly no other man within the movement or without it—not even Woodrow Wilson, whom, by the way, De Leon, dying before the post-war debacle, regarded as representative of the American *bourgeoisie* at its best—ever so thoroughly convinced himself that his every act was prompted by the highest of ideals, that his every opponent was a traitor to mankind.

Conscious of his own superiority over the well-meaning but none too clear-headed comrades about him and of his own complete mastery of the Marxian theory, De Leon was determined that this party, of which he soon became the unquestioned leader and mouthpiece, should hew to the correct intellectual line, let the chips of dissension fall where they may. Unlike Lenin, with whom he had much in common temperamentally and intellectually, he possessed nothing of the flexibility of the practical politician. The very word was for him synonymous with degradation and betrayal. Had he, six decades later, been faced with Lenin's problem of the immediate unworkability of the Communist program, the New Economic Policy with which the great Russian leader staved off defeat would never have been considered for a moment. De Leon would have gone down with the flag of uncompromising socialism flying high. He was, perhaps, the "purest"

[ 189 ]

scientist of revolutionary Marxism the world has ever known. Nothing in his life so well illustrates De Leon's intellectual implacability as his break with his beloved eldest son, Solon, many years later. The young man had been trained by his father in the service of the party. But one day he had the temerity to disagree with the elder De Leon regarding the exact fraction of the product of labor taken from it as surplus value. He was virtually disowned. Despite the staggering blow to his affection and intellectual pride when Solon joined the hated Socialist Party, De Leon showed no outward sign of dismay. "David had his Absalom" was his only comment.

Disregarding political campaigns, dull and more or less repetitious, and—for the moment—the constant guerrilla warfare within its own ranks, the career of the Socialist Labor Party after the coming of De Leon ranged itself into three major campaigns. First came the bitter and futile struggle to infuse the unions—first the Knights and then the energetic A. F. of L.—with socialism and to capture them for the Revolution; second, as a result of the failure of this program, to establish rival unions modeled upon socialistic principles; third, the fight to dominate, at least intellectually, the Industrial Workers of the World. We shall deal with only the first two efforts here.

Never before had such a concerted drive been made upon the labor unions as that undertaken by De Leon and his cohorts in the early '90s. De Leon himself joined the Knights and "bored from within" that body so vigorously that, until he was maneuvered out of his seat in 1895, he seemed at times within an ace of gaining control.

Meanwhile, his lieutenants conducted an equally intensive campaign within the Federation. The climax was reached during the panic of 1893 when a socialist, Thomas J. Morgan, introduced a resolution advocating "the collective ownership by the people of all the means of production and distribution." The resolution was carried! But it contained an unfortunate clause by which a referendum vote of the membership was necessary for its final adoption. This gave the hard-pressed Gompers and his forces time to rally their support. The referendum was blocked for a year and at the following convention the teeth were drawn from the resolution by an amendment which called only for the granting of public lands to the tillers of the soil.

Disillusioned and embittered by this defeat, De Leon drew back and launched the Socialist Trade and Labor Alliance, a model union body formulated on industrial rather than trade lines, with a definitely socialistic program. It was designed to supersede both the rapidly declining Knights and the growing A. F. of L. From the standpoint of strategy, it was probably the most unfortunate move ever made in American radical history. The unions, as we have seen, had already swerved sharply to the right after the Haymarket affair. Now, with the almost complete separation of the radicals from the rank and file of organized labor and the antagonisms engendered by embarking upon a policy of "dual unionism," the rift widened beyond all hope of repair.

The Alliance was not, of course, as its detractors of the Gompers type so vehemently proclaimed, the design of an archfiend, an *agent provocateur* out to wreck the unions by dividing labor's ranks. It was the brain-child of an altogether intellectual but nevertheless naïve man laboring under the delusion that the American worker was fundamentally radical and already on the eve of revolt against what the radicals, then as now, termed "the corrupt A. F. of L. machine." De Leon's workingman, as one of the leader's closest friends admitted after his death, was an idealized workingman, a powerful, benign giant in spotless overalls who stood with folded arms and head erect gazing fearlessly forward toward the collectivist society.

The Alliance, after creating a flurry among the more radically inclined unionists of New York—German mechanics, Jewish clothing workers and the like, came to naught. But it accomplished two definite things. It proved conclusively that the average American wage-earner was more interested in the immediate prospect of higher wages and shorter hours than in "throwing off the yoke of Capitalism" and it split wide open, not the American Federation of Labor and the expiring Knights, but the American socialist movement itself. A large group of De Leon's followers, many of whom had been chafing for some time under his domination of the party, and sincerely alarmed at the ever-widening rift between themselves and organized labor, stampeded and joined with other radical groups to form what was later known as the Socialist Party. But more of this later.

While the Socialist Labor Party was pursuing its stormy course in the '90s, changes of tremendous importance were taking place in America's economic life. By 1890 the frontier was little more than a romantic illusion. "Up to and including 1880," declared the Superintendent of Census in that year, "the country had a frontier of settlement; but at present the unsettled area has been so broken into by isolated bodies of settlement that there can hardly be said to be a frontier line." And the economic frontier was passing as well. The bulk of the nation's business and commerce might still be in the hands of loose aggregations of capital; the small capitalist, trader, manufacturer, storekeeper might still have a place at the board, but more and more the plates that passed his way had been cleaned of all but crumbs by the big fellows at the head of the table. The era of trustification had arrived and with it the Gilded Age—to borrow the graphic label of Charles Dudley Warner and Mark Twain—came into full flower. Viewed from one angle, it was a gay and dazzling decade; from another, an incredibly callous and sordid one. It reproduced the consciousless extremes of the early Industrial

Revolution thrown into sharp relief by the excesses and vul-garities of the unimaginative but socially ambitious coal, steel, railroad, copper, oil and meat-packing barons and their be-jeweled ladies. The triumphant American plutocracy had not yet learned the virtue—or the wisdom—of restraint. Confi-dent of its ability—demonstrated again and again—to beat revolt and protest to its knees, it flaunted its huge profits, its diamond-studded dog collars, fabulous entertainments, huge and hideous palaces, spurious art treasures before a gaping and frequently resentful world. Fortunes made in the '60s, '70s and '80s were used to buy titles for the daughters of sharp-eyed traders and steel-jawed industrial bandits. The last three decades of the nineteenth century give us a picture of American capitalism at its ugliest, but the '90s show it also at its most asinine. The years of depression between 1893 and 1897 witnessed some of the most fabulous exploits of the country's upper crust. They were also the heyday of child labor, sweatshops, the 66-hour week and tenement industry.

It was contrasts such as that provided by the Bradley-Martin ball, which turned the Waldorf-Astoria into a flower-bedecked Versailles, and vermin-ridden tenements in which thousands of half-starved people lived without bathing facilities of any sort that aroused the liberals and humanitarians to protest and awakened a "social consciousness" in many a middle-class breast. This indignation flowered in social service work, in the anti-child labor crusades led by Florence Kelley (who all during the '80s had been an active and vigorous figure among the American socialists), in legislative investigations (mostly sterile) into labor conditions, in the beginnings of the settle-ment-house movement. From Hull House in particular came reports which shocked even the hardened sensibilities of the '90s.

Little idea can be given [reads one of these reports in 1895] of the filthy and rotten tenements, the dingy courts and tumble-down sheds, the foul stables and dilapidated outhouses, the broken

[ 193 ]

sewerpipes, the piles of garbage, fairly alive with diseased odors, and of the number of children filling every nook, working and playing in every room, eating and sleeping on every window sill, pouring in and out of every door, seeming literally to pave every scrap of the "yard."

But the "heartbreaking '90s" present something more than a picture of industrial concentration, social ostentation and despair. This was also a decade of rebellion—of Homestead, Coeur d'Alene, Buffalo, the Tennessee coal strikes, the Debs Rebellion.

The newly formed Carnegie Steel Company, capitalized at $25,000,000, represented one of the outstanding triumphs of ascending capitalism, and the pride of the company was its million-dollar Homestead plant which, once it was under way, wrested the steel leadership of the world from England. Far from satisfied with his immense profits, Carnegie conceived the notion of breaking the power of the Amalgamated Association of Iron and Steel Workers, which had organized the men at the Homestead plant. He sent Henry Clay Frick, acting commander-in-chief of the Carnegie interests, a notice to be posted at Homestead announcing the company's intention to operate on a non-union basis after June 24, 1892, and hurriedly left for Europe.

As the day approached, both sides prepared for war. Frick wrote Robert Pinkerton for three hundred "guards." On July 1 the mills shut down. The Amalgamated threw a line of pickets around the Homestead plant. No one—not even the officers of the company—was allowed to enter. On July 6 a tugboat, with two covered barges loaded with Pinkerton men in tow, steamed up the Monongahela River to Homestead. Strikers armed with rifles, shotguns, stones and clubs rushed toward the dock. As the Pinkertons, brandishing revolvers, attempted to come ashore, shots rang out and their leader fell with a shattered hip. On the strikers' side two men fell dead.

The first blood unleashed passions which, on the side of the strikers, had been pent up for days. The Pinkertons were driven back to the barges. Attempts made to ignite the barges, to blow them up, failed; but after an all-day battle the Pinkertons surrendered and were driven out of town. Some ten men had been killed and about sixty wounded, both sides suffering about equally. But the strikers were still in possession of Homestead. Six days later, 8,000 militiamen arrived under Major-General Snowden. From then on, the locked-out workers fought a losing battle.

But the excitement was not entirely over. On July 23, an intense, intellectual-looking young Russian Jew burst into Frick's private office where Carnegie's "man of steel" was in conference with another executive, whipped out a revolver, and shot Frick in the neck. Before the intruder could be subdued, he also managed to draw a dagger and inflict a series of deep wounds upon Frick's hip and legs. When finally made captive by the combined office force, it was noticed that the would-be assassin was chewing something. His teeth were pried apart and a capsule containing fulminate of mercury discovered between them. Through bloody lips he muttered that he had hoped "to blow the whole room to hell." He was carted off to jail where it was discovered that his name was Alexander Berkman.

Frick staged a miraculous comeback. Thirteen days later he was back at his desk. His near-assassination had made of him something of a national hero. Berkman received a penitentiary sentence of twenty-one years. Strangely enough, Most denounced his act in the *Freiheit*; soon after, as a result, Emma Goldman horsewhipped Most at a meeting in Cooper Union.

The attempt to rescue Berkman during his imprisonment has been vividly described by Emma Goldman in her life story. It was as dramatically and naïvely conceived as might be expected from that devoted and inexperienced group that made up his New York friends and followers. Berkman, himself, had probably the finest mind among the anarchists in America. A sensitive, artistic and yet almost ascetic man, he was the very antithesis of Most, whom he disliked and distrusted. His book, *The Prison Memoirs of an Anarchist*, written several years after his parole in 1905, has become a revolutionary classic. It was also one of the first books—outside of medical and criminological literature—to discuss the problem of homosexuality in prison life.

Already in the '90s, anarchism was on the way to becoming more of an intellectual movement than the serious revolutionary force that it had been in the '80s. It had little influence in the labor movement, even though individual members were active in the various unions. The radical East Side Slavic Jews were just beginning to be won over from anarchism to socialism under the influence of the socialist *Abendblatt* and later, of the *Forward*. But there were numerous occasions, especially during the depression years, when all shades of radicalism joined hands in huge mass meetings in Union Square or Cooper Union. On such occasions the speakers might include John Swinton, Sergius Schevitsch, the socialist editor (husband of the beautiful Helene von Dönniges over whom Ferdinand Lassalle had fought the famous duel that had ended his stormy life), young Morris Hillquit, Emma Goldman and Voltairine de Cleyre, the young French Quakeress from Philadelphia who had renounced comfort for poverty, pacifism and anarchism and who, when she died, was buried beside the Haymarket victims in Waldheim Cemetery.

Down at Justus Schwab's saloon on First Street, libertarians and literary lights like Swinton, Ambrose Bierce, James Huneker and the ubiquitous and ever-needy Sadakichi Hartmann rubbed shoulders with the disciples of Bakunin, who talked of *Attentats*, and the disciples of Max Stirner, who discussed their egos. Though honest burghers and simple workers shuddered at the names of Most, Goldman, Berkman, their social superiors did not. Arthur Brisbane was something of an admirer of the intransigent Emma and sent her an inscribed copy of the biography of his father written by his mother. She had a number of other friends among the wealthy liberals. About 1890, an American journalist named George Kennan had brought back from Russia stories of the treatment accorded political prisoners in Siberia and the first "Friends of Russian Freedom" were organized in New York. William Lloyd Garrison, James Russell Lowell, Julia Ward Howe, Lucy Stone Blackwell and Lyman Abbott were among the members. They published a monthly journal called *Free Russia* and served to bring some of the most active of the Russian anarchists, who were also doing their bit for Russian freedom, into close contact with some of the foremost of the American libertarians.

The conflict at Homestead, serious as it was, proved to be but the initial shock in a great series of convulsions. While the steel battle was still raging, violence flared up in the West. The rich metalliferous mining region of Coeur d'Alene, Idaho, where powerful new combinations of capital had moved in, displacing the small operator and reducing the formerly more or less free and independent miner to the status of wage-earner, was the scene of bloody clashes involving striking miners and strike breakers, the militia and, finally, federal troops. It was the beginning of a desperate war that was to keep the Rocky Mountain states in an almost constant uproar for the next two decades. On the heels of the Coeur d'Alene outburst, 400 striking switchmen at Buffalo found themselves face to face with 8,000 state militiamen, and Tennessee coal miners, attempting to drive convict labor out of the pits, awoke to discover their whole region under martial law, their leaders jailed under indictments charging conspiracy, riot and murder. If there were any doubts left as to which side the organized State would favor in moments of industrial conflict, they were fast fading. Two years later, with the crushing of the Debs Rebellion, they were to be dispelled altogether.

At the beginning of the '90s, Eugene V. Debs, Grand Secretary-Treasurer of the Brotherhood of Locomotive Firemen, was well on the way to becoming a successful American labor leader. By dint of much hard work and an engaging personality, this tall, lanky man had struggled up from the ranks and was just at the point at which the average labor leader is content to settle down to the machinelike routine of conservative union officeholding. Debs, however, was cast in a different mold. He was an idealist with a tremendous emotional drive. He now reached the conclusion that the various railway unions must come together in order to present an effective front to their employers. When plans for federation within the Brotherhoods were defeated, primarily because of bad feeling between the firemen and engineers, Debs resigned his office and launched the American Railway Union, which was to be one big union open to all railway workers.

By the time the new organization was launched the country was in the throes of the 1893 depression and it had been in existence scarcely a year when trouble developed in Pullman, Illinois, a so-called "model town for working people" established by George M. Pullman, the "sleeping-car king," who was bitterly opposed to unionism. The "Pullman idea" was thoroughly feudalistic. The workers lived in Pullman houses, traded at Pullman stores, worshiped in Pullman churches, sent their children to Pullman schools and spent their off hours in Mr. Pullman's park or theater. So long as times were prosperous and wages adequate, the Pullman welfare scheme worked well. Pullman was rapidly gaining the reputation of an "enlightened capitalist." He was the Henry Ford of his day. With the coming of the depression, however, the Pullman Company slashed wages and discharged their men right and left, but they made no corresponding reductions in Pullman rents or in prices at company stores. The workers

[ 198 ]

failed to appreciate this brand of benevolence; they struck and appealed to the newly organized American Railway Union for aid.

Debs attempted to arbitrate but the Pullman officials would have nothing to do with him. He then ordered a boycott against Pullman cars. In two days all traffic between Chicago and the West was paralyzed. Debs warned against violence, but the workers, now feeling the full downward thrust of the depression, were in no mood for caution. Violence flared up all over the country. The great strikes of 1877 were recalled in the press. Business men generally, and those in Chicago particularly, raged. Neither fear nor fury was mitigated by the fact that Altgeld was still governor of Illinois. They immediately went over his head and appealed directly to President Cleveland for federal troops. The latter, in the face of vigorous and repeated protests from Altgeld, responded at once. Ten thousand soldiers appeared on the scene. Violence increased, some 2,000 railroad cars were wrecked and burned, company losses mounted until they were variously estimated at between fifty and a hundred million dollars. It began to look as though even the army could not stop the conflagration, when Debs and other union leaders were arrested under the Sherman Anti-Trust Law on charges of conspiracy. Released on bail, the courts issued an injunction enjoining them from doing anything to prolong the strike. The infuriated Debs struck back by issuing an appeal for a general strike and was promptly jailed again for contempt of court. The A. F. of L. declared that "the heart of labor everywhere throbs responsive to the manly purposes and sturdy struggle of the American Railway Union," but that its members were "as patriotic and law-abiding as any other class of citizens" and would not be placed in the false position of "open hostility to Federal authority." In short, there was to be no general labor uprising. The Pullman strike was promptly smashed and from this time forward the injunction became a chief weapon in the hands of the forces of law and order, the courts one of the most effective allies of Big Business.

The years between 1893 and the outbreak of the Spanish-American War were depression years that witnessed not only widespread labor disturbances, but the recurrence of those debtor-agrarian agitations that crop up in one form or another in the midst of every great depression.

The farmers had been restive and vociferous before the depression. More and more as the years passed, as farm machinery became more complicated and costly, as freight rates mounted higher, as urban wealth tightened its grip on the economic life of the country, the farmer found himself sunk deeper and deeper in debt. By 1890 farm mortgages had risen to a total of $1,085,995,960, corn was selling at from ten to fifteen cents a bushel in Kansas and was cheaper to burn than coal; cotton sold at five cents. It was high time, the farmers thought, "to quit raising corn and begin raising hell." A new anti-banker, anti-monopoly, anti-railroad, inflation movement was born.

The Populist movement (People's Party) started in Kansas, spread through the Middle West and into some of the states of the South. At its second convention held in Omaha in 1892, an independent presidential ticket was nominated and a party platform drawn up. In the following year, the party's candidate for President, General Weaver, received over a million votes. In 1894, the vote rose over half a million more; but in 1896, with Bryan as the Democratic candidate and the Free Silver issue paramount, the Populists backed the Commoner and thereafter their party rapidly disintegrated.

The People's Party was primarily a small-farmers' party but, as with the Greenbackers twenty years before, a definite bid was made for the support of the industrial workers. One section of its platform read:

Wealth belongs to him who creates it, and every dollar taken from industry without an equivalent is robbery. . . . The interests of rural and civic laborers are the same; their enemies are identical.

But this common bond was not apparent to the city worker, particularly the highly skilled unionist. Even the rank-and-file farmer was inclined to blame the high price he had to pay for manufactured articles upon high city wages. Populism failed to make much headway in the cities. But it did attract many of the erstwhile Nationalists and broke ground in the Middle West for the propaganda of a new Socialist Party after 1900.

Perhaps the most dramatic chapter in the social protest of the depression years was written neither by the militant Debs nor by the enraged farmers of the Middle West, but by a stubborn little visionary, Jacob Coxey, breeder of fine horses and a comparatively rich man. Coxey, while a Populist (he had been a Greenbacker in the '70s and '80s), worked out his own program for ending the depression. His basic idea was a gigantic highway construction project for the relief of unemployment to be financed by the government through a $500,000,000 issue of legal tender notes, but once started he kept on embroidering his plan until "Coxeyism," as it finally emerged, was as much a religion as an economic doctrine. He was aided by a Buffalo-Bill-like figure, one Carl Browne. Browne had been associated with Dennis Kearney in the anti-Chinese agitation on the Coast, but since that time he had beat his way about the country from one job to another. When President Cleveland persisted in ignoring Coxey's scheme for the rejuvenation of a deflated world, Coxey and Browne conceived the idea of sending "a petition to Washington with boots on."

On a chilly Easter morning in 1894, the procession filed through the streets of Massillon, Ohio, Coxey's home town. It included Coxey, his young son—Legal Tender Coxey—

Browne astride one of Coxey's fine horses, a straggling band of cohorts, and a rearguard, half as large as the Army itself, of newspaper reporters. The Army marched under the banner of the "Commonwealth of Christ." Other bands of Coxeyites converged on Washington from other parts of the country. The one that came from the Far West was the most formidable of all the contingents. It commandeered trains, descended on towns *en masse*, demanding to be fed, and though fairly good discipline was maintained, sent shivers down many an official spine. The rumors began to circulate that Coxey's 20,000 "prowling tramps" were thieves and murderers at heart. The forces of law and order threw every possible impediment in their path. Thousands of them never reached Washington—in fact, there were never more than a thousand of them in the Capital at any one time. The movement ended on a note of comedy when Coxey and a few of the faithful were arrested in Washington for trespassing on the White House lawn.

From the standpoint of labor and the radicals, Coxeyism was a meaningless gesture except as a symbol of widespread unrest. But by drawing some of the footloose workers into the movement, it undoubtedly set some of them to thinking of organization and of their rights. One of the marchers who started out with the western contingent but who dropped out before it reached the goal was the adventurous Jack London. Another marcher was Frederick O'Brien, who was later to start a South Seas movement with his *White Shadows in the South Seas*.

The wave of debtor-agrarian unrest reached its peak, however, not in Populism nor in Coxeyism, but in the Bryan campaign of 1896. This time the onslaught of the West against the Money Power drew the support of large sections of the industrial workers of the East. Even Debs, not yet a thoroughgoing socialist, supported Bryan, who was running on a platform which included opposition to "government by injunction." The battle was fought under the banner of the Democratic Party and it took all the craftiness of Mark Hanna, a three and a half million dollar levy on the banks for a Republican propaganda fund and the shipment of train-loads of Civil War veterans, waving the bloody shirt of the '60s, into doubtful territory to stem the tide that the young Bryan had set in motion at the Chicago Coliseum by his famous "crown of thorns" and "cross of gold" speech.

Bryan was defeated by only 600,600 votes, but in that great effort most of the forces of unrest had spent themselves. The depression was beginning to lift by the end of '96. The discovery of gold in the Klondike in '98, and the discovery also of the cyanide process by which gold could be extracted from hitherto unprofitable ore, had exactly the effect which Bryan had predicted for his free coinage of silver at 16 to 1. It increased prices. Corn rose from twenty-one to thirty-five cents a bushel. The farmers could "ease up." With '98 also came the Spanish-American War. The wheels of industry were set spinning again—some of them turning out paper-soled shoes and cans of putrid "embalmed beef" for soldiers. The country went forward eagerly to bear the "white man's burden" in the Pacific, to inaugurate a Richard Harding Davis-Theodore Roosevelt diplomacy in the Latin-American countries. American capitalism had graduated into a new—and probably final—stage. We had become an imperialistic nation.

Nationalism, Single Tax, Coxeyism, Populism, Bryanism —all these movements, coupled with the general *Weltschmerz* of the '90s, could not fail to stimulate sociological thinking and discussion among many thousands of Americans, and naturally some of these found their way, in due time, into more or less radical channels. Moreover, there were now intermediate stages between reformism and Marxism. The Nationalist, the Single Taxer, the Populist, inclined to move farther left, could do so gradually. Stimulated by the activities of the Christian Socialists in England and the earlier efforts of the Rev. William D. Bliss in Boston, Professors Richard T. Ely and George D. Herron organized the American Institute of Christian Sociology, designed to carry the Christian brand of socialism into the churches and colleges, and installed Professor John R. Commons as secretary. A somewhat similar organization sprang up in Chicago under the direction of Edwin D. Wheelock. The Christian Socialist movement raised a storm in conservative church and academic circles and a little later received an almost fatal blow when Professor Herron at Iowa College fell in love with Carrie Rand, daughter of the wealthy woman who was instrumental in founding the Rand School, and asked his wife to divorce him. The incident created a furor that seems scarcely comprehensible today. Clergymen, academicians and the conservative press seized upon it and magnified it to the proportions of a major scandal—for the purpose, of course, of showing that socialism was synonymous with "free love." Roosevelt whipped up sentiment by a vicious attack in the *Outlook*. The persecution lasted so long that Professor Herron and his new wife finally fled to Italy to live.

Socialism emerged in still another form in the '90s. In 1895, the American Fabian Society, stimulated by the activities of Beatrice and Sidney Webb, George Bernard Shaw, H. G. Wells, Annie Besant and other brilliant English figures, was formed. Dr. Bliss and Lawrence Gronlund were the moving spirits. An offshoot of the Fabian movement was the Social Reform Club in New York to which Charles Sotheran, Ernest Crosby, John Brisben Walker and W. J. Ghent belonged. Sotheran, a Yorkshireman, was a particularly interesting figure. Coming to America in the '70s already imbued with radical ideas—he had known Mazzini abroad—he joined what was later to become the Socialist Labor Party. All through its formative years he strove to broaden the scope and Americanize the program of that party. There was nothing of the fanatic in his temperament, however, and it was inevitable, although he was a veteran in the movement when De Leon entered it, that he should clash with that scholastic figure. De Leon, on one of his many heresy hunts, succeeded in getting Sotheran expelled for an article he was suspected of having written for the "capitalist press." "The charge of heresy," declared a body of Sotheran's radical friends, "sounds as if indited by the clergy of an established church, angry because he would not subscribe to the Thirty-nine Articles of Faith." Later, Sotheran, with J. G. Phelps Stokes, helped to found the People's Institute. Though he supported the new Socialist Party after its formation, he refused to join it. He was afraid, despite its repudiation of "De Leonism" that De Leon might some day influence its councils.

As the great winds of protest that blew in the '90s sent whirling eddies into every stuffy corner of our national life, William Dean Howells, whose New England novel, *The Rise of Silas Lapham,* hinted already at an awakening social consciousness in literary quarters, took a bold step forward. In 1890, with the publication of *A Hazard of New Fortunes,* he plunged into the New York maelstrom and dealt at some length with a street railway strike. Henry Demarest Lloyd set a precedent for and founded a school of social criticism in his *Wealth Against Commonwealth* published in 1894; and 1897 saw the publication of that merciless dissection of our *bourgeoisie, The Theory of the Leisure Class,* by Thorstein Veblen. At long last, the literary man, the journalist, the academician was beginning to survey the American scene with a curious and caustic eye.

All during the '90s, the Socialist Laborites, with De Leon standing firmly at the helm, had attempted to steer their course by the Marxian compass and to ignore the winds that were howling about their ears. De Leon, in the official party paper, the *People,* and his lieutenant, Hugo Vogt in the

*Vorwaerts*, blazed away at "pure and simple" unionism, nationalism and populism alike. Everyone but the loyal De Leonite was a "faker"; and let one of De Leon's closest comrades express the shadow of a doubt that the S. L. P. ship was a fraction off her course and he immediately became a "faker" too. The little movement—its membership never exceeded 6,000—was racked by heresy hunts, expulsions, internal campaigns of "purification." Already, during its brief lifetime, fights for the control of the party office and the official party paper—a powerful weapon in the hands of any dominant faction—had necessitated recourse to the courts and the calling in of the "capitalist police." Now, in 1899, a group gathered about the *New Yorker Volkszeitung*, the German organ of the movement, critical primarily of De Leon's trade-union policy, rebelled. On one occasion the opposition stormed the official offices and De Leon and his followers barricaded themselves within until the police arrived to rescue them. Blows were exchanged, furniture smashed, before the disturbance was quelled. The *Volkszeitung* group claimed the party name and for a while there were two S. L. P. tickets, two *Peoples*. The dispute finally reached the courts and the De Leonites were legally vindicated. The disappointed rebels withdrew and met in convention at Rochester, New York.

Meanwhile, from all the confused activities of socialistically inclined individuals outside the Socialist Labor Party—Left-Wing Populists and Nationalists, Fabians, Christian Socialists, even many pure Utopians with out-and-out colonizing schemes, a new socialistic movement was springing up. Its moving spirits at the outset were J. A. Wayland, editor of the *Coming Nation*, and Colonel R. J. Hinton, who had a pet scheme to inaugurate socialism by capturing a western state through colonizing the nation's socialists within its borders. They brought into existence the Brotherhood of the Coöperative Commonwealth which attracted the attention of Debs.

Debs, while in Woodstock Prison as an outcome of his

activities during the Pullman strike, had received a visit from the Milwaukee socialist leader, Victor Berger. Deeply impressed by Berger, he read the socialist literature which Berger sent him back from Milwaukee. While he did not become an enthusiastic convert overnight—he supported Bryan in 1896—the more humanitarian aspects of the socialist philosophy made a strong appeal to his warm-hearted, emotional nature. The Pullman strike had practically smashed his American Railway Union, but now he decided to pull the remnants of it together into some sort of political organization. Once out of jail, he welcomed the opportunity to join hands with the Brotherhood of the Coöperative Commonwealth. At Chicago, in June, 1897, the two organizations were welded together into a new party, the Social Democracy of America.

Colonizers, anarchists, trade unionists, a few clear-cut socialists, radicals of every description were represented at the Chicago convention. The colonizers were perhaps the dominant group and a committee was appointed which later endorsed a scheme to acquire 560 acres of land in the Cripple Creek region of Colorado. This was to be the site of a model coöperative commonwealth. But by the time the 1898 convention rolled around the more clear-headed socialists had gained in influence and numbers. They descended upon this second convention determined to capture it and to rule out all colonizing schemes. After a vigorous fight, in which they were defeated, they bolted and established still another new party —the Social Democratic Party of America. Its national executive board included Debs and Victor Berger.

In the meanwhile the bolting Socialist Laborites, headed by Morris Hillquit, Max Hayes and Job Harriman, and containing a considerable portion of the *Volkszeitung* following, were looking for some place to go. At their Rochester convention they made an appeal for unity to the Social Democrats. The latter viewed any contingent of the Socialist Labor

Party, even a seceding one, with considerable misgivings. To the western American radicals, De Leonism had all the connotations that the Papacy had for the members of the American Protective Association. But after many conferences and much wrangling a new united Social Democratic Party seemed on the point of emerging when a sudden rupture occurred that threatened the results of months of negotiation. For the moment, however, the two groups were bound together in legal wedlock whether they liked it or not. For they had already agreed to support Eugene V. Debs from the one group and Job Harriman from the other for President and Vice President, respectively, of the United States! It was now too late to separate and put two separate tickets into the field; so a temporary truce was agreed upon.

Working shoulder to shoulder through an actual political campaign accomplished what conferences, joint conventions, long star chambers sessions among the leaders could not. After the campaign and election—in which the two candidates had polled over 97,000 votes (the Socialist Labor Party vote fell to 34,000)—a new convention assembled in Indianapolis in 1901. A new platform was drawn up and adopted. The Socialist Party was born.

The career of Daniel De Leon and the history of the Socialist Labor Party in general should have made one fact clear to all American revolutionists thereafter—the fact that theoretical purity is not enough. If intellectual integrity and dogged devotion to Marxian precepts were sufficient to bring about the Revolution, De Leon would have had the whole capitalistic world crashing about his head. Instead, the very intensity of his doctrinal integrity isolated both himself and his party. Those who absorbed his message became and remained "sound Marxians." They kept the lamp of "uncompromising revolutionary socialism" alight through the confusing storms of many years. But there will always be too few of such to constitute a movement capable of instigating or directing a social revolution. When De Leon died in 1914, American labor scarcely knew that he had existed.

De Leon's tragedy lay in the fact that he was more Marxian than his Master. In the late '80s, Marx's co-worker, Engels, had written in a letter to Florence Kelley:

Our theory is a theory of development, not of dogma to be learned by heart and repeated mechanically. The less it is hammered into the Americans from the outside and the more they test it through their own experience . . . the more it will become a part of their flesh and blood.

PART THREE

# "YOURS FOR THE REVOLUTION"

# IX

---

## THE REVOLUTION BECOMES NATURALIZED

---

IN THE first years of the twentieth century the country seethed with insurgency. The Great American Illusion was beginning to die its slow death. It was to be resurrected, after a fashion, in the profit-sharing, dividend-disbursing, stock-speculating New Era which began after 1922, when stenographers saved their lunch money for a stake in General Motors, shipping clerks dreamed of cleaning up on American Can, and Italian fruit vendors saw themselves rising on a tide of Transamerica dividends. But at the turn of the century the American public was facing certain stern and inescapable realities.

The tentacles of that financial and industrial octopus which had seized upon the country's resources during and just after the Civil War now had their final stranglehold on industry, finance, agriculture and politics. By 1901, with the organization of the United States Steel Corporation, every important American industry had been trustified. The Sherman Anti-Trust Law had merely made the operations of Big Business a trifle more expensive and was giving rise to that Machiavellian monstrosity of evasion—the "holding company." Monopoly capitalism was graduating into finance capitalism. The day was fast approaching when even the Trust was to be little more than an industrial pawn in the game of international finance. The way out—and up—for more than an occasionally lucky or sufficiently ruthless few was closed. The Common People—represented in the cartoons as a small, bewildered, helpless gentleman constantly having his pockets picked —were faced by a powerfully organized, politically intrenched and socially unscrupulous aggregation of wealth and power at the moment of its complete triumph.

All through the '80s and '90s Big Business had been greedy and unashamed, and even in the early 1900s it had not yet learned to compromise with the public taste. The public relations counsel, as later personified in Edward Bernays and Ivy Lee, had not made his resplendent appearance. The business of building up an atmosphere of Service and Medicean benevolence about the operations of the Oil, Steel and Money Kings was yet to develop. The Captain of Industry was either beyond good and evil, like those robust old buccaneers, Jay Gould and Vanderbilt, who cared nothing for public opinion, or obviously sanctimonious hypocrites like "Divine Right" Baer who wept at investigations and regarded his overlordship of mines and railroads as a divine appointment. The industrial set-up was now sufficiently clear-cut to be unmistakable by anyone but Fourth of July orators. Even so safe and sane a labor leader as John Mitchell of the United Miners confided in 1903 that "the average wage-earner has made up his mind that he must remain a wage-earner."

All this is not to say that the average worker, farmer or small business man had any intellectual concept of what had taken place. But the violent and tragic '90s, with their industrial defeats and lost causes, had engendered in many thousands of Americans a dim and groping rebelliousness that was to express itself, for the most part, in futile efforts to set back the clock of industrial development, to shatter an economic pattern that had been in process of setting since the '70s. The battles of Coeur d'Alene, Buffalo, Pullman and the Tennessee coal regions and the effective use of state and federal troops against the strikers had illustrated the formidableness of the great combines as industrial antagonists and the fact that they could and would use the powers of the State to defend their privileges. The repeated use of the injunction in labor disputes had revealed the courts as additional allies of business. The hopes of the Gilded Age were dead or dying. And among the farmers was a similar state of disillusionment, in spite of the return of comparatively "good times"—a fact which was to account for the amazing midwest circulation of such journals as the militant *Appeal to Reason*.

If the industrial defeats of the '90s had left the wage-earners smarting under a deepened sense of injustice and the blow-up of his Populist dreams had left the farmer all dressed up for revolt and with no place to go, the middle and professional classes, feeling the tightening of the screws and reading the statistical data which now flowed from governmental and business bureaus, could see the pattern of American life hardening in its new mold. The world of modest competence, of comfortable security, of sound small business and assured rewards for industry and sagacity was shifting beneath their feet. In industry, God was definitely on the side of the most expensive machinery; in commerce, on that of the most effective combination.

The time was ripe for a new party, a new cause, a great movement of popular protest that would embrace both town and country, both urban and agrarian unrest.

In the thirty years that had elapsed between the organization of little sections of the First International and the Unity Conference of 1900, the revolutionary movement in the United States had consisted largely of foreign-born workers plus a contingent of native intellectuals and belated utopians. Now, in the first decade of the new century, it was to become naturalized, primarily through two organizations, the Social-ist Party and the Industrial Workers of the World. The task which De Leon had set himself but for which his own academic temperament had unfitted him was accomplished.

In an article written for the *Metropolitan Magazine*, when that high-powered monthly took its spectacular turn to the left in 1912, Morris Hillquit wrote in the classic Marxian strain:

> Socialism presupposes an advanced and concentrated state of industry, a powerful class of capitalists dominating the economic and political destinies of the country and a large army of industrial wage-earners in a precarious condition of existence and a clear-cut and conscious economic conflict between these classes.

To the hopeful radicals it seemed that all these conditions had now been fulfilled—all except, perhaps, such a clear-cut consciousness of the economic conflict as would lead to decisive action. It was this last subjective condition which they now girded up their loins to produce. The Great Propaganda Drive which was to flood the country with socialist "literature" in the next ten years was on.

It was impossible, of course, that any party dedicated to social revolution by whatever means should provide a single channel for such divergent and confused elements of discontent as existed at this time. The contradiction between the aims of the city wage-earners and those of the farmers, which had played havoc with all attempts at an American mass movement since the Civil War, was sharper in 1900 than in 1933. The farmer distrusted the labor unions almost as much as he did the eastern bankers. The small middle class felt itself the victims of both. Socialism, though directed ultimately against the whole system of private ownership, was most immediately concerned with the conditions of the industrial workers. Its advocates supported every strike. They believed in higher and higher wages, shorter and shorter hours. They regarded the demise of the small farmer and the little business man as inevitable. In spite of these facts, they were able to attract a certain percentage of both, because, in the confusions of the period, they offered the most direct and dramatic form of protest.

In general, the popular revolt of the early 1900s never quite reached the boiling point. It simmered in the muckrake crusades and the reform movements sponsored largely by a naïvely indignant middle class. It fed on the exposures in *McClure's, Everybody's, Cosmopolitan, Hampton's* and *Collier's* written by Ida Tarbell, Ray Stannard Baker, Lincoln Steffens, Charles Edward Russell and David Graham Phillips; on the insurance investigations of 1905, the stockyard stench raised by Upton Sinclair in 1906. It was reformistic, antimonopolistic, wistful with the typically American nostalgia for the old, independent way of life, the more simple and democratic past. It was directed at the pot-bellied Trusts—beef, steel, oil, railroad, money—with the huge dollar signs on their waistcoats, which now decorated the editorial pages of the Hearst newspapers—and at their political henchmen; not at a system, but at its most flagrant abuses. Young political Don Quixotes fresh from their college Liberal Clubs tilted at the windmills of vested interests, special privileges and dirty politics. Fired by the work of Jacob Riis and Jane Addams, begun in the past decade, young crusaders pledged themselves to careers of social service in city settlement houses, or inspired by Tom Johnson, "Golden Rule" Jones and Brand Whitlock set out to scotch the public utilities or to win the good fight for the initiative, referendum and recall. A literature of "social significance" reflected the preoccupations of the period. The problem play and the political or social novel flowered beside the journalism of exposure in the work of Winston Churchill, Robert Herrick, Frank Norris (in *The Pit* and *The Octopus*) , David Graham Phillips, and less directly, in the earlier work of Dreiser. There was little question but that Right would prevail. What the doctrine of biological evolution had been to the nineteenth-century dissenter, the doctrine of inevitable social progress was to the

[ 217 ]

dissenter of the twentieth. A movement that was to come to a head at Armageddon in 1912 took form and substance.

But not all the discontent and unrest of the period could find an adequate answer in the program of "Bust the Trusts" or in good government crusades against crooked politicians. For one thing, there existed, in this first decade, no strong national organization to unite the disaffected into one great national movement, sweeping up into its ranks even many of the more radical dissenters. Independence Leagues and Good Government combinations appeared in a number of cities; but not until 1912, when the new Socialist Party had a decade of intensive propaganda behind it, did the movement assume the dignity of a national party. And in the meanwhile, scattered throughout the country in the industrial centers, the mining and lumber camps, in the rural towns of the West, in colleges and in intellectual circles, the seeds of socialist agitation were falling on fertile soil. The accumulated agitations of the '70s, '80s and '90s, which had seemed to have borne so little fruit, were finding intellectual justification in the startling exposures of the reformers. The Nationalist movement had reached thousands of typical Americans with the message of an efficiency utopia. The persuasions of the Christian Socialists had lent to a philosophy long considered blasphemous an aura of spiritual and ethical values particularly potent in religious and academic circles. And the radicals themselves, or at least many of them, were learning to talk the American language, and were working with, rather than preaching at, the American masses. It was a moment when it seemed possible that all the radical forces—with the exception of the intransigent De Leonites—were to march steadily forward under one banner, that of a united Socialist Party.

While the number of citizens who wished to abolish capitalism was undoubtedly infinitesimal in comparison with the number who wished merely to remedy its abuses, the vote polled by Debs was to rise from 97,000 in 1900 to nearly a million in the year that Roosevelt summoned the hosts to the Progressive banner—and in that year more than 72 per cent of the Socialist membership was native-born. The Revolution, so it seemed, had taken root.

The new party had inherited groups and tendencies from all of the assorted radical movements of the past twenty years; but by 1901 the majority of the active American socialists were reacting violently against the fratricidal struggles, the scholastic dissensions and the heresy hunts which had marked the past ten years of radical history. The ghost of "De Leonism" so haunted the new organization through all its formative years that its members were ready to lean over backward to prevent the rise of a new "pope," another *People*. It was a reaction which drove them to the opposite extreme from the centralized, disciplined character of the Socialist Labor Party. Observing the fruits of sectarian isolation, they were more than ready to act on Marx's declaration that one movement was worth a dozen programs.

It was better—most of them were now convinced, intellectually if not emotionally—to build an organic united movement, even if a little confused and unorthodox, than a theoretically pure debating society remote from all contact with the American masses. The situation confronting them was not one of revolutionary crisis, demanding a single-minded unity of thought and action. Inspiring as the immediate future seemed, the Revolution was not around the corner. The job ahead was one of focusing the growing unrest of the workers and farmers on a revolutionary, rather than a reformistic objective. It was, in short, a propaganda job. A loose and inclusive heterodoxy would best enable the Socialists to summon the widest possible army to such a campaign.

That tendency to oversimplification and the substitution of adjectives for analysis, particularly strong among radicals, have tended to obscure the complex and diffused character of the dominant socialist organization throughout most of its career. It began as the attempted unification of native and foreign radical elements on a basis of fundamental principles. Though it was to be torn by those factional struggles to which all radical organizations seem inevitably doomed, its theoretical looseness enabled it to survive more or less intact for nearly twenty years. The party contained within its ranks devoted Marxian theoreticians whose orthodoxy was equal to De Leon's own and, on the other hand, evolutionary socialists akin to the British Fabians or the German Revisionists convinced of "the inevitability of gradualness." It contained incipient syndicalists to whom political action was a mere propaganda device and violence the essential weapon of revolution; it contained a smaller element almost as non-resistant as Mahatma Gandhi. There were remnants of utopianism tinged with populism, especially in the Middle West, of a metaphysical anarchism among many of the New York Slavs and the native "bohemians," of Christian communism, and a militant, "God-killing" atheism.

It was a combination that would undoubtedly have fallen to pieces in the face of a situation demanding swift and decisive revolutionary action. But such a situation was not at hand. And in the meanwhile the organization's base was broad enough to provide standing room for individuals as far apart in approach and temperament as Bill Haywood and Victor Berger, Jack London and Upton Sinclair, Debs and Professor George D. Herron. Its rank and file ranged from the palest pink to the deepest red. And about its base fluttered that lunatic fringe of dissent inevitably attracted to whichever radical flame happens to burn brightest at the moment— radical food, money and sex faddists, revolutionary psychopaths with pet schemes for undermining capitalism, cranks of every description, as well as a varied assortment of "spittoon philosophers" whose only contribution to the Revolution lay in incessant argument and theoretical speculations as they warmed the chairs of radical "reading rooms" throughout the nation. They were at once a source of contemptuous amusement and deep irritation to the hard-working and earnest revolutionary.

The new party's doctrinal elasticity did not prevent the rise of the usual internal differences, and a right, left and center developed almost immediately. The principal issues involved were the inclusion and character of "immediate demands"—social and labor reform planks—in the party program; the party's attitude toward the farmers (should it demand the immediate nationalization of *all* land, thereby antagonizing the small working farmer, or should it concede individual ownership to the latter?) ; the party's attitude toward "dual unionism"—that perennial bone of contention in all radical movements; toward coöperation with possible non-socialist labor parties; toward a party-owned press and control of elected officials. The factional divisions, especially in these earlier years, were rarely clear-cut and consistent— as they were apt to be in European radical movements. Many members could, and did, vote "right" on one subject and "left" on another. Thus the most "opportunistic" of the western party leaders was rigidly uncompromising in his demand for land nationalization ("no compromise with the petit bourgeois farmer") ; an eastern right-winger, a devotee of the German Social Democracy, helped to organize the "dual" I. W. W. in 1905. Debs, at the extreme left in his espousal of dual unionism, was as bitterly opposed—though for different reasons—as any Christian Socialist to many of the tactics advocated by another dual unionist, Haywood. Some of the academic left-wing theoreticians looked askance at both Debs' "sentimentality" and Haywood's "anarcho-syndicalism"—as did their spiritual father, De Leon. Compared with the European socialist organizations, the new party occupied a "centrist" position; and its own most representative centrist at the time was Morris Hillquit. At the extreme right stood Victor Berger and his Wisconsin band.

The history of political radicalism in the first two decades of the present century was to be, largely, the history of the Socialist Party. The "S. L. P." drawing its skirts ever closer about its theoretical purity and dwindling membership, was immediately overshadowed by the new alliance with its more youthful and enthusiastic membership, its popular native leadership. Both Debs and Ben Hanford, the party's national candidates in 1904 and 1908, were probably typical of the American working-class radical at his best. It is doubtful if either man had ever read the first volume of *Capital*, but the Revolution was in their blood and bones and they were there-fore—unlike so many of its more cerebral converts—inca-pable of "selling out" or forsaking it. Their socialism was dis-tinctively native, with all the populistic overtones which this implied in a country still so diffused in its economic character and in its forms of protest. Perhaps for this reason it was able to capitalize, for the first time in the history of American socialism, the disillusionment of the native individualist fac-ing a world in which individual opportunity was disappear-ing. During the first twelve years of its existence the new party made its most striking progress—as did the I. W. W. after 1905—not in the eastern industrial centers crowded with heterogeneous and still hopeful immigrant groups, but in the towns and the rural lumbering and mining districts of the West where restless Americans and the sons of earlier immigrant generations—Scotch, Irish, Germans, Scandina-vians, English, mostly—had come to the end of the trail.

When the vote polled by Debs as the candidate of the united socialist factions in 1900 rose to more than 400,000 in 1904, the jubilant radicals from Maine to California began to envisage that steady and inevitable progression in party strength which, on a strictly mathematical basis, would land

Debs in the White House by 1920—at which point the business of revolution would begin in earnest. Their enthusiasm was matched by the apprehension of their opponents. "The rising tide of Socialism" became the subject of magazine articles. It was confidently predicted, by a number of non-radicals, that within ten years the Socialists would constitute the American political Opposition.

Every new radical party draws into its ranks the younger, less experienced and more enthusiastic social rebels, undisciplined by failure and disappointment. The older radicals had already lived through that first enraptured stage of revolutionary optimism in the Social Democracy and the S. L. P. But even they were carried away by the evidences on every hand that the American proletariat was turning to the left. The quadrupling of the vote, the rapid increase in membership, the amazing growth of the socialist press in a few short years, were not the only indications of a revolutionary awakening. The period was no less propitious to the growth of organized labor, and in the labor movement itself the radical tide was rising.

In 1902, the 150,000 industrial unionists organized in the Western Labor Union (in which the Western Federation of Miners was the dominant factor) endorsed the Socialist Party and its aims. This was not remarkable because these western labor groups had always been socialistic in temper; but in the same year the citadels of craft unionism, the very aristocracy of labor, trembled under the radical onslaughts. The policy of "boring from within" was bearing fruit. At the New Orleans convention of the American Federation of Labor in 1902, a resolution submitted by the socialist and radical bloc, calling upon "the working people to organize their economic and political power to secure for labor the full equivalent of its toil and the overthrow of the wage system" was defeated only by a vote of 3,744 to 3,444. For the second time in its history, the most conservative labor body in the world came near to "capture" by the radicals. Thereafter, Gompers looked to his fences and a battle was on that was not to slacken until after 1915. But the radicals continued their successes among the rank and file. They dominated some of the most powerful of the International unions, such as the Machinists, and whole state federations, such as that of Illinois. The conservative Typographical Union had a strong enough radical bloc to send an outstanding socialist to every yearly convention of the A. F. of L. The same was true of Gompers' own Cigar Makers. With the exception of John Mitchell, the leaders of the powerful United Mine Workers were socialists. And scattered throughout the country were central labor bodies dominated by the left.

"In those days," writes David Saposs, "the conventions of the Federation were truly a parliament of labor where vital social issues were ably and learnedly discussed." They were also a battle-field on which two opposing social concepts fought for the soul of American labor. The radicals directed their fiercest bolts at the "unholy alliance" between the Federation officials and the National Civic Federation which had been organized in 1901 to bring capital and labor together and which Hillquit later described as "an organization founded by employers for the purpose principally and primarily of deadening the aggressive spirit of the American labor movement." Frightened by the tide of insurgency, labor officialdom assembled its steam roller. Denunciation of the socialists in the *Federationist* was followed by scathing answers in the radical press. Wrote Victor Berger in his Milwaukee journal: "Sam Gompers has more and more developed into an empty self-complacent old fool who does not see that the A. F. of L., from inertia and lack of movement, is hastening before his very eyes to a fatal apoplexy."

Berger was neither the first nor the last of the radicals to predict the Federation's rapid demise. But it was "delivering the goods" to its own skilled membership. What it lacked in social idealism it made up for in immediate effectiveness, and it continued to grow. Quite independently of the efforts of the socialists to commit it to more far-reaching aims, it was developing, in this first decade of the century—as a logical outcome of its own limitations, its own complementary brand of radicalism, a pragmatic anarchism uninspired by that idealistic social frenzy which had marked the Chicago trade union anarchists in the '80s. It was to be demonstrated in its most striking form in 1910 when hard-headed Democratic and Republican labor leaders, to whom the social revolution was a "pipe dream," together with a few labor anarchists, sought to supplement the strike and the boycott with dynamite.

While its union members bored from within the labor movement, a burgeoning socialist press and an amazingly well-organized propaganda machine bored from without, covering the land with pamphlets, leaflets, lecturers, soapboxers. By 1908 American socialism boasted four monthly magazines, twenty weeklies and two dailies in English, and ten foreign language dailies. In Chicago was a full-fledged socialist publishing house, the Charles Kerr Company, which had been publishing the *International Socialist Review* since 1900. From its presses poured major and minor revolutionary classics from ponderous three-volume editions of *Capital* (which the comrades religiously purchased by the thousands and then relegated to the position of honor on the parlor table) to little red-covered copies of the *Communist Manifesto, Value, Price and Profit* and the more popular works of the contemporary intellectuals. Leaflets and broadsides on the issues and outrages of the day were distributed by the million. But more important than any other propaganda medium of the period and undoubtedly the most influential agent in the Americanization of the Social Revolution was the *Appeal to Reason*.

No radical journal less essentially "homely" in its philosophy, less intemperate in its language, less sensational in make-up than the *Appeal* could have achieved a circulation of half a million when American socialism was still in its formative years. The *Appeal* was as American in quality as Daniel Shays, John Brown, Wendell Phillips, P. T. Barnum and Bernarr Macfadden. Its socialism was a strange blend of frontier militancy, Bellamy utopianism and revolutionary class consciousness. It was the product of its time and place— Girard, Kansas, in the first decade of the twentieth century. It could never have survived the World War—as the various attempts to revive it, notably by that mass-culturist, Haldeman-Julius, have proven. It was declining in 1916. In the neo-populist atmosphere of the Middle West in the early 1900s, it flourished like the green bay tree. For the Wolves of Wall Street it substituted "the System"; for permanent prosperity, the Coöperative Commonwealth. And its tone matched the militancy of the Rocky Mountain miners.

The *Appeal* was founded by J. A. Wayland, father of the Ruskin Colony back in the '90s and, for a radical, an incomparable promoter. Under Wayland and his editor, Fred D. Warren, there was built up the famous *Appeal* Army, the members of which were pledged to buy and distribute or sell a certain number of *Appeals* each week. When the *Appeal* issued its numerous special editions, such as the Anti-Trust edition in 1905, the Moyer-Haywood-Pettibone edition in 1906, it was the faithful *Appeal* Army which ordered and prepaid for more than 3,000,000 copies of a single issue. When the paper showed signs of financial stringency, it was the Army which poured its nickels, dimes and dollars into the breach. Wayland knew the secret of mass appeal as few radicals have ever known it, and he could undoubtedly have amassed a fortune in private enterprise. Instead, he committed suicide in 1912, leaving behind the message: "The struggle under the capitalist system isn't worth the effort. Let it pass."

The *Appeal's* constituency was not, of course, wholly agrarian. It had its cohorts in the fisheries of the West, the mining camps of the Rockies, the factories and railroad yards of the East. No flickering light of revolt on any horizon failed to attract its support and boundless enthusiasm. Many of the most prominent and some of the soundest of the radical writers contributed to its columns at various times. Debs had a weekly column that contained some of his most fiery propaganda. (It was in the *Appeal* that he issued, during the Moyer-Haywood-Pettibone affair, his famous call beginning "Arouse, Ye Slaves!" for an army of workers to free the prisoners forcibly.) But while the paper was a tremendous propaganda asset to the struggling Socialist movement, it was something of a liability as well, and many of the party intellectuals—both of the right and of the left—were inclined to regard it in much the same light as the intellectual devotee of capitalism regards our thoroughly capitalistic tabloids. Its wide circulation gave an undue leverage over party policy to a small and uncontrolled group in the Middle West. To the credit of the *Appeal* editors, it rarely took advantage of these opportunities and kept aloof, on the whole, from internal politics. But the ballyhoo with which it greeted each new prominent convert to the cause among the disaffected intellectuals who were already beginning that trek to the left that was to become a stampede in 1912, gave them a prestige out of all proportion to their knowledge and experience. Each young literary convert to the class struggle was immediately "captured" by the *Appeal*, built up by publicity and invited to tell all in its columns. Some of these finds—like Upton Sinclair—proved to be valuable assets. Famous journalists like Charles Edward Russell and Allan Benson, after their espousal of socialism, turned their first-rate talents to the service of the Revolution in trenchant weekly columns of exposure

[ 227 ]

—until they succumbed to Wilsonian idealism in 1917. But many of the *Appeal's* erstwhile Zolas were mere flashes in the radical pan, sources of subsequent embarrassment to the party and of deep irritation to the hard-working and unsung veteran propagandists. The *Appeal's* editors were devoted radicals but scarcely discriminating ones. Having boosted its circulation skyward with the serialization of Sinclair's powerful *The Jungle* in 1906, they attempted in later years to do the same thing with *Tarzan of the Apes*.

Another private enterprise in socialist journalism was *Wilshire's Magazine*. Gaylord Wilshire, its owner (after whom Los Angeles' leading boulevard is named), had made a fortune in Los Angeles real estate and billboards, a fortune which he subsequently sunk in radical propaganda and unprofitable gold mines. He was a handsome, black-bearded man with the voice and mannerisms of the old-line Shakespearean actor. He brought to the service of the Revolution the experience—and habits of mind—of the advertising campaigner. His billboards began to blaze with the slogan "Let the Nation Own the Trusts" and with challenges to Bryan to debate this issue with him. One of his circulation stunts was the offer of a free trip to Europe to the comrade who secured the most subscriptions to the magazine. (Tom Mooney won a special prize in 1908 and was given a trip to the Copenhagen convention of the Second International.) Though its circulation rose to 400,000, the capitalistic advertisers—to Wilshire's naïve surprise—failed to bite. *Wilshire's* went to the wall and the bulk of its owner's fortune went with it. Later, while living in England, Wilshire became a syndicalist. He was too much of a poseur ever to be popular with the comrades.

While the general public was being scandalized by the muckrakers' disclosures and the readers of the radical press were following the struggles of the eastern coal miners, the battles of Telluride and Cripple Creek, the stockyard strikes in Chicago, the political victories in Europe, the 1905 revolution in Russia, and were finding each week additional confirmation of the complete and inherent "rottenness of the whole Capitalist System root and branch," the party's scores of agitators were winning their tens of thousands. Its most able spokesmen were talking the language of the people. Most of them, indeed, could have talked no other. In the Rocky Mountain states, the mine leaders, Boyce and Haywood, together with Father Hagerty, the first Catholic priest to espouse the whole Social Revolution, were spreading the gospel. Haywood, in particular, epitomized the Revolution in the West—in a world which was still, in spirit at least, a frontier world. A hard-boiled, hard-drinking, hard-living, one-eyed giant, he was once described by Ramsay MacDonald as "a bundle of primitive instincts, a master of direct statement." He was the logical product of the undisciplined western mining region in which the lawlessness and violence of the copper and silver bosses bred a similar response in their workers—he-men and individualists for the most part, unbroken as yet to the machine process.

Active among the eastern coal miners was that ageless freelance agitator, Mother Jones. The old lady had begun her activities in the Knights of Labor in the '70s and had been "raising hell" ever since. She had just recently led the striking coal miners' children on a dramatic march to Washington. With never a spot on her white shirt-waist or a gray hair out of place, she had bobbed up in every major labor disturbance for thirty years. Hard-boiled and sentimental, fearless and vain (at eighty, she was still invariably rude to the younger and more attractive women radicals), she could fight like a tigress and swear like a trooper. She knew little of theory, socialistic or otherwise; and on several occasions, notably in 1916, she deserted to the Democrats. She hated John D. Rockefeller Jr. and John Mitchell of the United Miners with equal fervor.

Debs was, of course, the agitator *par excellence*. He combined the fire and fearlessness of Haywood with a warmth and sweetness that made him the most lovable of men. The party theoreticians were inclined—in private—to be a little contemptuous of him (his speeches, when read, were undoubtedly rhetorical and even sentimental, reminiscent of Robert G. Ingersoll, Eugene Field and his other nineteenth-century friends), but in his presence they found it difficult to resist him. Debs was utterly devoid of that egotism, that jealousy of personal prestige, that implacable hatred of actual and potential rivals, that has marked so many of the great revolutionaries from Marx down. In his commonalty he resembled the earlier Lincoln, rather than the windbag Bryan. He was at home among "the boys" in mining camps, railroad yards and around the cracker barrels of country stores—swapping yarns, denouncing "the System," getting a little lit. (All his life he waged a heroic battle against the temptation of alcohol, a battle that was inspired by his sense of responsibility to "the movement.") There was nothing of the plaster saint, the non-resistant Gandhi, the lowly Jesus about Debs. If he held aloof from the quarrels which racked his party from time to time and deprecated factionalism always, it was not for lack of positive opinions or fear of a fight. Some of these quarrels, as he undoubtedly realized intuitively, were transient and unimportant, the fruits of personal antagonisms, ambitions, neuroses, rationalizing themselves as intellectual issues. He hated dissension, even on important issues; but on matters which he considered fundamental, such as industrial unionism, he fought fiercely and consistently. For a man so impulsive, romantic and emotional as Debs, there was a strange consistency in his attitudes. As ready as any frontiersman for "direct action," he had little patience with the tactics of the anarchists. While he could call for a million men to march against Idaho in 1906 and revered the memory of John Brown, he was unalterably opposed both to individual terrorism and to sabotage. Though later his enthusiasm for revolutionary Russia was boundless, he was both temperamentally and intellectually unfitted for the rôle of a party Communist. His most intense hatred was reserved for an impersonal System. His fellow radicals might very well be mistaken, foolish, wrong-headed; but they were not, therefore, in his eyes, renegades.

While Debs, Hanford, Mother Jones, Haywood and an army of soap-boxers were carrying the message to the proletariat, the Revolution was gaining recruits on several other fronts. In 1908, Leslie M. Shaw, ex-Secretary of the Treasury, proclaimed in a speech oddly like one made by Vice President Coolidge fifteen years later:

Socialism is being taught on every hand and I am alarmed by the general trend of things in this connection. At our Chautauquas, the lectures are all preaching the doctrine. Teachers of sociology are doing the same thing. With a few exceptions they are socialists . . . and the few exceptions are anarchists.

Socialism had indeed invaded the universities and the churches. It was winning novelists, poets, playwrights and painters; it had its small but growing contingent of intellectuals; it had even its "millionaire socialists" (though not all of the men thus classified were actually in this category). When the Social Registerite, J. G. Phelps Stokes married the young Russian-Jewish cigar maker, Rose Pastor, the affair provided a feature writer's holiday. William English Walling and Robert Rives La Monte, two other upper-class converts —and like practically all upper-class radicals, extremely revolutionary ones—were the leading left-wing critics of the moment, already leaning toward syndicalism. It was Walling who organized the Friends of Russia in 1905 and rallied the liberals and radicals to the aid of the Russian Revolution. (The Friends sent the rebels a boatload of guns which never reached them.) It was La Monte whose debate with his friend,

[ 231 ]

H. L. Mencken, provided one of the outstanding left-wing literary events of the decade. Published in 1910, under the title *Men versus the Man,* it presented the case of collectivism against individualism. It disclosed the Sage of Baltimore in a mood that has since become habitual. "As between Communism, dominated by Robert Rives La Monte," he wrote, "and a democracy tempered by John D. Rockefeller, I am constrained to choose the latter." La Monte, on the other hand, foresaw "imminent revolution."

The work of a man whom La Monte called "the only sociologist America has produced (except the late Lewis H. Morgan)" was, with Veblen's *Theory of the Leisure Class,* becoming required reading for eager young radicals and feminists alike. In Lester Ward's *Pure Sociology* and *Applied Sociology* they were finding theoretical support from an unexpected quarter. When Ward spoke for them at the Rand School, emphasizing his view that "class distinctions depend entirely upon environmental conditions and are in no sense due to differences in native capacity," there was a distinct feeling that the anthropological angels were on their side. It was a period in which feminism and radicalism were practically synonymous and the fourteenth chapter of *Pure Sociology*, that long backward look at the position of women through the ages, became the bible of a whole generation of eager-eyed young women concerned with more "rights" than the mere right to vote.

The theological seminaries seethed with unrest and social criticism, inspired largely by Dr. Walter Rauschenbusch and Dr. Harry F. Ward. The Christian Socialist Fellowship was organized to "carry to the churches and other religious organizations the message of Socialism." In the colleges, instructors and professors were beginning that questioning of the economic gods that was to cost so many of them their jobs in the next decade. In 1906, the Intercollegiate Socialist Society, later to become the League for Industrial Democracy, was

[ 232 ]

organized by Upton Sinclair with Jack London as president and at one of its first meetings, at Yale, London, already a veteran in the movement, made a fiery confession of faith:

> I received a letter the other day [he told his audience]. It was from a man in Arizona. It began "Dear Comrade." It ended "Yours for the Revolution." In the United States there are 400,000 men, of men and women nearly 1,000,000 who begin their letters "Dear Comrade" and sign them "Yours for the Revolution. . . ." The Revolution is here and now. Stop it who can!

London and Sinclair were as yet the only outstanding novelists who were active socialists. No two men ever afforded a greater contrast—physical and spiritual. London was his own hairy-chested he-man; Sinclair, his own pale poet, Thyrsis. London was Rousseau's Noble Savage crossed with Nietzsche's Blond Beast and talking the language of behaviorism. In spite of that cerebral conversion to Marxism which inspired *The Iron Heel* and *The War of the Classes*, he was temperamentally more of an anarchist than a socialist. Handsome, charming, lovable, and irresistible to women, he was, like John Reed, a decade later, the conquering hero, the romantic rebel. But he did not, like Reed, die at the appropriate moment. In a little-known and early book, written with Anna Strunsky (who later became the wife of William English Walling) , may be found already the essence of that wish-fulfillment dream that was finally to carry London through the pages of Hearst's *Cosmopolitan* to the mastery of a rancho and blooded stock in the Valley of the Moon.

When *The Jungle*, that most effective exposé of the muckrake period, hit the eye of Theodore Roosevelt and the stomach of the nation (after it had already confirmed the worst suspicions of the readers of the *Appeal to Reason*) , Sinclair, the eternal utopian, was elevated to that position of literary crusader that he has maintained ever since. *The Jungle* was more than exposure. It was animated by a social passion that made it, almost accidentally and in spite of a bad ending, a really great book. In the few years following its publication, Sinclair was a young red Galahad in shining armor to his fellow radicals. If in later years he came to be taken less seriously, by both his comrades and the public in general, his own naïve and unconscious exhibitionism was largely to blame. An essential Puritan, he had, in this respect, all the naïveté of the Greenwich Village "free soul." It was not alone the readiness of the "kept press" to exploit the personal difficulties of prominent radicals that made Sinclair the perennial victim of the Sunday Supplement sensationalists. Sinclair's passion to tell all about himself, from his love-life to his diets, fed the flames. And yet, for all his strange intellectual contortions and enthusiasms—fasting, telepathy, anti-Kaiserism, technocracy, the New Deal—Sinclair has always maintained a certain intellectual integrity of his own that has made his fellow revolutionaries forgive his aberrations again and again. He has never, like the more brilliant and brittle Shaw, waxed equally enthusiastic over Lenin, Mussolini and Hitler.

Sinclair's Helicon Hall adventure was typical of the utopian innocence which still colored so much of the intellectual radicalism of the time. In this attempt of a group of forty socialists, anarchists, single-taxers and plain liberals to solve the problems of domesticity by community housekeeping back of the Jersey Palisades, the conservative press and pulpit immediately discerned another deep-laid plot against the sanctity of the American home. In the four months of its existence before the disastrous fire which put an end to the experiment, the Hall housed a striking assortment of members and visitors—Edwin Bjorkman and his wife, Frances Maule, Alice MacGowan and Grace MacGowan Cooke; Edith Kelley, the novelist, and Michael Williams who was to become the editor of the Catholic weekly, *Commonweal*; the anarchist, John Coryell, who was Bertha M. Clay—or at least one of the several ghost writers who produced the assembled works of that mythical lady, two or three Columbia University professors.

Resident for a while as furnace tenders and general handy-men were two young collegians named Sinclair Lewis and Allen Updegraff. The visitors ranged from William James and John Dewey to Jo Davidson, the sculptor, accompanied by the "hobohemian," Sadakichi Hartmann, who, when finally turned out into the snow, wrote protesting letters to the daily press.

But the routine work of the Revolution was proceeding with less fanfare on a much less publicized front. The radical watchwords of the decade were "Agitation, Education, Organization." Upon the rank-and-file members and their active sympathizers (the unsung privates to whom Ben Hanford assigned the name of "Jimmie Higgins") rested the burden of inaugurating the Coöperative Commonwealth. It was these who attended meetings and agitated in their unions, who distributed tons of radical literature, collected contributions for campaign funds, organized street meetings and stood on cold corners to help "swell the crowd"; who made door-to-door canvasses after hard working-days, addressed millions of envelopes, distributed bundles of *Appeals* or *International Socialist Reviews*, got their heads cracked in occasional encounters with the police, contributed to defense funds when some radical leader or soap-boxer got into "trouble." Factional bitternesses had not yet become so intense as to prevent common action in the face of attack or on certain memorial occasions. On the first of May each year or at some special occasion in between, the combined radicals—S. P'ers, S. L. P'ers, Wobblies, anarchists, left-wing unionists—forgot their differences for the evening to sing, dance, eat and drink together for the Revolution. All could sing the "Internationale"; all could sign themselves "Yours for the Revolution."

In 1908, the socialists were to discover that the progress of the Revolution depends as much upon the character of its opposition as upon enthusiasm, devotion and hard work among the radicals. In the presidential campaign of that year they made the most vigorous and intensive drive ever made by a radical party before or since. At tremendous sacrifices, a special train—the Red Special—was hired, and equipped with a battery of the best radical propagandists, for a swing around the country. Debs made from three to ten speeches a day (he was paid three dollars a day and his expenses). Huge crowds gathered at every station. Hall meetings, with paid admissions, overflowed in every city. Leaflets were distributed by the hundred thousand. Debs nearly died under the strain. But the Democratic candidate was William Jennings Bryan; and on the day after election it was discovered that the Socialist vote had risen only 20,000 over 1904. The rising tide was checked for the moment. It was to regain momentum in 1910.

In the first decade of the twentieth century the world of American radicalism was dominated by the Socialist Party. But the anarchists were far from inactive. They were divided into a number of schools (there is a germ of truth in the oft-repeated statement that there are almost as many kinds of anarchism as there are anarchists) and the movement shaded off into degrees of both social and artistic individualism in which it merged with the respectable doctrines of Single Tax, Jeffersonian Democracy or futurism. Thousands of vaguely radical individuals, especially in literary and artistic circles, to whom the Marxian doctrines with their coldly logical formulæ and their political implications offered no appeal, classified themselves as "philosophic anarchists." The phrase carried none of the proletarian atmosphere of militant, direct-action anarchism; it was in line with a respectable American tradition and it had at the same time a faint aroma of romantic danger which has always made the activities of the Russian nihilist so fascinating—from a distance—to middle- and upper-class *révoltés*.

[ 236 ]

American anarchism was divided principally into three schools: the individualist anarchists of the Proudhon-Tucker tradition (many of whom had now substituted the Single Tax for mutual banking schemes as a *modus vivendi*, and some of whom were members of the Democratic Party); the Tolstoyan or Christian anarchists, non-resistants, opposed to all forms of force; the communist-anarchists, followers of Bakunin and Peter Kropotkin. These last were the dominant and most active group, *the* anarchists, so far as the general public was concerned. Their best-known leaders were Berkman and Goldman.

Because, perhaps, of the diffused character of their philosophy, the various anarchist schools rarely displayed that distrust and bitterness toward one another that one invariably finds among the Marxian factions—a fact which made them pleasanter company, as a rule, than the latter. They were inclined to look upon any "libertarian" or "social idealist" who opposed authority and convention—from Paine, Thoreau, Walt Whitman, John Swinton to a dozen contemporary literary and artistic figures—as their own. Emma Goldman, probably the most implacable and quarrelsome of all the anarchist leaders, was able, in her autobiography, to say a word of praise even for Morris Hillquit, her outstanding socialist opponent, for his anti-war position in 1917.

At this time, however, Emma was dividing her time largely between lectures on the modern drama or birth control and vigorous and vituperative debates with leading socialists throughout the country on Anarchism versus Socialism. She was a fiery, effective and not always scrupulous debater; but there was nothing of the Jesuit about her. Whatever exaggeration or misrepresentation she may have indulged in (and her autobiography is full of the former, in particular) were the fruits of her own intense prejudices and capacity for self-deception. She was a thoroughly honest woman who could believe most implicitly whatever she wanted to believe. She had all the intensity, the emotional auto-intoxication, so common to the Russian-Jewish radical, intensified a millionfold. Words poured from her in a torrent; and she could brook no hint of opposition. But her enthusiasms and generosities were as warm—and as undiscriminating—as her prejudices. It was difficult to think of this square, firm-jawed figure in a spotless, white shirt-waist and neat black skirt, looking so much like a strong-minded *Hausfrau*, as the woman whom the American press, after the assassination of McKinley, had pictured and denounced as an archfiend, the leader of a band of skulking assassins. It was also difficult to think of her as the tender and maternal lover of the man who was to treat her so shabbily, and who accompanied her and managed her lecture tours at this time. Ben Reitman, with his wild, black hair, self-conscious sloppiness and purposeful childlikeness was doing his best to look and act the traditional vagabond-anarchist. His genius in disposing of anarchist literature at the Goldman meetings, however, betrayed him as a high-powered salesman of the first order.

The Goldman lectures on the drama of social significance drew the cognoscenti of Chicago, St. Louis, Kansas City and San Francisco. Limousines lined the street outside the lecture halls in a day when limousines were not plentiful. This combination of culture and revolution was the most élite gesture of dissent in pre-war American radicalism. Only an occasional bomb or pistol in the hand of some crack-brained or too literal disciple of Bakuninism shattered the comparative calm of anarchistic propaganda, as carried on by high-minded and idealistic little groups in New York and points west, and the nerves of their more sensitive friends. The day of the *Attentat* was about over, so far as the more orthodox anarchists were concerned.

There were a few of its new friends, however, to whom both the "propaganda of the deed" and the more bohemian aspects of anarchism had an irresistible appeal. The most prominent of these was Hutchins Hapgood, brother of Norman Hapgood, who celebrated the direct-action, pragmatic "labor anarchist" of the A. F. of L. in his story of Anton Johannsen, *The Spirit of Labor*, and the socially irresponsible, unmoral, nihilistic bohemian rebel in *An Anarchist Woman*, the story of the famous "Marie" and the pre-Greenwich Village-Lower Depths group that flourished in Chicago at this time. The two groups occasionally overlapped in personnel, and Hapgood, the product of respectability and Harvard, was naïvely fascinated both by the hard-boiled Rabelaisian Johannsen, who was later to figure in the McNamara affair, and by the "free souled" but essentially sentimental posturings of the "fallen woman" gone intellectual and revolutionary.

To counterbalance the somewhat turgid revolutionary *vie de Bohême* in Chicago, there was the Home Colony in the state of Washington, where, under the leadership of Jay Fox, another prominent American anarchist, a group of assorted radicals of all shades—but mostly Bakuninists—had gone back to the soil and were living the simple and wholesome life of voluntary coöperation on the shores of Puget Sound, raising chickens, vegetables and anarchist babies. Home Colony produced or attracted some of the most charming individuals and families among the American anarchists.

The alliance between anarchism and trade unionism had been effectively blown up by the Haymarket bomb in 1886. But the "propaganda of the deed," unembroidered by theoretical rationalization, had become, by 1910, a fairly habitual weapon among some of the more hard-pressed unions. It was one of the exigencies of their daily battle for existence in a time when profit-sharing schemes, employee representation and other concomitants of the New Capitalism had not yet appeared on the horizon. Here and there, however, the old alliance of the '80s had left certain curious vestiges. In California, for example, a powerful labor machine, centered largely about the building trades unions in San Francisco, was in the hands of what was undoubtedly the most corrupt labor leadership in America. And yet its two principal organizers—one of them the lieutenant of its politician-president, twice mayor of the city, who sternly suppressed any hint of rank-and-file dissent within its ranks—were declared anarchists of long standing. Up to 1911, in fact, the anarchists may be said to have been the brains of the conservative building trades organization in the West. The organization's conservatism, however, did not apply to method. Men who voted the straight Democratic ticket, went to early mass on Sundays and always supported Samuel Gompers at yearly conventions did not hesitate to use whatever weapons seemed most effective for the maintenance of their organization.

In 1910, knowing that the State of California could not continue to exist half slave and half free—in other words, Closed Shop in the north and Open Shop in the south—the San Francisco unionists, backed up by the entire A. F. of L., decided that Los Angeles, home of the ferociously union-hating Harrison Grey Otis and his band, must be organized. For practical assistance, they looked to the experienced officers of the Structural Iron Workers in Indianapolis, the most militant, though by no means radical, labor union in the country. Some time later, Otis' Los Angeles *Times* building was wrecked by dynamite. The accusation and arrest of the McNamara brothers, officials of the Iron Workers, followed.

The story of that famous case need not be retold here. Its culmination is more important. At no time in their history had labor and radicalism of every description been so united in a common cause as in the year 1911. The McNamara defense had behind it not only the entire resources of the A. F. of L., but the support of every radical organization and publication, the eloquence of every radical speaker and writer, the confidence of the American rank and file. The case had its political as well as industrial implications. One of the defense attorneys, Job Harriman, headed a socialist-labor ticket in Los Angeles, pledged to make that city safe for the Closed Shop. Both labor and the radicals were making a tremendous effort to elect Harriman and because of a general dislike of the fire-eating Otis and his candidates, labor stood an excellent chance of winning the election. The class lines in Los Angeles were tightly drawn.

Perhaps nothing has ever so stunned the labor and radical world as the McNamara confession just a few days before the election. Even among some of those few very close to the case who knew the brothers to be guilty, the idea of a confession, after the tremendous campaign of propaganda that had been waged in their behalf, seemed incredible. The announcement was followed by several suicides and cases of mental collapse among their followers. In Los Angeles, men broke into sobs in the courtroom or wandered dazed about the streets. Harriman campaign buttons filled the gutters. The confession had saved Southern California, in fact, all of California, for the Open Shop.

Undoubtedly William Burns and the prosecution "had the goods on" the McNamaras and their associates. Without a confession they might have hanged (though because of the tremendous sympathy for their cause, this is not certain), their associates would have been convicted, probably, of conspiracy. In any case, the mass of the workers would never have believed them guilty. They would have been labor "martyrs." With the confession, they received life and fifteen years' imprisonment, respectively, and their associates were convicted anyway. One of the brothers, at least, was willing to accept his fate and turned down Darrow's first suggestion of confession. Two of the several labor anarchists involved expressed themselves as quite ready "to take the rap." But in the meanwhile Lincoln Steffens, who had been covering the case—and who was still, like Darrow, a philosophic anarchist

—had been busily negotiating with the prosecution and the employers' leaders to settle the matter in a spirit of "brotherly love" and "the Golden Rule." In return for a confession— before election day—Steffens received the promise, which he naïvely accepted at face value, that the men would be granted sentences of imprisonment that would later be commuted, that there would be no prosecutions of their associates and that Capital would get together with Labor in Los Angeles to work out a more harmonious relationship. On the basis of these terms the McNamaras were persuaded that their confession would save the other labor men involved by Burns' evidence. They agreed. Except for the fact that the prosecution did not demand the death penalty, the agreements were never kept. J. B. McNamara is still serving his life sentence at San Quentin. If the *Times* dynamiting was a futile gesture, so far as the labor movement was concerned, the confession was almost equally so. Steffens' own story, in his autobiography, of his part in the affair furnishes an eloquent commentary on the rôle of the individualistic free-lancer in the labor movement.

# X

## SYNDICALISM—AMERICAN STYLE

THOSE same forces which at the beginning of the new century were stimulating the growth of radical political expression were also giving rise to a demand for more radical and aggressive unionism. The American Federation of Labor was growing rapidly, but its activities were confined almost exclusively to the skilled and semi-skilled trades, which, by the very logic of the machine process, seemed doomed to occupy a rôle of decreasing importance in American industrial life. Furthermore, the Federation was divided into craft unions which, however effective they might be in gaining immediate concessions for their limited membership, were rapidly becoming anachronisms in a world of giant corporations. By 1912 the A. F. of L. had brought only one-ninth of the wage-earners of America into its ranks and those were drawn largely from the ranks of skilled workmen in the untrustified industries. It was powerless in the realm of steel and oil, and was making no dent upon the rapidly growing automotive industry.

The De Leonites, as we have seen, had not waited for a more radical unionism to spring out of the objective conditions of American life; but, with their Socialist Trade and Labor Alliance, had attempted to create it synthetically in the image of their hearts' desire. The members of the new Socialist Party—at least half of whom were trade unionists—

had repudiated De Leon's tactics in this respect as premature and fatal in their effect upon the relationship between the radicals and the labor movement. But in the early 1900s, while the majority still clung to the policy of agitating *within* the existing unions, others, including some of the most influential men in the new party, were in favor of repudiating the A. F. of L. and all its works, of starting afresh to build militant, socialist unionism. The real impetus for such a movement, however, came from the Western Federation of Miners.

Since its inception in 1893, the year after the great strike at Coeur d'Alene, the Western Federation of Miners, which in 1902 came out definitely for socialism, had been involved in some of the fiercest and bloodiest labor battles the country had ever known. There was as yet no hint of "the new capitalism" in the western mining districts. Conditions, as in the eastern coal fields, were feudalistic; but the Westerners were a more militant, adventurous and essentially anarchistic lot than the coal miners of the East, many of whom were immigrants ignorant of their rights and easily awed by manifestations of authority. They were impatient of discipline and injustice alike, believers in direct action, individual and organized. Revolutionary by temperament and tradition, rather than collectivist by virtue of common experience with the machine process, they were, nevertheless, forced by the ruthlessness of their opponents into cohesive action of the most militant sort. In 1901 came the bitter strike of Telluride; in 1903-4 the still more bitter one of Cripple Creek. The Rocky Mountain states—Colorado, Montana, Idaho—became the scene of open warfare at which the country stood aghast. Battles were fought with dynamite and shotguns on both sides. Assassinations of mine bosses followed the murder of mine pickets; martial law was declared; the strikers were herded into bull pens; the radical press screamed indignant headlines. It was inevitable that this dramatic, lurid conflict would stir the imaginations and quicken the pulses of revolutionaries both

[ 244 ]

East and West. On the heels of the Cripple Creek strike a group of twenty-three men prominent in labor and radical circles met secretly at Chicago, issued a manifesto calling for a new labor-radical alignment, and at a convention six months later, also in Chicago, the Industrial Workers of the World was born.

Though French anarcho-syndicalism, through its converts among American intellectuals, was later to furnish what John Graham Brooks has called "a literary ritual" to the I. W. W., that organization was in its beginnings thoroughly native, essentially pragmatic and socialistic rather than anarchistic in character. It grew out of conditions—not theories—and was primarily the expression of that vague, passionate, rowdy, undisciplined spirit of protest that was beginning to make itself heard among the unskilled, footloose proletarian substratum ignored by the official labor movement, and among the hardfighting western mine workers, still imbued with the direct-actionist tradition of the frontier. Idealistically, it was the wish-fulfillment of those socialists, both in the old Socialist Labor Party and in the new Socialist Party, who, in their mounting despair over the narrow and conservative policy of "the corrupt A. F. of L. machine," had never relinquished the dream of establishing a revolutionary and "scientific" unionism as the industrial wing of the advancing socialist army.
Like the defunct Knights of Labor, after which it was patterned and from which its slogan—"An injury to one is an injury to all"—was derived, the I.W.W. was conceived as One Big Union, industrial in form, which was to sweep into its ranks *en masse* all workers, skilled and unskilled, regardless of "race, creed, color, sex, or previous condition of servitude." Unlike the Knights, however, or that more modern example of an industrial union, the United Mine Workers, the new organization was to be an extremely aggressive one, frankly revolutionary in spirit as well as "scientific" in form.

[ 245 ]

Basically, it was designed to give national scope to that militant, radical unionism which had sprung up in the metalliferous mining regions of the Rockies. "We come out of the West," declared "Big Bill" Haywood, who was the very personification of the spirit of the new movement, "to meet the textile workers of the East."

George Speed, one of the most devoted and astute of the western I.W.Ws (or "Wobblies," as the members of the organization came to be called), referred years later to this first official I.W.W. gathering as "the greatest conglomeration of freaks that ever met in convention." Certainly among the two hundred delegates present, representing an odd assortment of thirty-four scattered organizations and some forty trades, the lunatic fringe of the radical movement was more than well represented. But at the helm and dominating the convention were also some of the most able and experienced men in the labor and socialist camps. Charles Moyer, the brains, and Haywood, the spirit, of the Western Federation of Miners, and William E. Trautmann, of the United Brewery Workers, represented the only strong labor blocs. Debs, Ernest Untermann, a Socialist Party theoretician, A. M. Simons, the radical historian, Robert Rives La Monte, the young left-wing intellectual, Mother Jones and Lucy Parsons, widow of the Haymarket victim, were there.

Sitting in front of Debs [writes Haywood in his autobiography] was Daniel De Leon of the Socialist Trade and Labor Alliance, with badger-gray whiskers, a black spot on his chin. He had been eyeing his old antagonist, Debs, furtively and seemed charmed by what the leader of workingmen had to say. For years there had been a wide difference of opinion between Debs and De Leon. They represented extremes in the Socialist movement. I could feel what this difference meant when De Leon began to speak; he was the theorizing professor, while Debs was the workingman who had laid down his shovel on the locomotive when he took up the work of organizing firemen. Debs' ideas, while not clearly developed, were built upon his contact with the workers in their struggle. De Leon's only contact with the workers was through the

[ 246 ]

ideas with which he wished to "indoctrinate" them, to use his own word.

Thomas J. Hagerty, the radical Catholic priest, was much in evidence and helped to formulate the famous "Wobbly Preamble" with its spirited and uncompromising first line: "The working class and the employing class have nothing in common." Scattered throughout the hall were a dozen less well-known agitators with years of organizational experience behind them.

This combination of "revolutionary industrial unionists" was one inevitably doomed to schism. The Western Federation of Miners, while definitely socialistic at the time, contained also a strong direct-actionist, anti-political element which was destined to thrive in the atmosphere of the new organization. Delegates from small scattered locals and "clubs" represented every conceivable shade of radicalism from the purest anarchism to the most reformistic brand of socialism. De Leon was determined, naturally, to mold the new unionism into the likeness of his Alliance. The Socialist Party members, congenitally suspicious of him, were equally determined to prevent any such development. Nevertheless, speeches by Haywood, Debs and others glowed with revolutionary hope and promise—undoubtedly sincere at the moment—of solidarity forever. With Haywood's booming, "Fellow workers!" and Debs' fervid appeal for comradeship ringing in his ears, even De Leon, probably the bitterest factionalist the American radical movement had ever known, was moved to speak feelingly for unity.

"This is the Continental Congress of the working class," announced Haywood. "The aims and objects of this organization shall be to put the working class in possession of the economic power, the means of life, in control of the machinery of production and distribution, without regard to the capitalist masters. . . ."

The apparent union of the heterogeneous elements represented at the convention was made possible, as Paul Brissenden has pointed out, through "the binding influence of common antipathies," chief among which was the hatred of the old unionism as exemplified in the A. F. of L. A united front, however, can scarcely be maintained on such precarious foundations, and the enthusiastic delegates had barely adjourned before dissension broke out and various groups began jockeying for control. The first storm reached its climax in the 1906 convention. De Leon, whose influence had been steadily growing stronger during the intervening year, threw in his lot—for the time being—with the anti-political, direct-actionist element of the West, under leadership of Trautmann and Vincent St. John, in order to defeat the Socialist Party contingent. De Leon, who undoubtedly believed that once he had deposed the rival Socialists, he could easily outmaneuver the politically inexperienced Westerners, or "proletarian rabble" as he came to term them, emerged, apparently triumphant. He had sadly misjudged the temper of the anti-political bloc, however, and at the 1908 convention the Trautmann-St. John forces made short work of the "political incubus" of the Socialist Laborites.

Meanwhile, racked as it was by controversy, it is doubtful if the little organization would have survived its first stormy year if it had not been for a dramatic event that again brought Capital and Labor face to face and, for the moment, made the radicals forget their factional differences. This was the Moyer-Haywood-Pettibone case, the *cause célèbre* of the decade.

In December, 1905, ex-Governor Steunenberg of Idaho, who had been responsible for calling out the militia in the Cripple Creek strike, was killed by a dynamite explosion. Several weeks later, on the strength of a confession obtained from one Harry Orchard, a former bodyguard of Moyer, by James McParland, the Pinkerton detective who had been the nemesis of the Molly Maguires thirty years before, Haywood,

[ 248 ]

Moyer, George Pettibone and other officials of the Western Federation of Miners in Denver were kidnapped by Idaho officials, spirited across the state line and charged with Steunenberg's murder.

The illegal seizure of these men caused a wave of fury to sweep radical and labor circles. Debs, writing in the *Appeal*, gave vent to one of the most vitriolic and revolutionary editorials ever to come from his pen, in which he predicted that "if they [the mine owners] attempt to murder Moyer, Haywood and their brothers, a million revolutionists, at least, will meet them with guns." Giant mass meetings packed the halls and public squares of our major cities. Protest parades in New York lasted hours, with eighty to a hundred thousand marchers participating. Maxim Gorky, here on a visit and shortly to learn the meaning of American Puritanism when it was revealed in the press that he was traveling with a common-law wife, wired the defendants greetings from the workers of Russia. *McClure's* published Orchard's lurid autobiography in which he confessed to twenty-six murders, all of them alleged to have been committed at the instigation of the mine union officials.

Both the I. W. Ws and the Socialists threw practically all their energies into raising money for a defense fund which finally totaled $250,000. One of the highest powered batteries of legal talent ever to be employed in a labor case went into action: Clarence Darrow, then in his prime, prominent among the defense forces, and William E. Borah, then a promising young Idaho district attorney, taking up the cudgels for the prosecution.

Fifty special correspondents from America and England flocked to Boise to be on hand at Haywood's trial when it opened on May 9, 1907. The case dragged on for months in the full glare of national and international publicity, with ever-increasing excitement in the camp of the Revolution until politicians and employers began to grow alarmed. President Roosevelt, who earlier had branded Haywood and his comrades as "undesirable citizens" only to set thousands of their sympathizers to wearing buttons inscribed, "I am an undesirable citizen," unburdened himself to Senator Lodge of Massachusetts: "The labor men are very ugly and no one can tell how far such discontent will spread. There has been during the last six or eight years a great growth of socialist and radical spirit among workingmen and the leaders are obliged to play to this or lose their leadership."

Darrow's closing speech to the jury—a masterpiece of its kind—took eleven hours to deliver. "If at the behest of this mob," he declared, "you should kill Bill Haywood, he is mortal, he will die, and I want to say to you that a million men will take up the banner of labor at the open grave where Haywood lays it down, and in spite of prisons or scaffolds or fire, in spite of prosecution or jury, these men of willing hands will carry it on to victory in the end . . ."

Whether or not the jury believed this, the prosecution and the forces behind it were evidently in a mood to take it seriously. As the trial neared its end, it seemed obvious to many observers that the prosecution was "pulling its punches." Haywood was acquitted and later Moyer and Pettibone were freed. Orchard, the state's star witness, was then tried and received life imprisonment.

Haywood emerged from the Idaho murder trial the man of the hour in revolutionary labor circles, but the cause that was nearest his heart was not faring so well. The I.W.W. had, it is true, picked up some 10,000 additional members. In Goldfield, Nevada, working hand in hand with the Western Federation, it had organized every kind of worker from the nurses in the hospital to dishwashers, and had established a minimum wage of $4.50 for an eight-hour day. It had won a sawmill strike in Oregon, and a textile strike in Maine. But the imprisonment of Haywood had weakened the I.W.W's influence within the Western Federation when it was most needed. The factionalism which had lain dormant for a time was again rife and soon came to a head with the formal withdrawal of this strong labor bloc. Shortly after, the United Brewery Workers also withdrew. Both organizations eventually joined the A. F. of L. To the acute ear of many a laborite of the period, this loss of its strongest labor elements sounded the death knell of the I.W.W., but it struggled on to still another split and yet would not die.

Extremes met at the 1908 convention. On the one hand was the professorial De Leon with his coterie of faithful Socialist Laborites; on the other, a horde of migratory workers from the West, known as the Overalls Brigade, who poured into Chicago on freight trains singing, "Hallelujah, I'm a Bum!" The second paragraph of the original I.W.W. preamble had stated that the workers must come together on the *political* as well as on the *industrial* field. The Westerners, scorning politics—most of them, with no settled place of abode, were deprived of the ballot anyway—succeeded in stampeding the convention and eliminating the political clause. De Leon, declaring that "the barbarian begins with physical force; the civilized man ends with that when it is necessary," stormed out of the hall taking his little band of faithful adherents with him. The latter, somewhat against the veteran Marxist's wishes, set up their own organization which became known, because of the location of its headquarters, as the Detroit I.W.W., a more or less phantom body in the tradition of the old Socialist Trade and Labor Alliance. Its relation to the original, or Chicago, I.W.W., and of both these organizations to the A. F. of L., in connection with what was fast becoming the paramount issue of the day—political action versus direct action—was succinctly expressed by one of its leaders some years later in his testimony before the United States Commission on Industrial Relations:

Now a body [he declared] that repudiates the ballot naturally has to take something else, such as sabotage and direct action. Now the American Federation of Labor does not preach sabotage, but it practices it; and the Chicago I. W. W. preaches sabotage, but it does not practice it. . . . The position that we [the Detroit I. W. W.] take is that if we have the majority, and the capitalists' officials who count the ballots . . . refuse to count us in well,— then there will be a scrap. But we are going to test the peaceful method first.

The statement that the Chicago I.W.W. did not practice sabotage was, of course, not strictly accurate; but their open advocacy of it gave them a reputation for "lawlessness" entirely out of keeping with the facts.

The year 1908 marked a turning-point in the history of the I.W.W. Not only did the anti-political, direct-actionist wing, representative of the unskilled, migratory worker, come into its own that year, but Haywood made a trip abroad where he came into contact with many of the leading French syndicalists and returned to give more definite force and direction to the movement.

Syndicalism, unlike socialism and anarchism, is not a distinct social philosophy. A synthetic philosophy, an ideology —to use a favorite word of the modern Communist—was tacked onto it by a group of French intellectuals long after it had become an actuality in the labor world of Europe. In the most general sense of the term, syndicalism may be regarded as militant labor unionism dedicated to revolutionary rather than to ameliorative ends, and in this broad sense it has a history almost as old as that of utopian socialism. Even that most distinctive feature of modern syndicalist theory— industrial self-government by the producers (i.e., the workers) organized by industries—was a tenet of Robert Owen's Grand National Confederation of Trades Unions in 1834; just as the syndicalist fetish, the General Strike, was a feature of the Chartist propaganda a few years later. In 1869 a French

[ 252 ]

delegate to the First International (a Proudhonist) stated the fundamental syndicalist thesis when he declared that "the grouping of different trades in the city will form the commune of the future" and that government was to be "replaced by a federated council of *syndicats*," the French term for trade unions from which the word "syndicalism" is derived. In America, the Knights of Labor had shown syndicalist tendencies, particularly in their practice of sabotage during the great Southwest Strike, and the militant Chicago unionists, on the eve of the Haymarket debacle, were anarcho-syndicalists in spirit if not in theory.

Modern syndicalism, however, had its roots in France in the late '90s and early 1900s when the communist-anarchists, who had been extremely active in the Latin countries since the days of the First International, joined forces with a group of left-wing, anti-parliamentary socialists within the French General Confederation of Labor to form a powerful revolutionary bloc. The members of this bloc were, in the sectarian sense of the term, the first syndicalists, or—to phrase it with greater accuracy, since the anarchist influence predominated—the first anarcho-syndicalists.

It was primarily through their spectacular tactics, not by their powers of ratiocination, that these revolutionary trade unionists emblazoned their name across the red sky of Europe. Since 1895 the Confederation had been committed to the General Strike, but now a full-fledged anarcho-syndicalist program emerged, including not only the General Strike—to the syndicalist the weapon *par excellence* of the Revolution—but also the use of sabotage, boycotts, craft strikes and other forms of "direct action" aimed not merely at the employing class but at the State itself. Meanwhile, various sympathetic intellectuals, men like Georges Sorel, Hubert Lagardelle, Edouard Berth and Gustave Hervé, some of them drawing heavily upon the Vitalism of Henri Bergson, who was then at the height of his prestige, arose to endow the confused activities of the revolutionary unionists with a philosophic background in keeping with the temperamental, instinctive tendencies, as well as with the revolutionary traditions, of the anarchistically inclined Latin radical. The latter probably grasped few of the metaphysical implications of Sorel's "Social Myth" and other theories, but he welcomed this impressive support to his own impulses and experience. Syndicalism spread rapidly throughout Europe, taking on various socialistic or anarchistic modifications according to the environments it encountered, but gaining its firmest hold, outside France, in those two countries in which the Bakuninist tradition was strongest, Italy and Spain.

Though the syndicalists based their struggle on the Marxian conception of the class war and proposed the abolition of private ownership, they differed from the socialists in limiting the field of that struggle to the industrial front, "the point of production," alone; and the weapons of combat to the various manifestations of direct action. Unlike the conservative trade unionists, who in times of stress usually become pragmatic syndicalists, they conceived of the class struggle as conscious and continuous guerrilla warfare between the owners of industry and the workers, which would end only with the victorious culmination of the great General Strike. Meanwhile, every small strike—and the syndicalists believed in striking early, often and unexpectedly—contributed to the annoyance of the owning class and the training of the workers for the final conflict. To the socialists, on the other hand, the General Strike was merely one form of mass protest or aggression. (The use of the General Strike as a weapon against international wars, for instance, had been discussed at socialist congresses as early as 1891.)

Though some of the syndicalists called themselves "neo-Marxians," the predominant group, the anarcho-syndicalists, owed much more to Bakunin than to Marx. They were not concerned with the conquest, political or otherwise, of the

State (which, according to the Marxists, would gradually "wither away" only after a transition period of proletarian control had firmly established the foundations of the new social order). They aimed rather at its immediate and complete destruction and the substitution for it of a loose federation of highly autonomous, industrial units, each controlled by the workers enrolled therein. It was the old anarchist dream of decentralized, voluntary coöperation, but given an organic and functional industrial set-up, a conception which accounts for the bitterness with which many present-day syndicalists, like the "pure" anarchists, regard the highly centralized party dictatorship of Soviet Russia despite that country's recognition of their pet theory of industrial representation.

With the rise to power within the I.W.W. of the anti-political, direct actionists of the West and the return of Haywood from France to preach the doctrine of the General Strike and to stress—as the Communists do today—the revolutionary rôle of "militant minorities," the organization entered upon that phase of its career which was to make "syndicalism" a household word in American radical circles. Not that the average rank-and-file Wobbly ever came to have any real understanding of that term, much less of the underlying assumptions of French anarcho-syndicalism. Probably the majority of them never even heard of the latter nor of Sorel and its other high priests. A pamphlet entitled *Sabotage*, written in simple terms by Emile Pouget, assistant secretary of the French Confederation and translated by an Italian-born I.W.W. strike leader and poet, Arturo Giovannitti, came to circulate freely among them after 1912 and helped to acquaint them with many of the more subtle aspects of direct action. But, for the most part, syndicalist theory, except in those native aspects which already had been developed in the heat of many labor battles long before Haywood sailed for France, came to them second-hand from the lips of their leaders and from the more popular work of a number of American intellectuals, who, attracted by the spectacular qualities of the new unionism, attempted to do much the same thing for it in America that the French intellectuals had done for it abroad.

No mere factual account or theoretical analysis of their varied activities can convey the spirit and feeling of the Wobblies after 1908. The inadequacy of such treatment has been emphasized by John S. Gambs in *The Decline of the I.W.W.*

An organization which sang in deep-throated tones songs of sardonic humor and savage mockery; which evolved a vituperative cant of its own; whose picket lines were a thousand miles long; whose tactics of battle in free speech fights and harvest fields were unexpected and bold, which laughed with inimitable grim humor—such an organization cannot be completely understood unless some attention is given to its romantic side.

More than any other revolutionary organization which has sprung up in America, if not in the world, the I.W.W. came to represent the interests, the virtues and vices, the power and the limitations of the real underdog, of, to quote the earlier John Masefield—

> . . . the ranker, the tramp of the road,
> The slave with the sack on his shoulder, pricked on with the goad,
> .    .    .    .    .    .    .    .
> The sailor, the stoker of steamers, the man with the clout,
> The chantyman bent at the halliards . . .
> . . . the tired lookout.

From 1908, despite occasional heavy inroads—usually made at times of great stress—among the low-paid wage-earners of the East, particularly among the half-starved textile operatives of such towns as Lawrence, Massachusetts, and Paterson, New Jersey, the I.W.W. was primarily the organization of the footloose, migratory workers of land and sea, and particularly of the West. It was their phrases which lent color to its propaganda; their songs which "fanned the flames of discontent" from the harvest fields of the Dakotas to the forests of the Pacific Northwest, echoed along the waterfront and reverberated in the forecastles of American ships from San Francisco to Singapore; their voices which rose above Saturday night's tumult along the Main Stem proclaiming "the historic mission of the working class" from the vantage of a soap-box and drowning out the strains of the Salvation Army band on the opposite corner by a raucous rendition of Fellow-worker Joe Hill's *The Preacher and the Slave* with its sardonic promise of "pie in the sky when you die." Into the box cars, construction camps, bunk houses and hobo jungles of the land, they carried the Red Card and the Little Red Song Book. The haystack, the forecastle-head, the tree stump, the pile of ties in the shade of the watertank was their rostrum. They, more than any other element, made the organization their own, shaped its weapons to fit their own calloused hands, its ideals to express their own aspirations.

The tactics and philosophy of the I.W.W., as they evolved and crystallized through a long series of spectacular strikes and free-speech fights, can be understood only when considered in relation to this footloose element which more closely than any other American working-class group approximated that dispossessed proletariat who, in the Marxian phrase, had "nothing to lose but its chains." In settled industrial communities where the worker was usually a family man with a home, children, personal possessions, where, in short, his welfare was definitely linked with that of the community as a whole, the Wobbly program, as it gradually took shape after 1908, had little appeal. The organization that undertook to call a strike in such a complex community undertook a grave responsibility. Untold misery and hardship would be almost certain to follow if the strike were lost, and the organization responsible for calling it would then be likely to suffer a severe loss of prestige. The emphasis in such communities was, of necessity, laid upon careful planning and preparation, upon the accumulation of an adequate strike fund, stable organization and responsible leadership. The hastily called, spontaneous strike might succeed occasionally, but more often it failed. Without adequate funds and usually facing powerful combinations of capitalists who could afford to wait, the overhasty striker in such a community would almost inevitably be called upon to decide sooner or later whether he would accept the bosses' terms or starve together with his woman and children. After a few such experiences, he tended to become cautious—perhaps overcautious. He was not ready to "down tools" at the cry of every agitator who came along.

But in the harvest fields, lumber and construction camps, along the waterfront—in short, wherever the migratory workers congregated—the situation was vastly less complicated. If a strike promised to be long drawn-out or failed, the footloose worker, the "bindle stiff" as he was so often called, simply took to the road again where he spent a considerable proportion of his time anyway. Unlike the settled industrial worker with a home and family, he could afford—at least in those days—to maintain an attitude of almost chronic belligerency. If the sawmills were shut down and the lumber industry paralyzed, there was grain to harvest in the Dakotas, fruit to pick in the California valleys, gold to mine in Nevada. He shouldered his blanket roll and moved on. Often he was pitted not against a giant corporation, but against some individual farmer anxious to get his hay in the barn before a thunderstorm broke or some fruit grower to whom a slight delay might mean the loss of an entire crop. Under such conditions, the syndicalist tactics of striking early, often and unexpectedly worked to perfection. They suited the purposes of the American migratory worker much better, in fact, than they ever had those of the French industrial worker for whom they had been devised.

The I.W.W. was, to be sure, never composed entirely of this drifting, migratory element. It made surprising headway at times in the industrial East, particularly in the textile centers as has been noted. A large proportion of these eastern

[ 258 ]

recruits were unnaturalized immigrants without the vote to whom political socialism could have little appeal. Also most of them were low-paid unskilled wage-earners beneath the notice of the official labor movement as represented by the A. F. of L. It was the I.W.W. or nothing for them; and, though the organization was ill-suited to their needs in times of industrial peace, they turned to it in times of industrial war. The spectacular handling by I.W.W. leaders of great mass strikes, such as the Lawrence affair of 1912, with which we shall deal in the next chapter, swept Eastern industrial workers into the Wobbly ranks by the thousands; but once the excitement had died down, the organization could not hold them. It was too consistently revolutionary, too purely a fighting machine; it thrived only on action and conflict.

There was plenty of conflict to keep the Wobblies busy, however, during these eventful years. Haywood had scarcely rid himself of his sea legs before the organization was plunged into a series of strikes involving lumbermen, farm hands, glass workers, Mexican laborers, window cleaners, hop pickers and textile workers. None of these early strikes developed into great mass movements such as the new organization needed to bring it out of obscurity. In the summer of 1909, however, the Wobblies made their first bid for national fame when, in leading a strike of 8,000 employees of the Pressed Steel Car Company at McKees Rocks, Pennsylvania, they clashed with the Pennsylvania State Constabulary, one of the most ruthless anti-labor police forces in the country.

To the eastern workers, the Pennsylvania state troopers, or "Pennsylvania Cossacks" as the radicals called them, were the very personification of terrorism, but to the Wobblies, many of them veterans of western mine wars, any sort of eastern "policeman" was something of a joke. Early in the strike they quietly informed the state constabulary commander that for every striker injured or killed, the life of one of his men would be exacted in return. In the first head-on collision they made good their threat. About a dozen lives were lost on both sides, but when the shooting was over, the strike was won. The industrialists of the East had had their first good look at the Wobblies in action and it was not a sight to inspire pleasant dreams.

Meanwhile the organization was picking up in the West and was now to become identified with a new cause which more than any other, with the exception of the Lawrence strike, was to bring it into national prominence—the cause of "free speech."

The Spokane free-speech fight started with the drive of the Spokane authorities against the I.W.W. in the autumn of 1909. Halls were raided, street meetings broken up, speakers and organizers jailed, beaten and tortured. But for every Wobbly jailed or otherwise removed from the fray another appeared in his place. It was a phenomenon that was to be the feature of all such struggles thereafter. Wobblies from all up and down the Coast headed for Spokane. The affair took on the aspects of a mass pilgrimage, a barbaric invasion. Every freight train brought fresh recruits. Spokane was a town besieged. Its jails were jammed with five hundred singing Wobblies, including their nineteen-year-old Jeanne d'Arc, the dark-haired, blue-eyed Elizabeth Gurley Flynn, whose colorful and attractive personality cast a romantic glamour over the entire proceedings and did much to dramatize the event for the newspapers. Again, as in the McKees Rocks fracas, the Wobblies, by the very boldness of their tactics, emerged victorious. I.W.W. prestige in radical circles went up like a rocket.

Similar conflicts occurred later at Missoula, Montana; Everett, Washington; San Diego and Fresno, California, and many other points. The San Diego free-speech fight of 1912 was the most prolonged; the one in Everett, the bloodiest. The San Diego battle involved socialists, anarchists, single-taxers and free-lance agitators, for the authorities were determined to stamp out every type of "subversive" propaganda. During the summer-long battle of the intransigent soap-boxers, scores were imprisoned, beaten, tarred and feathered, ridden on rails. Ben Reitman, who turned up with Emma Goldman at the height of the disturbance, was branded by the vigilantes with lighted cigarettes and chased out of town. The San Diego jails resounded with the strains of "Hallelujah, I'm a Bum!" An official investigating committee sent by Governor Hiram Johnson turned in a report that blistered the forces of "law and order." After a clash in which one rebel was killed and two policemen wounded, the authorities backed down.

The struggle at Everett, four years later, was short and brutal. Three hundred Wobblies, protesting in behalf of A. F. of L. strikers and singing, "Hold the fort, for we are coming," journeyed by tugboat from Seattle to the port of Everett. Here they were met by armed deputies and Chamber of Commerce vigilantes. Seven Wobblies were killed and thirty-three wounded. The toll on the other side—only a few of the Wobblies were armed—was two dead and sixteen wounded. Over seventy Wobblies were arrested, charged with murder, some of them brutally tortured; but they won their fight. Free speech reigned in Everett.

The national reaction to these and other manifestations of the boldness and militancy of the new unionists was instantaneous and, among conservatives and radicals alike, violently emotional. To the former, the Wobblies, or "I Won't Works" as they termed them, were the very personification of criminal lawlessness, a menace to everything from the sacred rights of property to the sanctity of the American home. To the radicals —at least to the majority of them and especially to the more impatient, romantic temperaments in their midst—they epitomized the flaming rebel spirit and brought back to the American radical scene a fire and color which had been lacking since the spectacular rise and fall of communist-anarchism in the '80s. Not that the I.W.Ws, despite the enthusiasm they aroused in the average radical breast, were not subject to sharp and oftentimes scathing criticism by the assorted radicals outside their ranks. There were plenty of holes in the Wobbly armor and sharpshooters at points as far apart as Daniel De Leon and Victor Berger managed to find them with frequency and precision. Nevertheless, in discussing the Wobblies, the radical critic as a rule had to be almost totally blinded by partisan zeal not to allow a note of admiration to creep in. Whatever their shortcomings, and that they were many is a fact which almost any intelligent Wobbly today will admit, for sheer courage in action, for the ability to fight hard and, for the most part, openly and cleanly, and for their capacity —an attribute which more than any other perhaps won them the respect and loyalty of a considerable section of the American proletariat—to "take it on the chin," they have a record unparalleled in American radical history.

From a membership of 5,000 in 1908, the I.W.W. grew until it had at one time approximately 75,000 workers in its ranks; but it was always such a loosely-knit organization that such figures meant little. No other American radical organization has had such sudden ups and downs, has harbored such an unstable, restless rank and file. The average annual turnover in membership during the I.W.W's most active years has been estimated at 133 per cent and up to 1931 almost a million and a quarter red cards had been issued!

There was a considerable number of Wobblies who realized the significance of such figures and attempted to build on more solid foundations than those offered by the migratory, shifting elements which played such a dominant rôle in shaping policies and tactics. Most of these were centered around the Chicago headquarters or points east and became known as the "headquarters' group" or "job-ites" by the Westerners who regarded them with considerable antagonism. The headquarters' group, faced with conditions in the industrial East, naturally wanted to broaden the scope of the organization and

[ 262 ]

stabilize it by developing a program for settled industrial workers who were not in a position to wage incessant guerrilla warfare against "the bosses," to establish some degree of internal discipline and centralized control. The western rank and file, who were closer to the anarchist tradition, stood for decentralization. The controversy, variously called "the hoboes versus the home guards" and "the hall-cats versus the job-ites" ("hall-cats" referred to the homeless, migratory and often jobless element, which, having nothing else to do, hung about I.W.W. halls engaging in endless argument about the Revolution), became extremely heated at times, notably in 1913 and 1924. But even as early as 1909 the differences between the two groups were already acute.

An organization which taps the human reservoir at as low a level as did the I.W.W. is bound to draw off some of the dregs. The Wobblies drew to themselves many of the most courageous and unselfish fighters the revolutionary struggle has ever known, but they also attracted, inevitably, during their pre-war years, a certain number of opportunistic hangers-on, "panhandlers," "bums," and even a small semi-criminal fringe which found in the doctrine of sabotage a philosophic rationalization of its own personal impulses and practices. (When the organization's supreme test came in 1917, these were to desert it like rats leaving a sinking ship.)

The Wobblies' indiscriminate methods of recruiting, their low dues in comparison with the A. F. of L. unions', their willingness to take in anybody, so long as he wore overalls or showed familiarity with the seamy side of life, drew into their ranks thousands who had no real interest in, or understanding of, their aims; and, unlike the modern Communists, the Wobblies made little attempt to curb or direct these members by setting up internal discipline. Their informal and indiscriminate methods of recruiting are well illustrated by what they called "box-car unionization," though this particular method of adding to the rank and file was later repudiated. Wobblies,

[ 263 ]

finding themselves aboard some freight with time hanging heavy on their hands, would set out to "unionize" their fellow travelers. If the latter were not amenable to reason, they were likely to find themselves leaving the train at inconvenient times and places. It was almost impossible at certain periods for any itinerant to move about the West without a red card.

The rowdy, undisciplined, "I'm-a-Bum-ism" of the Wobblies, however much a source of inspiration and joy it may have been to the underdog of the camp, the box car, the "skid-road," was probably one of the organization's chief weaknesses in industrial communities where the average worker does not want to be a "bum." Moreover, the "bum" philosophy helped to weaken the morale within its own ranks, despite the unquestionable integrity of a large proportion of its members. So did the espousal of sabotage as a revolutionary weapon. No revolutionary movement is ever so idealistic and "pure" that weapons developed for use against the despised "capitalist class" will not—in times of internal stress—be turned to use by contending factions against each other. The Wobblies were no exception, and in their struggles with rival groups in the labor movement and even among themselves they resorted at times to the most deadly weapons in the syndicalist arsenal.

Yet, whatever their faults, the Wobblies had the saving grace of their lusty, Rabelaisian humor and their unquestioned courage. Their bark was usually worse than their bite. There was a blustering Paul-Bunyan-like quality about them. A little more effort to think things through, a little more brain-work and a little less action, undoubtedly would have stood them in good stead; but their lack of hairsplitting, fanaticism and religiosity made them good company. The American radical scene, to anyone who was familiar with it when the Wobblies were a force to be reckoned with, has seemed, ever since their decline, more than a little lonely.

# XI

## DISSENTERS' GOLDEN AGE

IF A graph were made of the rise and decline in America of that quality of mind which, for want of a better term, may be called "social consciousness," the peak unquestionably would occur in the year 1912. The wave of insurgency that had been rising since 1900 and that was finally to break on the rocks of the World War reached its crest in the year in which Roosevelt ran for President on a platform of Social Righteousness, Wilson unfurled the banner of the New Freedom, Debs polled 900,000 votes without benefit of national woman suffrage, the Lawrence strike put the word "syndicalism" on the front page of every newspaper, and Emma Goldman became one of the most popular lecturers on the American platform.

It was an extraordinary year in other ways, as Floyd Dell has pointed out in his recent autobiography:

It was a year of intense woman-suffragist activity. In the arts it marked a new era. Color was everywhere—even in neckties. The Lyric Year . . . contained Edna St. Vincent Millay's 'Renascence.' In Chicago, Harriet Monroe founded Poetry. Vachel Lindsay suddenly came into his own with 'General William Booth Enters Into Heaven' . . . 'Hindle Wakes' startled New York as it was later to startle Chicago. The Irish Players came to America. It was then that plans were made for the Post-Impressionist Show which revolutionized American ideas of art. In Chicago Maurice Brown started the Little Theatre. One could go on with evidences of a New Spirit come suddenly to birth in America.

Between 1910 and 1917 there were probably few intelligent Americans under forty who did not profess to some form of social, economic or artistic heterodoxy. To be a socialist, a syndicalist, an anarchist, a feminist or, at the very least, a left-wing liberal was merely to be in tune with the pre-war sociological infinite. The full flowering of the intellectual, artistic and "sexual" revolution did not occur until a few years after the sociological peak of 1912. It came at a time when the *Masses* had hit its full stride. But the Golden Age had begun in 1910; and in the pre-war years that followed, the release of such a flood of intellectual and artistic protest as the country had never seen before gave to the period the aspect of a radical renaissance. The intellectual, the artist, the poet, the journalist, the clergyman are the most articulate of rebels and a few such swallows can do more to create the illusion of summer than swarms of worker bees. The battles that were fought at San Diego and Everett, at Lawrence, Paterson and Ludlow, in the garment districts of New York and Chicago, were no more significant certainly than those of Cripple Creek and Homestead in the '90s, or of Pittsburgh, Passaic and Gastonia in a decade yet to come. But they were fought against a sounding-board of such far-flung and varied support and interest, such eloquent and picturesque championship, that they assumed epic proportions. It was the period in which art, journalism and the world of fashion discovered the Revolution; when large sections of the restive middle classes and smaller sections of the bored upper classes began looking to the left for release or for stimulation; when poets, playwrights, clergymen, editors and social leaders mounted soap-boxes or marched in picket lines to participate vicariously in the class struggle. When a popular monthly with its ear to the ground and its control vested in Harry Payne Whitney embraced the Coöperative Commonwealth, when Joseph Medill Patterson joined the Socialist Party and a Rockefeller pastor resigned from his pulpit to do likewise, when young Harvard men like John Reed embraced anarchism and arranged pageants for Paterson silk strikers, when Bill Haywood became the idol of Mabel Dodge's salon, the Revolution was looking up, socially speaking. It was also "news" in a sense in which it had never been before.

A history of that flight to the left that occurred between 1910 and the 1917 deluge might be written in terms of its journalism and of its various well-publicized intellectual activities in New York alone—the struggles of the New York *Call* as a Socialist daily, the brief and amazing capitulation of the *Metropolitan*, the tentative and timid radicalism of *Life* in 1912, the founding of the *Masses* and the revolt in Greenwich Village, Frank Harris' pursuit of Sex, Literature and the Revolution through the pages of *Pearson's*, the red romanticism of *Mother Earth* under Goldman and Berkman, the Marxian intellectualism of the *New Review*, the emergence of the *New Republic* to the right, and the brave beginning of the *Seven Arts*. It could also be told in terms of the Rand School with its classes of eager young boys and girls garnered from Kansas, Chicago, the lower East Side and the Bronx to imbibe the fundamentals of Marxism, of labor unionism and occasionally of folk-dancing; of the Ferrer School with its bright array of anarchist poets and painters; of Percy Stickney Grant's Sunday Night Forums, the Rev. Norman Guthrie's various radical gestures.

But though dozens of clergymen, hearing "the Call of the Carpenter," slammed church doors behind them and went about "arousing the lowly," though intellectuals and near-intellectuals left safe academic and editorial berths to become pamphleteers, agitators and radical educators, and though Art and Beauty danced for the Revolution at Webster Hall, all this was only part of the picture. The harder—and dirtier—work of the Revolution was being carried on elsewhere.

John Graham Brooks wrote in *American Syndicalism: The I. W. W.* in 1912: "No one can examine with any care the socialist leadership as it appears in political and other activities without seeing that we have to do with a movement that is in no proper sense 'foreign.' " And quoting a railway magnate to the effect that the only practical issue of the day was to "stave socialism off as long as possible," Brooks concludes: "There is much reason to believe that Socialism in its most revolutionary character is from now on to have its most fruitful field in the United States."

The radicals thought so too.

The socialistic drift that, for a time, seemed destined to become a landslide began in 1910 when Milwaukee went socialistic and Victor Berger was elected to Congress. The following year, Schenectady and a score of smaller cities and towns fell to the "reds." Among the Socialist officials in Schenectady was the General Electric Company's wizard, Charles Steinmetz. (The mayor's secretary was a young Harvard man named Walter Lippmann.) Throughout the country there were more than a thousand Socialists in office. Almost overnight, American socialism had passed into a new phase—a phase which the European radical parties had reached many years before. The problems of agitation for the Revolution were now complicated by problems of actual administration —a very different matter. It is a point at which all revolutionary movements make a definite turn to the right.

With its political successes there came, too, such floods of publicity—hostile, favorable, objective—as the bewildered radicals had never hoped to enjoy. Socialism became the favorite topic of magazine editors, the subject of sermons, lectures and of academic theses. A serial debate between Morris Hillquit and Father John J. Ryan ran in *Everybody's* under the title *Socialism—Promise or Menace*. "Prepare for Socialism" declared a leading article in the *Atlantic Monthly*. Sunday supplements ran riot with melodramatic radical symposia. The Socialist press flourished with five daily papers (one in

Lead, South Dakota, and another in Belleville, Illinois),
262 weeklies, and ten monthlies.

In the beneficent sunshine of so much attention, the party
membership expanded to nearly 120,000, its rolls bristled
with well-known names—literary, journalistic, academic,
theological—and the first gesture of protest that occurred to
the fledgling radical was to "join the Socialist Party." While
anarchism was still the more *recherché* movement, the Social
Registers of both New York and Boston were represented in
the party's left wing. But more important than any of this
was the fact that radical successes within the labor unions
were adding many a gray hair to the head of Gompers. In the
summer of 1911, just before the McNamara confession, the
radical bloc in the A. F. of L. convention polled a third of all
the votes cast for its candidate running against Gompers.

All this activity could not fail to impress the American
literary consciousness, and though the result was usually far
from happy from the literary point of view, a small but growing group of writers supplied the movement with some fairly
good fictional tracts. To the novels of Sinclair and London
could now be added Arthur Bullard's *Comrade Yetta* which
celebrated the birth and struggles of the New York *Call* and
the trials of the East Side clothing worker, Susan Glaspell's
*The Visioning*, several volumes by Reginald Wright Kauffman
and James Oppenheim, some of Fannie Hurst's early East
Side stories. Though David Graham Phillips was not an
avowed socialist, his two-volume *Susan Lenox* was hailed as
a sweeping indictment of "the system." Even Zoe Beckley,
who later introduced Queen Marie of Roumania to the
American public, turned out a light but purposeful little
propaganda novel celebrating the Rand School. Far above
all of these, as both literature and propaganda, stood Ernest
Poole's *The Harbor*. As is the case with so many autobiographical studies, it has remained its author's best book. The
story of its hero—his vague unrest, his coming into contact

with social and industrial realities in the great strike that ties up his beloved harbor, his hesitating conversion, his final immersion in that struggle—is the story of thousands of young, sensitive, groping middle-class men and women who in this period found themselves caught up by the tides of labor unrest and radical enthusiasms and plunged headlong into a movement which they but vaguely understood. It is a situation which was to repeat itself in the early 1930s.

The most astonishing evidence of the seriousness with which this leftward drift was being taken in high places was the conversion of the *Metropolitan Magazine*. Early in 1912, this most grandiloquent of popular monthlies announced that it had undertaken to "give socialism a hearing." It was somewhat as if the *Ladies' Home Journal* had united with Hearst's *Cosmopolitan* to endorse the Communist Party in 1932. That its backers, including the plutocratic Mr. Whitney, were merely sniffing the direction of the whirlwind and were preparing to ride it, the deterministic socialists never doubted for a moment. Nevertheless, when their leading spokesmen were invited to unburden themselves between pages of Richard Harding Davis, Fannie Hurst, Arnold Bennett, James Huneker, H. G. Wells and F. P. A., they were delighted at the opportunity to carry the battle into the camp of the enemy. Among the new radical contributors were Morris Hillquit, Algernon Lee (with a monthly column); W. J. Ghent, who envisaged fascism years before Mussolini or Hitler ever dreamed of it; Professor George D. Herron and Helen Keller. John Reed was roving correspondent and wrote from Mexico on "Villa, the Man of Destiny." Art Young sent monthly cartoons from Washington.

With its quarter of a million circulation (soon to mount to a million) the *Metropolitan* set out to convert the American business man, and incidentally its advertisers, to the proposition that the "social freedom" it advocated would mean "prosperity for all." Rebuking the merely progressive journals for their timidity, it remarked, unctuously: "They are innocuous; we are dangerous."

It was not, however, dangerous enough for the Socialists who were becoming increasingly irritated by its evasions and pretenses. Hillquit wrote an article—which the editors nobly published—in which he denounced the magazine's socialism as merely "vague humanitarianism." Socialism, he insisted, was a definite and concrete program "based on the class struggle." The editors replied that they abhorred the notion of the class struggle. The alliance was doomed. A year later "the Met" became the organ of Theodore Roosevelt and the preparedness patriots. In 1915 it sent John Reed, Fannie Hurst and Boardman Robinson to Europe as its war correspondents.

While the *Metropolitan* was flirting with socialism, *Life* had become a snug harbor for a number of radical cartoonists and humorists who were later to blossom forth in the *Masses*. Some of its drawings, notably "The Hand of Fate" by William Balfour Ker, would have damned it as anarchistic only a few years before.

While the Socialist band-wagon was becoming crowded, the I.W.W. was recovering from the blow to its strength dealt it by the defection of the Western Federation of Miners. At Lawrence, Massachusetts, in 1912, it caught the attention of the entire nation and set a pattern for all radically-led mass strikes thereafter.

The Lawrence strike began with the spontaneous walkout of thousands of unorganized textile workers, belonging to seven different nationalities, as a protest against a wage-cut. Within a few days, an I.W.W. organizer from New York, named Joe Ettor, appeared on the scene. He was soon joined by Arturo Giovannitti, the Italian poet and editor of *Il Proletario* in New York, and between them they organized the strikers. When they were arrested and jailed as "accessories before the act," after a girl picket had been shot in a riot, Bill

Haywood, Elizabeth Gurley Flynn, Carlo Tresca and William Trautmann came to Lawrence to take charge. The strike was dramatized as only the Wobblies could dramatize it—battles between police and strikers, mass picket lines, huge mass meetings, revolutionary songs, flying banners, nation-wide publicity and appeals for support. Food, clothing, money poured in from the united radicals and liberals throughout the country. Victor Berger hammered in Congress for a Congressional investigation. Lawrence and the I.W.W. became front page news in every daily paper.

The cause of the textile workers has always been one to arouse quick sympathy even among the fairly conservative. The industry was still tarred with the brush of early nineteenth-century industrial barbarity. In the public mind it was associated with the horrors of the industrial revolution. Liberals protested, clergymen denounced the mill owners, wealthy clubwomen came to Lawrence—some of them all the way from California—to observe the battle and to offer their services as pickets. Feature writers arrived on every train. Public sympathy reached a climax when the children of the strikers, who were being sent to friends of the cause in other cities in order that they might be well cared for, were torn from their parents at the railway station by Lawrence police, the parents beaten and arrested. The Congressional investigation was voted.

The fateful note of the Lawrence strike [writes John Graham Brooks] was not in that distracted city. It was in the impression made on almost every outside investigator. It was in the throb of fellow-feeling, not for managers or for stock-holders, but for strikers deprived of organization. In more than eighty articles in every variety of publication from the *Atlantic Monthly* to the great dailies, this sympathy appeared.

The strike was won in March with an increase in wages. The Wobblies had won their first major battle with capitalism. The American public had learned a new word—"syndicalism." The movement was riding high. The *Nation* commented in May of that year:

Seldom has publicity come so suddenly and so lavishly to any movement as to the Syndicalist movement. Before the Lawrence strike and for several weeks after the strike was underway, there must have been very few people in this country who knew what the Syndicalist theory stands for and what was the I.W.W. organization in which the Syndicalist philosophy is embodied in this country. Today there is little excuse for ignorance on that subject.

There was even less excuse when, in the following year, the great silk strikes in Paterson, New Jersey, repeated the drama of Lawrence, and again brought the Wobblies into the headlines. In Paterson, both I.W.Ws, the Detroit and Chicago factions, were active, hurling recriminations at each other's heads. But so far as the public was concerned, the I.W.W. spelled the followers of Bill Haywood.

In November, 1912, Ettor and Giovannitti, now national figures, were acquitted of the charges against them. In the same month, Eugene V. Debs polled 900,000 votes. His gains were phenomenal in the Far West, smaller proportionately in New York; but after this year, the party's center of gravity swung eastward. Twice later, in 1920 and 1932, the radical vote was to rise to a slightly higher level, but only after woman suffrage had doubled the number of voters.

At the very height of their strength and influence, the radical forces were subjected to the strain of a major internal conflict—the great sabotage controversy that helped to sever the ties that had bound the political actionists and the revolutionary unionists together.

Although the I.W.W., as an organization, had taken a definitely anti-political turn in 1908, thousands of its members still voted the Socialist ticket and many remained members of the party. Haywood was on the party's National Executive Committee. But by 1912, and particularly just after the

Lawrence strike, anarcho-syndicalist influence was at its height. It had captured the imaginations of some of the most articulate and eloquent of the left-wing intellectuals. It had become, in fact, the new radical fashion. The philosophy was to have its purest expression later in a comparatively insignificant movement supported by the anarchists and led by William Z. Foster, but it came nearer to claiming the industrial unionists and American intellectuals as its own at this time than in any other period.

When the intellectual, the artist, the member of the leisure class turns to the left, he usually turns to the extreme left. In socialism, he was usually to be found in the extreme left wing from whence he turned enthusiastically to syndicalism. In communism, he is more likely to be a Trotskyist than a Stalinist. Action, color, drama, the uncompromising defy, the extreme revolutionary gesture are more likely to fire his imagination and fit his mood than the dull, plodding business of building step by step, of zigzagging progress. The dramatic fight of the I.W.W. at McKees Rocks had as early as 1908 aroused the enthusiasm of many left-wing writers. By 1912, André Tridon (principal exponent of French syndicalism in America, who was later to become a psychoanalyst), William English Walling, Robert Rives La Monte; John Macy, the literary critic; Frank Bohn and other radical journalists were familiarizing the American radicals with the theories of the French syndicalist philosophers. Though Haywood had brought back with him from France the germs of syndicalist theory, they had done little more than strengthen an already existing anti-political drift in the I.W.W. Now, however, radical discussions bristled with French words and phrases—*sabotage, la grève générale,* etc. A practice which wage-workers had always indulged in more or less instinctively, but had rarely talked about, was elevated, verbally at least, to the status of a major tactic. Pouget's book, translated into English, sought to define the meaning and philosophy of the term "sabotage." It could mean, in fact, almost anything which "slowed up" production, from loafing on the job to ruining the product or putting the machinery out of order. But hoarse-voiced soap-boxers, expounding it to lumberjacks, miners and harvest hands throughout the West in the typical I.W.W. idiom, embellished it according to their own temperamental biases. In California a little group of Wobblies started a publication called the *Wooden Shoe* which contained dark references to the "sab-cat." Farmers, small-town business men, chiefs of police saw, heard and were horrified. Most of it was sheer talk, the western Wobbly's instinctive sardonic bravado, his "bad-man" hangover. But the organization was to reap the fruits of this verbiage in 1917 and after, while the A. F. of L., which has undoubtedly practiced more sabotage than the I.W.W. ever talked about, was reaping the fruits of its discretion.

All this anarcho-syndicalist heresy, particularly when expounded by the violently outspoken Haywood, was certain to arouse the ire of the bulk of the Socialist membership, especially now that the party's parliamentary tendency had been strengthened by political victories. It had taken them years to dissociate themselves from anarchism in the public mind. Now the ghost of Bakunin seemed stalking again. A speech made by Haywood at Cooper Union brought the matter to a head. An amendment to the party constitution outlawing the advocacy of sabotage and other forms of violence was proposed. The left-wing forces, including the group of writers gathered about the *International Socialist Review*, rallied about Haywood to defeat the measure. Right and center united to support it, as did a few of the more radical leaders who believed that the advocacy of sabotage as a *doctrine* had a demoralizing effect upon the workers, that it encouraged reliance on guerrilla tactics rather than upon class solidarity, and invited the attention of *agents provocateurs*. This last view was expressed by Debs who, while agreeing with Haywood's contention that the worker need have "no respect for the property rights of the profit-takers," went on to say:

> This does not imply that I propose making an individual law-breaker of myself. . . . I am opposed to sabotage and "direct action." I have not a bit of use for the "propaganda of the deed." These are the tactics of anarchist individualists, not of socialist collectivists. . . . My chief objection to all these measures is that they do violence to the class psychology of the workers and cannot be successfully inculcated as mass doctrine.

The amendment passed and the following year Haywood was recalled from the Socialist Executive Committee.

The sabotage quarrel was the culmination of a growing irritation between two radical groups that had been rapidly moving in opposite directions while their membership continued to overlap. It was a misfortune for both groups. Socialistic influence within the I.W.W., which had been, on the whole, a steadying influence, dwindled; the syndicalist tendency, less attuned to the realities of an increasingly mechanized environment, was temporarily strengthened. On the other hand, the withdrawal of Haywood was accompanied by a decline within the Socialist Party of its more militant and uncompromising elements which had acted as a check upon the swing to the right. That such a fierce and far-reaching battle should have been staged upon a comparatively irrelevant and passing issue is typical of at least half the internal struggles among the radicals. In 1917, the sabotage clause was removed from the Socialists' constitution as "no longer an issue." Three years later the I.W.W. declared at its twelfth convention that the organization "does not and never has believed in or advocated either destruction or violence as a means of accomplishing industrial reforms" and went on to explain its attitude in words that were reminiscent of those used by Debs in 1912.

While the syndicalist issue was racking the socialists, a division was occurring among the syndicalists themselves. In

[ 276 ]

1911, the I.W.W. had sent as a delegate to the International Trades Union Conference at Budapest a young man who had joined the organization in 1909 after expulsion from the Socialist Party. This was William Z. Foster. In Europe, Foster, like Haywood before him, came into close contact with the French syndicalists, who—unlike their American comrades—worked within the existing trade unions. Foster returned convinced of the folly of "dual unionism." Failing to convert the I.W.W. to the policy of "boring from within" the A. F. of L., he resigned and, together with a group of anarchists and some scattered radical unionists, formed the Syndicalist League of North America. The anarchists, with their fear of any centralized authority, had never looked with much favor upon the I.W.W., decentralized as that organization was. They supported the new League with enthusiasm. It was, according to *Mother Earth*, "an organization of active propagandists formed for the purpose of spreading the ideas of syndicalism, direct action and the general strike among the organized and unorganized workers in America." Its influence remained negligible, although later, when its name was changed to Trade Union Educational League, it enlisted the support of a much larger body of radical unionists. It was as the head of this latter organization that Foster caught the eye of Moscow in 1920 as the man best fitted to lead the trade union cohorts of communism in America and his organization, passing through another metamorphosis, became the Trade Union Unity League, the American division of the Red International of Labor Unions in Moscow.

By 1912 the activities of the anarchists were largely educational. As a group, they had graduated from the conspiratorial stage and they were probably attracting more artists and poets than workingmen. They were, on the whole, rather more charming, colorful and exciting as personalities than the rank and file of either socialism or syndicalism. These last were, or aimed to be, mass movements. Anarchism stressed the individual. If it drew a larger lunatic fringe than any other type of radicalism, it did so for the same reason that it also drew the artist, the idealist, the mystic, the bohemian. It was, socially speaking, the extreme gesture, and this was a gesture which also recommended itself to the social dilettante, the revolutionary play-boy and play-girl. Though its leaders and devoted workers were anything but dilettantes, there were plenty such who fluttered in their wake.

In 1911, with the Rand School booming as a center of socialistic light and learning, a little group of New York anarchists established the Ferrer School in memory of the Spanish educator, Francisco Ferrer, who had been executed two years before by the Spanish government. Its moving spirits were two gentle and indefatigable laborers in the anarchist vineyard, Leonard Abbott, an associate editor of *Current Literature* (and formerly on the staff of the *Literary Digest*), and Harry Kelly, who had assisted Peter Kropotkin on the anarchistic *Freedom* in London. The school started in an old building on Twelfth Street near Fourth Avenue with two teachers and one pupil, but the accession of the three Konrad Bercovici progeny—Free Love, Gorky and Liberty—and of four other budding young anarchists soon raised the attendance to eight. Adult classes were highly successful from the start. Will Durant, fresh from a Jesuit seminary and in the first throes of his radical enthusiasms, took over the instruction of the younger brood, all of whom had been raised without benefit of discipline. Manuel Komroff was the school's secretary; Lola Ridge, the poet, its organizer. Robert Henri and George Bellows donated their services for the art classes. A number of other well-known artists both attended and taught. Though the school soon became the rendezvous of all the more extreme New York radicals, Abbott managed to gather a large list of distinguished lecturers. By this time, too, Freud had been translated, Havelock Ellis and Ellen Key were the authors of the hour, and in general sex was taking on a seriously revolutionary air. Manuel Komroff, whose bottomless store of affectionate Ferrer School memories is a source of unending delight to radical gatherings in a less wide-eyed decade, recalls an occasion on which young Durant undertook to speak on this very subject to the assembled comrades. At the conclusion of his address, an earnest little cloak-maker arose from her chair at the rear of the hall and announced indignantly:

"Comrade Speaker, you talk about revolution, but I been in this here sexual movement for over twelve years and I ain't seen no progress yet."

In 1915, the school was moved to a farm at Stelton, New Jersey. Many of the families of its thirty pupils settled in the neighborhood and something of a colony was formed. The school's character became less specifically anarchistic, more generally radical and experimental. It still flourishes.

In the year 1913, a new note could be heard in the revolutionary symphony. It was a gay note. The year was one of depression, of losses of membership by both socialists and syndicalists; and in the grim winter of 1913-14, there were bread riots on the East Side, unemployed demonstrations throughout the country, and in New York City Frank Tannenbaum and a few other Wobbly leaders led the unemployed from Rutgers Square to St. Alphonsine's Church demanding food and shelter. The churchmen and the newspapers called for police clubs, but over at St. Marks-in-the-Bouwerie, the intrepid descendant of Fanny Wright and his Socialist Fellowship fed the rioters.

But this was also the year in which the Revolution discovered the lighter (and possibly baser) side of its nature and learned to laugh. It marked the wedding of humor and economics, sex and sociology, Freud and Marx. Greenwich Village, and its little replicas throughout the country, became aware of the class struggle; and though the class struggle was to be no less grim and unrelenting for that fact—as witness Ludlow, Colorado, a year later—it was to be embroidered with satire and poetry, irony and art. The responsibility for this new note lay chiefly with the *Masses*.

The *Masses* had begun its career back in 1911, first under the editorship of Thomas Seltzer and then of Piet Vlag, a former cook in the Rand School restaurant. But it was not until early 1913 that it assumed the policy, format and editorship that were to make it the chief organ of that whole vaguely social-minded literary and artistic upheaval that marked the years between 1912 and 1917. The spirit of that upheaval, as described later by James Oppenheim, expressed itself in "Socialism, sex, poetry, conversation, dawn-greeting, anything so long as it was taboo in the Middle West."

Writing of the period in her anthology of *Masses* and *Liberator* poetry, *May Days,* Genevieve Taggard remembers that—

The air was clear and exciting and the hour was the hour of seven on a spring morning. May Days indeed. . . . Dignity was not the fashion. Boredom, ennui were not the fashion. There was so much to be said, done, thought, seen, tried out. The youth of the land was getting out of doors and all the winter taboos were being broken.

> Bliss was it in that dawn to be alive
> But to be young was very heaven.

With Max Eastman, just resigned from Columbia University, at the helm, the *Masses* stated a credo that was to set the tone of the new literary and artistic sophistication, a sophistication which in a post-war and depression world fairly blushes with youth and innocence.

A free magazine owned and published coöperatively by its editors. It has no dividends to pay and nobody is trying to make money out of it. A revolutionary and not a reform magazine; a magazine with a sense of humor and no respect for the respectables; frank, arrogant; impertinent; searching for the true causes; a magazine directed against rigidity and dogma wherever it is found; printing what is too naked and true for a money-making press; a magazine whose final policy is to do what it pleases and conciliate nobody, not even its readers. There is a field for this publication in America. Help us find it.

But for all its defiant "a revolutionary and not a reform magazine," for all its proletarian title, the *Masses*' appeal was not to the worker, but to the restless and yearning sections of the middle, intellectual classes, just beginning to greet the dawn of a new day. It was "caviar to the general," too playful for the actual class struggler. For those who had time to be both gay and rebellious, it led the way. To the older of these, it gave a sense of pleasurable shock; to the younger, a sense of pleasurable wickedness and daring. To quote Miss Taggard again:

It hit few class or economic sore spots—not because it did not aim at them but because class fear in the reader had not been genuinely aroused. . . . This magazine was so obviously the voice of a harmless minority. Although its editor pounded away at the distinction between reform and the seizure of economic power by the working class, he failed to keep them separate in the mind of the middle-class intellectual because events themselves had not yet made them separate.

*May Days* itself, with half its poems as devoid of social implications as the contents of any "pure" poetry journal, is as eloquent of the catholic tastes of the *Masses* editors as were the *Masses* drawings, ranging all the way from nudes by Pablo Picasso to the vigorous social cartoons of Boardman Robinson. The nudes, in fact, predominated, leading a cynical columnist to remark:

They draw nude women for the *Masses*
Thick, fat, ungainly lasses—
How does that help the working classes?

The ancient Art versus Propaganda controversy did not fail to rack the *Masses* staff from time to time; but the list of the magazine's contributors in its early days indicates how far this controversy came from that recriminatory stage it was to reach in the early '30s. Among the magazine's contributing artists—some of them co-editors—were Maurice Becker, George Bellows, Glenn Coleman, H. J. Glintenkamp, Jo Davidson, Arthur B. Davies, Cornelia Barns, Hugo Gellert, Robert Minor, Boardman Robinson, John Sloan, Art Young, Frank Van Sloun, Horatio Winslow. Among the writers, the variety of whose style and viewpoints was even more striking, were Sherwood Anderson, Edwin Bjorkman, George Creel, Floyd Dell, Arturo Giovannitti, Walter Lippmann, Ernest Poole, Upton Sinclair, Lincoln Steffens, Louis Untermeyer, John Reed, Will Irwin, Edna St. Vincent Millay, Mary Heaton Vorse, Susan Glaspell, James Oppenheim, Daniel Wilbur Steele, Amy Lowell, E. E. Cummings, William Ellery Leonard, Edmund Wilson, Carl Sandburg, John Dos Passos, Vachel Lindsay, Margaret Widdemer, William Rose Benét and a host of others. Howard Brubaker wrote regularly those paragraphic commentaries which are now a weekly feature of the *New Yorker*. Charles Erskine Scott Wood's ironic *Heavenly Discourses* appeared here before they were gathered into book form.

Max Eastman's editorials were probably, from the viewpoint of the Revolution, the soundest part of the *Masses* program. The tall, slender, handsome Eastman, with his prematurely gray hair, his romantic reputation, was the veritable John Barrymore of American radicalism and with his own interests divided equally between poetry and politics, art and economics, was himself the perfect embodiment of the *Masses* spirit. After the coming of Floyd Dell as managing editor in 1914, the feminist, psychoanalytic, birth-control, sexual-freedom note was emphasized. Both Eastman and Dell were feminists as well as socialists (Eastman had organized the first Men's League for Woman Suffrage and with other brave masculine souls had marched down Fifth Avenue to the jeers of their less advanced brethren) ; but Dell was especially concerned in those days with what Havelock Ellis has called "the sexual rights of women" and it was these, even more than the right to vote, which were exercising the feminine readers of the *Masses*. All over the country a Floyd Dellian youth was poring over tomes by Ellis, Stekel, Long and Robie, and candlelit tea-rooms echoed with discussion of the erogenous zones and similar intimate matters. Young women from Kansas, California, Georgia and Maine burned their candles at both ends and called upon friends and foes to see the lovely light. In such matters the note of the period was defiant, rather than flippant as in the post-war years; and for all this defiance, the Quatz' Arts gaiety at Webster Hall, the self-conscious seeking after "experience," the interminable sociological-erotic conversations, it was, unlike the post-war moral and social nihilism that succeeded it, essentially "wholesome."

Through the pages of the *Masses*, in cartoons, caricatures, articles, poems, editorials, marched the pageant of America's pre-war years—as seen through youthful radical eyes—usually gay, sometimes tragic, but always exciting. The great suffrage parade down Fifth Avenue with Inez Milholland, the beauty of the woman's movement, astride a great white horse; the Provincetown Players in a Macdougal Street stable under the guidance of George Cram Cook; Margaret Sanger's first birth-control agitations, her arrest, and later—when the movement had gained more support—a great birth-control meeting in Madison Square Garden; the organization of the powerful Amalgamated Clothing Workers under the leadership of Sidney Hillman as an independent industrial union of the formerly helpless and driven sweatshop workers; the invasion of Mexico, the growth of the *Forward* under Abraham Cahan.

Here, too, was the grim story of Ludlow, Colorado, where two years of bitter and violent struggle in the coal fields dominated by the Rockefeller interests culminated when the militia fired upon and then set fire to the tent colony occupied by the families of the striking miners, killing thirteen women and children. A wave of horror swept the country. In an East Side tenement three young anarchists were blown up as they were manufacturing a bomb intended, so it was claimed, for John D. Rockefeller. Upton Sinclair and a group of friends picketed the Rockefeller offices on lower Broadway. The United States Commission on Industrial Relations, under Frank P. Walsh, then investigating labor conditions and industrial disturbances throughout the country, called John D. Rockefeller Jr. to the stand. The whole subject of the Colorado coal situation was uncovered in a series of dramatic sessions. It was an experience the younger Rockefeller was never to forget. The Rockefeller dynasty suddenly became aware of public opinion. But the oil family was not the only one to have its nose rubbed in the muck of American industrial realities. The hearings of the Industrial Commission were anything but orthodox and they drew the indignant fire of conservatives and liberals alike. The *Nation* raved at its rough-and-ready tactics and denounced Walsh as a "blatherskite." Academic social work circles, with their fetish of "scientific objectivity," were equally shocked. But the Commission, or at least part of it, with its experienced and irreverent publicity staff, was out to present the nation with a picture of the seamy side of its industrial life—and it did it. J. Pierpont Morgan, Bill Haywood, Samuel Gompers, ditch diggers, soap-boxers, efficiency experts, miners, social workers, union organizers followed one another on the witness stand. Never before had the cream of America's financial, industrial and social aristocracy found itself in such close proximity to the sources of its well-being. At one hearing the venerable and dignified R. Fulton Cutting found himself listening to the story of a Polish striker from the agricultural fertilizer company in which he, like the Rockefeller Foundation, was a controlling stockholder and which had recently cut wages to $1.60 a day. If American capitalism developed

[ 284 ]

a "social conscience" about this time, it was largely as a result of the Commission's hearings.

But meanwhile war had cast its shadow over the world.

The shock to American radicals in the month of August, 1914, came not from the war itself—unlike many of the liberals and pacifists, they did not look upon world war as "the Great Illusion"—but in the collapse of the revolutionary opposition, the triumph of nationalism over internationalism in the camp of the Revolution abroad. With the declaration of war in Europe, American socialists waited with bated breath for the reverberations of that international solidarity that was certain to be affirmed by the hosts of the Second International as it had been in 1912 when the Balkan War had threatened to engulf all of Europe. The announcement that the German socialists had voted the war credits was like a bolt from the blue. The capitulation of the Belgian and French radicals, and, a little later, of the British Labor Party had much the same effect upon the radicals in the United States as had the McNamara confession three years before. It was altogether unbelievable. War-time censorship still excluded all news of vigorous anti-war minorities in all the belligerent countries.

If only the extreme right wing of the European radicals had been reported as flocking to the colors, the news would have seemed more credible. The American right, not yet involved to any serious extent in the responsibilities and ramifications of a major national party, occupied a position considerably to the left of the German, French, British and Belgian right; and the average American socialist had always looked with a certain degree of antagonism at some of the more conservative leaders of European socialism. But what made the news that came through from Europe doubly astounding was the nature of the pro-war desertions. American radicals read of the capitulation of Gustave Hervé, the most

[ 285 ]

violent anti-militarist in Europe; of Léon Jouhoux, head of the French General Confederation of Labor and a host of other French and Italian syndicalists and anarchists; of Benito Mussolini, fiery editor of *Avanti!* and leader of the extreme left wing of Italian socialism who was already urging Italian participation in the war and who was soon to be expelled from the party. How explain the fact that Jaurès, a fairly moderate socialist lay dead from an assassin's bullet as the price of his anti-militarism while Jules Guesde, the leading revolutionary Marxian of all France had accepted a seat in the war cabinet? How account for the fact that in England, Henry Hyndman, the uncompromising old war-horse of the British Socialist Party and England's nearest approach to a Daniel De Leon, had been violently chauvinistic while the frankly opportunistic MacDonald remained a pacifist? But more amazing still was the acquiescence, a little later, of the grand old man of anarchism, Peter Kropotkin. The situation was not to be explained on a rationalistic basis. It sprang from those emotional and temperamental biases which the radicals were too prone to overlook. In America they were to be confronted with equally illogical contradictions before the war was over.

The danger that America would be drawn into the war was sensed almost immediately by both radicals and pacifists and they centered their energies on a drive to check the martial spirit. In 1915, the Socialists passed a resolution which read: "Any members of the Socialist Party, elected to office, who shall in any way vote to appropriate moneys for military or naval purposes or war, shall be expelled from the party." The aggressive Hungarian-Jewish pacifist, Rosika Schwimmer, "sold" Henry Ford the idea of the Ford Peace Ship and, gathering together the most amazing assortment of radicals, liberals, pacifists and a contingent of highly amused newspaper reporters, together with a generous sprinkling of cranks, set forth on that ill-starred and rather ridiculous venture of

1915 to pacify a warring world into a mood of sweet reason-ableness. It was a venture that was to leave Ford with a deep-rooted anti-Semitic complex which later released itself in the *Dearborn Independent* and involved him in serious legal dif-ficulties.

At first the radicals and pacifists seemed to be fighting wind-mills. In spite of his passing indignation over "the rape of Belgium," the average American was obviously all for neu-trality. Theodore Roosevelt and his friends were bellicose, of course, and their utterances found a refined echo in the *New Republic*.

The *New Republic*, by the way, furnished an interesting side-light on pre-war liberalism. It was originally conceived by Herbert Croly, Dorothy and Willard Straight as the voice of a neo-Bull Moose progressivism, but, as one of its first edi-tors, Walter Lippmann, has pointed out, the European War, which began on the day its offices opened on a quiet block in West Twenty-first Street, changed all that. By the time its first number reached the stands, "the old World of the Bull Moose was shattered." But the *New Republic* was an event. It sounded a new note in intellectual liberalism. In comparison with its style and format, the *Nation*—still under the editor-ship of Harold DeWolf Fuller—seemed absurdly stodgy. It provided a haven and a mouthpiece for a group of intellectuals who looked upon themselves as leaders of a liberal—even, at times, a daringly radical—crusade, men like Lippmann, Croly, Walter Weyl, George Soule, Francis Hackett (as liter-ary editor), Alvin S. Johnson, Philip Littell, Straight him-self. All of them were to flounder pathetically in those first eventful years of the World War, though Weyl was probably the most clear-headed of all the American Progressives. At the outset, the *New Republic* was pro-Roosevelt, anti-Wilson, adopting the attitude that America should have protested the invasion of Belgium. A little later, however, when Roosevelt began to attack Wilson and Bryan, holding them personally

[ 287 ]

responsible for the reported rape of nuns in Mexico, the *New Republic* liberals began to suspect that their hero's judgment might not be exactly sound. The reaction which set in was soon to make them as ardent converts to the New Freedom as they had been to Roosevelt's New Nationalism. After the death of Straight, Mrs. Straight established a trust fund to support the magazine and its board of editors indefinitely (a fact which caused Mencken to refer to those liberals who managed to drop anchor there as "the kept idealists of the *New Republic*"). The first editorial board was largely of Croly's choosing. Later it became self-perpetuating, vacancies being filled by the vote of the board itself.

The anti-militarism campaign, however much a mock-battle it may have been at the outset, became a grim enough affair by 1916. After the sinking of the *Lusitania*, the jingoes rallied their millions. Preparedness parades sponsored by Chambers of Commerce, patriotic societies and business clubs wound their way through flag-bedecked streets. The radicals, pacifists, friends of Irish and other freedoms staged their counter-demonstrations. But preparedness had become a burning issue. It was still respectable to oppose war as such (Wilson was to win reëlection on the slogan "He kept us out of war"), but to oppose arming for "national defense" was to be anti-American.

A tragic event in San Francisco added fresh fuel to the jingoistic flames. A bomb exploded during a preparedness parade killing ten and wounding forty persons. A private detective, employed by the power companies, saw an opportunity to turn the local tide of patriotism to good account and directed suspicion at two men whom he had been shadowing for months. One of them was a militant and energetic young radical and trade unionist, something of a lone wolf in the San Francisco labor movement—Tom Mooney; the other was an adventurous young man with no particular convictions of radicalism who had been vaguely associated with Mooney and who had once served a brief prison term after being convicted of transporting dynamite—Warren Billings. Both were arrested in an atmosphere of almost insane hysteria, tried and convicted on testimony every word of which has since proved to have been perjured. Billings was given a life sentence. Mooney was sentenced to hang. Later revelations and the intercessions of President Wilson, after the case had become an international scandal, caused Mooney's sentence to be commuted to life imprisonment. For eighteen years, the combined forces of radicalism and liberalism have hammered at the doors of Justice in a futile effort to liberate the two men. Workers have demonstrated, world-famous figures in art, literature and science have lent their influence, nationally known lawyers have donated their services to the cause. So far, all these efforts have been defeated by official cowardice in California.

The radicals were not alone in sensing the drift toward war. In September, 1915, Senator La Follette had declared:

> With our manufacturing interests extending enormous credits to the Allies, with our money interests committed to keeping the bonds of the Allied governments good, we are underwriting the success of the cause of the Allies. We have ceased to be neutral in fact as well as in name.

American industry and finance could no longer afford to have the Allies lose. But popular sentiment was still against intervention. The 1916 presidential campaign was actually fought on that issue. The Socialist candidate, Allan Benson, ran on a special anti-preparedness, anti-militarist platform. But so did Wilson, and because the war danger loomed so ominously, because Wilson's "pro-labor" record recommended him to so many wavering radicals as well as liberals, he cut heavily into the Socialist vote.

During that same eventful year when industry was humming with Allied war orders, the number of strikes throughout the country nearly drove the war news from the front pages of the daily papers. A great rail strike threatened to tie up transportation. There were undercurrents of unrest everywhere. The Irish and the Hindus were plotting their respective freedoms in New York, Boston and San Francisco and were being arrested and brought to trial for violating American neutrality. That they were being aided, in some cases, with German funds was, of course, obvious. England's extremity was their opportunity and they were making the most of it —as had the Americans in 1812. Their secret organizations, especially those of the Hindus, were honeycombed with British Secret Service representatives who reported their activities to the Department of Justice. It was all colorful, melodramatic, underground. The more Irish of the Irish-Americans, brushing up on their Gaelic and indulging in early Sunday morning rifle practice, were eagerly awaiting the proclamation of the Irish Republic. The Easter Rebellion in 1916, the execution of its leaders, including the socialist James Connelly, the arrival of the famous Irish labor leader, socialist and republican, Jim Larkin, in America, drew the Irish patriots closer to the American radicals. During all the years of his exile here, Larkin acted as a connecting link between the two groups. He was the kind of radical that is found only in Ireland. He combined Marxism with Catholicism, Irish patriotism with internationalism, irrational prejudices with economic logic. A tall, rugged figure with a gift for violent invective, a love of poetry, a strain of mysticism, a hatred for the "politician" type of Irishman both in Ireland and in America and an uncompromising honesty, he was a fish out of water in the American labor movement.

The suffragists were also busy during this year. They had divided into two camps, and the more militant section was picketing the White House, breaking into jail and following the example of the English militants generally. They were also making the suffrage issue dominant over all others, and in the presidential campaign, they supported Hughes against Wilson because Wilson had failed to push their fight with the Democratic Congressmen. There is irony, certainly, in the fact that Inez Milholland, the radical feminist, should have died as the result of overexhaustion while campaigning in the West for Charles Evans Hughes.

In March, 1917, news of the first Russian Revolution sent a thrill of hope through both radical and liberal worlds. At least, the last vestiges of absolutism were cracking. It also relieved the Allies of the moral incubus of Czarism in their crusade for world democracy. Russian exiles throughout the world began to turn their faces homeward. In New York, a dark, wiry, nervous Russian Jew who had been a leader in the 1905 Revolution and who had been contributing recently to the Russian socialist paper in New York, *Novy Mir*, but whose name was scarcely known outside Russian radical circles, was given a farewell dinner by his comrades. His name was Leon Trotsky.

In April, the United States entered the World War. Six Senators and fifty Representatives, including the Socialist, Meyer London, and the one Congresswoman, Jeannette Rankin, voted against the declaration.

# XII

## WAR AND THE RADICALS

THE swift march of events in April, 1917, introduced no such confusion into American life as that tragic sequence of July, 1914, had introduced into the lives of millions of Europeans. No invading armies thundered at our gates; no guns boomed in the distance; no tramp of armed men echoed through our streets at night. About the only hysteria that followed close upon the heels of America's plunge into the World War was to be found in the newspaper headlines. Despite the rejoicings of the militarists, the Anglophiles, the Rooseveltian liberals of the *New Republic* and the wails that went up from the pacifists and the pacific liberals who only five months before had voted for Wilson on the strength of Bryan's slogan, "He kept us out of war," it must be recorded that in the days which witnessed the launching of "the greatest crusade in all history," the American people, taken by and large, were unmistakably apathetic. From the close of that historic week in April until George Creel and his staff of high-powered publicity and advertising experts undertook the campaign to "sell" the war to the American people, an almost ominous quiet settled over the land. When the floodgates were finally unlocked, it was apparent that this period of relative calm had done nothing to decrease the fury of the torrent destined to pour through them. But the radicals already had had time to determine what their attitude toward the war was to be. Unlike their European comrades, who were so suddenly caught up in a whirlwind of wild alarms and rumors, they were, for the most part, in no mood to be stampeded. Socialists, Socialist Laborites, I.W.Ws, anarchists, all generally opposed the war and all worked out a *modus operandi* of opposition in accord with their own position and theories. All came to suffer persecution at the hands of the authorities, all had their "renegades" as they termed them.

Sensing the drift toward war, the Socialist leaders, early in 1917, sent out a call for an Emergency Convention. The delegates converged on St. Louis in April, with the obvious intention of protesting against American participation. But they were twenty-four hours too late. When the convention was called to order on April 7, the United States was technically at war.

Any doubts that may have existed about the Socialists' attitude were soon set at rest. The Committee on War and Militarism submitted three reports. The first, or majority report, drawn up by a subcommittee headed by Hillquit, was approved by a vote of 140 delegates out of the nearly 200 in attendance. It spoke in no uncertain terms:

The Socialist Party of the United States in the present grave crisis solemnly reaffirms its allegiance to the principles of internationalism and working-class solidarity the world over, and proclaims its unalterable opposition to the war just declared by the government of the United States. . . . As against the false doctrine of national patriotism we uphold the ideal of international working-class solidarity. . . . We brand the declaration of war by our government as a crime against the people of the United States and against the nations of the world. In all modern history there has been no war more unjustifiable than the war in which we are about to engage.

The manifesto went on to pledge the party to "continuous, active and public opposition to the war" . . . "unyielding opposition to all proposed legislation for military or industrial conscription . . . vigorous resistance to all reactionary measures, such as censorship of the press and mails, restrictions of the rights of free speech, assemblage . . . constant propaganda against military training . . . widespread educational propaganda to enlighten the masses as to the true relation between capitalism and war."

Two minority reports were brought in, one by Louis Boudin, a leading Marxian theoretician, and the other by John Spargo, a popular Socialist author. Boudin's resolution differed only in a few respects from that of the majority. (He could never have brought himself to sign anything, no matter how satisfactory, written by his lifelong antagonist Hillquit.) The Boudin resolution received thirty-one votes. Spargo's resolution was definitely pro-war. It received but five votes. When the majority report and a revised minority resolution (stating, in effect, that now that a state of war existed, further opposition to it was useless) were submitted to a referendum vote of the party membership, the majority report—to be known as the St. Louis Proclamation—was overwhelmingly approved. Approximately 21,000 votes were cast for it, about 350 against.

In spite of the near unanimity of its membership on the subject, the party was not to emerge unscathed from this crisis, and, as in Europe in 1914, the character and personnel of the deserting contingent was altogether surprising. It cut across right, left and center. It was completely unrelated to the previous utterances and actions of its members. With the adoption of the anti-war manifesto, or soon thereafter, the exodus of the intellectuals began. Notable among the pro-war deserters were Upton Sinclair, who was later, however, to recant publicly; A. M. Simons, who had bitterly denounced the European socialist deserters in 1914 for their "cowardedly compromise"; William English Walling and Robert Rives La Monte, the two left-wing, syndicalistic critics; W. J. Ghent; John Spargo, a right-wing author and speaker; Charles Edward Russell; Allan Benson, who had been the party's presidential candidate only the year before; J. G. Phelps Stokes, the millionaire Socialist; W. R. Gaylord, a former state senator in Wisconsin, and a group rallying around the *Appeal to Reason*, which changed its name to the *New Appeal* and became pro-war.

The degree of apostasy varied with the apostates. Simons, who claimed that the American party had been scuttled by "German nationalistic jingoes and anarchistic impossibilists," joined with Gaylord to bring the "treasonable" character of the St. Louis Proclamation to the attention of the authorities. Spargo, who as a young man in England had protested against the Boer War at the risk of his life and who as late as 1915 had stated: "It is easy to affirm international solidarity in times of peace . . . but the test of our faith comes with war and the threat of war," became the most furious of jingoes. Sinclair, in his letter of resignation, was more reasonable—and more prophetic: "I intend to go on working for Socialism as long as I can," he wrote, "and when this crisis is past, when the breakdown of the Prussian caste system seems to me to have progressed far enough, I may come back and ask you to take me in again. . . . Yours for the Social Revolution——"

The St. Louis Convention, meeting the day after war was declared, threw the deliberations of the Socialists into bold relief, but their stand was little different from that taken, officially or unofficially, by the other radical groups. In the syndicalist ranks there were no outstanding deserters among the Wobblies (most of the syndicalist intellectuals had remained in the Socialist left wing). But among the anarcho-syndicalists, William Z. Foster, then organizing the stockyard workers in Chicago for the A. F. of L., supported the pro-war position of Gompers; and even, a little later, carried on a Liberty Bond campaign in his union. Foster undoubtedly took this position with his tongue in his cheek; but later still, in 1919, when as an organizer for the steel workers in Pittsburgh he was subjected to cross-examination by a Congressional Committee on his war position, he was obliged to reaffirm his admiration for President Gompers and emphasize his own war-time patriotic services. The opportunism of 1917-18 was to plague him down into the 1930s.

If the line of demarcation between anti- and pro-war radicals cut across factional lines, it was the intellectuals in both right and left who seemed particularly vulnerable. To the former, the idealistic overtones of Wilsonianism were irresistible. To the latter, the War, like the Revolution, provided color, mass action, melodrama, and exerted that exaggerated attraction which any such spectacle has for those who lead protected, cerebral lives. Though both groups rationalized their conduct, their reactions were essentially those of the common man. They no longer saw the war as a struggle between contending capitalistic forces; it was Civilization versus Barbarism, Democracy versus Militarism, Culture versus *Kultur*. They could now stand shoulder to shoulder with Gompers who at the 1917 A. F. of L. convention declared that "as a lifelong pacifist" he was "a fighting man."

The liberal intellectuals flocked to the colors almost *en masse*. In that bitter essay on "The War and the Intellectuals" written by Randolph Bourne, that young radical-liberal whose untimely death robbed American social criticism of one of its finest minds, is recorded the intellectual debacle of the year 1917. "Only in a world in which irony is dead," writes Bourne, "could an intellectual class enter war at the head of such illiberal cohorts in the avowed cause of world-liberalism and world-democracy." The *New Republic* actually hailed the declaration of war as the demonstration of the power of an "intellectual class to shape American policy and mold American life." It considered itself, evidently, the principal organ of that class. Walter Lippmann captained the bright young lights of erstwhile progressivism and liberalism into the Military Intelligence Service, the War Industries and Labor Boards, and similar shell-proof sectors of the united democratic front. The *Nation*, not yet under the editorship of that hereditary pacifist, Oswald Garrison Villard, and in spite of its fifty-two years of liberalism, declared: "War has come, and we must all face it, steadfastly and cheerfully."

By the time the first Liberty Loan drive rolled around, the anarchist artist, George Bellows, was producing the most ferocious of the atrocity posters.

Spasmodic attacks upon the radicals began almost at once, but they did not partake of the nature of a concerted drive until after the passage of the Espionage Act on June 15, 1917. The very next day the *American Socialist* was barred from the mails and the witch-hunt was on. The Socialists, because of the widespread publicity given their anti-war declaration, the I.W.Ws, whose activities "at the point of production" were particularly obnoxious now that every emphasis was being laid upon speed of production, and the anarchists, because of their terrifying reputation, bore the brunt of the attack. Socialist headquarters in several cities were sacked by mobs of soldiers and sailors. Little Socialist and I.W.W. branches in smaller towns were driven underground or completely out of existence. The Rand School directors were indicted and fined $3,000 for publishing Scott Nearing's pamphlet, *The Great Madness*. Radical journals of every hue were denied mailing privileges. Every letter addressed to the Milwaukee *Leader* was turned back to the sender by the post-office censorship.

In July, 1,200 striking I.W.Ws and their sympathizers in Bisbee, Arizona, were corralled in a ball park by armed business men and mine officials, then herded into cattle cars and shipped out into the desert. In Tulsa, Oklahoma, seventeen of their comrades were tarred, feathered and left half-dead in barren country. In Butte, Montana, Frank Little, an I.W.W. organizer and a cripple, was dragged from his bed by masked men, taken to a railway trestle and hanged. On September 5, every I.W.W. hall in the country was raided and a few days

[ 297 ]

later over a hundred and sixty Wobblies, including Haywood, Elizabeth Gurley Flynn and Arturo Giovannitti, were rounded up in Chicago and held for trial on charges of treason.

In an article which appeared in the *Masses* at this time, John Reed, mentioning, among other matters, the holding up of that lively journal and eighteen other publications by the Post Office Department, the trial and conviction of Emma Goldman and Alexander Berkman on charges of obstructing the draft, the attack of soldiers and sailors upon the Boston Socialist headquarters and the Bisbee deportations, wrote:

> In America the month just passed has been the blackest month for freedom our generation has known. With a sort of hideous apathy the country has acquiesced in a régime of judicial tyranny, bureaucratic suppression and industrial barbarism which followed inevitably the first fine careless rapture of militarism.

The war-time persecutions were not, of course, confined to radical circles. The mildest pacifists, the most lukewarm liberals, the Germans who had always voted the Democratic or Republican ticket straight, the poor devils who were unable to buy as many Liberty Bonds as the community patriots thought they should, found themselves classed with "Reds and other traitors." In academic and clerical circles, hysteria was rampant. God, ethics, history, philosophy, culture were all on our side. To express the shadow of a doubt was treason. Consequently the stand taken by men like John Haynes Holmes, Judah L. Magnes, the liberal New York rabbi, and Norman Thomas; the critical appraisal of the government's policy by Professors J. M. Cattell and H. W. L. Dana of Columbia, stand out in bold relief. With the dismissal of Cattell and Dana from Columbia, Charles Beard resigned and even John Dewey, though thoroughly pro-war, was moved to protest. Throughout the country other men and women were dismissed from universities and secondary schools for attending pacifist meetings, ministers were unfrocked or tarred and feathered for expressing Christian doubts.

With war no longer an academic question, many of the pre-war pacifists rallied behind the President. But with the older peace societies shattered, more aggressive ones came to the fore. The most influential of these was the People's Council of America for Peace and Democracy. Its program was inspired largely by the Russian Soldiers' and Workmen's Councils which had just published their extremely sane peace demands anticipating in many respects Wilson's famous Fourteen Points. (Much was made of this "Russian origin" later by the famous Lusk Committee in a report in which everyone connected with the People's Council from Dr. David Starr Jordan to Jane Addams was set down as a "dangerous Red.") The new alliance drew pacifists, socialists, liberals, anarchists, I.W.Ws, single taxers, utopians, men and women from every walk of life, into a united front to fight for an early peace without victory. But in spite of its eminently non-treasonable program—and possibly because its 2,000,000 members and the support it received in high places made it seem particularly effective—it aroused as much frenzied opposition as the outspokenly revolutionary groups. Soldiers, sailors, Department of Justice agents descended upon its meetings. Scott Nearing, its organizer, found halls denied him in all the principal cities and was arrested in several of them. Individual members faced social ostracism and the loss of their jobs. The organization was denied the right to hold its convention in Minnesota; meeting in Illinois, the delegates were dispersed by troops.

In the Middle West, still another non-revolutionary organization, the Non-Partisan League, was being hounded with all the fury directed at the eastern anarchists. The League had been organized by A. C. Townley in 1915 when the wheat belt, and particularly North Dakota, was seething with unrest. It represented the political revolt of the farmers against

[ 299 ]

the owners of the grain elevators, the flour mills, against the bankers, the Chambers of Commerce, and it proposed to elect farmers' representatives to office by securing their nomination on the major party tickets at the primary elections. By 1918 the League had nearly 200,000 members, mostly in Minnesota, Montana, South and North Dakota, and completely controlled the last-named state, having elected the governor, Lynn Frazier, the majority of the legislature, as well as several Congressmen, in 1916. But like the People's Party in the '90s, the League's program had its industrial demands, and what was more important still at the moment, it called for a peace program that "will make an end of war by creating a world democracy . . . a United States of the World, by consent and not by conquest." To the middle-western patriots, stimulated by propaganda from Minneapolis, St. Paul and Chicago, Townley and his cohorts combined all the evils of Prussianism with the menace of Revolution. They suffered accordingly.

With the enforcement of the Conscription Act and the Espionage Law, much of the energy of the radicals and the more militant pacifists was absorbed in efforts in behalf of the conscientious objectors, free speech, free press and free assemblage. Out of the American Union Against Militarism, which had been organized to combat the preparedness propaganda of 1915-16, emerged the National Civil Liberties Bureau (now the American Civil Liberties Union), with Roger N. Baldwin as director, L. Hollingsworth Wood, a Quaker, as chairman, and Lillian D. Wald, Amos Pinchot, Crystal Eastman, A. A. Berle, Zona Gale, Norman Thomas, Jane Addams, Dr. Jordan and Rabbi Wise among its sponsors. In a pamphlet published just before the post-war red hysteria of 1919-20, listing hundreds of cases of mob violence and persecution under the espionage and treason laws, the Bureau has left us a graphic picture of those war-crazed years—German farmers whipped to make them subscribe to the Red

Cross; I.W.W. organizers, Non-Partisan Leaguers, Socialists lashed, tarred and feathered; meetings of the Friends of Irish Freedom broken up by mobs; a woman indicted under the Espionage Act for a discourteous reception to a Red Cross solicitor; Kate Richards O'Hare, a Socialist lecturer, sentenced to five years in prison for an indictment of war (she later wrote a scathing exposé of conditions in the prison at Jefferson City, Missouri, where she and Emma Goldman were incarcerated; and her charges, although almost unbelievable, were later substantiated by impartial investigators); religious pacifists of the International Bible Students Association beaten and tortured; the gentle Dr. Jordan howled down and threatened with mob violence by hoodlums in Baltimore; Rose Pastor Stokes sentenced to ten years for a letter on war profiteering; a pastor of a Mt. Vernon, New York, church arrested for refusing to ring his church bells to celebrate an Allied victory; the Minnesota Socialist candidate for governor sentenced to five years for anti-war campaign speeches; a sixty-eight-year-old farmer tarred and feathered for refusal to buy more Liberty Bonds when he had already bought $5,000 worth; an I.W.W. organizer in New Jersey hanged to a tree by the chief of police and local business men and cut down only after he had lost consciousness.

While a sobering document in the main, the Civil Liberties pamphlet had its lighter moments. A Socialist editor in Alaska went valiantly off to jail for printing the line: "We must make the world safe for democracy if we have to 'bean' the Goddess of Liberty to do it." One Waldemar Czapanski was sentenced to ten days in jail for laughing at a group of rookies drilling at the San Francisco Presidio. A New Yorker was given ninety days for spitting on the sidewalk near some visiting Italian army officers.

With the war fever at its height, radicalism or pacifism in the smaller towns and rural communities was almost suicidal.

But in the larger cities, and particularly in New York with its great foreign-born populations, the situation was less tense. Here, by force of numbers, the radicals could remain vocal. In the case of the Socialist Party, its losses in the hinterlands were more than made up for by its gains in a few big cities. In September, 1917, Max Eastman wrote in the *Masses*:

> Upton Sinclair's prediction that the Socialist Party will be wiped out of existence because it braced itself to fight something is not in accord either with probability or fact. Having dwindled to 67,000 in April, the membership of the Socialist Party increased in May and June to 81,000 and bids fair to reach 100,000 by July.

Several factors contributed to the Socialist growth at this time. The party's war opposition drew into its ranks many of the more radical pacifists. The fall of the Czar had aroused new hope in the breasts of many tired Russian-born radicals and liberals who hastened to reaffirm their faith by taking out a red card. Irish and Hindu nationalists and their many sympathizers, animated more by hatred of British imperialism than by socialistic conviction, helped to swell the Socialist audiences, and some of the more radical Irish Republicans, influenced by the socialism of Jim Larkin, even joined the party. In Wisconsin and other sections of the country with large German populations, the party also picked up, although for the most part the real pro-German was already in too dangerous a position to jeopardize himself still further by leaning even slightly to the left. Unless he happened to be a convinced radical, he usually stayed as far away from "the Reds" as possible.

In a remarkable campaign for the New York mayoralty in the fall of 1917—a campaign in which the Socialists' anti-war position was played up at immense rallies packing Madison Square Garden to the doors—Morris Hillquit polled over 150,000 votes, the highest ever recorded for a New York Socialist candidate up to that time. The Socialists caught the Tammany Tiger napping and sent ten legislators to Albany, seven members to the New York Board of Aldermen. This marked the high tide of the radicals' anti-war campaign. A new factor had now entered into the international situation. On November 7, 1917, came news of the second Russian Revolution—the Bolshevik Revolution—and the birth of the first working-class republic. Russia became the revolutionary fatherland; its cause became the cause of the international revolutionaries.

The highly idealistic proposal of "peace without victory" embodied in Wilson's Fourteen Points, issued two months later, and Germany's continued assaults upon the New Russia between the November revolution and the signing of the Brest-Litovsk treaty, turned a number of radicals, particularly the Slavic ones, violently pro-Ally. In March, 1918, the *Nation* declared that some of the "most pronounced radicals now talk of volunteering for service against the Germans." The *Masses*, meanwhile, had been suppressed; but in the *Liberator*, which had succeeded it, Eastman and Dell, burning with enthusiasm for the Soviets and disarmed by Wilson's peace proposals, announced their endorsement of "the war aims outlined by President Wilson and by the Russian People." A few months later, Eastman declared that he was "willing to take the risk of accepting him [Wilson] as a member of the Socialist Party," and began an agitation to have the party alter its St. Louis resolution. (Wilson had not yet sent American troops to Siberia.)

While the official attitude of the Socialists as expressed in the anti-war resolution was never changed, certain individual members were not unresponsive to these new currents. The party's aggressive declaration of principles had aroused no responsive echo in the breasts of the American workers now enjoying better pay and working conditions than they had ever known. Like the official labor movement, they were whooping it up for the war which brought such expanded pay envelopes, joining enthusiastically in the various red hunts. Effective "mass opposition" to the war was a revolutionary daydream. Except for what little support they received from middle-class liberals and pacifists, and from some of the foreign-born wage-earners, the Socialists and I.W.Ws were more isolated from American labor than at any time in their history. Now, with so many of the radical needle-trades workers in New York assuming a pro-Ally attitude, the gulf seemed to be widening. In New York, in particular, the *Liberator's* suggestion for the restatement of the party's war position gained momentum. The seven Socialist aldermen in New York voted to support the third Liberty Loan, justifying their vote on the ground of Germany's attacks on Russia and the nature of Wilson's peace terms. In the West, radical anti-war sentiment suffered no such abatement. There were rumors that Debs, whose emotions had been deeply stirred by the Russian upheaval, was wavering. But the now rapidly aging man soon put an end to all speculations. Taking the platform at a Socialist state convention in Canton, Ohio, he delivered a scathing two-hour denunciation of "the Junkers in the United States" as well as in Germany, praised the courage and loyalty of his imprisoned comrades, spoke warmly of the I.W.W. and the Bolsheviks and referred to patriotism as "the last refuge of a scoundrel." The speech was framed deliberately in defiance of the Espionage Act and Debs knew fully what it entailed. Two weeks later he was arrested in Cleveland, tried, convicted and sentenced to ten years in the federal penitentiary. Facing the broad-jowled, grim-faced trial judge, the old agitator, just before sentence was pronounced, declared:

Your Honor, years ago I recognized my kinship with all living beings, and I made up my mind that I was not one whit better than the meanest of earth. I said then and I say now, that while there is a lower class, I am in it; while there is a criminal element, I am of it; while there is a soul in prison, I am not free. . . .

[ 304 ]

Upon appeal, the conviction was upheld by the Supreme Court, Justice Holmes delivering the opinion. Debs was sent to Moundsville, West Virginia, and then, because of rumors that an attempt would be made to rescue him, to the more formidable bastille in Atlanta.

A year later, the Socialists, meeting in national convention in New York City, named Debs as their presidential candidate in the wildest burst of enthusiasm a radical convention had ever shown. The country was flooded with campaign posters picturing a bald, smiling man in prison garb against a background of iron bars. That year Convict 9653 received approximately a million votes, the highest number ever recorded for an American Socialist candidate.

During the closing years of the war, the federal government closed in rapidly on the radicals. Five national officials of the Socialist Party, including Victor Berger, were indicted under the Espionage Act, declared guilty and sentenced to twenty years in the federal prison at Leavenworth. Judge Kenesaw Mountain Landis, who tried the case, was later reported as saying:

> It was my great displeasure to give Berger twenty years at Fort Leavenworth. I regret it exceedingly because I believe that the laws of this country should have enabled me to have Berger lined up against a wall and shot.

Though the convictions were later set aside by the Supreme Court, Berger, who had again been elected to Congress from Wisconsin, was expelled by an almost unanimous vote when that body convened in April, 1919. He carried his fight back to his constituents and was reëlected; but again, more than a year after the Armistice, his seat was denied him.

A few weeks after the indictment of the Socialists, over a hundred I.W.W. leaders, rounded up during repeated federal raids, were brought to trial in Chicago. Among the defendants were Bill Haywood, Vincent St. John, George

[ 305 ]

Andreytchine, now a Soviet official, Ralph Chaplin and Charles Ashleigh, Wobbly poets (the latter an English dandy of a sort who worked occasionally on various capitalistic dailies) , and others comprising the brains and backbone of the organization. Nearly 10,000 specific crimes were charged against them. Ninety-three of the defendants were found guilty. Sentences, imposed by Judge Landis, ranged from twenty years to ninety days. Heavy fines were added for good measure. Haywood and some of the others appealed and after almost a year in jail were released under heavy bail. Haywood's health was poor and a twenty-year jail sentence was analogous to life. In the spring of 1921, after the loss of their appeal, Haywood and several other defendants "jumped" their bail and fled to Russia. Although many of the Wobblies resented their action, and particularly Haywood's desertion to communism, the organization assumed full responsibility for the bail. In spite of the fact that the I.W.W. was shot to pieces and barely able to maintain itself, it succeeded by prodigious effort in paying back $66,000 of the forfeited bond, which had been guaranteed by radical sympathizers. The Wobblies may have sneered at "bourgeois ethics," but in a crisis they never let their friends down.

The government's victory at Chicago was a signal for similar action all over the country and mass trials of I.W.Ws were soon under way in Omaha, Spokane, Wichita and Sacramento. They came to trial in such an atmosphere of prejudice in California that forty-three of them resorted to a "silent defense." Filing into the courtroom each day, they sat with folded arms and sealed lips, refusing to accept legal aid or to utter a single word in their own behalf.

While the Chicago trial was still under way, a lighter note was introduced into the court records of those days at the *Masses* trial. Max Eastman, Floyd Dell, the rotund and lovable Art Young and Merrill Rogers of the *Masses* staff were accused of conspiracy to violate the Espionage Act. A con-

tributor, Josephine Bell, had been included in the indictment on the basis of a poem she had written about Emma
Goldman. At the opening of the trial, Hillquit, a defense
attorney, handed the poem to the judge, claiming it contained
nothing illegal. His Honor read it and, handing it back to
Hillquit, demanded: "Do you call that a poem?"

"It's so called in the indictment, your Honor," replied
Hillquit.

"Indictment quashed," declared the judge.

All in all, the trial was a gala affair. George Creel came up
from Washington to testify in behalf of the defendants. The
courtroom was crowded with the New York intelligentsia.
The atmosphere was like that of a New York first night. Art
Young fell asleep while his case was being argued, and on
awaking, completely relaxed, dashed off a sketch of a snoring,
Kewpie-like figure of a man and labeled it: "Art Young on
trial for his life."

The jury disagreed and the *Masses* group, including John
Reed who had just returned from Russia, were tried again.
Once more the jury disagreed and the government gave up
the case as a bad job.

Although Eastman faltered in his stand during the course
of the two trials, he steadied himself at the end. In a closing
speech to the jury in his own behalf, he said, apropos of the
St. Louis declaration:

As a member of the party that adopted it, and as an American
citizen who still dares to believe in his rights, I have no hesitation
in telling you that I endorse that resolution. And although subsequently, during the last winter and spring when Germany was
invading Russia, I passed through a period of extreme doubt and
was almost ready to lay the resolution aside as an expression of
abstract principle . . . that period of doubt has passed.

> Quit your crying, baby,
> Lonely little waif,
> Papa's in an iron cage

To make your future safe;
All the other daddies
Have gone and left their wives,
And all the kids on our street
Are playing with their knives.

Byelo, little baby,
Let your crying cease,
You'll go to jail with Papa,
If you disturb the peace;
Close your little eyelids,
Don't you peep nor yell,
Half the dads in Christendom
Have died and gone to hell.

The above lines, part of a lullaby written in prison during the World War by an American conscientious objector, Floyd Hardin, to his baby, illustrates an attitude of mind unknown during any previous war in our history. The majority of the conscientious objectors in the World War were not—it is true—of this type. As in the Civil War, they were religious pacifists—Dunkards, Mennonites, Quakers, etc. These, for the most part, were set down by the War Department as "sincere objectors"; and, except in the case of some of those whose religious scruples would not allow them to accept any form of non-combatant service, were well-treated. A precedent had been established for them. But the so-called "political objector" was in a different boat. The War Department, the military officers, draft boards—except for an occasional enlightened individual here and there—had no idea what to do with them. The easiest course was to label them "Reds," "pro-Germans," "slackers," "yellowbacks," and treat them accordingly. Despite the none-too-strenuous efforts of Secretary of War Baker and a few of his aides to bring some sanity to bear on the problem presented by this new type of "C. O.," this was just what was done in most cases.

In the main, it was only the more militant pacifists and radicals of long standing who, like some of the religious objectors, were prepared to go to jail for their convictions. Many of the radicals took a more or less pragmatic view of the situation and either fled the country or failed to register and took their chances on being caught. The majority of those who fled crossed the border into Mexico. This contingent included a large number of intellectuals, artists, writers, camp-followers of *la vie de Bohême* and *Masses* contributors. One of the latter established a Slackers' Hotel in Mexico City which became a haven for Socialists, I.W.Ws and anarchists from the States. Some of those who stayed in the country were picked up by the Department of Justice, but a surprising number managed to dodge about the country and escape detection.

The "C. Os" who faced the music are of more concern to us here. The stir they created was entirely out of proportion to their numbers. They were made up of a little band here, an individual there, subjected to scorn, ridicule, spat upon, badgered with questions as to what they would do if the Huns attacked their grandmothers, given twenty-year sentences for refusing to peel potatoes, pricked with bayonets, made to stand at rigid attention until they dropped in their tracks, immersed head down (at least two of them received this treatment) in the filth of latrines. One of them, while in chains in a solitary cell, received notification that he had been awarded the Carnegie medal for bravery for risking his life to save a drowning woman just before war was declared. A few died from the effects of beatings or confinement in damp, unheated cells. One, a brother of Hugo Gellert, the artist, committed suicide as the result of inhumane treatment. Evans Thomas, a brother of Norman Thomas, risked his health and life by going on strike in behalf of a group of non-resistant religious pacifists who were being subjected to particularly brutal treatment. Later strikes of a different nature—"mutinies," the War Department called them—developed among the Wobblies and other radicals at Fort Leavenworth. By an amazing display of courage and solidarity, they forced the prison offi-

[ 309 ]

cials, supported by the entire machinery of the War Department, to back down, and won for themselves and other prisoners important concessions. The Wobbly group even established its own "house organ," known as the *Can Opener,* within the prison.

The record of the treatment of the "C. Os" in America is not, to be sure, one of unmitigated brutality. Secretary of War Baker, something of a liberal, attempted to standardize the treatment of both political and religious objectors, to clarify their position in relation to the government. But the response to whatever rules he laid down in the matter varied with the temperaments of the officers in charge of the various cantonments and prisons. Some of the worst brutalities occurred at Camp Funston and Fort Riley under the command or supervision of Major-General Wood. The famous "hole" and bread-and-water diet at Alcatraz Island in San Francisco Bay were reminiscent of the Spanish Inquisition. At Camp Grant a number of men were tortured. An occasional intelligent or humane official here and there, however, refusing to believe that the few recalcitrants in his charge endangered the success of the war program, tended to take the matter somewhat lightly. A now well-known writer, after refusing to obey orders and disrupting the life of an entire camp by assimilating a degree of irresponsibility that enabled him to put liquid soap in the soup and to wander off in the hills to write poetry whenever "K. P." duty irked him, found himself carrying a note from his commanding officer to the camp physician, the burden of which was, "For God's sake, find something wrong with this man!" The physician promptly discovered flat feet and our hero was relieved of all further responsibility to make the world safe for democracy.

Much of the brutal treatment to which the conscientious objectors were subjected by petty guards and officials was condoned by Y.M.C.A. secretaries and army chaplains. In his carefully documented book on this subject, Norman

Thomas quotes a letter from one objector who writes, in part:

I think it was a common experience of conscientious objectors that their most bitter and intolerant enemies in the army were the chaplains and the Y.M.C.A. men. No doubt there were individual exceptions, but I believe this enmity was the general rule. I think these representatives of "the church in arms" must have felt that the very existence of the conscientious objectors implied a vital criticism of the whole program of these militant churchmen.

Speaking from his own experience, Thomas testifies, "It was easier to talk with military officials and representatives of the War Department on this subject than with high officials of the Christian Church." Military officers, he concludes, were usually realists; the average churchman, a romantic patriot and complete sentimentalist.

At no time, even after the Armistice, was it possible, in the United States, to prevail upon such an array of notables to sign a petition for amnesty as took action in behalf of the conscientious objectors in England—men like Hilaire Belloc, Arnold Bennett, George Bernard Shaw, Arthur Henderson, John Galsworthy.

In light of the fact that the war objectors were frequently considered a little "off their heads" by a number of officials with whom they came in contact, it is interesting to note that in intelligence tests, both religious and political objectors far excelled the general average of the enlisted men. The "absolutists," (i.e., those who refused any form of non-combatant service) a large percentage of whom were "politicals," surpassed the average for commissioned officers.

The Armistice in November, 1918, which brought such joy and emotional release to a war-weary world, was celebrated with particular joyousness among the radicals because with it had come the news of the revolutions in Germany and Austria. Here was a certain degree of compensation for the black years of slaughter and reaction. Counter-revolution had not yet raised its head. At home, the war had at least brought victory to the Woman Suffrage cause and though that victory was to be of no particular service to the Revolution in general, it disposed of an issue which had engaged the energies of thousands of radical women for many years— and divided the victorious suffragists into two warring camps. The radicals now turned their energies to the release of their war-time martyrs.

The amnesty campaign that followed the war made little immediate headway. Victory had enhanced rather than softened patriotic passions and prejudices. The returning heroes were the loudest in their denunciation of political prisoners. Post-war hysteria was to surpass that of 1917.

At the end of 1921, the easy-going opportunistic Harding issued a pardon for Eugene V. Debs. The Democratic liberal, Wilson, had refused even to consider such action. Debs went back to Terre Haute like a conquering hero. The whole town turned out to greet him.

The last of the political prisoners were not released until the end of 1923. Several of the Wobblies had contracted tuberculosis and died soon after regaining their freedom.

American radical organizations, though subjected to the severest test in their history, had survived the war. They were now, however, to be torn asunder in a great post-war schism.

# XIII

## THE GREAT SCHISM—THE THIRD
## INTERNATIONAL

BACK in 1889, the Second International had been organized as a loose federation of socialist and radical labor parties. By 1900, it had affiliated groups in twenty-seven countries and in 1914 it represented about 12,000,000 radicals throughout the world. It included every kind of radical labor group from the Russian Bolshevists (the majority faction of the Russian Social Democratic Party) on the left to the mildly socialistic British Labor Party on the extreme right. Both Socialist and Socialist Labor parties of America were represented in its councils. It urged and tried to bring about radical unity in each country. It made no attempt to enforce it. In 1914, when its largest groups, the British, German, French and Belgians, had deserted to their respective colors, it had practically fallen to pieces.

In 1919, the Third International was organized, receiving its impetus and inspiration from the second Russian Revolution. It admitted only the extreme left wing of the radical army. The Second International had been built, for the most part, on the basis of a gradual approach to socialism. The Third arose unmistakably on the base of the revolutionary *coup d'état*. The time and place of its birth, Moscow, 1919, precluded consideration of any other program.

It was this year which marked the division of the revolutionary forces into two warring camps—socialist and communist, little factions of which were to split off and conduct their own private hostilities. Factional struggles and bitter ones had marked the whole history of the radical movement, but the struggle of 1919 was to tear its ranks completely asunder, and to inject into the relationship between the warring Marxians a venom and bitterness wholly unprecedented even in radical history. During the fourteen years which have elapsed since that fateful year, the subject of the schism itself and everything relating to it has become so overladen with emotion, legend and rationalization that its original sources have become more or less obscured; and to discuss it with any degree of objectivity is to invite attack from all sides.

The issue which divided the revolutionaries into separate communist and socialist camps was concerned only incidentally with support or opposition to the World War. Both groups had their quota of "social patriots." The present leader of French communism not only supported the French government in 1914 but was sent on special missions to persuade, first the Italian socialists and then the Russian Bolsheviks to support the Allies. The war merely widened a breach which had existed for years between two opposing concepts of revolutionary action. The Russian Revolution gave sufficient prestige and power to one of these groups to enable it to establish its own, separate international organization. The Third International was the child of Russian revolutionary experience, but it had had its theoretical roots in almost every nation long before 1917.

For the key to the new alignments which took place in 1919, however, it is necessary to turn once more to Europe in the war period.

From the very beginning of the war there had been minority groups of socialists in all the belligerent countries which had opposed it. These had consisted, for the most part, of members of the center and the left. The center was represented in Germany by such leaders as Kautsky, Ledebour, Haase; in France by the followers of Jean Longuet (Marx's grandson) ; in Austria by those of Fritz Adler; in England by a section of the Independent Labor Party. At the extreme left in Germany were Luxemburg, Liebknecht (the younger), Mehring, Rühle; in France, Monette and his followers; in Russia, the Bolsheviks with their leader, Lenin, in exile. Later, the Italian, Bulgarian and American socialists opposed the war by official majorities.

Late in 1915, the Italian and Swiss socialists undertook to bring the anti-war groups in the various warring and neutral countries together at a conference in Zimmerwald, Switzerland. Lenin, who was present at the conference, wanted to start a new International immediately but was voted down. The following spring the same group held another conference at Kienthal, this time to begin a concerted drive for peace in all the warring countries. The pro-war socialists were vigorously denounced and Lenin's views received somewhat more support than at Zimmerwald, but no actual move was made for a new international organization.

By this time the world was showing the first decided signs of war-weariness. The anti-war minorities were gaining strength. In Germany, the Centrists formed the Independent Socialist Party; the extreme left, the Spartacus Bund. In Austria, Fritz Adler, the Independent leader, had shot the Premier as a protest against war-time absolutism and received surprising expressions of sympathy. The French anti-war minority was promoting strikes. In the French army as in the Russian there were signs everywhere of a mutinous spirit. The first Russian Revolution in March and the entry of America into the war in April aroused hopes of an early peace and intensified the peace drive.

In November, the second Russian Revolution electrified the world, the Bolsheviks made overtures for peace, Germany continued its attacks on Russia and for the first time the German Social Democrats refused to vote the war credits. In France, the followers of Longuet were gaining strength over the majority. The Bolsheviks finally made a separate peace with Germany at Brest-Litovsk.

In October of 1918 revolutions occurred in Bulgaria, Hungary and Austria. In November came the Armistice and the revolution in Germany. The war was over; the Second International lay dismembered; the Third was not yet born. In the words of Lewis Lorwin in his study of the two Internationals: "A scorn and hatred unparalleled in the history of the Socialist movement filled the hearts of the members of the various factions for one another."

Whether or not the German Social Democrats could have turned the republican revolution of November, 1918, into a social revolution similar to that of Russia in 1917 or whether, if they had, the revolution could have sustained itself in the face of a triumphant Allied army on its soil is a matter for argument. The Allies were no longer too preoccupied elsewhere to give adequate support to a counter-revolution, nor had Germany the advantage of Russia's huge size and comparative isolation. The Communist dictatorship inaugurated in Hungary by Bela Kun four months later, with the support of the Socialists and a complete lack of resistance from the liberals under Count Karolyi, was starved out by the Allies and viciously suppressed by the counter-revolutionists and the Roumanian army. The Soviet Republic, set up in Bavaria in April by the Independent Socialists under Kurt Eisner, lasted but three weeks. A similar attempt made by the Finnish Independents was also short-lived. But at least, that program of nationalization which Lenin had suggested to the Kerensky government after the first Russian revolution could have been inaugurated, the Junker estates broken up. The Germans were half-starved, but they were also desperate. As in 1914, the Social Democrats hesitated, compromised and threw in their lot with the Weimar Republic. Having committed themselves to its defense, they were obliged thereafter to move steadily to the right.

The Russian communists unquestionably expected the World War to be followed by social revolutions, at least in Europe. Their own precarious position in 1918-19 made such an outcome seem almost necessary to their survival. And in 1919, with the whole world seething with political and industrial upheavals, the crisis in capitalism appeared to have arrived. The time was ripe to rally the returning soldiers, the war-weary masses to the banner of the World Revolution—and to prevent, at the same time, the revival of the Second International. The eyes of the advance guard of the revolution were now turned hopefully toward Russia. In this new and final stage of the revolutionary struggle, Russia was expected to lead the way. A wireless went out from Moscow, calling for an international congress to meet in that city on March 6, 1919, to form a new revolutionary International.

The first congress of the Third International was held in a room in the Kremlin. Most of the delegates were without credentials, owing to the blockades and the disorganized state of the radical movement in general. Many of them represented factions rather than parties. The chairman of the convention was Gregory Zinoviev, probably the most Jesuitical sectarian the modern radical movement has produced. Though he was later to be deposed by his comrades, his position at the helm of the Third International during its first five formative years was an unmitigated misfortune for the whole international movement. The new International called upon the workers of the world "to rise as an organized mass," to disarm the bourgeoisie, form workers', peasants' and soldiers' councils, organize red armies and establish the dictatorship of the proletariat. It attacked not only the pro-war right but the anti-war center, the Independents of Germany and England, the followers of Longuet in France. It

[ 317 ]

did not, however, adopt as war-like an attitude as it was to assume a year later.

Between the First and Second Congress of the Third International, the prospect of a world revolution, or at least of revolutionary upheavals in several countries, appeared even brighter. Europe and America were torn with strikes. In Germany and Finland there had been Spartacide and Independent uprisings; in Hungary a communist dictatorship had come and gone; in France were rumblings of a general strike; in Italy the revolutionary tide that was to lead to the seizure of the factories in September was rising. The Second Congress of the new International met when the whole world seemed to be turning leftward. The Independents of Germany, Austria and England, the syndicalists of France and Italy, the I.W.W. of the United States were represented. "We are living in an epoch of civil war; the critical hour has struck," declared the Congress. It was in such a mood of confidence and triumph that the famous Twenty-one Points, or conditions of admission to the Third International, were laid down.

The Twenty-one Points were clearly intended to establish the authority of the Comintern (the Communist International) as the "general staff" of the Social Revolution. They were presented to the organized radicals of the world in the spirit of "take them or leave them" and only those groups which took them *in toto*, agreeing to expel all dissenting or vacillating elements from their midst, were eligible for admission. Among those centrist leaders mentioned by name as undesirable were Kautsky, Hilferding, Adler, Longuet, Hillquit. In the Twenty-one Points the new International served notice of warfare, not only upon international capitalism, but upon all non-communist radicals, and the socialists in particular, of whatever shade.

Zinoviev has been quoted as stating at this time that the leaders had "racked their brains in vain to invent ten conditions more to make it more difficult to join," but that "their inventive faculties could do no more." No more was needed, however, to alienate all but the completely orthodox, those who subscribed to the theory that the revolutionary struggle had entered a stage practically of civil war demanding unquestioning adherence to a centralized international authority, and a tightly organized and rigidly disciplined army. The German and British Independents withdrew. Throughout the world splits occurred in the socialist and syndicalist ranks between those willing and those unwilling to endorse the Moscow program. The Italian Party, which had already enthusiastically endorsed the Third International, now split on the acceptance of the Twenty-one Points. (It was this division in the ranks of the vigorous Italian movement which paved the way for the triumph of fascism in 1922.) A number of the French and Italian pro-war socialists embraced communism and denounced their former anti-war comrades as renegades. The syndicalists and the anarchists denounced both the socialists and the communists. Dissension, charges, countercharges filled the air.

Early in 1921, eighty delegates of the left and center groups which had failed to submit to the Moscow program met in Vienna and formed a Union of Socialist Parties which became known as "the Second and a Half International." It called for a flexible program that would not "restrict the proletariat to using democratic methods only, as is done by the so-called Second International, nor prescribe the mechanical imitation of the methods of the Russian peasants and workingmen's revolution as the Communist International would like to do."

But by 1921 the force of the post-war labor unrest had partially spent itself and at the Third Congress of the Third International in Russia, Lenin testified to the fact that international revolutionary developments had "slowed down." The tone of the conference was quite different from that of

[ 319 ]

1920. The emphasis of discussion lay upon the internal situation in Russia, rather than on world revolution. A new and very different slogan, "Make capitalism serve the workers!" was heard. The Kronstadt Rebellion had taken place and the New Economic Policy was about to be enunciated. The following year the Communist International was to call for a "united front" with "the betrayers" of the right and center. The reaction had set in.

All these events had their repercussions, of course, in the United States.

The second Russian Revolution had aroused the most intense enthusiasm among the radicals of all shades and organizations—socialists, syndicalists, anarchists. To the American radicals who had watched in despair the spectacle of their European comrades butchering each other on three fronts, who had seen their own members persecuted and imprisoned, their organizations harried, their press almost destroyed, Russia stood both as a justification of faith and a flaming symbol of hope. Here was the first Working-Class Republic, the revolutionary ideal made real. The attacks of the Allied-financed counter-revolutionary armies upon the Bolsheviks, the landing of troops at Murmansk, and later in Siberia, aroused their bitterest indignation. In socialist, I.W.W. and anarchist meetings throughout the country, the very word Russia was greeted with storms of applause. Before the bitter conflict of 1919 had arisen—not over approval or disapproval of Bolshevist methods in Russia, but over a whole restatement and redirection of revolutionary thought and method, and submission to the authority of the Third International—the revolutionary forces were united as they had never been before in their enthusiasm over the Russia victory. (Up to the schism of late 1919, Morris Hillquit, who was later to become anathema to the Communists, acted as legal adviser to the Soviet Government Bureau in the United States.)

The Russian revolutionary methods and the philosophy of revolution from which they sprang had made a deep impression upon the American left by the end of 1918. They served as a justification for opinions and attitudes expressed for many years by the group of left-wing intellectuals centered for a time around the *New Review* and whose best-known spokesman was a young man named Louis Fraina. Now, in these optimistic days at the close of the World War, when the whole world seemed to be turning upside down, when the old socialism of the Second International seemed so obviously inadequate in the face of new and acute situations, when the whole revolutionary movement needed to be rebuilt along sharper, clearer and more militant lines, these views gained prestige and adherents.

The drama of the Russian Revolution had captured the radical imagination of the world. Few among the American radicals doubted at this time that the American soldiers would return in that same mood of embittered disillusionment which had marked the returning armies of Russia, Austria, Germany, even of France and England; that the inevitable post-war adjustments would bring on violent industrial conflicts. The older slogans of soap-boxers and agitators generally gave way to new ones gleaned from the chronicles of revolutionary events abroad—"All power to the Soviets!" etc. Little socialist and I.W.W. groups throughout the country transformed themselves into "soviets" and talked the language of the Russian crisis. Workers' and soldiers' councils were formed. There were even references, at times, to the "American peasantry." The radical world set out to remodel itself in the Russian image in preparation for the final conflict.

The industrial state of the nation in the year 1919 was such as to give some credence to the theory that the United States, as well as Europe, was entering upon a revolutionary crisis.

Labor, intrenched and strengthened during the war years, was showing its teeth. Though its mood was not revolutionary, it was decidedly aggressive, reflecting the wave of militancy then sweeping the working-class world. The year saw more than 2,000 strikes and lockouts involving more than 4,000,000 workers. No wonder the left-wing hopes rose higher! The general strike in Seattle, the great steel strike, the police strike in Boston, even the Actors' Equity strike in New York—when for the first time American "artists" forgot their dignity and discovered their pride—seemed like the first skirmishes of the Revolution.

The Seattle General Strike, though carried out by "regular" A. F. of L. unions, took on a definitely revolutionary hue because of the generally radical tone of Seattle labor and because it was immediately labeled a "revolution" by Mayor Ole Hanson and the local business men. It was the first strike of its kind in the United States and it tied up all industry and business in Seattle. No street cars ran, even restaurants, theaters, barbershops were closed. The strikers themselves kept order with unarmed labor guards, closed all saloons, distributed milk through the Milkmen's Union, food through their own distributing centers. The strike was a demonstration of solidarity with the water-front workers. It was called off when it had served its purpose.

The Great Steel Strike represented labor's one militant drive against the Steel Trust, its one great effort to organize the unskilled immigrant labor so viciously exploited in the steel mills. It was led by William Z. Foster, backed up by the leaders of the Chicago Federation of Labor and, through their influence, by the A. F. of L. It involved more than 400,000 workers in the most feudalistic industry in the nation. The Steel Trust answered with its habitual weapons, thousands of armed guards, the state constabulary, sheriff's posses of small business men. Strikers were shot, women and children clubbed. As usual, all liberal and radical opinion—and in this case, even religious opinion—was mobilized behind the strikers. But American Steel has never had to bother about public opinion. It had power and money and it used both. The Strike Fund of $400,000 was soon exhausted, the strikers faced starvation. The A. F. of L. lost what little enthusiasm it had had for the strike in the beginning. In January, 1920, the strike was called off. A little later, Foster went to Moscow.

The labor unrest of 1919 expressed itself also in politics. In Chicago, the same men who had backed Foster and the steel strike organized a Labor Party which, in 1920, turned into a Farmer-Labor Party with a presidential candidate in the field. But by this time the reaction had set in. Its candidate, Parley Christensen, polled only a quarter of a million votes. The farmer-labor party movement retained strength only in Minnesota.

In the year 1919, probably eight out of ten of the American radicals were thoroughly disillusioned with the Second International, with most of its leaders and with the type of gradualist, parliamentary theory which dominated it. They were ready for some new, more aggressive leadership, a totally new international alignment. Both the Socialists and the I. W. W. had hailed enthusiastically the second Russian Revolution, the Sparticists and Independent uprisings in Germany, the Bela Kun government in Hungary; they had denounced the murders of Liebknecht and Luxemburg. The Socialists had sent delegates to a conference at Berne in 1919 in which the old International leaders participated but later they had repudiated the Conference and had approved, by an overwhelming majority, a resolution to the effect that "the Socialist Party shall participate in an international conference called by, or in which, participate the Communist Party of Russia and the Communist Party of Germany." Moscow had not yet adopted the Twenty-one Points and the efforts of the

Independents to effect a union of all radical socialist groups which would "exclude the so-called social-patriotic elements of the socialist movement in all countries and include the Bolshevik socialists of Russia," still held promise of revolutionary unity.

But in the meanwhile, the Manifesto of the First Congress of the Third International had appeared in the United States with its thesis that the imperialist war was "passing into civil war," its call for concentration upon "mass action, with its logical result—direct conflict with the governmental machinery in open combat." Thousands of the American radicals who were ready to join hands with Moscow in the new International, who accepted in general the criticism of the older socialism, the need for a restatement of aims and methods and the doctrine of the proletarian dictatorship, even the eventual necessity of "civil war," were dubious, nevertheless, about the appropriateness of this diagnosis and prescription to the American scene in 1919. At the right, were other members who repudiated it altogether. But thousands more, some of whom had already arrived independently at the view taken by the Russian leaders, were ready to accept the new program *in toto* and began a campaign to commit the American movement to the new leadership and tactics—realizing that in so doing it would be necessary to split off or expel all recalcitrant elements. A Left Wing was organized within the party, with its own platform, membership cards and dues and the fight was on. The backbone of the Left Wing was the socialist foreign language federations.

At the height of the party's strength, in 1912, the membership of these federations had not exceeded 16,000 in a total of 120,000 members. In 1919, fifty-three per cent of the organized socialists were members of the foreign-speaking organizations. The Slavic branches in particular had grown by leaps and bounds since 1917. The importance which this fact was to assume in the schism which followed and in the organization of American Communism may be gleaned from the fact that out of a total Communist Party membership announced in 1925 as 16,325, only a little over 2,000 were members of the English-speaking sections.

The launching of the organized Left Wing to capture American socialism for the Third International and to reorganize it upon a basis of the Left Wing program initiated the fiercest struggle in the history of the Revolution in America. As usual, it became surrounded immediately with an aura of abuse, recriminations, personal attacks and extraneous charges on both sides. Had the crisis appeared at a time when the left wing forces of the world were less intoxicated with the heady wine of Russian victory and the imminence of world revolution, had the issues involved been kept clarified, the alignments which finally took place would have been far more logical, the bulk of the radical following would not have been lost to both communism and socialism, and the next eight years of radical history would have been less a tale told by an idiot, full of fury and dissension and signifying almost nothing. Some of the dogmas of 1919 were to be the heresies of 1922; the faithful of 1922, the heretics of 1927. The "dominant socialism" of the pre-war years which was dying a natural death in 1918 was given life, vitality and prestige by the extravagances and frenzy of its critics in 1919.

The lengthy Left Wing Manifesto and Program presented to American socialism for its unqualified endorsement by its newly organized Left Wing began with the following statement: "The world is in crisis. Capitalism is in process of disintegration and collapse," and went on to an analysis of war and imperialism, the Second International, moderate socialism, the proletarian revolution, American socialism, the A. F. of L., political and mass action, and ended with a call to the proletariat to rally to the banner of the Communist International. It took note of the rise of the new labor party but denounced "laborism" as a snare and a delusion. Much of its

[ 325 ]

analysis was both apt and brilliant. Some of it was sheer romanticism. In its survey of the American labor scene and history it found little to praise except the essentially anarchistic Western Federation of Miners in the '90s. Its contention that "the temper of the workers and soldiers, after the sacrifices that have been made during the war, is such that they will not endure the reactionary conditions so openly advocated by the master class" was certainly the product of undue optimism. The American soldiers were returning in that mood of bumptious super-patriotism that was to make of these "buddies" the most active red-baiters of the next two years. The widespread strikes, except perhaps in Seattle, were inspired by the usual immediate dissatisfactions rather than by revolutionary ardor. Denouncing "moderate socialism" in general for failing to turn "an imperialistic war into a civil war—into a proletarian revolution," the Manifesto denounced American Socialism in particular for failing to carry out the implications of the St. Louis Proclamation and for coöperating with such bourgeois pacifist organizations as the People's Council both during the war and in a general demand for amnesty after it. The *Revolutionary Age*, the principal left-wing organ declared regarding these prisoners: "We don't want amnesty for them. We want them to be released by the industrial might of the proletariat, by class conscious action." Unfortunately the proletariat was not interested in them.

There were many thousands of radicals who were in complete agreement with the general tenor of the left-wing analysis but who were not convinced that the revolutionary situation in the United States was as advanced as the Manifesto implied, who were not ready to denounce as traitors to the Revolution all those who questioned its wisdom or to cry "Kolchak" even at their right-wing opponents some of whom happened at the time to have sentences of twenty years' imprisonment hanging over their heads as a result of their war-time activities. But the Manifesto had to be accepted or rejected in its entirety. The struggle for control that followed its dissemination was marked by subterfuge, illegality, slander, on both sides. The Left Wing caucus was well organized and had back of it almost the entire foreign-language membership. The administration was in control of the party machinery and proceeded to use it to hold its control. It accused the Slavic federations of fraudulent voting and suspended them. It reorganized locals as fast as they joined the Left Wing. The Left, which pinned its faith to "militant minorities" and jeered at democracy, howled about democracy and fairness. The Right, which adhered to the principles of democracy and fair play, used direct action and all the methods of dictatorship.

The whole quarrel came to a head in Chicago where the Socialist Party had called an emergency convention for August 30, 1919. Here the army of the Revolution was split three ways. It developed that there were two Left Wings. One, led by Fraina, the backbone of which were the foreign-language federations who regarded themselves as the only real Bolsheviks in America, bolted the original Left and formed the Communist Party. (Its convention hall in Chicago was christened "Smolny Institute" after the Bolshevik headquarters in Petrograd.) The remaining majority of the Left first tried to capture the Socialist Convention for Communism. Headed by John Reed, some of their delegates invaded the convention but after a short skirmish, the feature of which was a fist fight between the impetuous Reed and the equally impetuous Julius Gerber, the capitalist police swooped in and restored order. The Left Wing majority delegates then withdrew to a hall downstairs, declared themselves to be the real Emergency Convention of the Socialist Party, and then reorganized themselves as "The Communist Labor Party of the United States." It included most of the

English-speaking members of the original Left Wing and a large number of veteran American radicals.

Meanwhile, the zealous Communist Party, so dominated by the foreign-born radicals, had laid the foundation for still another split. To its convention had come the delegates from the expelled Michigan branch of the Socialist Party, which had been among the first of the Socialist groups to join the original Left Wing. The Michigan delegates, hopelessly outnumbered by the Slavs and unable to get a word in edgewise, left the convention to form a little communist party of their own. The result of this schism within a schism was the Proletarian Party of America, a tenacious little group of "scientific" revolutionists still going its lonely Marxian way.

But long before this development took place and two months after the organization of the Communist and the Communist Labor parties, the tide of the post-war red hysteria was at its height. In the new witch-hunt, communism of every shade and variety was driven underground.

The state of the world in 1919 was not, as we have seen, such as to inspire peace and confidence in the heart of the Tory. The Soviet régime in Russia, despite daily rumors of its downfall, seemed to grow more firmly intrenched from month to month. Hungary had turned red, if only temporarily; Italy was flirting with sovietism, and even British labor was showing an alarming militancy. The whole international horizon was taking on a bright red glow. In America strikes were multiplying daily, the returning soldiers were clamoring for their jobs. The country seethed with an uncrystallized unrest. But patriotism was still rampant and this was an opportune moment in which to drag a few red herrings across the trail. Hundred per cent Americanism, Jew-, Negro- and, particularly, alien-red baiting became the order of the day.

The drive against "alien anarchy" and "Bolshevism," known as the Palmer Red Raids and the Deportations Delirium, exceeded anything of the sort the country had ever seen before. The hysteria which accompanied the riots of 1877, the May Day demonstrations of 1886, even the war in 1917-18, paled by comparison. For a precedent it is necessary to turn to England at the time of the French Revolution. Just as the English Tories of those stormy times saw a Jacobin lurking behind every hedgerow, America's big and little business men, Legionnaires and professional Nordics now saw a Bolshevik behind every set of whiskers. Every gathering of a handful of foreign-born workers in some obscure hall became a menace to American institutions. Every sizable package in the mails was a potential bomb. It was the sort of hysteria that men in high places and of uneasy conscience, financiers who had waxed fat on a blood-drenched world, manufacturers who had reaped a golden harvest from shoddy goods, contractors and government officials involved in shady deals, could turn to good account—and did.

Spies and *agents provocateurs* penetrated every inch of the radical terrain. Halls and workers' schools, especially those where Russians congregated, were raided, the furnishings smashed. Mass arrests were made on John Doe warrants issued by the thousand. Men and women, many of whom, in the words of one investigator, "didn't know the difference between Bolshevism and Rheumatism," were torn from their families, held incommunicado for weeks, beaten and abused. Those who could produce proof of citizenship were finally released. The others, if they could be connected in any fashion with communism or anarchism, were held for deportation. To connect them thus, Department of Justice agents went so far as to forge names to false confessions and to beat them with blackjacks. One Andrea Salsedo, after being held in secret confinement for eight weeks in the offices of the Department of Justice in New York City, committed suicide by jumping from a fourteenth-story window.

Those finally to be deported were concentrated at Ellis

[ 329 ]

Island. The group, numbering 249 persons, included Emma Goldman and Alexander Berkman, both recently released from prison. Early on the morning of December 21, 1919, they were herded aboard an old army transport, the *Buford*, afterwards known as the Soviet Ark, which sailed under sealed orders. The man who signed the deportation order was Louis F. Post, formerly editor of Henry George's single-tax paper and now Assistant Secretary of Labor. The "reds" were being sent back "where they came from." The Red Raids continued for a time unabated, with a large part of our foreign-born population in a constant state of dread and terror.

On Armistice Day, 1919, with one-hundred-per-cent Americanism at its height, a procession of American Legionnaires had made its way through the streets of Centralia, Washington, and had come to a halt before the I.W.W. hall. Repeated raids had been made against the Wobblies in the Pacific Northwest all during the war because of their activities among the lumber workers. In Centralia, in particular, the feeling between the business elements and the Wobblies had grown tense. Now, with the town full of returned soldiers and patriotism rampant, the Wobblies were to be put in their place. Just what happened after the parade halted became the subject later of pages of conflicting testimony. The state claimed that the marchers had merely halted to close up their ranks and that they had been fired upon without provocation. The defense claimed that the parade had been deliberately routed past the hall—which was in an out-of-the-way part of town—that the Legionnaires had broken ranks, rushed the hall and that the Wobblies had fired in self-defense. Four Legionnaires were killed and several wounded. Eleven Wobblies were rounded up. One, himself an ex-soldier, was taken from the jail by a mob, horribly mutilated and then hanged. Seven of the prisoners were tried, convicted of second-degree murder and sentenced to from twenty to forty years in prison. Six of the jurors later made affidavits that they had been threatened and terrorized into voting for conviction.

A farcical note was introduced into the great crusade against the Red Menace when New York State, not to be outdone by the federal government, appropriated $30,000 to finance the activities of the famous Lusk Committee. The Lusk Report on seditious activities fills two enormous volumes. Two more are devoted to "constructive measures" such as criminal syndicalism laws, deportation rulings, Boy Scout activities, Americanization campaigns. The first two volumes are probably the only ones that were ever read.

The New York investigators set out to blast radicalism sky high. What they succeeded in doing was to gather together and have published at the expense of the state one of the most valuable source books on red revolution ever to occupy a niche in any radical's library. They added just enough interpretation to the facts so laboriously assembled to make themselves the laughing stock of the country. Here were all the resolutions and manifestoes the radicals had been shouting from the housetops for years revealed as aspects of a diabolical conspiracy. Private correspondence of humanitarians, liberals, radicals, most of it seized in spectacular raids on various organizations, was reproduced in facsimile as the most damning of evidence. Led on by dark hints calculated to render him breathless with excitement, the reader was let down by such items as the following: "Enclosed please find petitions," "You will be surprised to hear I saw your nice wife yesterday in Milwaukee," or "I shall be very glad to accept your invitation to act upon the Council of the Emergency Peace Federation." The high spot of the whole dire proceedings was reached with the reproduction of a postcard written by Jane Addams aboard the Ford Peace Ship bearing the single line: "We don't know where we're going but we're on our way."

The data gathered by the Committee, despite all the hilarity it caused after publication, was drawn on heavily by the

New York authorities during the Red Raids. It was made the basis of the expulsion of five Socialist assemblymen from the New York legislature in 1920—over the protests of the Bar Association of New York City, Charles Evans Hughes, Ogden Mills, and other conservatives who had managed to keep their heads. The red hysteria mounted all over the country until even men and women of liberal views who traced their ancestry back to the *Mayflower* hesitated before appearing on the street with a copy of the *Nation* or *New Republic* under their arms. In the spring of 1920, Attorney-General Palmer received some severe setbacks. Assistant Secretary of Labor Post, who, in spite of the fire directed at him from the left, had been under even stronger fire from the right because of his liberal interpretations of cases that came to him for official review, was threatened with impeachment by the Palmerites. The effort collapsed and the country began its gradual swing back to "normalcy" under the ægis of the Ohio gang. The public lost interest in the Bolsheviks. The Red Raids petered out.

As they did so, the Socialists met in New York City and nominated Debs for President. All during the past year, members of the Left Wing, by this time members of one of the two Communist parties, had visited Debs at Atlanta, urging him to espouse their cause. The old man, grieving over the schism that was racking his party and with close friends on both sides, could not, for all his enthusiasm for Russia, see eye-to-eye with the Communist leadership; and repeated attempts to convert him after his release from prison, until the time of his death in 1926, failed.

In 1920, the Socialists were still confronted with the problem of their international affiliation. The Twenty-one Points had not yet arrived from Moscow and the party convention went on record for adherence to the Third International but declared its opposition to any "formula such as the dictatorship of the proletariat in the form of soviets." The arrival of the Moscow answer a little later put an end to all attempts by the Socialists to find a berth within the Third International. The split was complete and final. Debs wrote in the *Liberator*:

The Moscow comrades have arrogated to themselves the right to dictate the tactics, program, the very conditions of propaganda in all countries. It is ridiculous, arbitrary, autocratic—as ridiculous as if we were to dictate to them how they should carry on their propaganda.

The I.W.W. was now to go through much the same inner struggle. Since 1917, it had hailed the new Soviet Republic as the realization of the syndicalist ideal. Several of its leaders including Bill Haywood and Bill Shatov, who was to become the great railroad builder of Russia, were well on their way to becoming enthusiastic Bolsheviks and after their arrival in Russia sent back glowing reports to their American comrades. In 1919 the Wobblies had voted to affiliate with Moscow, and the following year they sent a delegate to the Congress of the Third International. Here it became apparent that the Communist policy of highly centralized party dictatorship was not the I.W.W. idea of the new industrial society. Moscow frowned upon syndicalism, its Red Trade Unions were to be definitely under the party thumb. It sought the allegiance of the I.W.W., or rather of its membership, but it also sought to "liquidate" the I.W.W. as an independent organization. The Wobbly delegate returned with a highly unfavorable report and the I.W.W. reconsidered its affiliation. "We endorse the Third International," its resolution declared, "with reservations as follows: that we take no part in parliamentary action whatsoever and that we reserve the right to develop our own tactics according to conditions prevailing."

The next four years of Wobbly history were to be devoted very largely to struggles with the communist unions. The little Socialist Labor Party also refused to be liquidated and continued on its way.

When the period of the Great Schism had passed, the revolutionary movement in America lay dismembered. The great bulk of its membership—in all camps—disheartened and tired by the long, internal conflicts, the incessant wrangling, had dropped out of the movement altogether. They were to constitute an army of tired radicals in the years ahead.

# XIV

## EBB TIDE IN THE BOOM DECADE

THE war decade had ended in a blaze of industrial and political unrest among the workers, of confusion and division in the camp of the Revolution, red hysteria and super-patriotism among solid citizens and politicians, a cocky, triumphant, "we-won-the-war" attitude among the returning heroes, and a thoroughgoing disillusionment on the part of the intellectuals.

Though Harding was elected on the slogan of "Back to Normalcy" in 1920, the real "post-war era" with all its familiar connotations of manners, morals and ideas did not begin until after the depression of 1921. It took nearly three years to deflate the American labor movement after its war-time honeymoon with capital under the ægis of the National War Labor Board. The A. F. of L. nearly doubled its membership between 1917 and 1923. During the remainder of the boom decade, it was to go steadily downhill.

The beginning of the new decade found wages still high, but living costs were proportionately higher. As the war industries subsided, unemployment increased, wages of the unorganized went down but the cost of living stayed up. Organized labor showed no willingness to yield an inch of its conquered territory. American industry had piled up sufficient profits to tide it over a long period of inactivity, and in its efforts to restore economic "normalcy" it could afford to take certain losses. The post-war depression of 1921 provided just the opportunity it needed to "shake down" a too-bumptious and growing labor movement. The slump went far enough to do just that before the New Era was inaugurated.

America had come out of the war sitting on top of the world. It had wrested financial leadership of the nations from England; through its war-time and post-war loans, American capitalism—however much of an isolationist the average American might feel politically—had become an important factor in Europe's industrial life. The country had lost nothing but the lives of the men and boys who had died in France and Belgium; and most of those who returned had not yet lost their illusions. They were now being organized in the American Legion.

If the strikes and political protests of 1919 and 1920 were indications of continued belligerency and hope in the labor and radical ranks, the defensive struggles of 1921-22, with five million unemployed in the country, were indications of desperation. These were the years of another great coal strike, the battle of Logan County, West Virginia, the Herrin Massacre in Illinois, the cotton-textile strikes in New England, the lockout of the Amalgamated Clothing Workers, the great railway shop strike. If labor was being deflated, so was radicalism. In the seven years of the New Era which followed, organized labor was shorn of most of its militancy, radicalism of most of its influence.

The various communist parties and sects were leading a romantic but futile underground existence and assailing each other, nevertheless, with the utmost bitterness. The Socialist Party, in spite of the large vote polled by Debs in 1920, was shot to pieces as a result of two years of internal struggle and the final split in its ranks. The I.W.W., with most of its leaders still in jail (and even among these a schism had occurred over the acceptance of individual clemency), was still bleeding from its war-time wounds and was torn asunder by controversies with the communists. The anarchists, reading the bitterly disillusioned reports that came from Berkman and Goldman in Russia and shocked at the repression of the anarchists in the revolutionary Fatherland, were in the depths of despair. Some of them became converted to the principle of dictatorship and embraced communism. But all the radical groups were now facing a handicap more formidable than persecution and internal dissension—the rising tide of what newspapers and politicians loved to call "unprecedented prosperity." It was a period in which the post-peace treaty disillusionment of so many erstwhile idealists expressed itself either in cynical conformity, a tongue-in-cheek willingness to play the game and make one's pile while the making was good, or by the despairing merrily-I-go-to-hell, lost-generation gesture of escape that was to furnish the dominant note for the literature of the 1920s.

The despairs of the post-Versailles period were, after all, the despairs of the literary, artistic, liberal and radical worlds. In America, at least, this mood was not shared by the common man who saw in the New Era a possible opportunity to recapture, without struggle and organization, something of his war-time prosperity, an older independence. Even though he descended occasionally into that army of 1,800,000 technologically unemployed that attended even the high peak of our national prosperity, the hum of industrial activity, the general spirit of optimism and the talk about him of easy money created always the illusion of imminent escape. The psychological frontier was being born again in the minds of vast numbers of Americans.

In our various sick and slightly unsteady industries—coal, textiles, agriculture, etc.—a large section of the working population was wholly untouched by the general upswing; many of them were, in fact, in a worse condition than at any time in the past thirty years. There were organized but unskilled groups, even in the railway industry—such as the maintenance-of-way employees—earning as little as 17 cents an hour. In the lower strata of the labor world, millions were receiving, as usual, far less than the earnings agreed upon by governmental bureaus as a "health and decency" minimum. But most of these were inarticulate, unorganized or badly organized, accustomed to living on the ragged edge. Their grievances were drowned in the general prosperity chorus.

To the middle class, the small and somewhat bigger business men, the new hordes of high-pressure salesmen and executives, the new business professionals and their families, the period was one of unprecedented smugness and complacency, a country-club Babbittry at its most effulgent. The old and new rich—however much they sighed romantically over lost naïvetés, snorted with Mencken at the "booboisie," or aped the new decadence of the literary expatriates of Montparnasse—continued to enjoy their privileges heartily; and a new, young post-war generation, experimenting with bootleg liquor, sex, higher education, sports models and such other extravagances and comforts as no previous younger generation had ever known, was having the time of its young life.

One of the most eloquent commentaries on the intellectual mood of the early post-war years, when the various gestures of despair and criticism had not yet hardened into a stereotyped mold, was contained in a volume edited by one of the brightest of the bright young men of the period, who a little later was to head the flight of the disgusted intellectuals to France—Harold E. Stearns, a name as familiar to the intelligentsia of 1922 as is that of Edmund Wilson in similar circles in the 1930s. *Civilization in the United States* was subtitled *An Adventure in Intellectual Coöperation* and it surveyed the American scene from thirty-three different angles. Among its contributors, each speaking for his or her particular sector of the cultural front, were Lewis Mumford, H. L. Mencken, George Jean Nathan, Robert Morss Lovett, Robert Lowie,

Van Wyck Brooks, Deems Taylor, Conrad Aiken, Walter Pach, George Soule, Elsie Clews Parsons, Katharine Anthony, Hendrik Van Loon, Ring Lardner and Ernest Boyd. Its keynote was set by the editor in his preface: ". . . the most moving and pathetic fact in the social life of America today is emotional and esthetic starvation. . . . We have no heritages or traditions to which to cling except those which have already withered in our hands and turned to dust." In a chapter on radicalism in America, George Soule remarked: "Economic radicalism never looked—on the surface—weaker than it does in the United States today."

To the weekly journals of opinion—the *Nation* and the *New Republic*—had now been added a third, the *Freeman*, probably the most refined gesture in liberal journalism the United States has ever seen. The *Freeman* was financed by the packing-house millions of that part of the Swift family into which Francis Neilson, its editor-in-chief, had married. With Ben Huebsch as publisher, Alfred Jay Nock as its shining editorial light (his column signed "Journeyman" contained some of the best critical writing of the period), Van Wyck Brooks as literary editor, and Lewis Mumford and Suzanne La Follette on its editorial staff, the *Freeman* was a joy to the literary sensibilities of its day. Its almost excessive gentility in make-up, an open-faced, headline-less conservatism that would have paved its way into the very best of English clubs, rendered it altogether unattractive to a proletariat educated to read as it runs. But the *Freeman* was not edited for the proletariat. Nock set its socio-economic tone and—for all its verbal protestations of extreme radicalism "in the sense of getting at the root of things," its lofty attitude toward radical and liberal politics—its economic program of philosophic anarchism and single tax would no more have offended Thomas Jefferson than it did the more "civilized" members of the Union League Club. Such rarefied journalism is an expensive plaything and the *Freeman* could not possibly have paid its way. It expired when Mrs. Neilson grew tired of providing for it.

The popular social and literary note of the period was to be struck, of course, by the *American Mercury*. It was a note first sounded by Sinclair Lewis in *Main Street* and it was to reverberate down into the 1930s. It is too familiar to need elaboration. When stage directors distinguished their stage collegians from other members of the cast by having them make their entrance with the familiar green *Mercury* sandwiched jauntily under one arm, the Menckenian vogue had reached its height. It was to vanish in the second winter of the Great Depression.

The radical hiatus in the three years that followed the Great Schism was reflected graphically in the pages of the *Liberator*. In spite of essential differences in temperament that existed between himself and the more dogmatic Left Wingers in 1919, Eastman had espoused the communist cause. But the state of American communism at this period was scarcely such as to inspire great enthusiasm, and except in its tone toward Soviet Russia and the Russian leaders, the *Liberator* was in no sense an orthodox communist journal. Many of its earlier contributing editors had dropped away; others held altogether aloof from internal politics of the period; still others, who were later to become leading communists, were as yet anarchists or syndicalists. The magazine was declining. The playful mood of the Revolution had long since passed (though in Chicago, the scene of a literary renaissance about this time, a type of hobohemian-literary radicalism was having a recrudescence in Jack Jones' Dill Pickle Club). A new spirit was abroad, sharper, more dogmatic, more specifically partisan. A new vocabulary of revolution was being coined. During 1921-22, before Eastman resigned all editorial responsibilities to go to Russia, his more liberal mood still pervaded the *Liberator's* editorial policy. Thus Debs' criticism of the Third International was printed along

[ 340 ]

with enthusiastic chronicles of communist activities abroad and sonnets to Lenin and Trotsky. Early in 1921 appeared the story of John Reed's tragic death in Moscow, of his burial in the Kremlin, and, a little later, one of the first calls for help from the Sacco-Vanzetti Defense Committee.

This case, which was to end so tragically six years later, was as yet scarcely talked of outside of anarchist circles. It had grown out of the Red Raids and the death of Salsedo in 1920. Nicola Sacco, a shoemaker, and Bartolomeo Vanzetti, a fish-peddler, had been friends of Salsedo and had been under suspicion as "dangerous reds" during the Palmer régime. When two men were shot at South Braintree, Massachusetts, in a payroll robbery—a quite conventional crime of the sort that two idealistic anarchists would be the last persons in the world to commit—and the murderers were reported to be Italians, a hopeful Department of Justice agent on the trail of red revolution in Massachusetts, conceived the notion that these two anarchists were the guilty parties. He had caught them in the act—a quite natural one at the time and under the circumstances—of trying to conceal anarchist literature and they had betrayed at the time "a consciousness of guilt." On the basis of evidence that was flimsy, prejudiced and psychopathic, in an atmosphere of tight-lipped, respectable New England hatred of foreigners and radicals, and before a judge whose name has since become synonymous with a cold, self-righteous sadism, these two humble Italians came to trial and were convicted on July 14, 1921. But the long, six-year "passion of Sacco and Vanzetti" had barely begun. Within a few years the case was to arouse the sympathy of the whole liberal, radical and working-class world.

While the fortunes of American radicalism were at low ebb, they received from an unexpected quarter a sudden financial windfall that was to help tide over the lean years a number of causes and institutions. The angel in the case was the twenty-year-old heir of a Wall Street financier, Charles Garland, who, as a Tolstoyan anarchist, refused to accept a legacy of $900,000 on the ground that he had not earned it. The friend who finally persuaded young Garland to accept the money and turn it into a fund to be administered for the benefit of deserving liberal and radical causes was Roger N. Baldwin, director of the American Civil Liberties Union. The Fund thus set up was officially named the American Fund for Public Service, but has rarely been called anything except "the Garland Fund." It consisted largely of stock in the First National Bank of New York City and, though Garland had specified "that the money should be distributed as fast as it can be put into reliable hands," the amazing boom in stocks that followed increased the fund (it was estimated at more than $2,000,000 at one time) faster than it could be disbursed.

All the principal radical and liberal groups were represented on the Fund's first administrative board, but Baldwin's personality dominated that body as it has the Civil Liberties Union. His temperamental asceticism, backed up by the same quality in Scott Nearing, another member of the board, had as much to do perhaps as the steady rise in bank stocks with the fact that the money was not distributed as fast as young Garland had expected it to be.

Baldwin, incidentally, is both a representative and a somewhat lonely figure in contemporary American radical and liberal life—a spiritual heir of the New England Puritans turned Abolitionists, intellectuals, reformers, revolutionists, and translating all their emotional drive, their pristine religious fervor, their capacity for martyrdom into social channels. There are few of the type left (although the Sacco-Vanzetti case was to stir a surprisingly large remnant in Massachusetts to action) and Baldwin, for all his clipped and hard-boiled modern efficiency, is their representative *par excellence*. Possessed of a tremendous store of nervous energy and almost entirely lacking in what may be termed a "private life," his ability to drive those about him, as well as himself, to the point of exhaustion in the service of the cause has earned him the title of "slave driver" among the individuals who at one time or another have been members of his staff. His earlier radicalism was in the Tucker philosophic anarchist tradition. Later, he was to go to jail as a conscientious objector and join the I.W.W. for awhile, but his later radicalism, embracing at the same time the cause of civil liberties and proletarian dictatorship, is difficult to label. Through his influence any number of nice old Quaker ladies in Philadelphia, Back-Bay Bostonian liberals and philosophic young men of the order of Charles Garland have been induced to contribute generously to the most "subversive" causes. As the watchdog of the Garland Fund, he has earned more gratitude and at the same time made himself the target of more abuse than any other liberal-radical of his day.

Among the organizations and causes which leaned upon the Fund during these years of rising stocks and falling militancy were the Sacco-Vanzetti and Mooney-Billings defenses, anti-lynching campaigns in the South, workers' education, Southern textile and New York fur and garment strikes, the birth-control movement, anti-militarist propaganda, the Vanguard Press, Federated Press and the *New Masses*. The New York *Call*, which had struggled along for sixteen years on the nickels and dimes and hard work of its socialist supporters, was given $54,000 with which to blossom out as a "regular" labor newspaper and expired three months later. Several radical novelists received sustaining funds while completing their masterpieces. The money kept piling up faster than it was doled out. In the ten years between 1922 and 1932, $2,126,000 was given away or loaned—often as bail to strikers.

But not all the requests for aid came from radicals. Cranks of every sort applied for personal consideration. Most amus-

[ 343 ]

ing of all were the applications of the United States Flag Association (Calvin Coolidge, Honorary President), the National Boy Scouts (Herbert Hoover, President) and still another patriotic organization with Hamilton Fish, Jr. on its board of directors.

By 1932 the Fund, deflated by the stock crash, was practically gone.

The fortunes of American communism, in the two or three years between its birth in 1919 and the final emergence of the Workers Party at the end of 1922, constitute—depending upon one's point of view—either the most humorous or the most discouraging chapter in the later history of the Revolution. Driven underground so soon after their formation, the communist factions divided their energies between bitter verbal assaults on each other's revolutionary integrity, charges and protestations to Moscow, and the issuance of fiery proclamations, bristling with references to civil war, armed insurrection and revolutionary mass action, to an indifferent American proletariat. The romantic aspects of an underground existence, so like that of the Russian revolutionists prior to 1917, was reflected in the tone of American communist propaganda during the entire period of its illegality. It was addressed to a proletariat which had no existence outside the wish-fulfillment dreams of its writers. The communist organizations of this time, as George Soule pointed out in his article, "Radicalism," "found their reason for being, chiefly in the logic which originated in Moscow and Berlin, rather than in the American situation."

As later exposés of Department of Justice activities during 1920 were to indicate, underground communism probably included one Secret Service operative or *agent provocateur* to every three legitimate members and some of its more flamboyant utterances were undoubtedly due to this influence. Two of the most active of the communist leaders of the period

—one of them the leader of the Left Wing rebellion the year before—were accused by co-members of being in the employ of Palmer and in one case, at least, the charge was substantiated by public confession in 1925. But even among the most sincere, if not the most realistic, of its devotees, revolutionary romanticism was at its height, and in spite of the dangers implied in the existence of the various state criminal syndicalism laws, many of the comrades were unquestionably having the time of their lives. The necessary secretiveness of the movement—so long as it talked in terms of imminent revolution—the knowledge of its membership that its party ranks were infested with spies, the attempt to walk the path of the triumphant Russians, all tended to add glamour and drama to this conspiratory period. Robert Minor, by now the most orthodox of adherents, suddenly blossomed out as an incipient Trotsky with a little goatee and visored cap, refusing even to speak to his former, non-communist associates. Other leaders adopted the gestures and mannerisms of Lenin, Bukharin or Zinoviev. Until the coming of Foster, the movement had no leader with any wide experience in, or understanding of, the American labor movement.

By the end of 1921, however, as it became apparent that capitalism was once more stabilizing itself for an indefinite period and as the red hysteria subsided, the American communists began to realize the futility of their position. A more reasonable mood asserted itself and with it came the desire for a united front. "It cannot be denied," conceded the *Communist* at this time, "that the Communist Party in America practically does not exist as a factor in the class struggle."

The organization of a united Workers Party to act as the legal political expression of communist activity won the support of all but a small section of the "undergroundists." In 1922 a call was sent out for a convention to be held in the woods near Bridgman, Michigan, in August, for the purpose of liquidating the underground Communist Party with its inflammable reputation and preparing for a legal existence. The elaborate secrecy which surrounded this move was superfluous, for at least one of the delegates was a Department of Justice agent who had been supplying Washington with copies of all secret communist documents for more than a year. Seventeen of the delegates were arrested, including William Z. Foster, who had now thrown in his lot with the new party. This affair put an end to underground communism. Henceforth, the Workers (Communist) Party was to be the official representative in America of the Third International.

The program and spirit of the new Workers Party were not, in many important respects, the program and spirit of the revolutionary Left Wing of 1919. There was little talk of insurrection. The party was prepared to fight for immediate ends, "on questions of bread and butter, on housing, on labor organizations, wages and hours." In coming up for air, American communism was, at the same time, coming down to earth.

The international red tide of 1919 had receded, and in Russia the urban strikes and the rebellion of the Kronstadt sailors in 1920 had been followed by the New Economic Policy. With the permanent revolution indefinitely postponed, with the need for consolidating the position of Russia paramount, the Third International was sending out calls for a "united front" of communists, socialists, anarchists, syndicalists, for "a battle against the misery of the hour." The policy soon found its echo in the United States. In the *Liberator* for December, 1922, appeared an article by Robert Minor entitled, "We want a Labor Party!" And in its convention of that month, the Workers Party called for a United Political Front.

It was in such a conciliatory mood and as the result of a new interpretation of the American situation by the Comintern that the Workers Party affiliated with, and then captured what was left of, the Farmer-Labor Party, which had been organized in 1919. A year later, at a St. Paul convention, when the Minnesota Farmer-Labor Party initiated a move for a presidential campaign, much the same thing happened. An attempt was made by the now communist-controlled Federated Farmer-Labor Party to reach an agreement with the group that was already backing La Follette as a third party candidate. "The campaign will allow us to enter the third party wherever the opportunity presents itself, to form a left wing within it, and split it away from the third party," declared an American communist leader in the party's press service. But the victims of this proposed strategy were as able to read English as were the party members. La Follette denounced the communists. The Federated Farmer-Labor Party finally endorsed the candidacy of William Z. Foster. Soon thereafter, it quietly expired.

As is usually the case when the radicals arbitrarily "capture" some more conservative labor combination, the captured non-radical elements simply melted away, leaving them holding little more than a new name. The revolutionaries had not yet learned to forego the outward display of conquest in favor of coöperation and a more effective, if less spectacular, friendly pressure toward the left.

Meanwhile, for the first time since 1912, a third party movement had been launched. To the Conference for Progressive Political Action in 1922 came delegates from the railway unions—its chief instigators—from the more radical A. F. of L. unions, the Amalgamated Clothing Workers, the Non-Partisan League, the Farmer-Labor Party. The Conference attracted progressives and liberals of every hue as well as the Socialists, who had hitherto spurned all labor and farmer alliances. The Workers Party also sent delegates, but these were refused admission. The railway men, who dominated the Conference, were concerned primarily with the "Plumb Plan," a scheme for "industrial democracy" in railroad management, rather than with a labor party. But by 1924 they were prepared to back La Follette as a presidential candidate. In the campaign of that year the bulk of the liberal, radical and labor forces of the country, including the A. F. of L., was behind the Wisconsin Progressive and Burton K. Wheeler, his running mate. The Socialists, though far from enthusiastic about the La Follette program, put all their resources into the campaign—a fact for which the Communists, who had by now returned to their own partisan politics, bitterly denounced them. It turned out to be a La Follette, not a Labor campaign. Its dominant note was Progressivism. Many of the Progressives actually expected a La Follette victory. His five million votes seemed to the radicals a tremendous achievement, a promising start for a third party movement. But to La Follette and his friends, so long accustomed to Congressional victories, to the railway unions and the more conservative labor leaders, the result was bitterly disappointing. Within a few weeks after the election the whole alliance had blown up. The Progressives, a little frightened by their own daring, returned to the Republican Party; the Laborites to non-partisanship; the Socialists to their independent politics. The third party movement was to lie dormant for another decade.

With the exception of at least two magnificent battles in behalf of unorganized textile workers and a steady campaign in the labor ranks conducted by Foster and his lieutenants, the history of American communism in the five years before the crash consists largely of internal struggles which were reflections, for the most part, of party conflicts in Russia. In the field once dominated by the I.W.W., the party was showing effectiveness, realism and daring. But in the field of theoretical propaganda and internal politics, it was displaying all the weaknesses of its position as the least favored child in the international communist family. Puny and unpromising when compared with most of its brother parties in Europe, treated with a certain amount of contempt by its parents in Moscow (who kept an official observer on hand to guide its destinies and report on its progress), trying to function on a theoretical basis that had little relation to its actual environment in the boom decade, it naturally sought to compensate for its comparative ineffectiveness and to win parental favor by a doctrinal "regularity," an imitative activity and vocabulary that were pertinent only to critical situations existing in Europe, or to certain factional differences within the Soviet Union. American communism, during this period, is intelligible only in relation to its position as a link in the international communist chain.

Twenty years before, when the Socialist Party had been fashioned as a weapon of agitation and propaganda, capitalism in America, as elsewhere, was still hale and hearty, for all the germs of self-destruction which may have lurked behind its aggressive, imperialistic front. However hopefully it looked forward to the inevitable collapse of capitalistic economy, the new party, like the Second International with which it was affiliated, was organized, not for war, but for persuasion and preparation. It was a function that permitted the maximum of decentralization, the minimum of discipline, authority, doctrinal regularity.

The Third International, and with it American communism, was a weapon forged for revolutionary crisis at a time when it seemed that the walls of the capitalistic Jericho were on the verge of tumbling down. It was, in the words of its own declaration, "the International of Action." The walls had already tumbled in Russia; they were cracking in half the nations of Europe. The final stage in the capitalistic cycle, it seemed, had been reached. Revolutionary Russia had shown the way. When the moment for action arrived, when the storm of revolution broke among the returning soldiers, the starving workers and a disgruntled peasantry, a small, determined, disciplined group had ridden and then harnessed the whirlwind. In the face of the failure of the Second International, here was success. After the disillusionment and hopelessness of the war years, here was promise. It was inevitable that the new International and the forces that grouped themselves around it should bear the imprint of the Russian experience. The old, easy-going, gradualist days were over. The grim, fighting days were at hand. International communism was organized on this basis.

Although the inauguration of the New Economic Policy in Russia had marked a strategic retreat from the position of 1919-20, an acknowledgment of the fact that the World Revolution was not yet at hand, the Third International continued nevertheless to be "the general staff" of the international communist army. With two thirds of the communists of the world in Russia, Russian communism naturally dominated it by virtue of both numbers and prestige. In its Executive Committee was found the apex of that centralization of authority to which all communist organizations, "dominated by an iron discipline which is quasi-military in its severity," submitted as a condition of admission to the International.

The "democratic centralization," the iron discipline and quasi-military character of all official communist organizations is the logical corollary of a belief in inevitable and more or less imminent catastrophic revolution. If the triumph of the working class is to be achieved by a revolutionary *coup d'état*, a mass insurrection or civil war, in which the owning class will fight to the last ditch for the retention of its privileges, only a highly disciplined army, accustomed to unquestioning obedience to its chosen leaders, can act quickly and effectively to take advantage of a revolutionary situation which may arise from another world war, a prolonged labor disturbance, an economic crisis, the actual collapse of capitalism itself. A battle cannot be won if the general must stop to argue with his soldiers. Once power has been achieved, the same centralization of authority and discipline in the ranks is required to subdue or extirpate the bourgeoisie (and also other radical factions) to enforce the party dictatorship ("the conscious will of the proletariat") during the transition from capitalism to communism. As some such situation may occur at any time, it is natural that the orthodox communist should be dominated always by a "war-time" psychology, and that in the pre-revolutionary interim which remains, he should carry on "a merciless warfare" (one of the most frequently used phrases in the communist vocabulary) against all unorthodox elements which are likely to question the party decisions when the critical hour arrives. A war-time psychology is one which also permits the end to justify the means, not only in revolutionary struggles with capitalism, but in the internal struggles within the party itself. For each contending faction inevitably identifies its ends with those of the Revolution, its rival's ends with those of counter-revolution and betrayal.

Unfortunately, the very characteristics which make of any group or organization an effective instrument of warfare—class or otherwise, which enable it to act quickly and decisively in a crisis, are frequently those which make for schism, dissension, Jesuitry in times of comparative peace. Revolutionary fervor becomes doctrinal religiosity. With emphasis on faith rather than on works, centralized authority takes on the aspects of an ecclesiastical hierarchy. Communist organizations throughout the world were fashioned as instruments of revolutionary struggle. All but a few of them, however, were destined—in the years between 1923 and 1929—to operate on that basis of watchful waiting and peaceful preparation which had characterized the pre-war years. This was particularly true in the United States. Communist history in the next five years was to be very largely a history of schisms, excommunications, papal bulls, summonses to Moscow.

The first of the major internal battles after the emergence of the united Workers Party revolved, for the most part, around the party's farmer-labor activities, its flirtation with the third party movement, sponsored by its unquestioned leader at this time, Charles Ruthenberg, and opposed by Foster and his followers. At the party convention, held at the height of the controversy, Foster's views received the support of two thirds of the delegates. But Ruthenberg had behind him the Comintern's official representative, the former Hungarian commissar, "John Pepper" (later discredited and expelled from the International). Moscow upheld the Ruthenberg group and the party decision was set aside. Foster bowed to the decision, some of his followers left the party, but most of them deserted to the victor. Foster was to have his revenge four years later.

In 1926-27 the great Stalin-Trotsky controversy rocked the entire communist world. Not only Russia's internal policy was involved, but the policy and control of the Third International as well. It was a quarrel with angles too numerous to be considered in detail, but fundamentally it involved the question of whether revolutionary Russia, acting through the Third International, should constitute itself the spearhead of an aggressive revolutionary struggle throughout the world or whether the energies of Russian communism should be devoted to the "building of socialism in one land," to strengthening and consolidating Russia's position in a capitalistic world, with an ever-widening gulf between its interests and functions and those of the Third International which it actually controlled. All the implacable bitterness, the accusations, the name-calling, the stern suppression of dissent which had accompanied the struggle with dissenting elements from 1917 to 1920 came into play in this inner controversy. Stalin and Trotsky each hurled Lenin's written and spoken opinions of the other at each other's head, and each faction claimed, of course, to be working within the orthodox Leninist tradition. The quarrel reverberated in every little communist party throughout the world. In the United States, a minority, including Foster, inclined to Trotskyism. The outstanding

Trotskyist was James Cannon, a former I.W.W. When the Trotsky cause was manifestly lost and the brilliant Left Oppositionist finally banished, Foster swung over to Stalin and advocated the expulsion of the American Left. Led by Cannon, the latter group organized the Communist League, the American branch of the International Left Opposition and its paper, the *Militant*, became the official Trotskyist organ in the United States.

Though not altogether lacking in the element of personal ambition, the Stalin-Trotsky struggle was a "legitimate" one, in the sense that it involved definite and important issues, divergent revolutionary points of view. It had, therefore, a dignity which so many factional quarrels among the radicals have not. Trotsky's theory of "permanent revolution" was, of course, conceived long before 1917. Stalin seemed supported, in the international field at least, by the logic of current events. In no other nation of the world in 1927, except in China, did there appear the ghost of a revolutionary possibility. In domestic matters, Stalin conceded the validity of most of Trotsky's arguments in favor of a more aggressive internal policy by his intensive drive for collectivization and his vigorous pushing of the Five-Year Plan.

During the course of the long Stalin-Trotsky controversy, Ruthenberg died in New York and was succeeded, not by Foster, who was still under a cloud for his former Trotskyist sympathies, but by a young intellectual named Jay Lovestone. Foster's own forces were divided, his influence negligible. At a party convention called in New York in 1929, the quarrels of the past two years were brought to a head for final decision. Foster stood practically alone. The convention was a complete triumph for the Lovestone-ites. Then, out of a clear sky, arrived a cablegram from Moscow. It decreed that the minority should be the majority and named Foster as the party leader. Lovestone was summoned to Moscow for discipline. He had been guilty of several "right deviations" (notably in advancing the theory that American capitalism was still unripe for a revolutionary crisis); but more important, in a conflict which had developed between Stalin and Bukharin—both of whom two years before had fought shoulder to shoulder against Trotsky—Lovestone had backed the position of Bukharin and so had become identified with what was known as the Right Opposition which was now being disciplined or expelled. As had been the case with Foster four years before, the bulk of Lovestone's followers deserted to the new leadership. The voice of the Comintern was the voice of God.

The result of this latest deviation and its suppression was a Right (or International) Opposition organized outside the official party. Lovestone became its American leader; the *Workers Age*, its official organ in the United States. Its criticism of the official party position was, on most issues, the exact opposite of that of the Left (Trotskyist) Opposition. In international matters it contended for less centralization of authority in the Comintern, more consideration for the specific conditions and differences of development in different nations. In Russia, it opposed what it considered the too-rapid and ruthless pushing of the collectivization program and advocated a relaxation of the party domination over the trade unions.

The American working class was now confronted with three communist organizations, in addition to the little Proletarian Party which had gone its own independent way since 1920. In the heat of the controversies which accompanied these various schisms, the most appalling charges were flung by right, left, and center. To the party rank and file, most of whom believed whatever they read in the *Daily Worker*, both Cannon and Lovestone were renegades, crooks, betrayers of the Revolution and of Soviet Russia. In the heat of the fight, one party leader declared that "fairness is a conception imported from a hostile class; it belongs to the columns of the

*Nation* and the *New Republic*." Thus were post-war revolutionary ethics distinguished from the ethics of liberalism.

To turn back from these fratricidal wars to the field in which the Revolution, under communist leadership, was actually making some headway is like coming from a noisy and odorous room out into the clear air.

Early in 1926, after a ten-per-cent wage-cut in an already shockingly low wage-scale, 16,000 textile workers in the woolen mills around Passaic, New Jersey, went on strike. The strike, which was to last an entire year, was a better organized and even more dramatic edition of the one in Lawrence in 1912. It repeated all the Lawrence phenomena—the great mass meetings conducted in several languages, mass picketing, revolutionary songs, continuous activity, the mobilization of the radical, liberal and labor opinion of the nation behind the strikers. This time the principal leader was no experienced and hard-bitten Wobbly agitator, but an intense young Jewish intellectual, a graduate of Harvard Law School, Albert Weisbord. About him was gathered a devoted little band of communist lieutenants, including several foreign-born agitators, zealous young revolutionaries from New York, and a seasoned veteran in charge of the administration of relief. Communist slogans and phraseology were not flaunted, the strike leadership was known as the United Front Committee. Its efforts were aided by the attitude of the mill owners and by the incredible stupidity and brutality of the local and state police. Mass meetings and picket lines were broken up, strikers, including women and children, were ridden down, beaten up, drenched from fire hoses in zero weather. Even reporters from the New York dailies were beaten, their cameras smashed—a fact which turned almost the entire daily press to the side of the strikers and gave a New York tabloid the excuse to send its reporters and camera men to Passaic in an armored car. Money poured in from all over the country, bakers' unions sent truckloads of bread; the Amalgamated Clothing Workers, as usual, sent fat checks; socialist, anarchist, I.W.W., communist, liberal speakers addressed mass meetings from the same platform or marched in the picket lines. Artists, writers, clubwomen, prominent churchmen visited the scene and went back to New York to arouse sympathy and raise money for the strikers.

The Passaic strike—in spite of the fact that its organization and partial victory were to be no more lasting than those of Lawrence—marked the outstanding achievement of American communism in the '20s. It was handled with wisdom, skill and a lack of demagoguery that permitted the most genuine united front American radicalism was to know between 1919 and 1933.

The communist-led strike in Gastonia, North Carolina, two years later was in many respects a southern replica of Passaic. But the southern strikers were natives with something of their mountaineer spirit still unbroken by years of undernourishment on their sterile patches and later in the mill villages, and they lacked the patience of the Slavic immigrants who composed the bulk of the Passaic strikers. They were accustomed to "toting" guns and settling their grievances in their own way; and, though their leaders warned repeatedly against violence, the invasion of their tent colony by the authorities, after emotions had been roused to fever pitch by repeated raids upon their relief store, resulted in the fatal shooting of the chief of police. The strike leaders were arrested for conspiracy; another typical labor trial was staged in an atmosphere of intense prejudice and—as the leaders were Northerners—southern hostility; the defendants were sentenced to long prison terms. With years in a southern prison ahead of them, a horrible prospect certainly for young and innocent men, the communist organizers "jumped" their bail and sought refuge in Russia as had Haywood and his companions eight years before. It is impossible not to sympathize with the Gastonia leaders, but "bail jumping" among radicals is a serious matter. It strengthens the position of the courts, which are already inclined to set bail for radicals at excessively high figures, decreases the amount of bail available for future emergencies, and causes radical sympathizers to hesitate before coming to the rescue in similar cases thereafter. In the case of the Gastonia defendants, communist sentiment in America was divided between approval and disapproval of their act. The dwindling Garland Fund was the chief loser. There was some talk at first of the Comintern and then of the American communists assuming the responsibility, but actually only $253 was ever paid back.

Between the Passaic and the Gastonia strikes, the seven-year battle to save Sacco and Vanzetti had come to its tragic close. No radical, labor or political case in history—except possibly the Dreyfus case—had ever so stirred the hearts and minds of millions of men and women throughout the world. International demonstrations, mass protest meetings, mile-long petitions, pleas, appeals to the higher courts, to Governor Fuller of Massachusetts, to President Coolidge, finally to individual justices of the United States Supreme Court, all were in vain, all crumbled before a withered, tight-lipped, senile old man who found in the cold letter of the law a means of venting prejudices so deep that it is doubtful if he ever knew that he had them. What were the lives of two simple Italians when the majesty of the law and the dignity of the great state of Massachusetts were at stake? On the eve of the execution, radicals and liberals flocked to Boston, attempted to parade, to hold mass meetings on the Common, to picket the State House. Hundreds of them were carted off to jail. In New York, London, Paris, Madrid, Moscow thousands congregated before bulletin boards, massed to hear radical speakers in the squares. Isadora Duncan threatened to dance nude on the steps of the American embassy in Paris. She was, fortunately, dissuaded. Bombs went off in remote places. All explosions—even that of a bootleg still in the Italian section of Boston—were attributed to "Sacco-Vanzetti sympathizers." Charlestown prison, where the world-famous prisoners awaited the chair, bristled with machine guns. On the fatal night of August 22, 1927, powerful searchlights swept the surrounding scene and every approaching street ended in a glittering forest of bayonets. Between 12:15 and 12:30 A.M., the light inside the prison went dim—twice.

Probably never before had the death of two individuals affected so many people in every quarter of the globe. The shoemaker and the fish-peddler had become symbols of human heroism and dignity. Vanzetti's parting words to Judge Thayer were to echo around the world:

If it had not been for these things, I might have live out my life talking at street corners to scorning men. I might have die, unmarked, unknown, a failure. Now we are not a failure. This is our career and our triumph. Never in our full life could we hope to do such work for tolerance, for joostice, for man's onderstanding of man as now we do by accident. Our words—our lives—our pains—nothing! The taking of our lives—lives of a good shoemaker and a poor fish-peddler—all! That last moment belongs to us—that agony is our triumph.

# XV

## MARX REDIVIVUS—
## THE REVOLUTION AND THE AMERICAN SCENE

T HE crash of 1929 shattered a world in which the Revolution—at least in the United States—had seemed almost an academic issue, although this fact was not to be realized until almost a year later. There had been "depressions" before. Every American adult had lived through several—1907, 1913, 1921. That this one, coming on the heels of the long and dazzling Boom Decade might mark the end of an era became apparent only toward the end of 1930. As the breadlines lengthened, as the army of unemployed multiplied steadily, as each optimistic pronouncement from Washington fell flat in the face of statistical evidence and increasing misery, a new note crept into academic, journalistic, periodical and even popular discussions. Doubters and critics of capitalism, leftward-leaning professors of sociology and economics, social planners, heterodox intellectuals, political and industrial Cassandras of every shade emerged from their ten years' obscurity or lethargy and gained a hearing in unexpected and even thoroughly orthodox quarters. The Profit System suddenly ceased to be sacrosanct. It had become a subject for searching and critical examination. The old gods were being deflated. The intellectuals began looking about for new ones; their gaze shifted slowly toward the left. Books on "the Russian experiment," mostly friendly or at least objective, poured from the presses.

To the assorted radicals, accustomed by now to their snail's progress and to their general isolation from a largely indifferent working class, the crash, with the depression which followed it, was at once a justification of their Marxian faith, a signal for mobilization and a supreme opportunity. In spite of the private difficulties of their own members, all of the radical groups were immediately galvanized with a new ardor. The tired radicals of a decade evinced a renewed interest in their old faiths. The hopes that had waned in the past nine years when the permanent revolution seemed temporarily shelved, were burgeoning again among the communists. Among the discouraged socialists appeared a note of optimism absent since the campaign of 1920. Capitalism had, to be sure, survived serious crashes before, but this one was another matter. The system was no longer on the up-and-up, a youthful and resilient organism. It had reached a decidedly overripe maturity. In the past ten years the world in general had grown increasingly unsteady on its economic legs, and during that time European capitalism had been heading slowly but obviously toward the abyss. American capitalism, caught at last in the snarls of its own inherent contradictions, was now hastening in the same direction. The collapse of the industrial and financial structure of the United States, the strongest link in the imperialistic chain, might well be the beginning of the end.

By the end of 1930, "the System" was proving to the hilt every charge the intransigent radicals had ever made against it, and the objective conditions favorable for the rapid growth of a revolutionary climate of opinion were at hand. The radicals had learned from experience that their organizations do not, as a rule, increase their membership during periods of depression, but such periods, if prolonged, breed disillusion, unrest, resentment—fertile soil for the radical seed. Argument, abstract logic were no longer necessary. They had only to point their fingers at the spectacle of breadlines and bursting granaries and cry, "Look!" A child could see that the System had failed to work. Its industrial, financial and political spokesmen, shorn of their boom-tide confidence and authoritativeness, stood nakedly revealed to the public gaze in all their essential puerility. The Mitchell, Insull, Kreuger, Wiggin exposés (surprising to no one who had read Gustavus Myers' *History of the Great American Fortunes* or who remembered the Pujo exposures of 1913) were yet to come, but by 1931 utterances from on high were already being received with that typical American rejoinder, "Oh yeah?"

The Crisis in Capitalism found the forces of the Revolution in the United States more divided than at any time in their history. The Socialist Party was still the most influential politically, polling by far the largest vote. Since the death of Debs it had had no leader of outstanding appeal to American workers. Norman Thomas, one of the directors of the League for Industrial Democracy (successor to the Intercollegiate Socialist Society), had risen rapidly in its councils since the war years, and he had a large and devoted following, particularly in collegiate, professional and liberal religious circles. He made no pretense of being a scientific Marxian, and was in many respects something of a thorn in the side of the older and more orthodox leaders headed by Hillquit. For all his theoretical heterodoxy, however, he stood, on several issues, slightly to the left of the party Marxians; and, by 1930, in spite of the handicap of his ministerial and Princetonian past, he was the Socialists' most popular spokesman. During the boom years, the party had done little more than mark time and carry on routine agitation. The organization had never recovered from the effects of the war and the schism which followed. Both the vote and the membership had fallen seriously since 1920.

The official Communist Party had emerged from six years

of internal strife with its membership cut in half from the 1924 figure, and was just beginning to put its house in order again. It had gained applause and support for its fights in Passaic and Gastonia, it had organized a number of left-wing unions (since 1928, its attitude toward dual unionism had shifted somewhat), and it was devoting a considerable portion of its energies to winning the support of the Negroes—a field which the Comintern had indicated as one of the most promising in the American labor scene. But in spite of the fact that it basked in the reflected light of the prestige gained by Russian communism, its intensely sectarian tactics, its bitter attacks upon all those who differed a hair's breadth from "the party line," kept aloof from it thousands who were in sympathy with its ultimate purposes. Its political strength was still negligible.

The two Communist Oppositions, the Left and the Right, were little more than agitational centers within the communist orbit. Their propaganda was directed largely at the party itself, rather than at the non-radical public. The little Proletarian Party frankly regarded itself as a Marxian educational society; the Socialist Labor Party, still pursuing its ethereal De Leonite way, was actually little more than that, although it still put up candidates and carried on campaigns. The I.W.W., torn asunder by struggles with the communists during the early '20s, was now only a shadow of that former rowdy and picturesque self that had aroused so much interest and apprehension between 1910 and 1917.

Still another group had appeared upon the scene—the Conference for Progressive Labor Action. Its membership consisted, for the most part, of teachers and graduates of the Brookwood Labor College, young men and women from the ranks trained for service and radical leadership in the labor movement. Around it gathered a group of former communists (some of them expelled from the party for various "right deviations"), a number of "militant" socialists. The Conference members, popularly known as "the Muste-ites," after their leader, A. J. Muste, stood halfway between the official Communists and the official Socialists. They were, in a sense, attempting to Americanize communism, regarding the Moscow direction of the party's policy as fatal. They were also agitating for a militant labor party to include all the radical and left-wing groups.

It was these groups which now faced the possible collapse of capitalism, or at least a combination of objective conditions which seemed ready-made for their purposes.

That mood of profound disillusionment which the radicals had anticipated with the crash of 1929 did not actually generate until the middle of 1931 and did not reach its crest until the summer of 1932. Even then it did not manifest itself where they had every right to expect it—among the dispossessed proletariat standing in endless breadlines, drooping on park benches, huddled hopelessly in cheerless rooms.

Perhaps no phenomenon of the depression has been so frequently commented upon as the mood in which twelve to fifteen million unemployed accepted their plunge into the incalculable misery and degradation of the early '30s. During the first year of the depression, they were buoyed up, perhaps, by the promises of the professional optimists, by the hope of speedy recovery. After a year or more of steadily increasing insecurity, desperation, undernourishment, broken pride, the fight seemed to have gone out of them. In no previous depression had the unemployed remained so patient, so abject—possibly because in no other depression had relief—of a sort—been quite so well organized.

The picture was not one of unrelieved apathy, of course. Among the employed and partly employed, subject to repeated wage-cuts which left many of them scarcely better off than the unemployed recipients of relief, there were sporadic strikes, attempts at resistance. The aggressive spirit was most

[ 363 ]

pronounced in Detroit where radical leadership was also the most active. Here both unemployed demonstrations and strikes against wage-cuts took on at times the color of minor rebellions, culminating in the clubbing and shooting of demonstrators at the Ford plant in March, 1932. Elsewhere, in the steel industry, in the coal fields of Pennsylvania and West Virginia, and still later at Harlan, Kentucky, there were "labor troubles" of various sorts, led by Communists, Socialists, Muste-ites, I.W.Ws. In general, these were merely continuations of old struggles rather than the direct fruit of the crisis. On the whole, labor, both organized and unorganized, could scarcely afford to be aggressive with a thousand men clamoring for every job.

In the larger cities, particularly in New York and Chicago, the radicals, and especially the Communists, whose methods were particularly fitted for demonstration purposes in times of crisis, were making considerable headway by 1932 among the unemployed. Huge mass meetings were staged, hunger marches and unemployed parades drew not only the radical faithful but thousands of the hungry, the footloose, the vaguely resentful into their ranks. The espousal and dramatization of the Scottsboro case by the Communists won them a considerable following, or at least a sympathetic hearing, among the Negroes, probably suffering more than any other group from the ravages of the depression. Thousands of unemployed were organized into unemployed councils or unemployed leagues. In a number of cities, evictions were followed by riots, the more aggressive demonstrators fought back when attacked by police. Union Square, in New York City, was as usual the center of almost continuous turmoil and anything resembling a proletarian uprising was confined largely to the seasoned veterans of this section. During the summer, the Bonus Army staged its march to Washington. But though it was cheered on and abetted by the Communists, intent on winning the support of the ex-soldiers, it was not, even after the tear bombs and bayonets of Anacostia Flats, concerned with the Revolution.

The summer of 1932 saw the beginnings of the presidential campaign and what one politician so graphically described as "the peak of the depression." It saw also—in two distinct and widely separated quarters far from the proletarian front —the peak of insurrectionary sentiment in the United States since the eventful years of the '70s.

The farmers of the nation, and particularly of the Middle West, had not shared in the prizes of the Boom Decade. Since the fat years of the war and immediate post-war period, their fortunes had steadily declined, their indebtedness had steadily mounted. Now, facing foreclosure, ruin, the loss of their middle-class status after a ten-year battle to maintain it, they suddenly turned to direct action with all the readiness of the pioneer unbroken to the machine process. The Corn Belt seethed with revolt. The Farm Holiday movement arose and gained headway; mortgage foreclosures were forcibly resisted, judges and bank lawyers were threatened with violence, milk was dumped by the thousand gallons along the roadside. All this was occurring, not among the long-peonized share-croppers and dispossessed farmers of the South and Southwest, but among the formerly comfortable owning farmers of Iowa, Nebraska and Wisconsin, the backbone of the American body politic. Here was sabotage such as the Wobblies had never dreamed of. Here was radical action without benefit of radical theory. The urban radicals of the East hailed the farm insurrection as the first skirmishes of an agrarian revolt, many of them forgetting for the moment that direct action is not necessarily social revolutionary. The agrarian with a stake in the soil was the traditional American rebel fighting in a traditional American cause, the same cause for which his predecessors had fought with flintlocks in Bacon's and Shays' rebellions, with ballots in the '70s, '80s and '90s. He was trying to hang onto his land and to get higher prices for his product. But whatever his motivation and its end, here, at any rate, was action, resentment, refusal to starve quietly, to give up without a fight.

If the revolt of the farmers was a heartening demonstration of instinctive militancy, it was by no means the most striking phenomenon of the great depression. If revolution seemed in any sense imminent in 1932—and that it did in certain quarters was betrayed by the fact that a number of apprehensive gentlemen were stocking their country homes with canned goods in preparation for a possible state of siege—it was because it had won its most ardent converts in the most articulate section of the population. The real revolution of 1932 occurred on the intellectual front, and had its reverberations throughout the whole urban upper- and middle-class world. The American intellectuals, as we have seen, had turned to the left at regular intervals ever since 1840, but never quite so clamorously as in the third year of the Great Depression.

Though the working class had shown, on the whole, a surprising lack of interest in the propaganda of the Revolution, the urban middle and professional classes, more shattered psychologically than the workers by the effects of economic breakdown, had been toying with both its theory and its vocabulary. Even in times of comparative prosperity, the average worker enjoys little sense of security. His boom days are usually punctuated by unemployed intervals, his work is seasonal or unsteady, he is rarely able to save enough to tide himself over a "bad break." He teeters habitually on the edge of a social precipice and he becomes accustomed to danger. To members of the professional and middle classes, raised, for the most part, in an atmosphere of comparative security and accustomed to a definite place in the social sun, the economic exuberance and expansion of the '20s had opened up new frontiers which had relieved to some extent the overcrowding in their ranks. Their own confidence had never, as yet, been seriously shaken. When their world was rocked to its foundations in the early '30s, they were, quite naturally, the first to think and talk of revolution. Unaccustomed to privation and uncertainty, they were unable to realize, or to credit, the "splendid patience of the poor."

By the autumn of 1932, it was the engineers, architects, newspaper and advertising men without jobs, teachers with drastically cut salaries, doctors without patients, lawyers without clients, writers and artists without markets, overworked social workers and even dispirited bond-salesmen who were talking darkly about the breakdown of capitalism. Among big and little business men one heard repeatedly that "if something doesn't happen soon there's going to be a revolution in this country." The American intellectuals discovered, or rediscovered, Karl Marx, and that turn to the left which was to take on the nature of a stampede began. Æsthetes and academicians, getting their first taste of the class struggle, became revolutionary theoreticians overnight. Erstwhile New Humanists and Spenglerians, devotees of Mencken, Gurdjieff or Keyserling, blossomed out as Marxian critics and proletarian artists, and proceeded to tell the battle-scarred veterans in both these groups what it was all about. As a result of this agitation on the intellectual and artistic front, the Revolution in general and communism in particular became the fashionable gesture of the moment. Socialism was more popular in upper middle-class and academic quarters, but communism flourished in literary and artistic circles and in the higher brackets of the social scale.

The unusual preoccupation of so many of the American intellectuals with the class struggle in the early '30s was not, of course, as superficial as the gestures made by their numerous admirers and camp-followers in high and low places tended to indicate. Economic and social issues had become the compelling issues of the moment. The ivory towers, the academic cloisters of the world had been struck by the lightning bolts of the social thunderstorm. Many of their occupants had once served brief apprenticeships to the Revolution in their younger and more hopeful days. Now they were returning to the left with renewed faith and vigor. Others, critics like Edmund Wilson and novelists like John Dos Passos, had been moving steadily and intelligently toward the Marxian beacon light even before the crash of 1929. Men like Dreiser, who had been vaguely but warmly sympathetic toward the struggle of the workers, now found themselves galvanized into indignation and action. Still others, shocked out of their habitual æsthetic, philosophical or journalistic preoccupations by the obvious bankruptcy of the prevailing order, turned wholeheartedly and sincerely to a cause which alone seemed to offer them spiritual and intellectual nourishment, a satisfying set of values, and did so without setting themselves up immediately as the prophets and schoolmasters of the new dispensation. The ablest and intellectually soundest of these were among the least contentious and fire-breathing of the new left-wing intellectuals. The horrendous vocabularies, the revolutionary clichés and the hairsplitting scholasticism which have done so much to make the new Marxian intellectualism slightly ridiculous in the past few years and which would have caused Marx himself to turn over in his grave were to be found principally among the little radical Phi Beta Kappas who followed in their wake.

As the presidential campaign progressed in an atmosphere of mounting disillusionment, agrarian rebellion, middle-class unrest and intellectual revolt, the hopes of the two major radical parties had every reason to rise higher. Hoover was politically discredited. Roosevelt was certainly not the object of any intense or widespread enthusiasm. Both Norman Thomas and William Z. Foster spoke to huge and enthusiastic gatherings throughout the country. To the banner of the former rallied an imposing array of sociologists, economists, liberal journalists, ministers, several playwrights, columnists, satirists. An even more imposing group of well-known playwrights, novelists, poets, critics, painters and the left wing of the *New Republic's* board of editors came out for Foster and communism, and a pamphlet called *Culture and the Crisis* was issued in their name.

Just at this time a new economic formula made its sudden appearance in the public prints and the manner in which it was received indicated how ready the American public had become at this time to try anything but revolution. Technocracy had, to be sure, a typically American appeal. Though its vocabulary was not altogether intelligible, it talked in terms of power, energies, mechanics, efficiency, elimination of waste, and these, even more than its utopian promise of $20,000-a-year incomes, were calculated to capture the American imagination. Howard Scott, its progenitor, had been a familiar figure in radical-bohemian circles for many years— during which time he had been pouring forth his scorn on the radicals' schemes of mass revolution and demonstrating that twelve revolutionary engineers in strategic places could bring capitalism to its knees in three days. Coming now from the hallowed precincts of Columbia University, backed up by an imposing array of academic sponsors and assistants, his theories took on an authority and dignity that made Scott the man of the hour. A technocracy craze swept the country. The newspapers were full of it; whole magazines were devoted to it; fierce controversies ranged around it. Veblen's *The Engineers and the Price System*, which contained the essence of technocratic theory, was republished and became a bestseller. Scott himself helped to kill the movement several months later in a rambling, incoherent and confused speech that was broadcast throughout the country. A few stubborn admirers hoped, and claimed, that their idol was somewhat "tight" when he made it. But a new prophet had toppled from his pedestal. The new panacea died a rapid death.

The result of that showing of hands involved in the presidential election of 1932 was probably more surprising to the apprehensive conservatives and the enthusiastic revolutionary converts than to the more seasoned radicals. The Socialist vote had quadrupled, the Communist vote had doubled since 1928—and both candidates of the left had probably polled many more votes than were counted for them. Nevertheless, in the disillusioned '30s while the American workers were receiving the worst bludgeoning in their history, the farmers were embittered and the professionals aroused as never before, the combined vote of the Socialists, Communists and their left-wing liberal supporters had shown only a slight increase over that polled by the united Socialists in the pre-woman suffrage year of 1912.

The militancy of the first three depression years had been, primarily, the militancy of the American middle and professional classes fighting against extinction. Only a small proportion of both the rural and urban insurrectionists was looking for either Mr. Foster's proletarian dictatorship or Mr. Thomas' confiscatory capital levy. They wanted changes, to be sure, but changes that would restore their former security, not plunge them into a social upheaval that might eliminate them altogether. Like the workers, they had no program but they were ready to support anything which seemed to offer change and relief. They turned to the New Deal. The Roosevelt landslide was an electoral mandate for immediate action of some kind; the NRA was the administration's answer to that mandate.

The promotion of revolution in the United States has always been an uphill job. We have our own tradition of radicalism, but it is not a tradition of collectivist radicalism. Anarchism is undoubtedly the philosophy most native to the American temperament. The country attracted the restless individualist. The frontier itself and then the memory of it

[ 370 ]

defeated for many years the inexorable collectivist logic of the machine process. In the words of Benjamin Stolberg, in the *Nation*:

The frontier fixed and arrested these sesquicentennial views [the doctrines of eighteenth-century libertarian individualism] in the American subconscious which explains why today we have such a tragic time in thinking through the Socialist demands of a new revolutionary epoch, the demands of social planning in a world of social anarchy. After the geographical frontier was closed, we carried over its spirit of individualism and adventure into finance, industry and labor. Our capitalism in the '80s and '90s was a buccaneer capitalism and our labor leaders during the formative years of the American Federation of Labor were primitive tribal chieftains, each craft a tribe, who fought back with desperate guerilla tactics.

Marxism got off to a bad start in the early '70s. It did not become acclimatized and infiltrate the native labor movement as it did in other countries. The social revolutionary movement never completely lost its dilettante character—even after the objective conditions of American social and industrial life became increasingly friendly to what the communists call "the radicalization of the masses."

After 1912, though American socialism was predominantly native in membership and vocabulary, its propaganda and program were patterned upon the dominant Germanic tradition of gradualness, of slow steady progress which called for a quiet purposefulness and patience totally alien to the impatient, excitement-craving American temperament—and which seemed particularly uninspiring in the post-war years. The American has little historical perspective. He wants action and results and he wants them quickly. If they are not forthcoming he turns to something else, a trait that has helped to junk so many hopeful third-party beginnings.

The coming of communism offered to those who wanted it plenty of "action," but it offered them so much else besides that they did not want, that it too made little progress. If socialism spoke with an exotic accent, communism scarcely spoke English at all. But its chief drawback lay in the fact that it came wrapped in the garment of a medieval religiosity that made the Society of Jesus look like a college Liberal Club in comparison. It was a church, not a movement, and a church which operated under the thumb of a college of cardinals four thousand miles away. For a decade while the party was rent with schisms and heresy-hunts, while each gesture of Moscow attuned to the realities of the Russian situation was matched in miniature by a similar gesture in New York, thousands of convinced radicals and potential recruits sickened and turned away. If the socialists underestimated the streak of almost primitive emotionalism, the possibility for mass excitation which existed in the American working class, the communists overestimated its class consciousness, its readiness for revolt. Their tendency to confuse a riot with a revolution gave to many of their activities an unreal and histrionic air. The average worker was more inclined to be amused than impressed.

At the present time, as in the past, the Socialist Party contains the most diverse shades of radicalism. On its extreme left are certain "militants" as convinced of catastrophic revolution and a proletarian dictatorship as are the Communists, but who refuse to accept the leadership of the Third International in American revolutionary affairs. At its extreme right are members whose "gradualness" and loyalty to democratic procedure rival those of the British Labor Party. The membership as a whole varies between these two extremes. The party's official position seems predicated upon the idea that while the necessity for a violent conquest of power *may* be forced upon the radicals by a stubborn ruling class, this is a contingency to be avoided if possible, that it is preferable first to attempt this transformation by democratic methods.

Regardless of theoretical validity, the weakness of this position at the present time lies in the fact that capitalism itself is moving toward forms of administration which cut off the possibility of peaceful transition. While the workers might, if they were sufficiently militant now, clip the wings of an emergent fascism before it had time to gain strength, there is as yet little indication of any such political awakening. Though fascism is not an inevitable prelude to a social revolution in America, it is obvious that in such a period of economic disintegration as the present a radical party must be prepared for the collapse of democracy. By continuing to function only as a propaganda and agitational machine, it leaves itself unprepared for the exigencies of warfare, for leadership in time of crisis. The party's future effectiveness probably depends upon a more complete break with the undramatic gradualist tradition which has identified it with the failures of European social democracy and a closer affiliation with the more leftward-looking native farmer and labor elements.

While the events of the past few years have reinforced the Communist's certainty of the imminence of the final revolutionary conflict and the collapse of capitalism, American communism has had to adjust itself meanwhile to the fact that the American workers are not yet ready to fight for a Soviet America. In doing so, it has right-about-faced from many of its earlier tactics. It bores from within trade unions, seeking to capture their membership, and organizes dual communistic unions. It carries on a particularly intensive campaign among the Negroes and in line with a thesis enunciated by the Comintern has declared its support for a separate Negro republic in our "black belt"; that is, in those states and counties where the Negro population predominates. It fights with the ex-soldiers for the bonus, with the unemployed for larger relief grants, with the farmers for higher prices and with "bourgeois pacifists" in anti-war and anti-fascist demonstrations. The party has been most successful and most realistic in its organization of unskilled agricultural workers in the West, of mill workers in the East.

It is here that it shows the most promise and deserves un-stinted praise. And yet, though communism as a philosophy has won the sympathy and interest of thousands who were antagonistic or indifferent to it a few years ago, most of these sympathizers hold aloof from the party itself because of disagreement with its methods, the almost psychopathic vindictiveness of its press. Since the collapse of German communism, with its 6,000,000 adherents, in the face of the Nazi offensive, and on order from the Comintern, the party has adopted a somewhat less belligerent tone and has sought to engage in various "united front" movements with other radical groups. But the theory that all non-communist party radicals are "social fascists" and "renegades" does not square with the new tactic of a united front. Undoubtedly one or the other will have to be abandoned.

Since the presidential election of 1932 and in spite of the optimism which accompanied the earlier months of the Re-covery Program, sentiment for a radical American third party movement—labor or farmer-labor—has spread rapidly. It has fed largely upon the conviction that capitalism has passed the stage in which it can be stabilized, that the acute-ness of the economic situation and the drift toward world war and fascism necessitate the union of all those aggressive labor, farmer and professional elements which can be molded into an effective instrument of social change. The first expres-sion of this sentiment crystallized when the League for Inde-pendent Political Action, a liberal-radical coalition under the leadership of Professor John Dewey, initiated a third party movement in Chicago. As was inevitable, there was a sharp cleavage between the liberal and radical forces and the Farmer-Labor organization which emerged has remained in a tentative stage. Three months later, the Conference for Progressive Labor Action, at a convention in Pittsburgh, launched the American Workers Party, a new "revolutionary American party of workers and dirt farmers." It became, in

[ 374 ]

effect, a communistic party with an American orientation, unaffiliated with any International. The new organization will probably draw into its ranks many of those unaffiliated revolutionary intellectuals for whom the *Modern Monthly*, the Marxian journal edited by V. F. Calverton, serves as a mouthpiece.

Though the combined vote of the Socialist and official Communist parties may constitute a fairly accurate gauge of the *conscious* opposition to capitalism in the United States at the present time, it is in no sense a measure of potential revolutionary strength under the strain of continued or recurring depression. Nor does the numerical weakness of the revolutionary movement, with its repeated dissensions and schisms, its bitter internal animosities, its all too human mistakes and failings, constitute an insuperable barrier to its final triumph. (In Russia prior to 1917, the Bolshevik Party was but one of five or six small, wrangling revolutionary groups, all aiming at the same general end but differing violently as to methods of achieving it.) To counterbalance these is the real courage and devotion of its members and the fact that at this particular juncture in social development, the rebels are working—historically speaking—on the side of the angels. In the general direction toward which they are pointing may well lie the only alternative to social chaos. While in America, the radicals of all shades have seemingly made very little progress, American capitalism itself has been laying the groundwork for social revolution. Today millions who never before questioned its premises or its soundness are beginning to suspect its bankruptcy.

The events of the post-election year, the inadequacy of the NRA to remedy a situation which is inherent in a profit economy, have done nothing to stem the rising tide of social unrest. It becomes increasingly apparent that the American Bourbon has learned nothing and that our national labor leadership has learned little since 1929. But whether or not, in the critical period ahead, the American worker will turn hopefully to the left, instead of despairingly to the right, may depend largely upon the wisdom and adaptability of the American radicals.

So far, their propaganda in the United States has succeeded in winning an important segment of the American intellectuals and these have a valuable and important function to perform on the cultural front of any mass movement. But the most urgent problem now confronting them is to convince the man on the job, on the farm, on the park bench, that he can trust the radical leadership, that it knows what it is about, and that he and his fellows are capable of building a new society. Unlike the intellectuals, he does not idealize the proletariat.

It is useless as yet to direct his attention to Russia inspiring as its achievements may be, for though Russia has no unemployment, the American worker does not consider the physical status of the Russian worker a superior one and he is too pragmatic to weigh in the balance the Russian's future possibilities. Nor—in the midst of his own desperate situation—can he be stirred by such slogans as "Defend the Soviet Union [or the Chinese Soviets] from Imperialist Invasion." He is not convinced that he has any stake in either and he will probably be ready to rebel in his own behalf a decade before the Communists have succeeded in persuading him of this fact. Furthermore, he is a realist and is not concerned with those fine points of theoretical and tactical differences to which the radicals devote so much of their time and attention. He wants to be sure that the forces of revolt once set in motion will resolve themselves to his advantage.

If American radicalism is to overcome its own isolation and take advantage of labor's renewed aggressiveness under the Recovery Program—as it failed to take advantage of its disillusionment during the past three years—it would seem ob-

[ 376 ]

vious that there must be some change in its propaganda and tactics. Its indictments of the present order are unanswerable, but this evidently is not enough. Though capitalism may be doomed, socialism or communism is not necessarily the next step, nor are these any longer the only alternatives to "bourgeois democracy." Fascism, too, can take advantage of a revolutionary situation; and though a fascist capitalism may also be doomed to shipwreck on the rocks of its own inherent contradictions, it can survive long enough to wipe out or so cripple all radical opposition that when the strategic moment arrives there will be no group with sufficient strength and vitality to take hold.

It is possible that if the Social Revolution in America is going to triumph over capitalism this side of the abyss, it will do so by somewhat the same methods used by the Russian communists. But there is some significance surely in the fact that so far the communist program of seizure of power by small militant minorities has been most successful in two countries that have been predominately peasant in population—Russia and China. That it would encounter special difficulties in nations with large and aggressive middle classes, with a highly developed and complicated industrial life, only a few communists will admit. Even so intelligent a convert as Mr. John Strachey cannot forebear to indulge in much wishful thinking on the subject. In spite of the evidence offered by the triumph of Hitlerism in Germany, contemporary radicalism continues to underestimate the virility and the capacity for action of the middle classes.

It must be obvious, too, that while the capture of Petrograd and Moscow by a handful of purposeful communists, backed up by some thousands of soldier-workers, meant the capture of political power over all of Russia, the taking of New York, Washington or Chicago in a nation where each geographical section is so highly intregrated both politically and economically as in the United States would mean very much less, and might leave a very formidable St. Louis, Cleveland and San Francisco to be reckoned with, to say nothing of a large and militant class of Kulaks in Iowa, Nebraska and Wisconsin. The result would be merely prolonged civil war. If the *coup d'état* is to be the weapon of revolution in the United States, it will certainly require not only a high degree of strategic skill and technical knowledge, but a widespread and popular support a thousand times greater than that needed by the revolutionaries in Russia, where the great mass of the peasantry was indifferent to, and largely ignorant of, what was happening in the capital. The larger and more politically aggressive a nation's middle class, the wider and stronger the base of its revolutionary movement will need to be. The transition from capitalism to communism, once power has been achieved, would be a much simpler business in the United States than in Russia, because the new society would start with all the advantages of modern industrialization. The achievement of that power is a more complicated matter. It was one thing to liquidate Russia's small and youthful bourgeoisie. It would be quite another to liquidate the American bourgeoisie even though the depression has reduced many of its members to a proletarian status. For all of these reasons, revolutionary unity would seem to be more important in the accomplishment of an American revolution than theoretical purity.

Marx once wrote in one of his most clear-sighted moments:

The development of socialist sects and the development of a genuine labor movement have at all times been in inverse ratio. If sects exist with a measure of historic justification for their existence it but indicates that the working class has not yet ripened for an independent historic movement. But when the working class reaches that maturity, all sects become a reactionary phenomenon.

# SELECTED BIBLIOGRAPHY

ADAMIC, LOUIS. *Dynamite.* Viking. 1931.

*American Labor Year Book.* (Published annually.) Rand School.

ASBURY, HERBERT. *The Gangs of New York.* Knopf. 1928.

AVELING, EDWARD AND ELEANOR MARX. *The Working-Class Movement in America.* Sonnenschein. London. 1891.

BEARD, CHARLES A. AND MARY R. *The Rise of American Civilization.* Macmillan. 1927.

BEER, M. *The Life and Teaching of Karl Marx.* Translated by T. C. Partington and H. J. Stenning. National Labour Press, Ltd. London, 1921.

BELLAMY, EDWARD. *Looking Backward, 2000–1887.* Houghton Mifflin. 1898.

BIMBA, ANTHONY. *The History of the American Working Class.* International Publishers. 1927.

BOUDIN, LOUIS N. *The Theoretical System of Karl Marx.* Charles H. Kerr. 1910.

BRISBANE, ALBERT. *Social Destiny of Man.* Stollmeyer. 1840.

BRISSENDEN, PAUL FREDERICK. *The I. W. W.: A Study of American Syndicalism.* Columbia University. 1919.

BROOKS, JOHN GRAHAM. *American Syndicalism: The I. W. W.* Macmillan. 1913.

BUCHANAN, JOSEPH R. *The Story of a Labor Agitator.* The Outlook Company. 1903.

CHAMBERLAIN, JOHN. *Farewell to Reform.* Liveright. 1932.

*Civilization in the United States.* Edited by Harold E. Stearns. Harcourt, Brace. 1922.

CODMAN, JOHN THOMAS. *Brook Farm: Historic and Personal Memoirs*. Arena. 1894.

COLE, G. D. H. *Robert Owen*. Ernest Benn. London, 1925.

COLEMAN, MCALISTER. *Eugene V. Debs*. Greenberg. 1930.

COMMONS, JOHN R., and Associates. *History of Labour in the United States*. Macmillan. 1918.

*Daniel De Leon: The Man and His Work*. (A Symposium.) New York Labor News Co., 1926.

DELL, FLOYD. *Homecoming: An Autobiography*. Farrar & Rinehart. 1933.

*Documentary History of American Industrial Society*. Edited by John R. Commons and Associates. Arthur H. Clark. 1910.

DWIGHT, MARIANNE. *Letters from Brook Farm: 1844–1847*. Vassar College. 1928.

ELY, RICHARD T. *The Labor Movement in America*. Thomas Y. Crowell. 1886.

FAULKNER, HAROLD UNDERWOOD. *Economic History of the United States*. Macmillan. 1928.

FINE, NATHAN. *Labor and Farmer Parties in the United States, 1828–1928*. Rand School. 1928.

FRANKFURTER, FELIX. *The Case of Sacco and Vanzetti*. Little, Brown. 1927.

GAMBS, JOHN S. *The Decline of the I. W. W.* Columbia University Press. 1932.

GEORGE, HENRY. *Progress and Poverty*. (Abridged) Vanguard. 1926.

GOLDMAN, EMMA. *Living My Life*. Knopf. 1931.

GOMPERS, SAMUEL. *Seventy Years of Life and Labor*. Dutton. 1925.

GREELEY, HORACE. *Recollections of a Busy Life*. The Tribune Association. 1873.

HALLGREN, MAURITZ A. *Seeds of Revolt*. Knopf. 1933.

HAYWOOD, WILLIAM D. *Bill Haywood's Book*. International Publishers. 1929.

HILLQUIT, MORRIS. *History of Socialism in the United States*. Funk & Wagnalls. 1903.

HUNT, HENRY T. *The Case of Thomas J. Mooney and Warren K. Billings*. National Mooney-Billings Committee. 1929.

Hunter, Robert. *Violence and the Labor Movement.* Macmillan. 1919.

Laidler, Harry W. *A History of Socialist Thought.* Thomas Y. Crowell. 1927.

La Monte, Robert Rives, and H. L. Mencken. *Men versus The Man.* Henry Holt. 1910.

Laski, Harold J. *Communism.* Henry Holt. 1927.

Lenin, Nikolai. *Imperialism* and *The State and Revolution.* Vanguard. 1926.

Lewis, Lloyd, and Henry Justin Smith. *Chicago, the History of Its Reputation.* Harcourt, Brace. 1929.

Lloyd, Henry Demarest. *Wealth Against Commonwealth.* Harpers. 1894.

Lorwin, Lewis L. *Labor and Internationalism.* Macmillan. 1929.

Lyons, Eugene. *The Life and Death of Sacco and Vanzetti.* International Publishers. 1927.

McMurray, Donald L. *Coxey's Army.* Little, Brown. 1929.

Martin, Edward Winslow. *The History of the Great Riots.* National Publishing Co. 1877.

Marx, Karl. *Capital: The Communist Manifesto and Other Writings.* Edited with an introduction by Max Eastman. Modern Library. 1932.

Marx, Karl. *Capital: A Critique of Political Economy.* Translated by Ernest Untermann. Charles H. Kerr. 1909.

Marx, Karl. *Revolution and Counter-Revolution.* Sonnenschein. London, 1904.

*May Days: An Anthology of Verse from Masses-Liberator.* Chosen and edited by Genevieve Taggard. Boni & Liveright. 1925.

Mumford, Lewis. *The Story of Utopias.* Boni & Liveright. 1922.

Nomad, Max. *Rebels and Renegades.* Macmillan. 1932.

Nordhoff, Charles. *Communistic Societies of the United States.* Harpers. 1875.

Noyes, John Humphrey. *History of American Socialisms.* Lippincott. 1870.

Oneal, James. *American Communism.* Rand School. 1927

Owen, Robert Dale. *Threading My Way.* G. W. Carleton & Co. 1874.

Pataud, Emile, and Emile Pouget. *Syndicalism and the Co-opera-*

*tive Commonwealth.* Translated by Charlotte and Frederic Charles Oxford. New International Publishing Co. 1913.

PERLMAN, SELIG. *A Theory of the Labor Movement.* Macmillan. 1928.

PODMORE, FRANK. *Robert Owen: A Biography.* D. Appleton & Co. 1924.

POST, LOUIS F. *The Deportations Delirium of Nineteen-Twenty.* Charles H. Kerr. 1923.

*Revolutionary Radicalism.* Report of the Joint [N. Y.] Legislative Committee Investigating Seditious Activities. [Lusk Report.] J. B. Lyon Co. 1920.

RÜHLE, OTTO. *Karl Marx: His Life and Work.* Translated by Eden and Cedar Paul. Viking. 1929.

SACHS, EMANIE. *The Terrible Siren.* Harpers. 1928.

SCHLÜTER, HERMAN. *Lincoln, Labor and Slavery.* Socialist Literature Co. 1913.

*Selections from the Works of Fourier.* Translated by Julia Franklin with an introduction by Charles Gide. Sonnenschein. London, 1901.

SIMONS, A. M. *Social Forces in American History.* Macmillan. 1913.

SINCLAIR, UPTON. *American Outpost: A Book of Reminiscences.* Farrar & Rinehart. 1932.

SOTHERAN, CHARLES. *Horace Greeley and Other Pioneers of American Socialism.* Mitchell Kennerley. 1915.

STEFFENS, LINCOLN. *The Autobiography of Lincoln Steffens.* Harcourt, Brace. 1931.

SWIFT, LINDSAY. *Brook Farm: Its Members, Scholars, and Visitors.* Macmillan. 1900.

THOMAS, NORMAN. *The Conscientious Objector in America.* Huebsch. 1925.

TRIDON, ANDRÉ. *The New Unionism.* Huebsch. 1917.

TROLLOPE, FRANCES. *Domestic Manners of the Americans.* Dodd, Mead & Co. 1927.

TROTSKY, LEON. *Dictatorship vs. Democracy.* Workers Party. 1922.

VEBLEN, THORSTEIN. *The Theory of the Leisure Class.* Macmillan. 1899.

VIZETELLY, ERNEST ALFRED. *The Anarchists: Their Faith and Their Record.* John Lane. 1911.

[ 382 ]

Ware, Norman J. *The Labor Movement in the United States: 1860–1895*. D. Appleton & Co. 1929.
Waterman, William Randall. *Frances Wright*. Columbia University. 1924.
Wright, Edward Needles. *Conscientious Objectors in the Civil War*. University of Pennsylvania Press. 1931.
Young, Art. *On My Way*. Liveright. 1928.
Young, Arthur Nichols. *The Single Tax Movement in the United States*. Princeton University Press. 1916.

## PAMPHLETS

*The Draft, or Conscription Reviewed by the People* (1863) ; *A Concise History of the Great Trial of the Chicago Anarchists in 1886* by Dyer D. Lum (Socialistic Publishing Company) ; *The Accused the Accusers: The Famous Speeches of the Eight Chicago Anarchists in Court* (Socialistic Publishing Society) ; *Federal Aid in Domestic Disturbances* (Supplemental to Senate Document 209, 57th Congress, 2d Session) ; *Manifesto of the Communist Party* by Karl Marx and Frederick Engels (Charles H. Kerr) ; *The Two Internationals* by R. Palme Dutt (George Allen & Unwin, London, 1920) ; *Daniel De Leon* by Arnold Petersen (New York Labor News Co., 1931) ; *Sabotage* by Emile Pouget, translated by Arturo Giovannitti (Charles H. Kerr, 1913) ; *Proletarian and Petit-Bourgeois* by Austin Lewis (Industrial Workers of the World) ; *The Story of Mooney and Billings* (National Mooney-Billings Committee, 1929) ; *War-Time Prosecutions and Mob Violence* (National Civil Liberties Bureau, 1919) ; *In Prison* by Kate Richards O'Hare (Frank P. O'Hare, 1920) ; *The Trial of Eugene V. Debs* by Max Eastman (The Liberator Publishing Co.) ; *Seeing Red* by Walter Nelles (American Civil Liberties Union, 1920) ; *Since the Buford Sailed* (American Civil Liberties Union, 1920) ; *Report upon the Illegal Practices of the United States Department of Justice* (National Popular Government League, 1920) ; *Amnesty for Political Prisoners* (American Civil Liberties Union, 1920) ; *Was it Murder? The Truth About Centralia* by Walker C. Smith (Northwest District Defense Committee, 1922) ; *Facing the Chair* by John Dos Passos (Sacco-Vanzetti Defense Committee,

1927) ; *The Passaic Textile Strike* by Mary Heaton Vorse (General Relief Committee of Textile Strikers, 1927) ; *The Second Congress of the Communist International as Reported and Interpreted by the Official Newspapers of Soviet Russia* (Government Printing Office, 1920) ; *Program of the Communist International* (Workers Library, 1929) ; *Culture and the Crisis* (League of Professional Groups for Foster and Ford, 1932) ; *The Communist Position on the Negro Question* (A Symposium) ; *Communist Election Platform* (Workers Library, 1932) .

# INDEX

[ 390 ]

Walling, William English, 231, 274, 294

*War of the Classes, The* (London), 233

Ward, Dr. Harry F., 232

Ward, Lester, 232

Warren, Josiah, 18, 79, 120, 154

Waterman, William Randall, 26

Wayland, J. A., 206, 226, 227

*Wealth Against Commonwealth* (Lloyd), 169, 205

Weisbord, Albert, 355

Weitling, William, 80, 81, 85, 90, 102

West, William, 87, 88, 126

Western Federation of Miners, 223, 244–247, 250, 251, 271, 326

Western Labor Union, 223

Weydemeyer, Joseph, 85, 90, 100, 102

Whitby, Richeson, 25, 26, 28

Wilkinson, Jemina, 7

Wilshire, Gaylord, 228

Wilson, Edmund, 282, 368

Wilson, Woodrow, 189, 256, 285, 288, 289, 292, 299, 303, 312

Wisconsin Phalanx, 68

Woman in the Wilderness Community, 7

Woodhull, Victoria, 121–124, 126, 155

*Woodhull & Claflin's Weekly,* 122–124

*Workers Age,* 354

Workers (Communist) Party (*see* Communist Party), 344–349, 351–357

*Working Class Movement in America, The* (Avelings), 180, 181

Working Man's Advocate, 41–44, 81, 88

Working Men's Party, 38–45

Workingmen's Party of the United States, 144, 149, 150

Wright, Camilla, 22, 25, 27, 33

Wright, Frances, 21–33, 39, 40–44

Yellow Springs Community, 19, 20

Young, Art, 270, 282, 306

Zimmerwald Conference, 315

Zinoviev, Gregory, 317, 318

Zoar Community, 8